I wrote before in this spot that using color was hard for me, but lately I really like it!

I'm so glad! I hope to continue learning new skills.

Enjoy volume 11!

Naoshi Komi

NAOSHI KOMI was born in Kochi Prefecture, Japan, on March 28, 1986. His first serialized work in *Weekly Shonen Jump* was the series *Double Arts*. His current series, *Nisekoi*, is serialized in *Weekly Shonen Jump*.

NISEKOI:
False Love
VOLUME 11
SHONEN JUMP Manga Edition

Story and Art by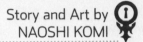
NAOSHI KOMI

Translation ✐ Camellia Nieh
Touch-Up Art & Lettering ✐ Stephen Dutro
Design ✐ Fawn Lau
Shonen Jump Series Editor ✐ John Bae
Graphic Novel Editor ✐ Amy Yu

NISEKOI © 2011 by Naoshi Komi
All rights reserved.
First published in Japan in 2011
by SHUEISHA Inc., Tokyo.
English translation rights arranged
by SHUEISHA Inc.

Printed in the U.S.A.

Published by VIZ Media, LLC
P.O. Box 77010
San Francisco, CA 94107

10 9 8 7 6 5 4 3 2 1
First printing, September 2015

www.shonenjump.com   www.viz.com

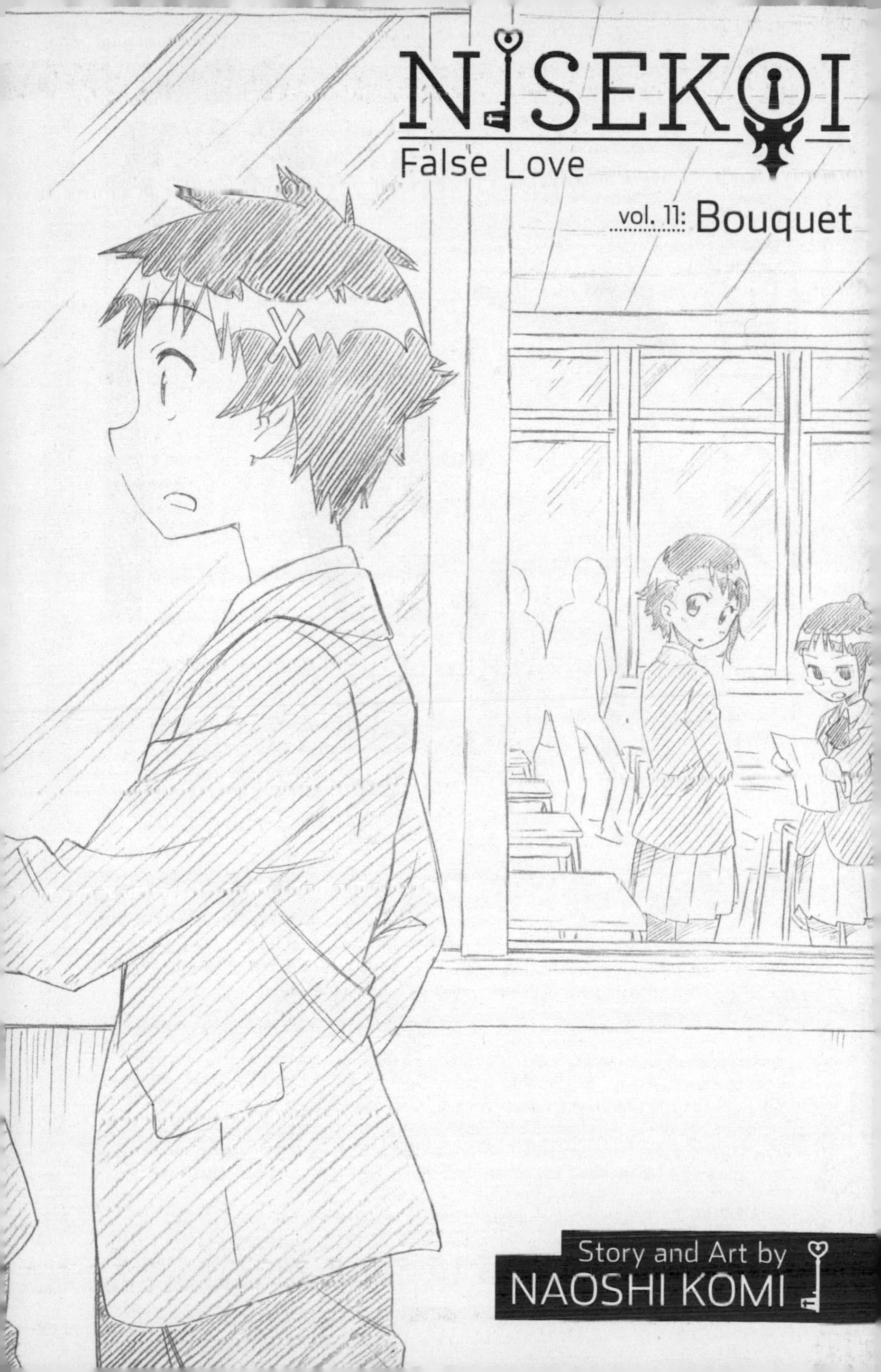

NISEKOI
False Love
vol. 11: Bouquet

Story and Art by
NAOSHI KOMI

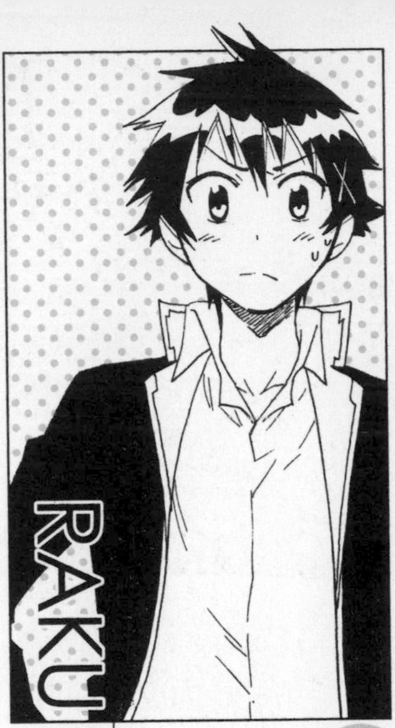

RAKU ICHIJO

A normal teen whose family happens to be yakuza. Cherishes a pendant given to him by a girl he met ten years ago. Has a crush on Kosaki.

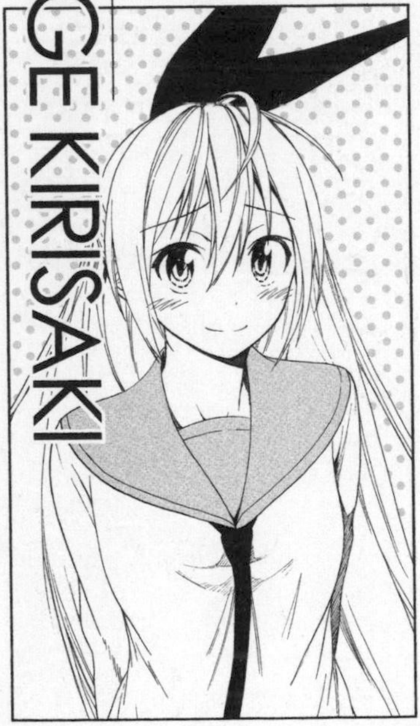

CHITOGE KIRISAKI

A half-Japanese bombshell with stellar athletic abilities. Short-tempered and violent. Comes from a family of gangsters.

CHARACTERS & STORY

Raku Ichijo is an ordinary teen...who just happens to come from a family of yakuza! His most treasured item is a pendant he was given ten years ago by a girl whom he promised to meet again one day and marry.

Thanks to family circumstances, Raku is forced into a false relationship with Chitoge, the daughter of a rival gangster, to keep their families from shedding blood. Despite their constant spats, Raku and Chitoge manage to fool everyone. One day, Chitoge discovers an old key, jogging memories of her own first love ten years earlier. Meanwhile, Raku's crush, Kosaki, confesses that she also has a key and made a promise with a boy ten years ago. To complicate matters, Marika Tachibana has a key as well and remembers a promise ten years ago.

Between Ms. Kyoko quitting her job to get married and some intense encounters with Kosaki's sister, Haru, Raku's life is as hectic as ever. When a stray ball almost hits Chitoge, Raku protects her and gets hit in the head, losing his memory! Chitoge and the others will do anything to help him recover his memory, even though they're somewhat intrigued by his new ultrapolite personality.

KOSAKI ONODERA

A girl Raku has a crush on. Beautiful and sweet, Kosaki has no shortage of admirers. She's a terrible cook but makes food that *looks* amazing.

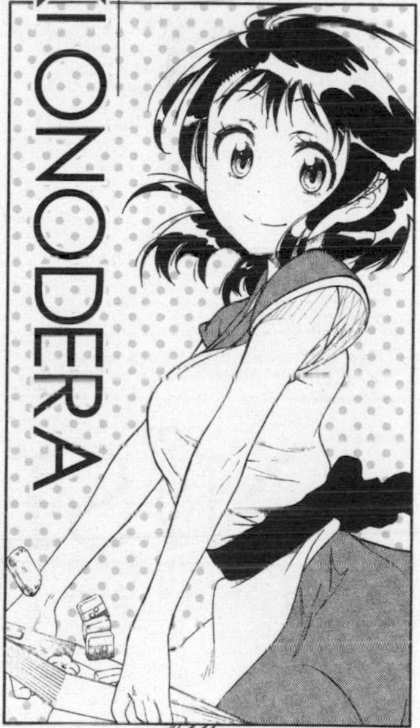

MARIKA TACHIBANA

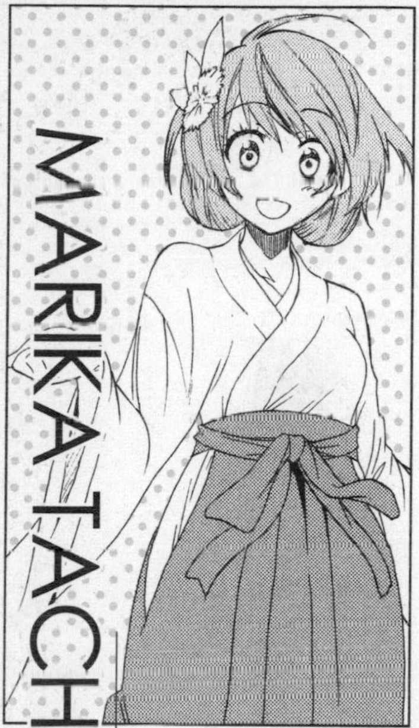

Daughter of the chief of police, Marika is Raku's fiancée, according to an agreement made by their fathers—an agreement Marika takes very seriously! Also has a key and remembers making a promise with Raku ten years ago.

SHU MAIKO

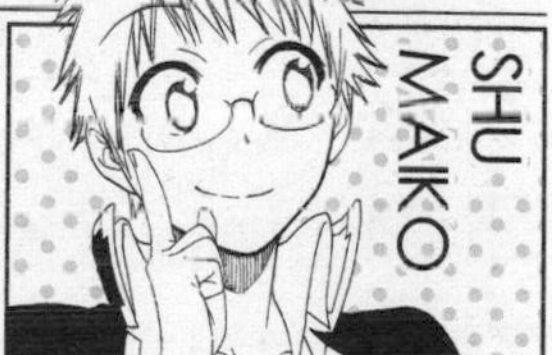

Raku's best friend is outgoing and girl-crazy.

SEISHIRO TSUGUMI

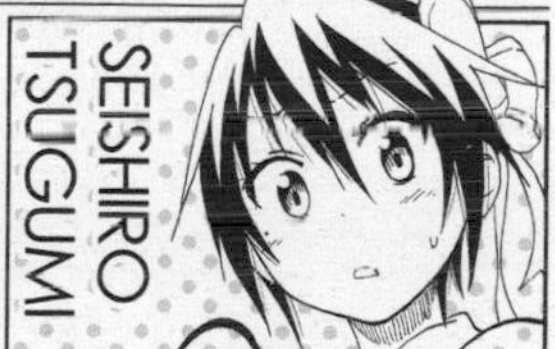

Trained as an assassin in order to protect Chitoge, Tsugumi is often mistaken for a boy.

RURI MIYAMOTO

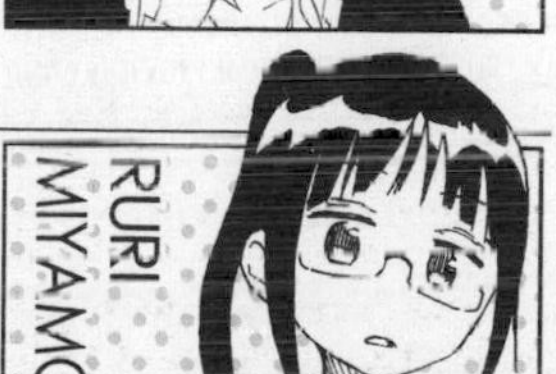

Kosaki's best gal pal. Comes off as aloot, but is actually a devoted and highly intuitive friend.

HARU ONODERA

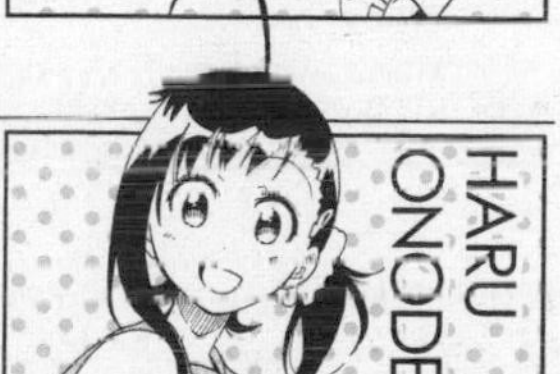

Kosaki's adoring younger sister. Has a low opinion of Raku.

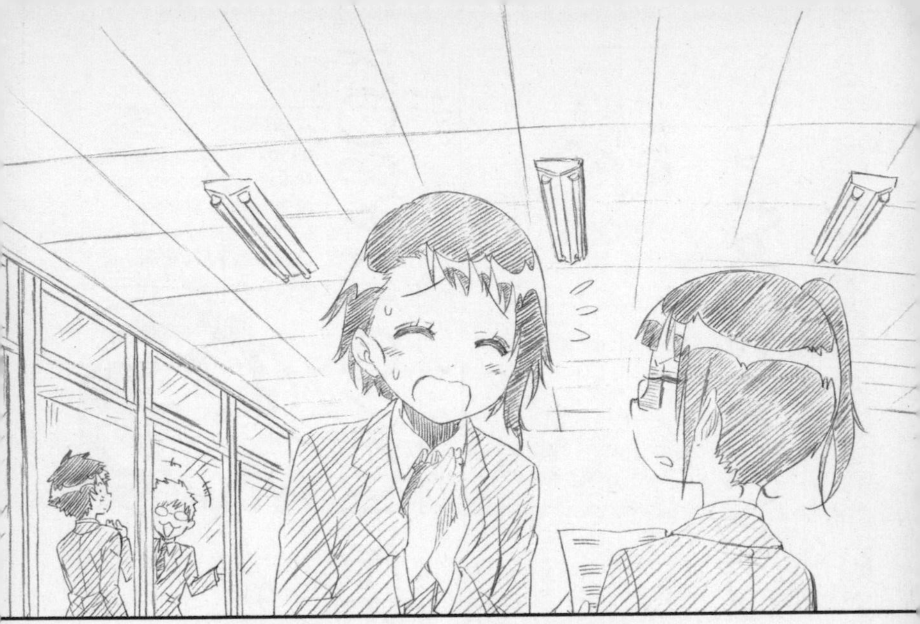

NISEKOI
False Love

vol. 11: Bouquet

TABLE OF CONTENTS

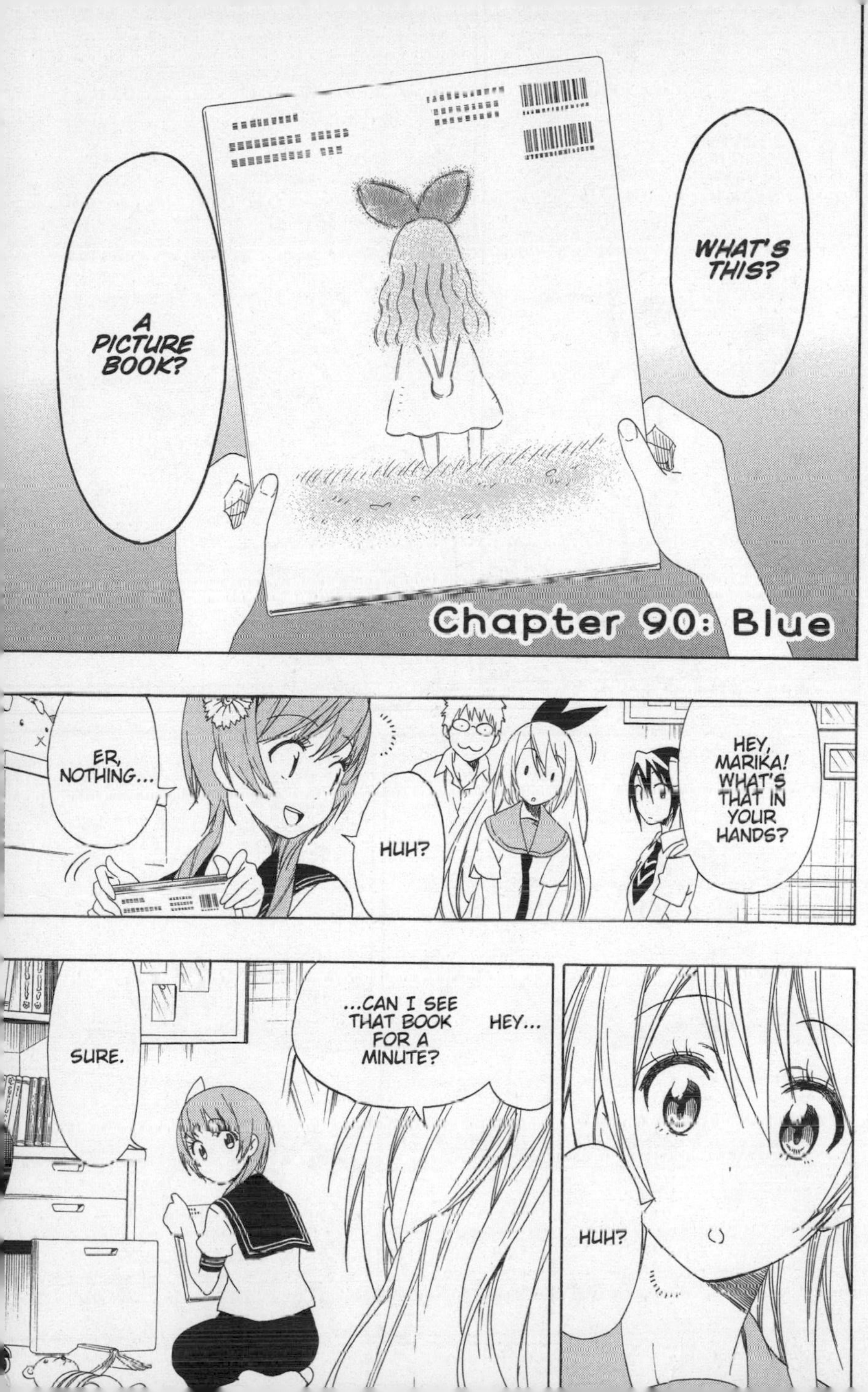
WHAT'S THIS?
A PICTURE BOOK?
Chapter 90: Blue
HEY, MARIKA! WHAT'S THAT IN YOUR HANDS?
HUH?
ER, NOTHING...
HUH?
HEY...
...CAN I SEE THAT BOOK FOR A MINUTE?
SURE.

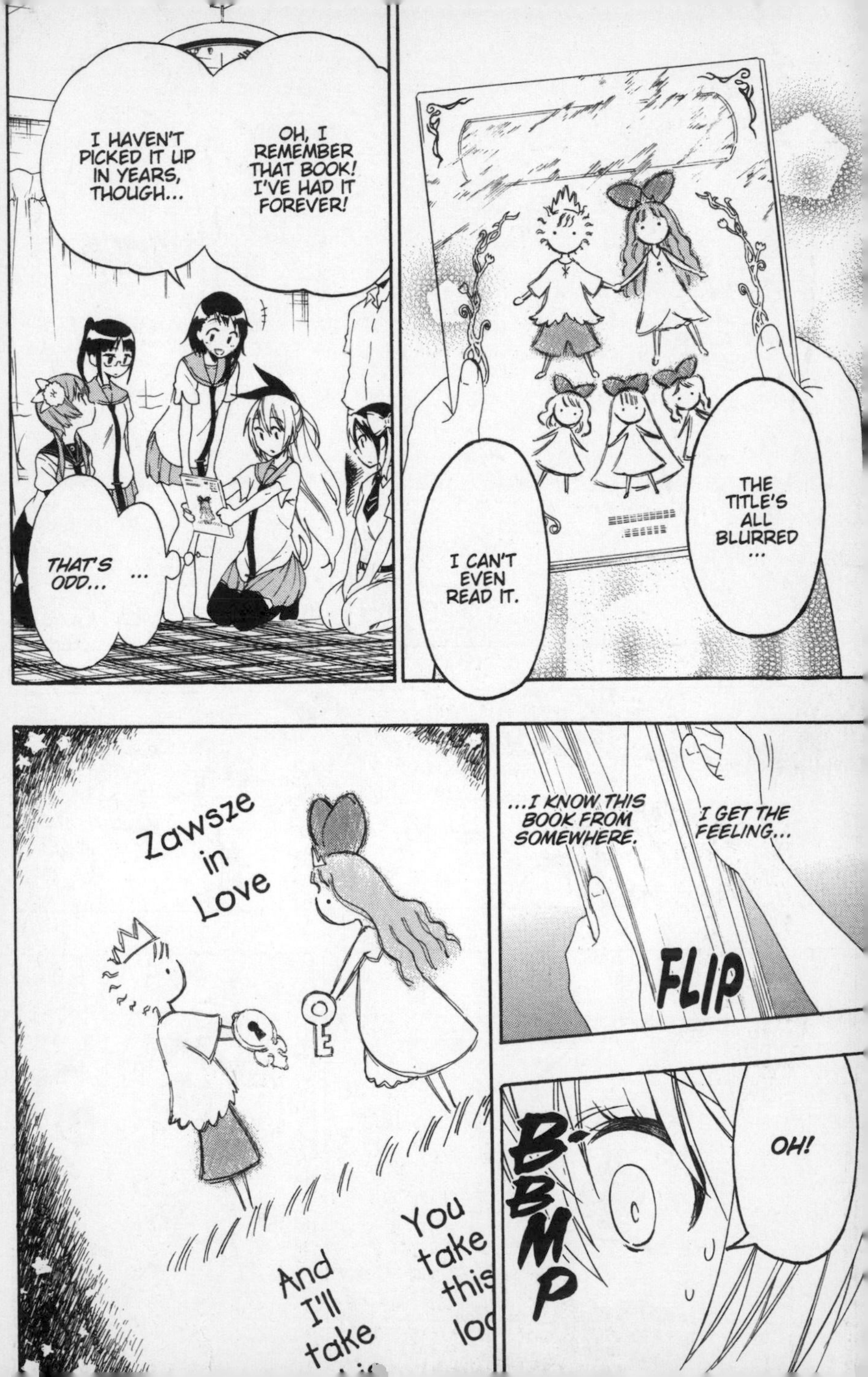
THE TITLE'S ALL BLURRED ...
I CAN'T EVEN READ IT.
OH, I REMEMBER THAT BOOK! I'VE HAD IT FOREVER!
I HAVEN'T PICKED IT UP IN YEARS, THOUGH...
...
THAT'S ODD...
I GET THE FEELING...
...I KNOW THIS BOOK FROM SOMEWHERE.
FLIP
OH!
B-BMP
Zawsze in Love
You take this loc
And I'll take

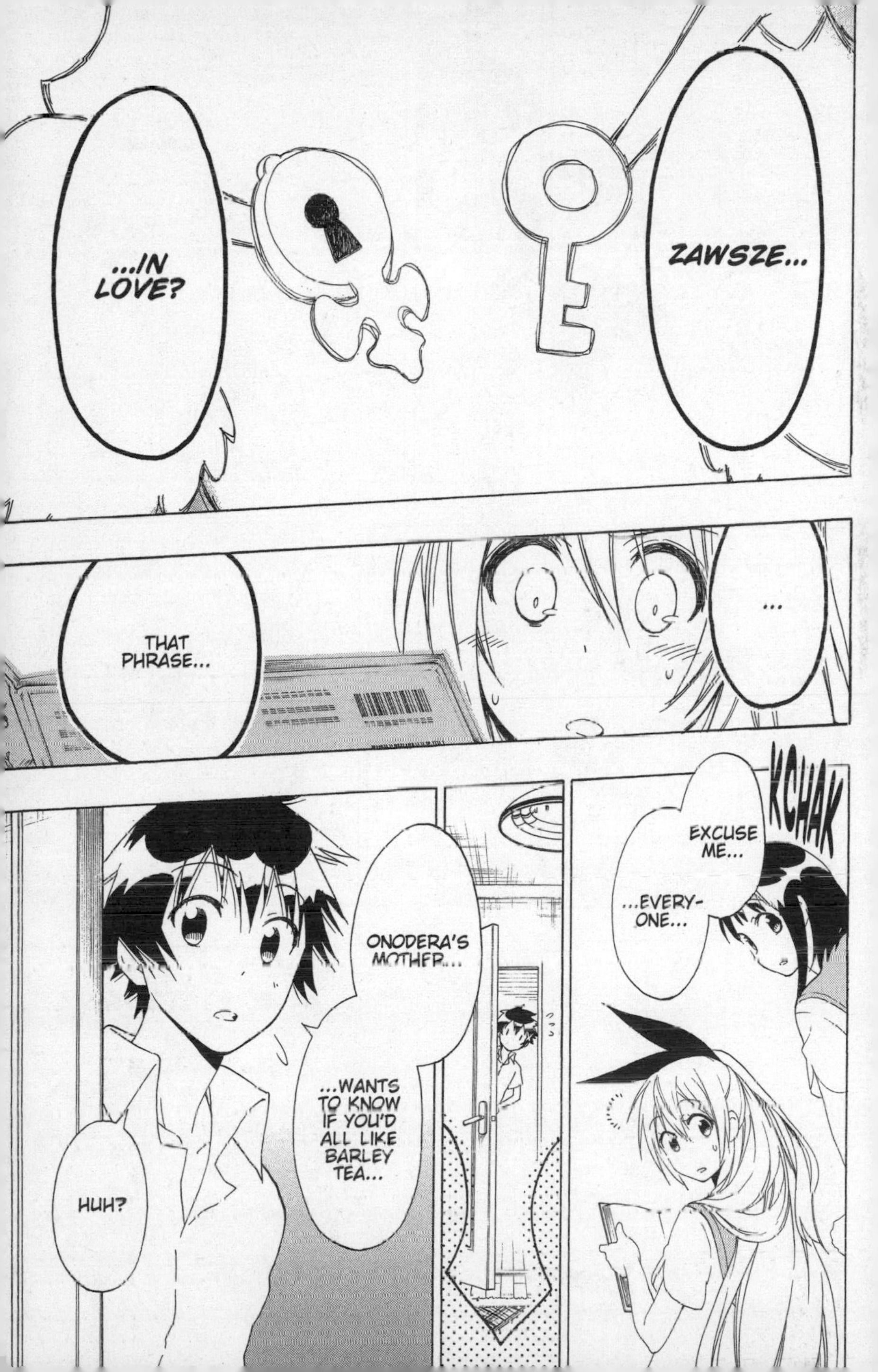
ZAWSZE...
...IN LOVE?
...
THAT PHRASE...
KCHAK
EXCUSE ME...
...EVERY-ONE...
ONODERA'S MOTHER...
...WANTS TO KNOW IF YOU'D ALL LIKE BARLEY TEA...
HUH?

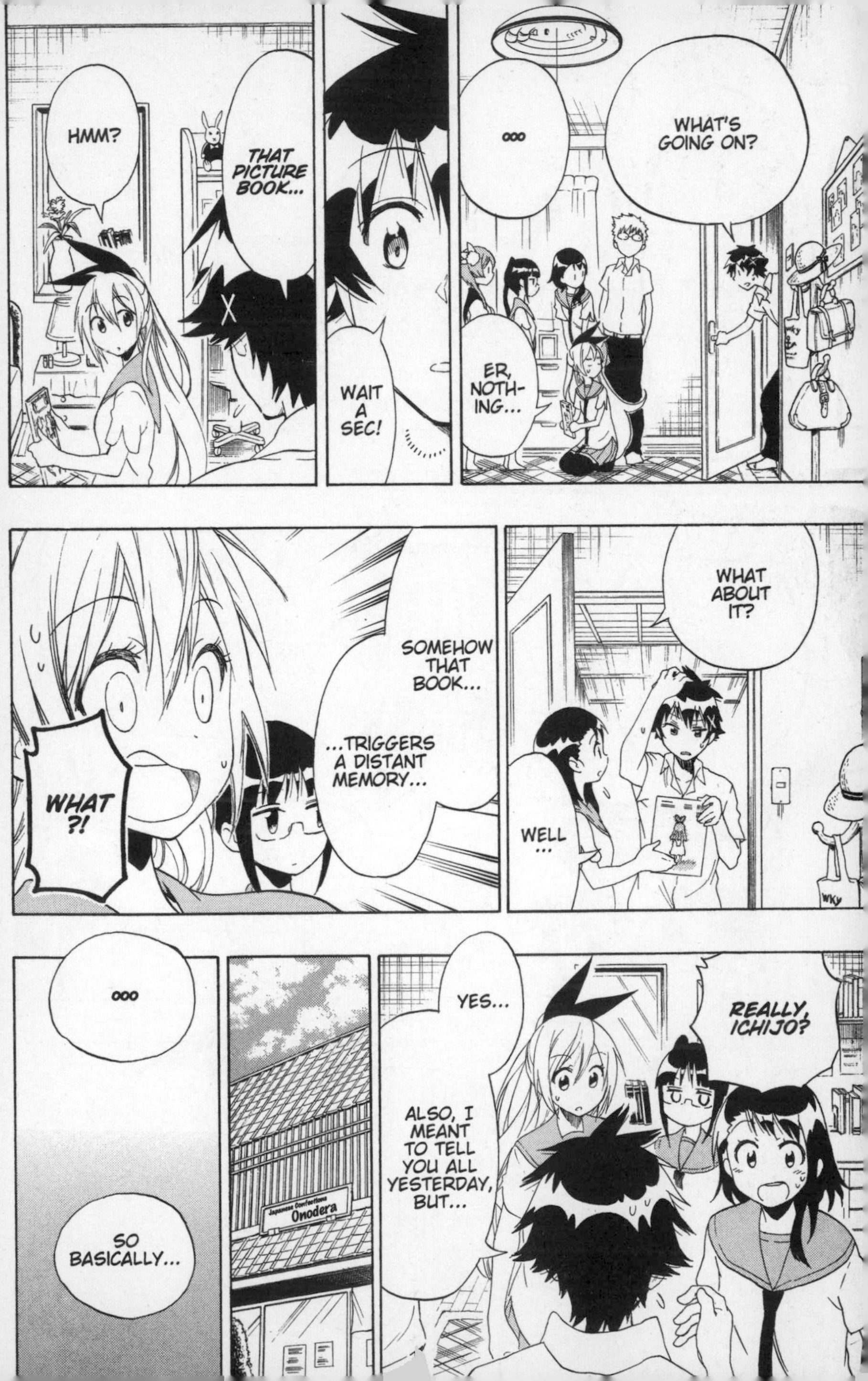
WHAT'S GOING ON?
...
ER, NOTH-ING...
WAIT A SEC!
THAT PICTURE BOOK...
HMM?
WHAT ABOUT IT?
WELL...
SOMEHOW THAT BOOK...
...TRIGGERS A DISTANT MEMORY...
WHAT?!
REALLY, ICHIJO?
YES...
ALSO, I MEANT TO TELL YOU ALL YESTERDAY, BUT...
Japanese Confections
Onodera
...
SO BASICALLY...

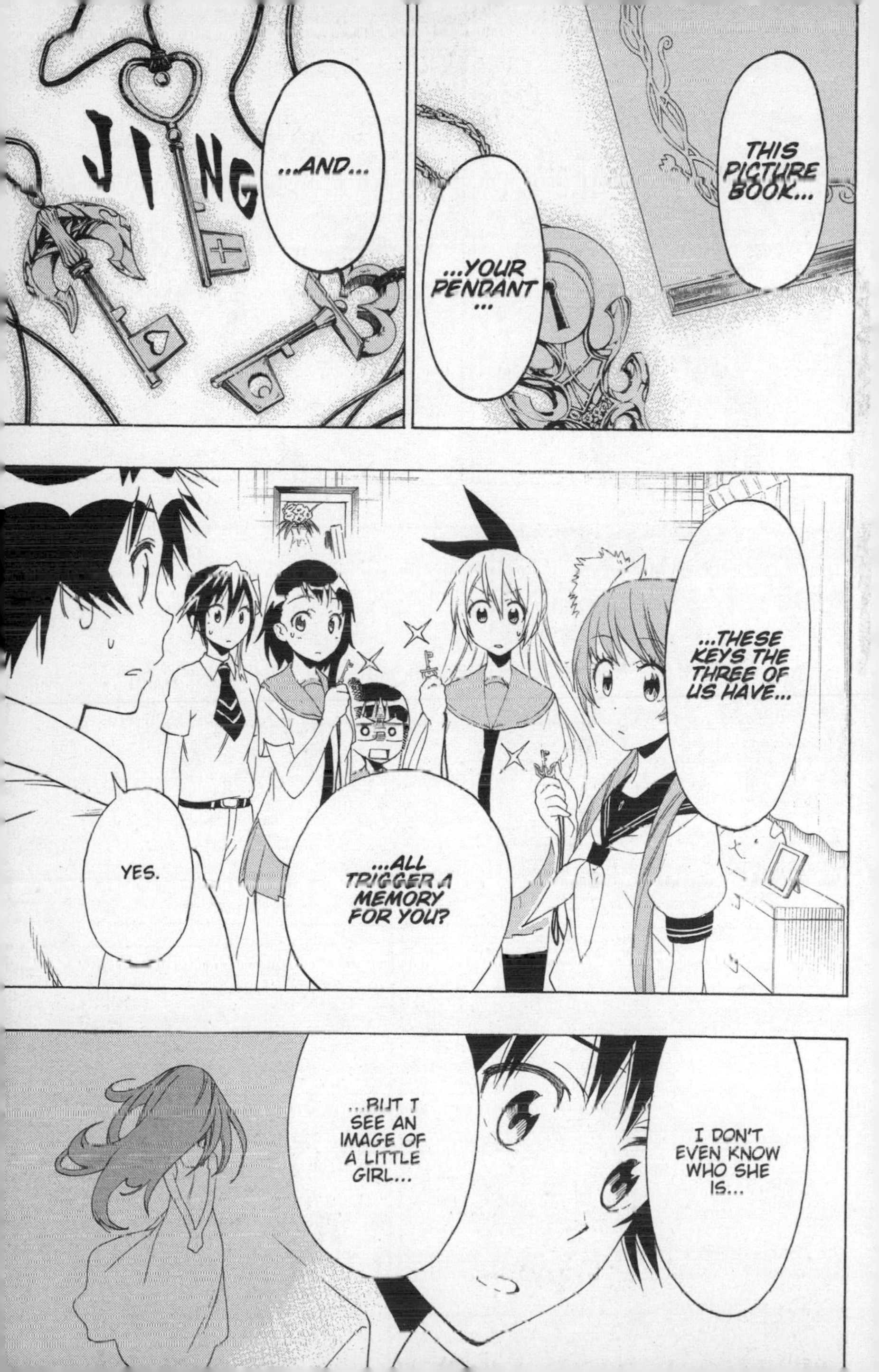
THIS PICTURE BOOK...
...YOUR PENDANT...
...AND...
JING
...THESE KEYS THE THREE OF US HAVE...
...ALL TRIGGER A MEMORY FOR YOU?
YES.
I DON'T EVEN KNOW WHO SHE IS...
...BUT I SEE AN IMAGE OF A LITTLE GIRL...

...THE GIRL YOU MADE THE PROMISE WITH TEN YEARS AGO?

IS SHE...

?

WHAT PROMISE?

PROMISE?

JOLT

GLARE

WHY DIDN'T YOU TELL ME?

Oh!

I'M SORRY!

KOSAKI, YOU NEVER TOLD ME YOU MIGHT BE THE GIRL ICHIJO REMEMBERS!

THAT'S INCREDIBLE.

I DIDN'T REALIZE YOU AND RAKU ICHIJO HAD A CONNECTION TEN YEARS AGO...

...MAYBE THERE'S SOME KIND OF CONNECTION.

IF THE BOOK REMINDS HIM OF THE GIRL HE MADE THE PROMISE WITH...

PROBABLY!

RAKU TOLD ME.

WELL, YEAH.

DID YOU KNOW ABOUT ALL THIS, MAIKO?

Most of it, anyway.

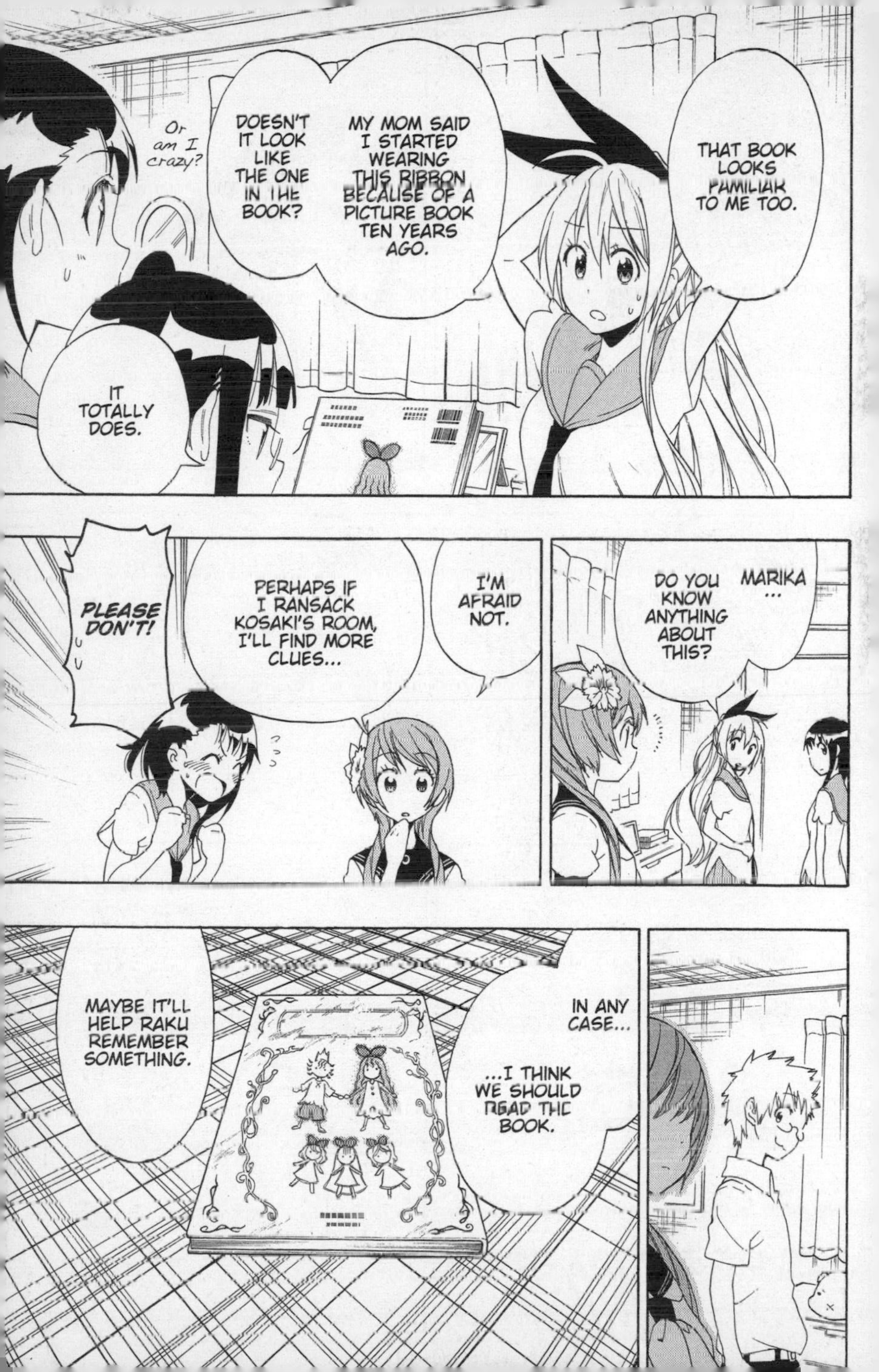
THAT BOOK LOOKS FAMILIAR TO ME TOO.
MY MOM SAID I STARTED WEARING THIS RIBBON BECAUSE OF A PICTURE BOOK TEN YEARS AGO.
DOESN'T IT LOOK LIKE THE ONE IN THE BOOK?
Or am I crazy?
IT TOTALLY DOES.
MARIKA...
DO YOU KNOW ANYTHING ABOUT THIS?
I'M AFRAID NOT.
PERHAPS IF I RANSACK KOSAKI'S ROOM, I'LL FIND MORE CLUES...
PLEASE DON'T!
IN ANY CASE...
...I THINK WE SHOULD READ THE BOOK.
MAYBE IT'LL HELP RAKU REMEMBER SOMETHING.

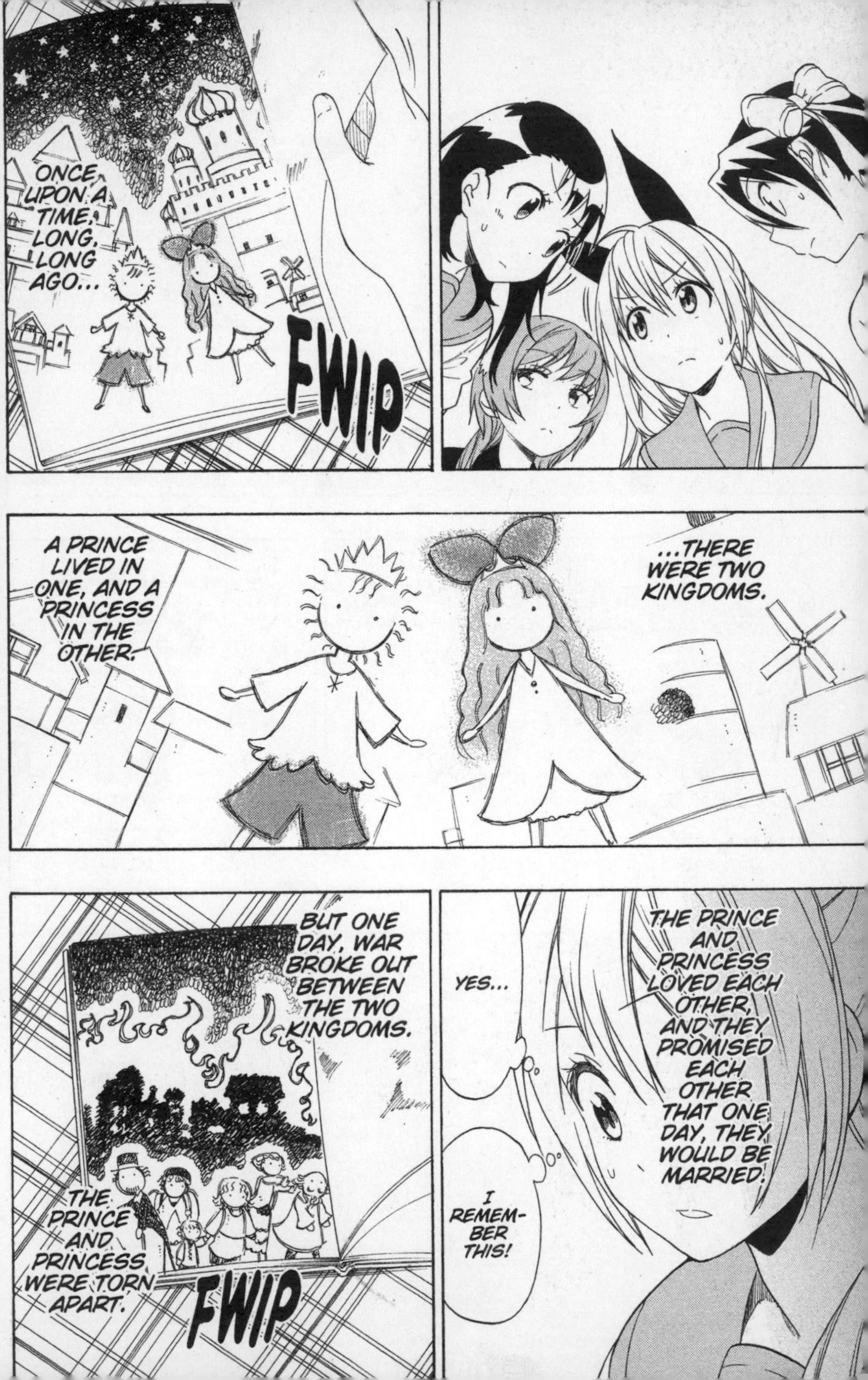
ONCE UPON A TIME, LONG, LONG AGO...
FWIP
...THERE WERE TWO KINGDOMS.
A PRINCE LIVED IN ONE, AND A PRINCESS IN THE OTHER.
THE PRINCE AND PRINCESS LOVED EACH OTHER, AND THEY PROMISED EACH OTHER THAT ONE DAY, THEY WOULD BE MARRIED.
YES...
I REMEM-BER THIS!
BUT ONE DAY, WAR BROKE OUT BETWEEN THE TWO KINGDOMS.
THE PRINCE AND PRINCESS WERE TORN APART.
FWIP

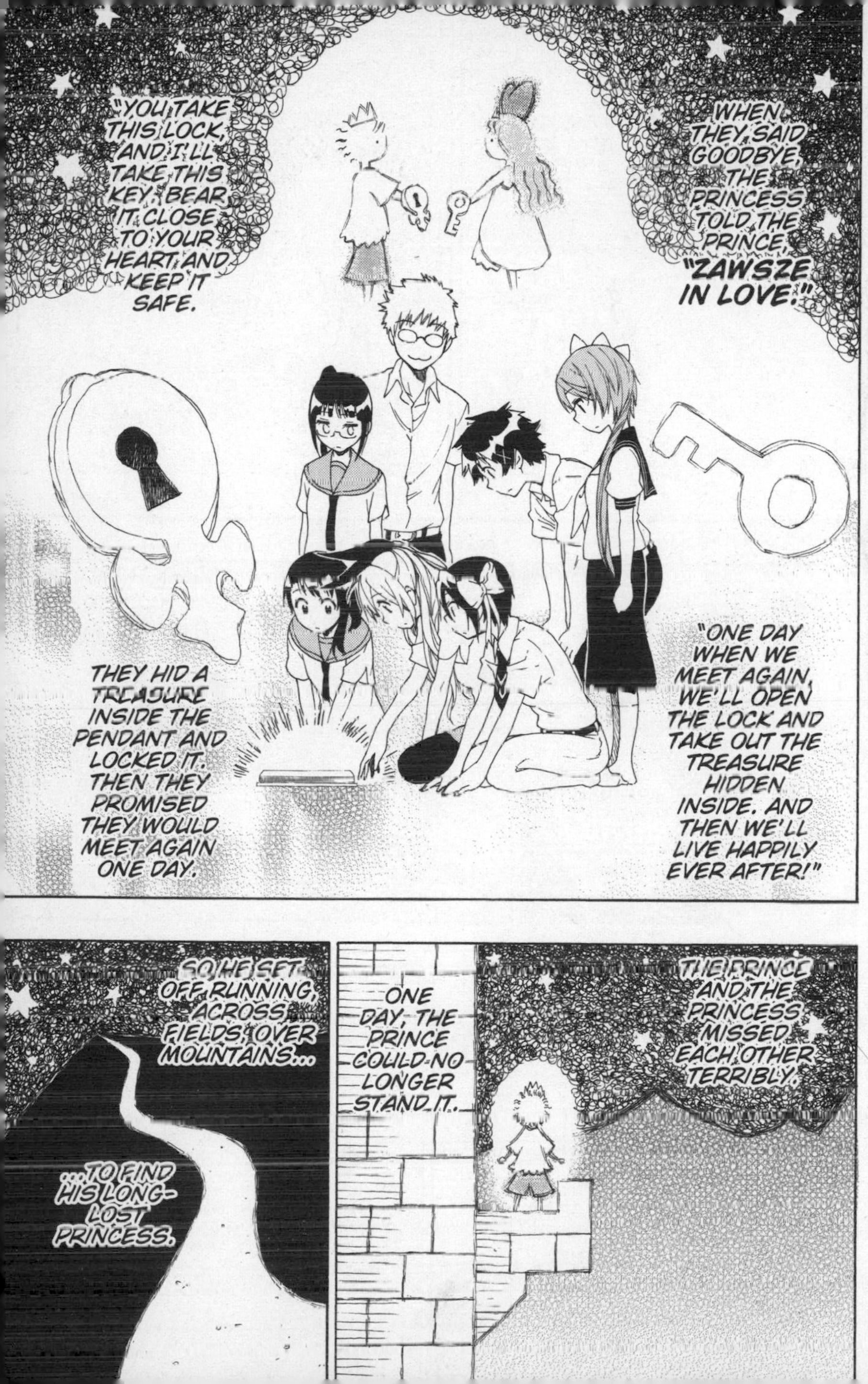
WHEN THEY SAID GOODBYE, THE PRINCESS TOLD THE PRINCE,
"ZAWSZE IN LOVE."
"YOU TAKE THIS LOCK, AND I'LL TAKE THIS KEY. BEAR IT CLOSE TO YOUR HEART AND KEEP IT SAFE.
THEY HID A TREASURE INSIDE THE PENDANT AND LOCKED IT. THEN THEY PROMISED THEY WOULD MEET AGAIN ONE DAY.
"ONE DAY WHEN WE MEET AGAIN, WE'LL OPEN THE LOCK AND TAKE OUT THE TREASURE HIDDEN INSIDE. AND THEN WE'LL LIVE HAPPILY EVER AFTER!"
THE PRINCE AND THE PRINCESS MISSED EACH OTHER TERRIBLY.
ONE DAY, THE PRINCE COULD NO LONGER STAND IT...
SO HE SET OFF RUNNING, ACROSS FIELDS, OVER MOUNTAINS...
...TO FIND HIS LONG-LOST PRINCESS.

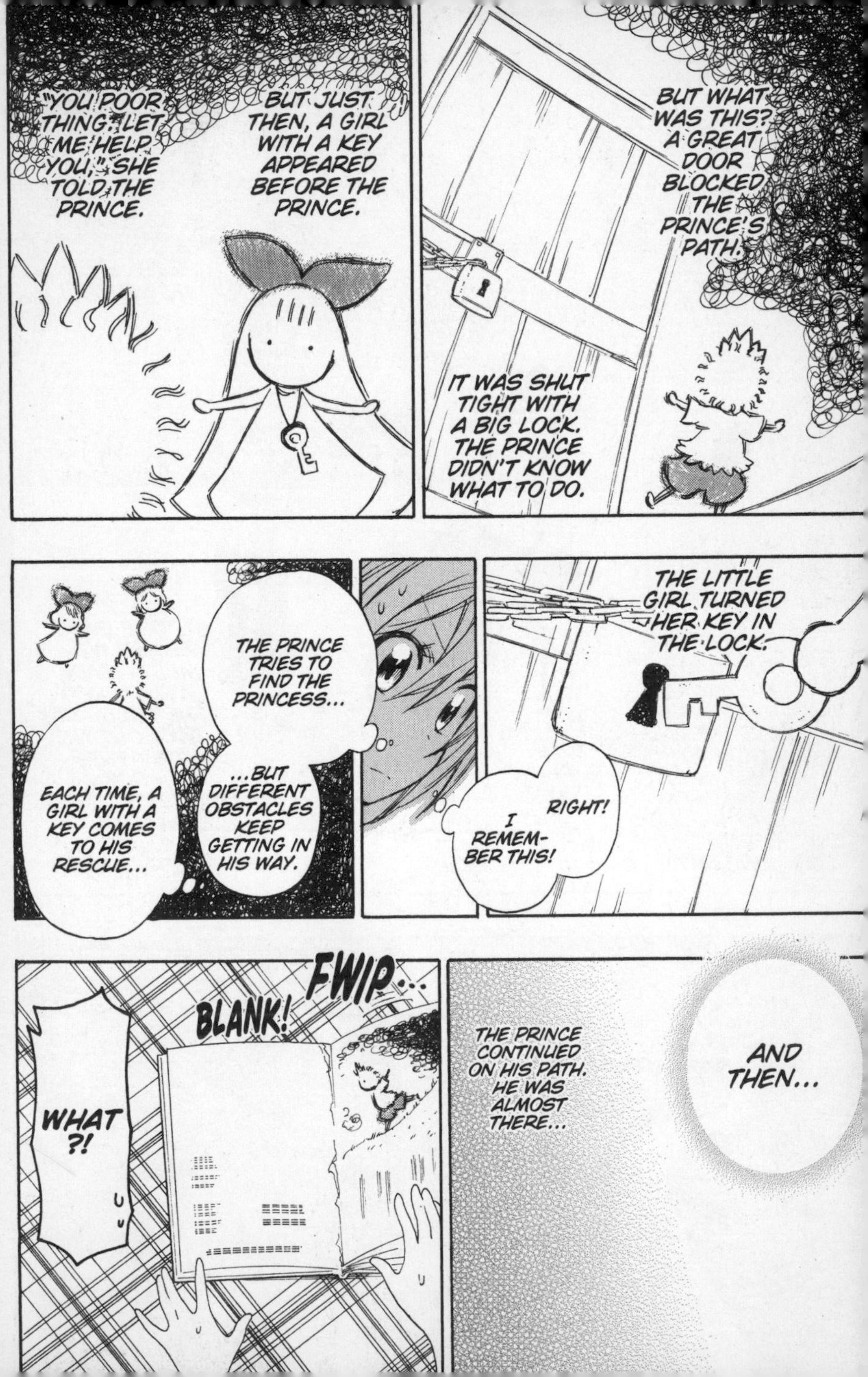
BUT WHAT WAS THIS? A GREAT DOOR BLOCKED THE PRINCE'S PATH.
IT WAS SHUT TIGHT WITH A BIG LOCK. THE PRINCE DIDN'T KNOW WHAT TO DO.
BUT JUST THEN, A GIRL WITH A KEY APPEARED BEFORE THE PRINCE.
"YOU POOR THING. LET ME HELP YOU," SHE TOLD THE PRINCE.
THE LITTLE GIRL TURNED HER KEY IN THE LOCK.
RIGHT! I REMEMBER THIS!
THE PRINCE TRIES TO FIND THE PRINCESS...
...BUT DIFFERENT OBSTACLES KEEP GETTING IN HIS WAY.
EACH TIME, A GIRL WITH A KEY COMES TO HIS RESCUE...
AND THEN...
THE PRINCE CONTINUED ON HIS PATH. HE WAS ALMOST THERE...
FWIP...
BLANK!
WHAT?!

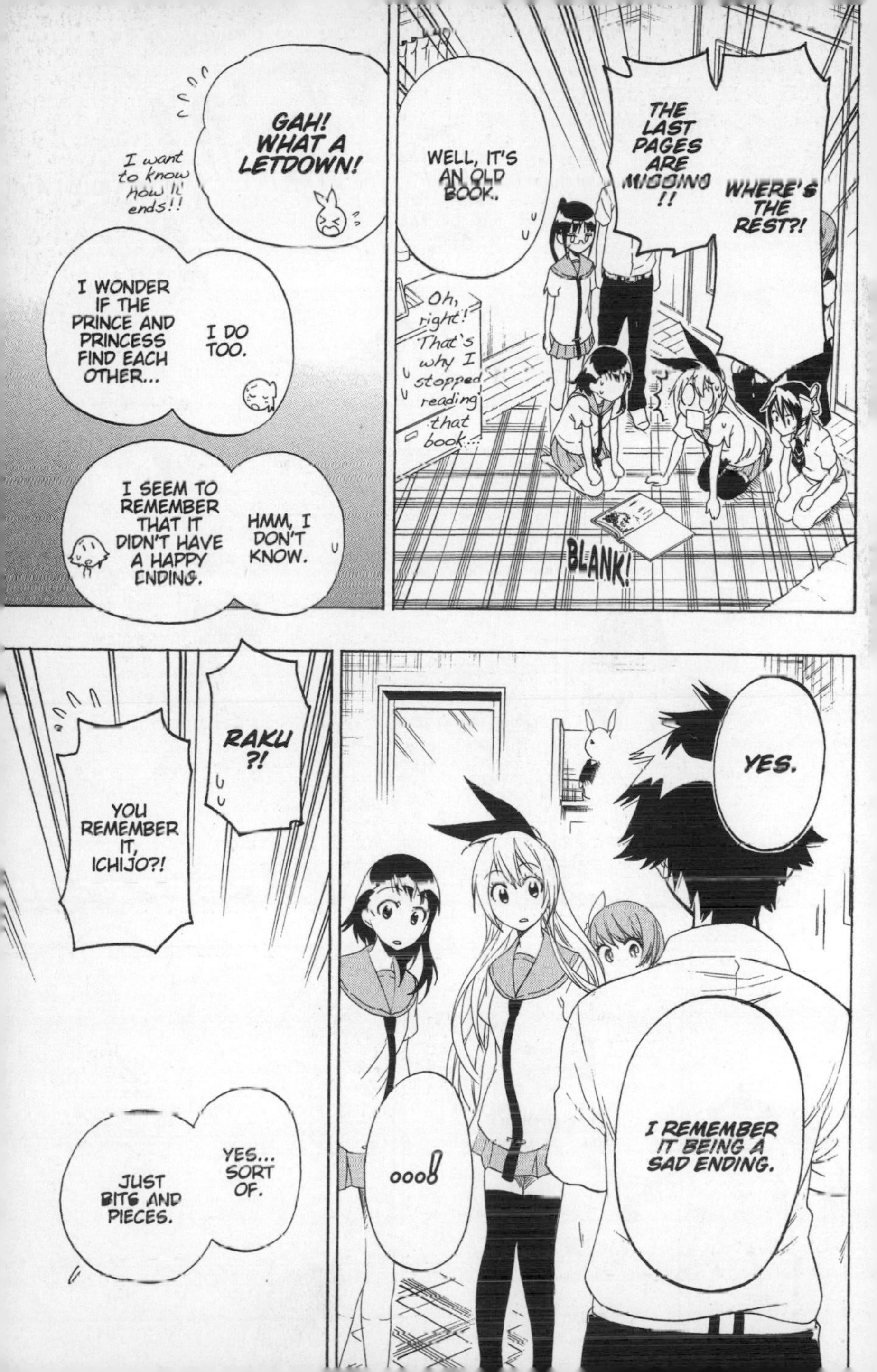
THE LAST PAGES ARE MISSING!!
WHERE'S THE REST?!
WELL, IT'S AN OLD BOOK.
Oh, right! That's why I stopped reading that book...
BLANK!
GAH! WHAT A LETDOWN!
I want to know how it ends!!
I DO TOO.
I WONDER IF THE PRINCE AND PRINCESS FIND EACH OTHER...
HMM, I DON'T KNOW.
I SEEM TO REMEMBER THAT IT DIDN'T HAVE A HAPPY ENDING.
YES.
I REMEMBER IT BEING A SAD ENDING.
ooo!
RAKU?!
YOU REMEMBER IT, ICHIJO?!
YES... SORT OF.
JUST BITS AND PIECES.

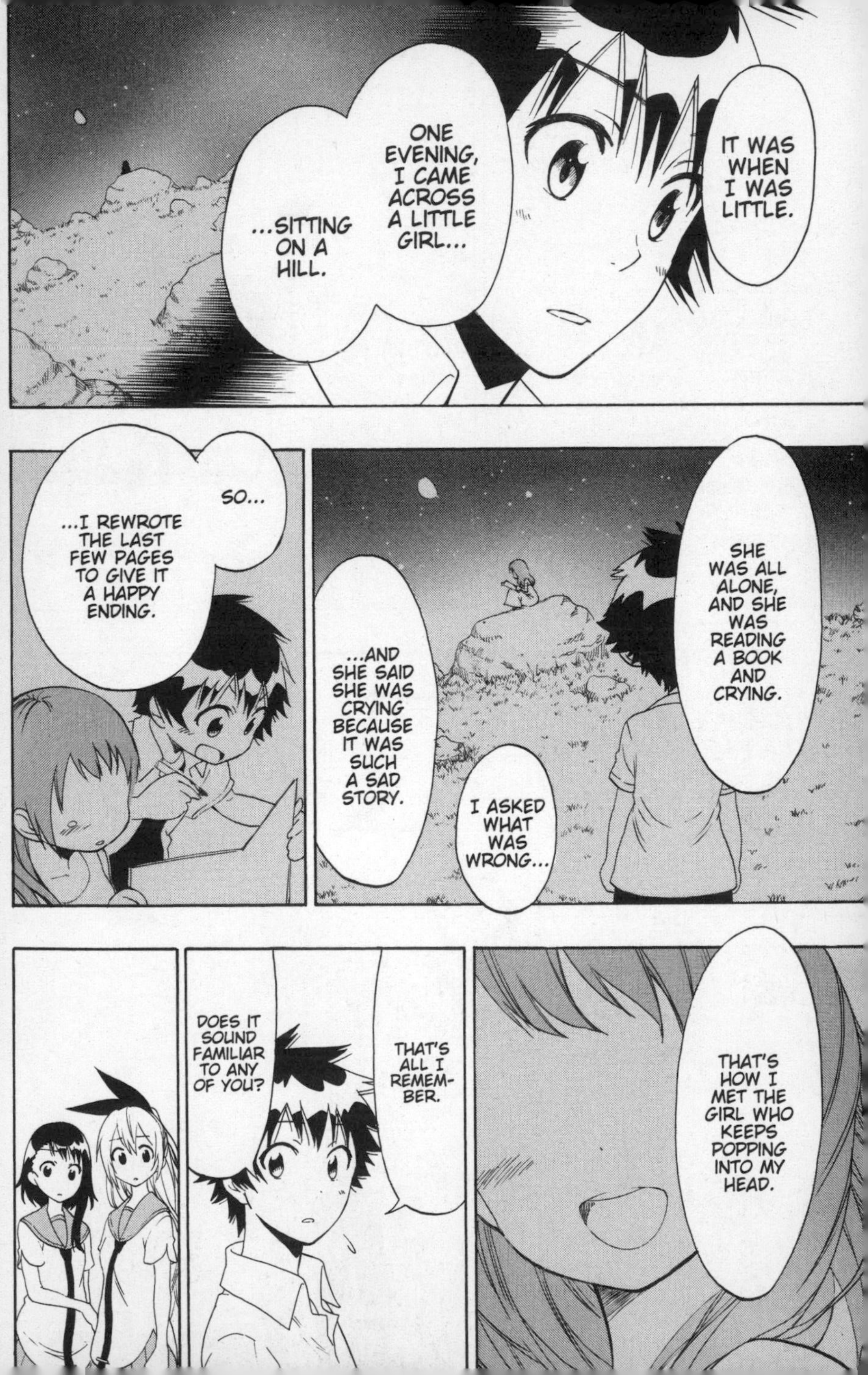
IT WAS WHEN I WAS LITTLE.
ONE EVENING, I CAME ACROSS A LITTLE GIRL...
...SITTING ON A HILL.
SHE WAS ALL ALONE, AND SHE WAS READING A BOOK AND CRYING.
I ASKED WHAT WAS WRONG...
...AND SHE SAID SHE WAS CRYING BECAUSE IT WAS SUCH A SAD STORY.
SO...
...I REWROTE THE LAST FEW PAGES TO GIVE IT A HAPPY ENDING.
THAT'S HOW I MET THE GIRL WHO KEEPS POPPING INTO MY HEAD.
THAT'S ALL I REMEM-BER.
DOES IT SOUND FAMILIAR TO ANY OF YOU?

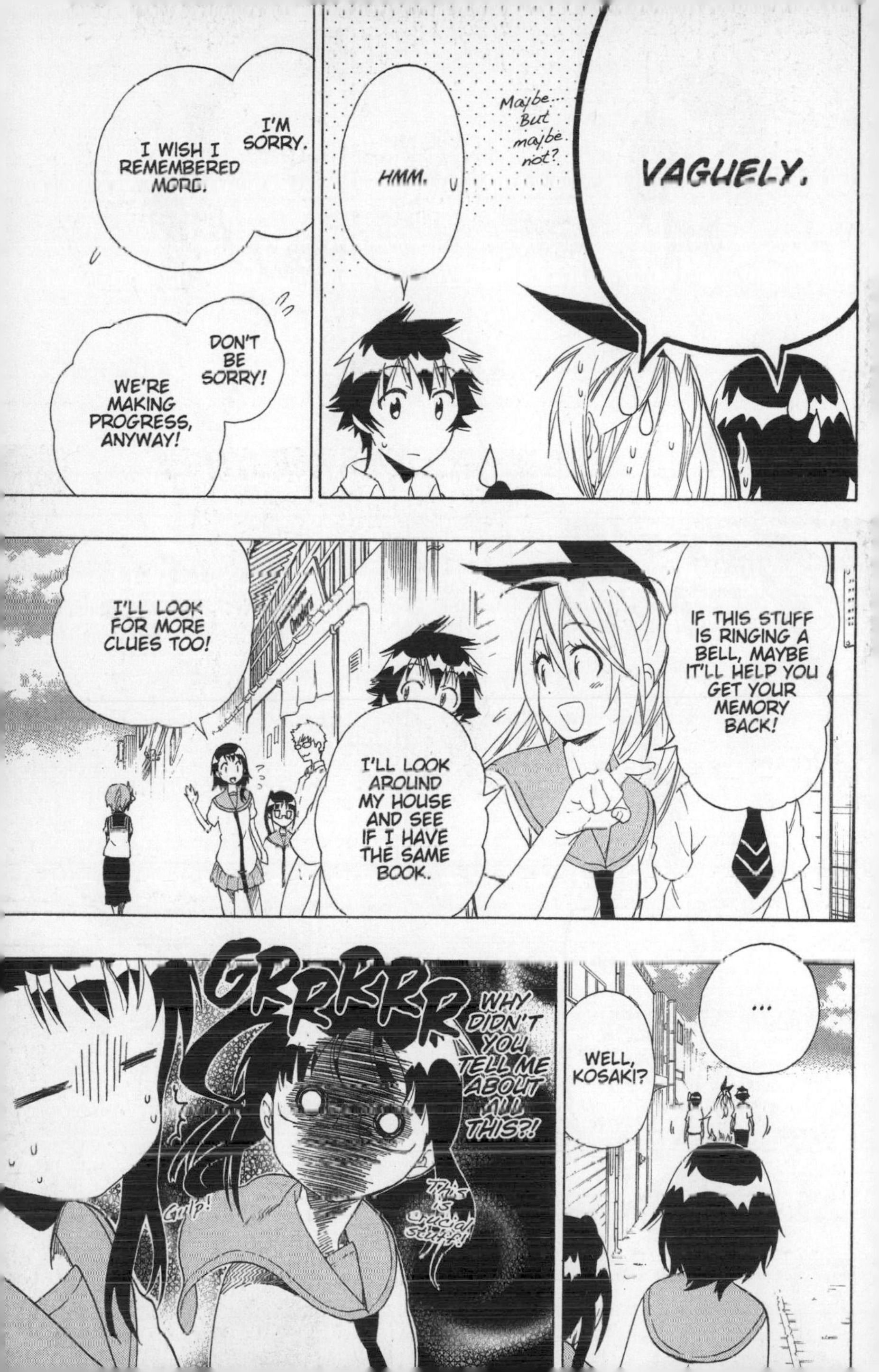
VAGUELY.
Maybe... But maybe not?
HMM.
I'M SORRY.
I WISH I REMEMBERED MORE.
DON'T BE SORRY!
WE'RE MAKING PROGRESS, ANYWAY!
IF THIS STUFF IS RINGING A BELL, MAYBE IT'LL HELP YOU GET YOUR MEMORY BACK!
I'LL LOOK AROUND MY HOUSE AND SEE IF I HAVE THE SAME BOOK.
I'LL LOOK FOR MORE CLUES TOO!
...
WELL, KOSAKI?
GRRKRR
WHY DIDN'T YOU TELL ME ABOUT ALL THIS?!
This is crucial stuff!
Gulp!

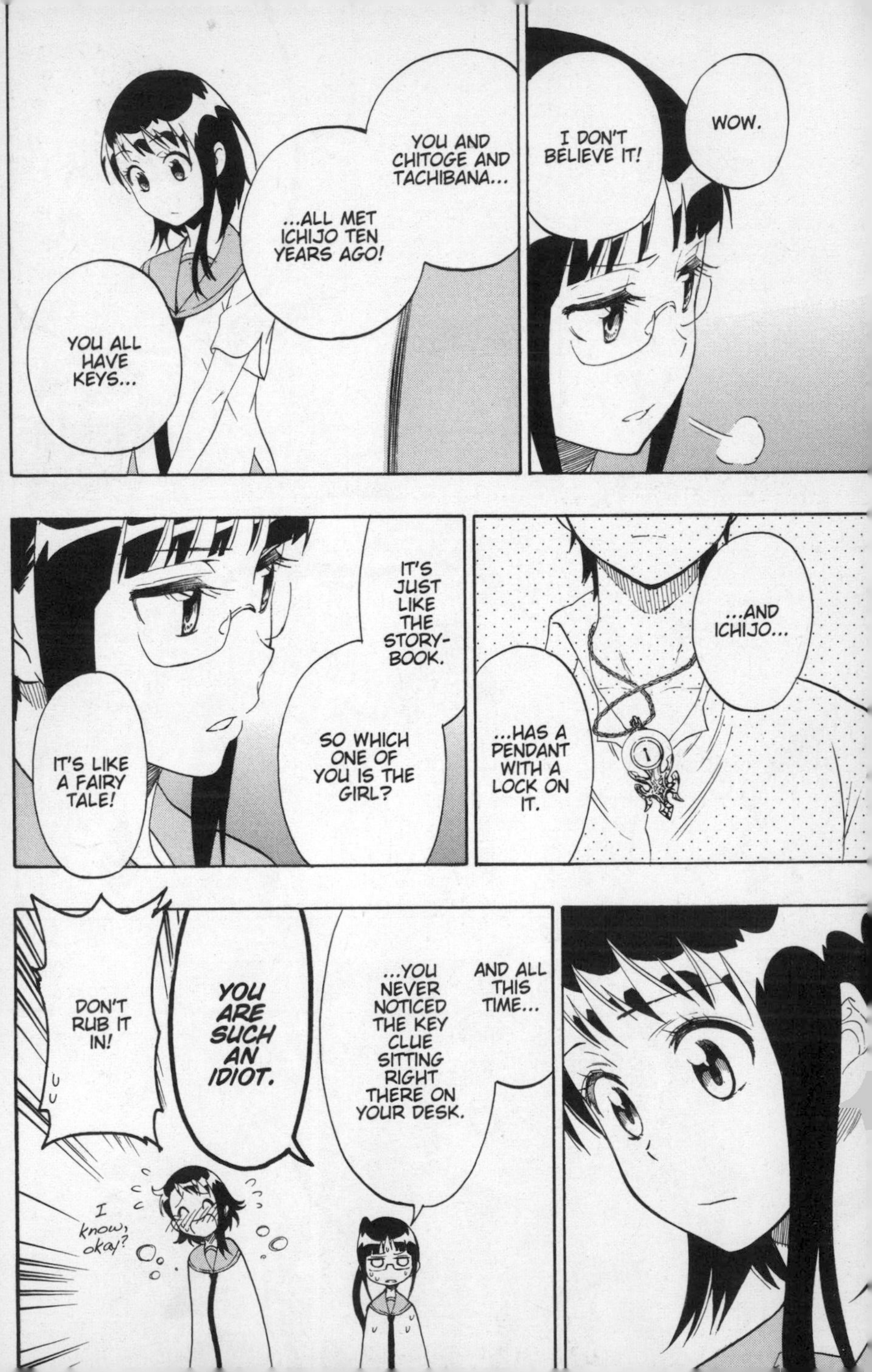
WOW.
I DON'T BELIEVE IT!
YOU AND CHITOGE AND TACHIBANA...
...ALL MET ICHIJO TEN YEARS AGO!
YOU ALL HAVE KEYS...
...AND ICHIJO...
...HAS A PENDANT WITH A LOCK ON IT.
IT'S JUST LIKE THE STORY-BOOK.
SO WHICH ONE OF YOU IS THE GIRL?
IT'S LIKE A FAIRY TALE!
AND ALL THIS TIME...
...YOU NEVER NOTICED THE KEY CLUE SITTING RIGHT THERE ON YOUR DESK.
YOU ARE SUCH AN IDIOT.
DON'T RUB IT IN!
I know, okay?

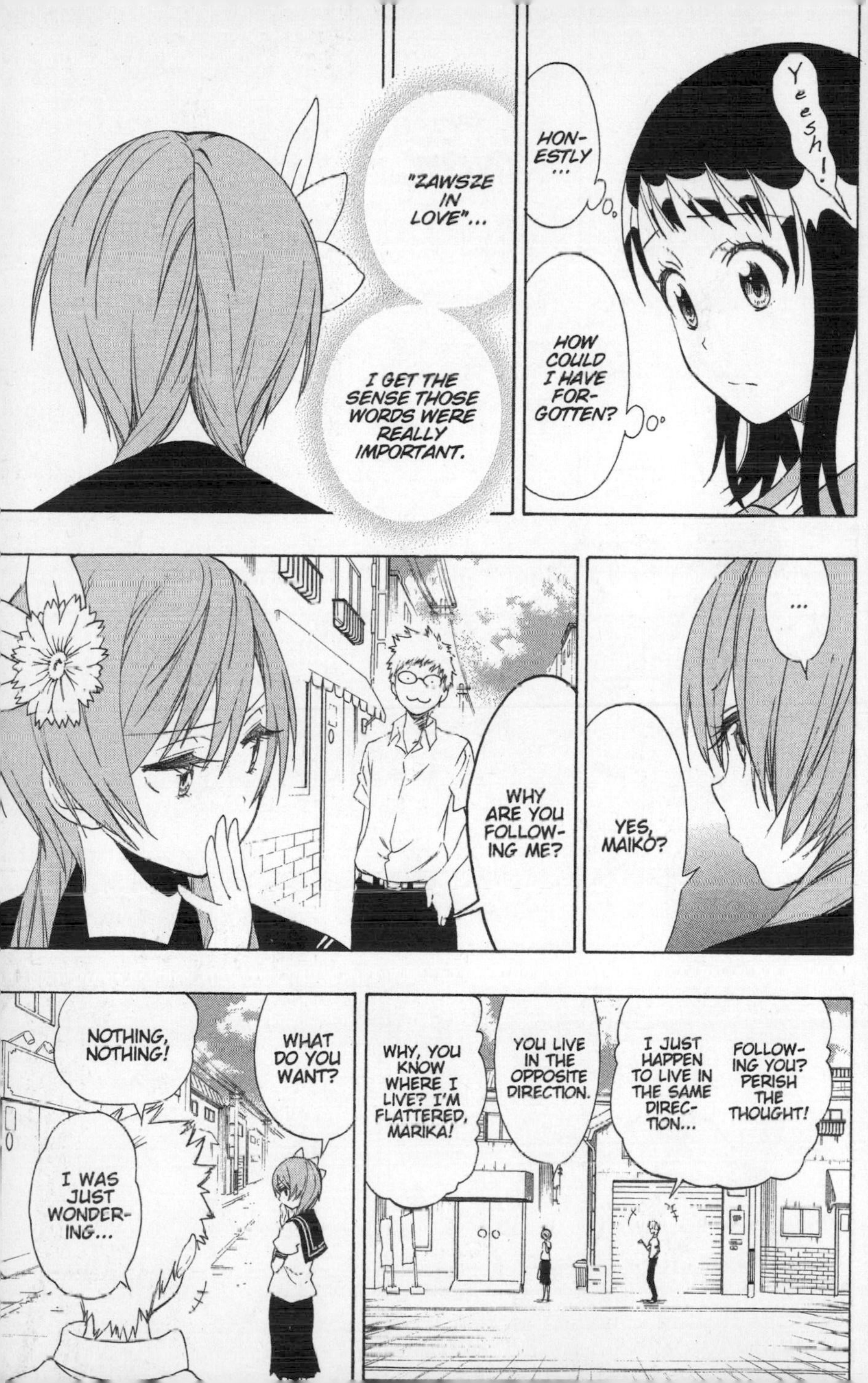
Yeesh!
HONESTLY...
HOW COULD I HAVE FORGOTTEN?
"ZAWSZE IN LOVE"...
I GET THE SENSE THOSE WORDS WERE REALLY IMPORTANT.
...
YES, MAIKO?
WHY ARE YOU FOLLOWING ME?
FOLLOWING YOU? PERISH THE THOUGHT!
I JUST HAPPEN TO LIVE IN THE SAME DIRECTION...
YOU LIVE IN THE OPPOSITE DIRECTION.
WHY, YOU KNOW WHERE I LIVE? I'M FLATTERED, MARIKA!
WHAT DO YOU WANT?
NOTHING, NOTHING!
I WAS JUST WONDERING...

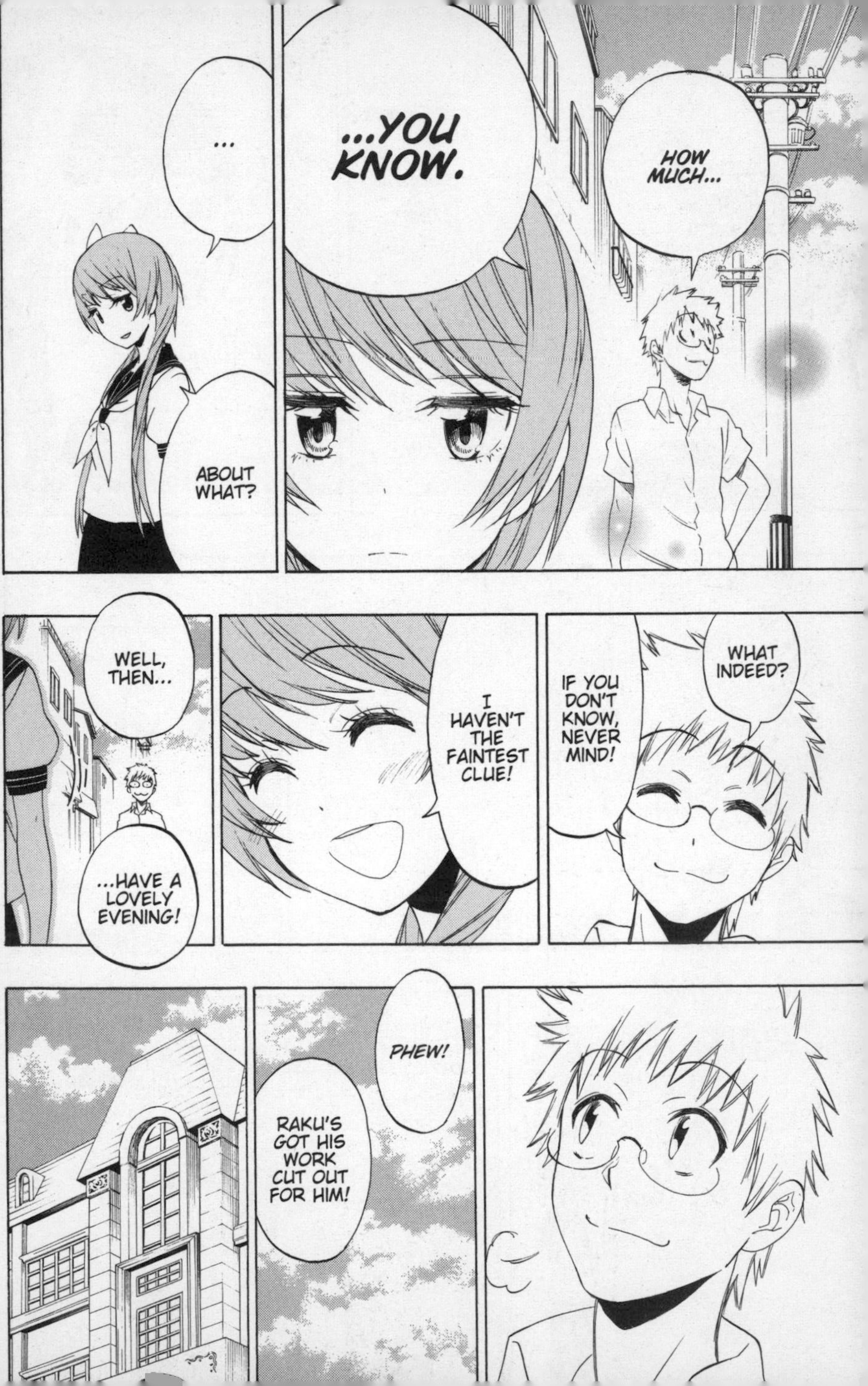
HOW MUCH...
...YOU KNOW.
...
ABOUT WHAT?
WHAT INDEED?
IF YOU DON'T KNOW, NEVER MIND!
I HAVEN'T THE FAINTEST CLUE!
WELL, THEN...
...HAVE A LOVELY EVENING!
PHEW!
RAKU'S GOT HIS WORK CUT OUT FOR HIM!

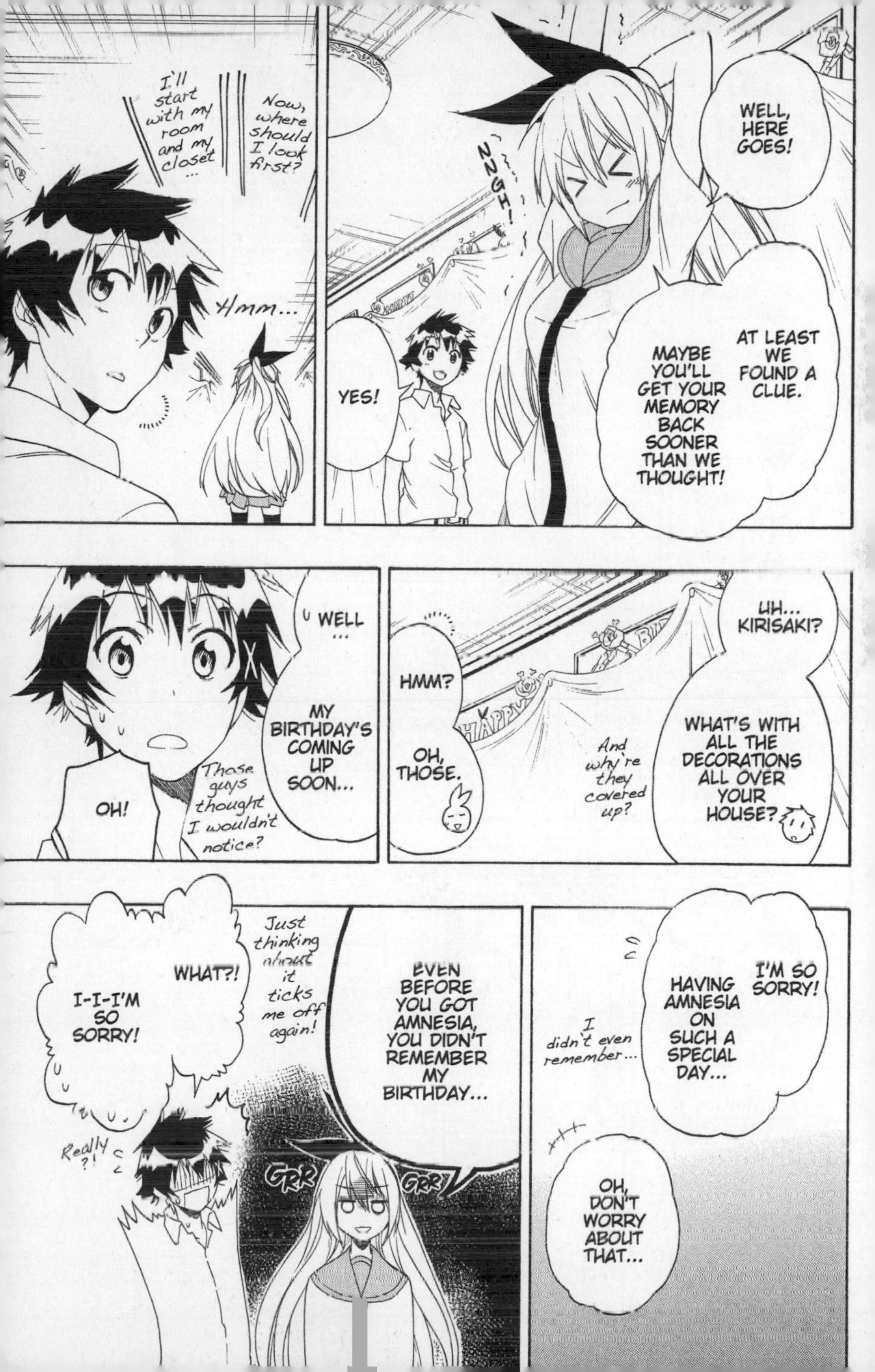
WELL, HERE GOES!
NNGH!
AT LEAST WE FOUND A CLUE.
MAYBE YOU'LL GET YOUR MEMORY BACK SOONER THAN WE THOUGHT!
YES!
Now, where should I look first?
I'll start with my room and my closet...
Hmm...
UH... KIRISAKI?
WHAT'S WITH ALL THE DECORATIONS ALL OVER YOUR HOUSE?
And why're they covered up?
HMM?
OH, THOSE.
WELL...
MY BIRTHDAY'S COMING UP SOON...
Those guys thought I wouldn't notice?
OH!
I'M SO SORRY!
HAVING AMNESIA ON SUCH A SPECIAL DAY...
I didn't even remember...
OH, DON'T WORRY ABOUT THAT...
EVEN BEFORE YOU GOT AMNESIA, YOU DIDN'T REMEMBER MY BIRTHDAY...
Just thinking about it ticks me off again!
GRR
GRR
WHAT?!
I-I-I'M SO SORRY!
Really?!

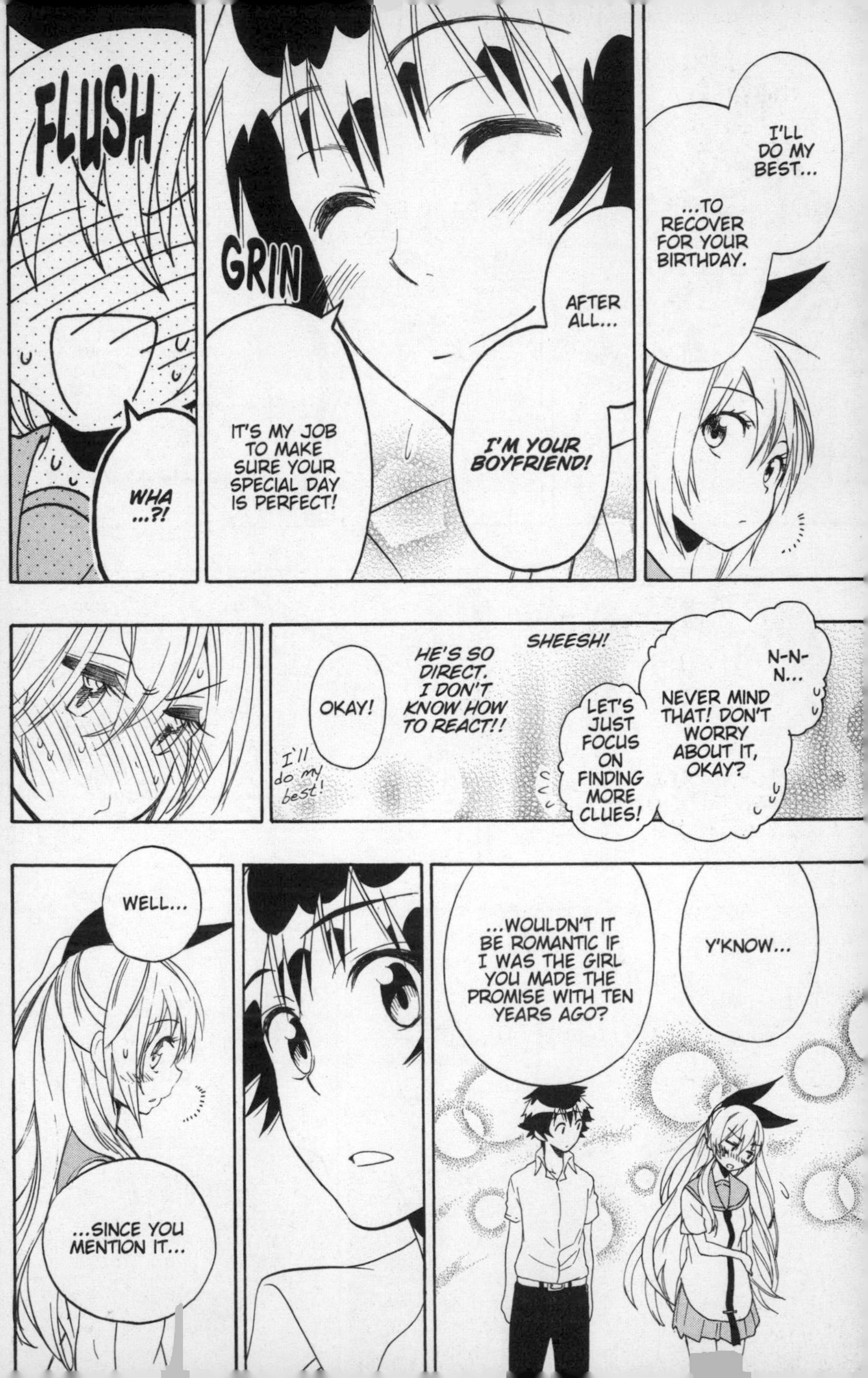
I'LL DO MY BEST...
...TO RECOVER FOR YOUR BIRTHDAY.
GRIN
AFTER ALL...
I'M YOUR BOYFRIEND!
IT'S MY JOB TO MAKE SURE YOUR SPECIAL DAY IS PERFECT!
FLUSH
WHA ...?!
N-N-N...
NEVER MIND THAT! DON'T WORRY ABOUT IT, OKAY?
LET'S JUST FOCUS ON FINDING MORE CLUES!
SHEESH!
HE'S SO DIRECT. I DON'T KNOW HOW TO REACT!!
OKAY!
I'll do my best!
Y'KNOW...
...WOULDN'T IT BE ROMANTIC IF I WAS THE GIRL YOU MADE THE PROMISE WITH TEN YEARS AGO?
WELL...
...SINCE YOU MENTION IT...

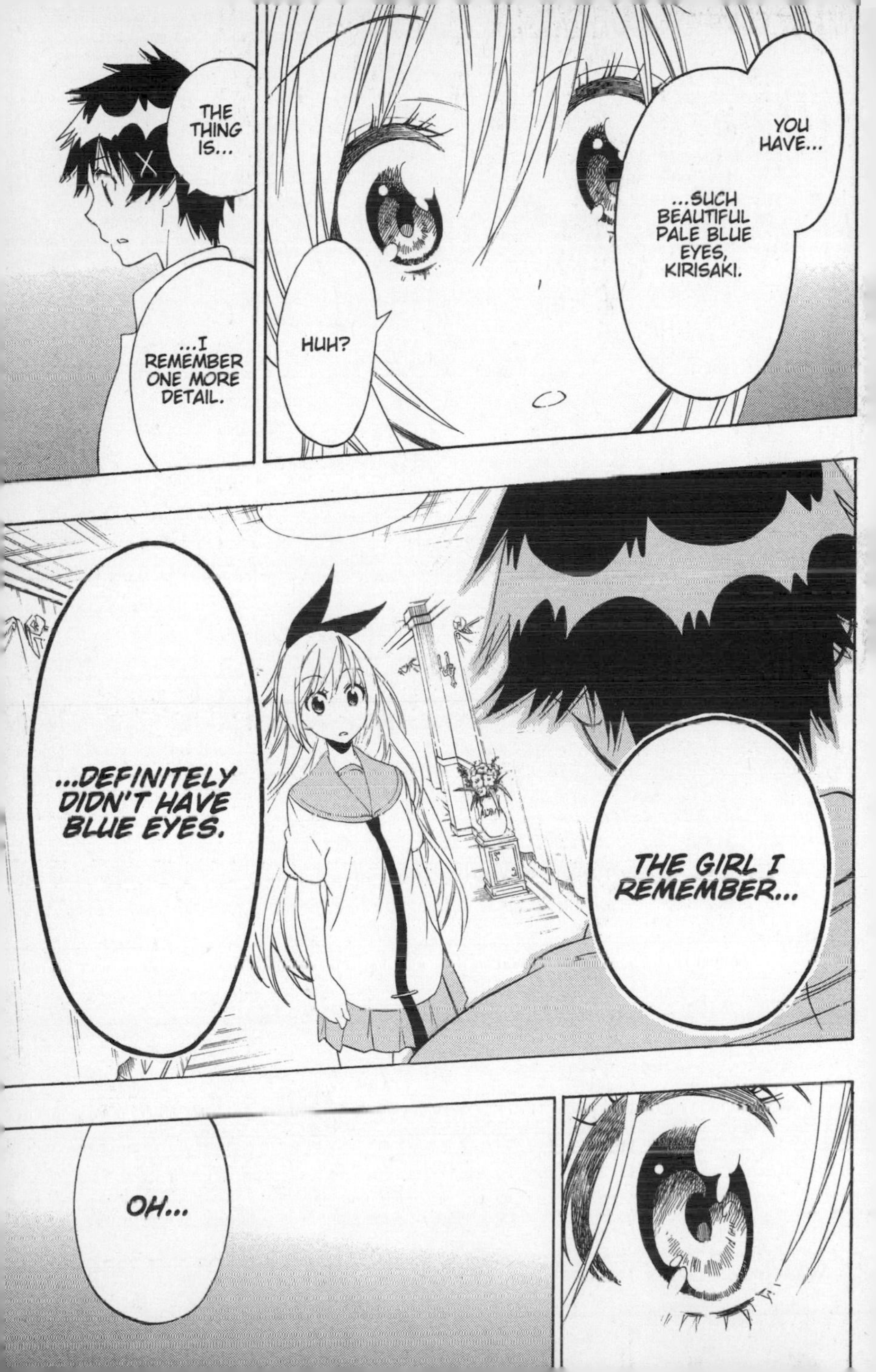
YOU HAVE...
...SUCH BEAUTIFUL PALE BLUE EYES, KIRISAKI.
HUH?
THE THING IS...
...I REMEMBER ONE MORE DETAIL.
THE GIRL I REMEMBER...
...DEFINITELY DIDN'T HAVE BLUE EYES.
OH...

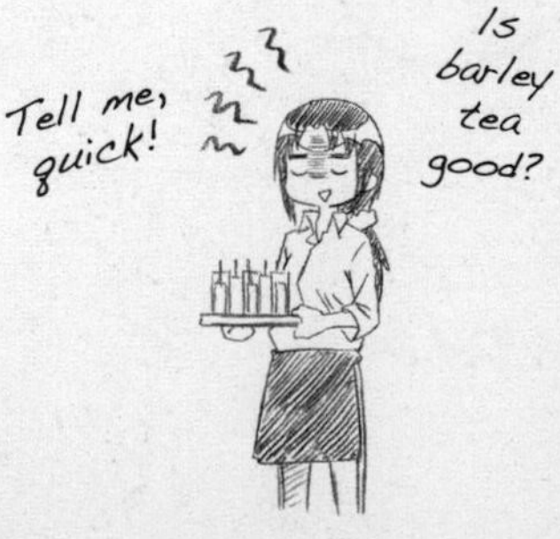
Is barley tea good?
Tell me, quick!

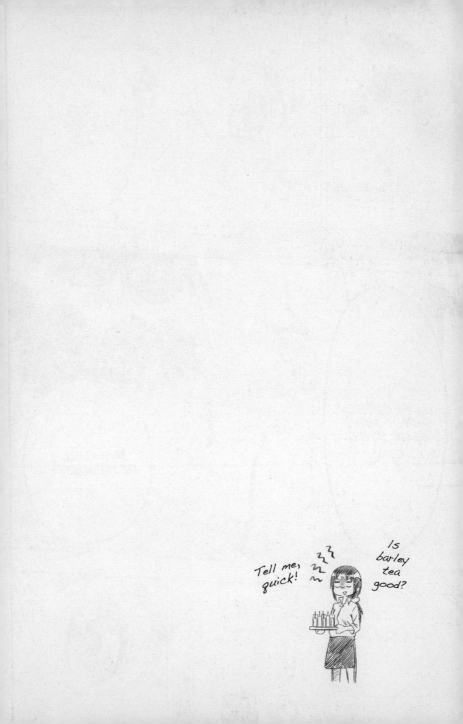

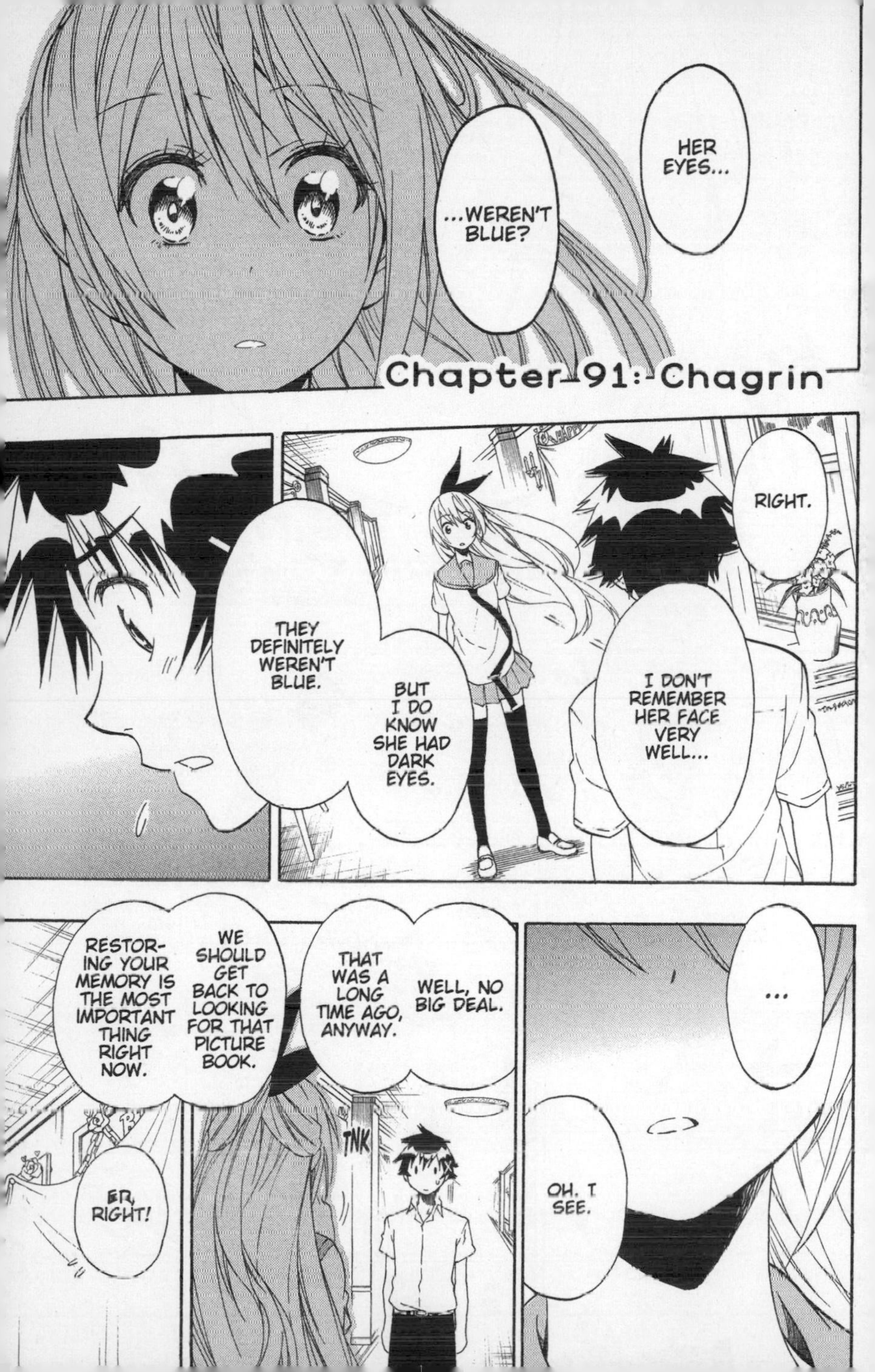
HER EYES...
...WEREN'T BLUE?
Chapter 91: Chagrin
RIGHT.
I DON'T REMEMBER HER FACE VERY WELL...
BUT I DO KNOW SHE HAD DARK EYES.
THEY DEFINITELY WEREN'T BLUE.
...
OH. I SEE.
WELL, NO BIG DEAL.
THAT WAS A LONG TIME AGO, ANYWAY.
WE SHOULD GET BACK TO LOOKING FOR THAT PICTURE BOOK.
RESTORING YOUR MEMORY IS THE MOST IMPORTANT THING RIGHT NOW.
TNK
ER, RIGHT!

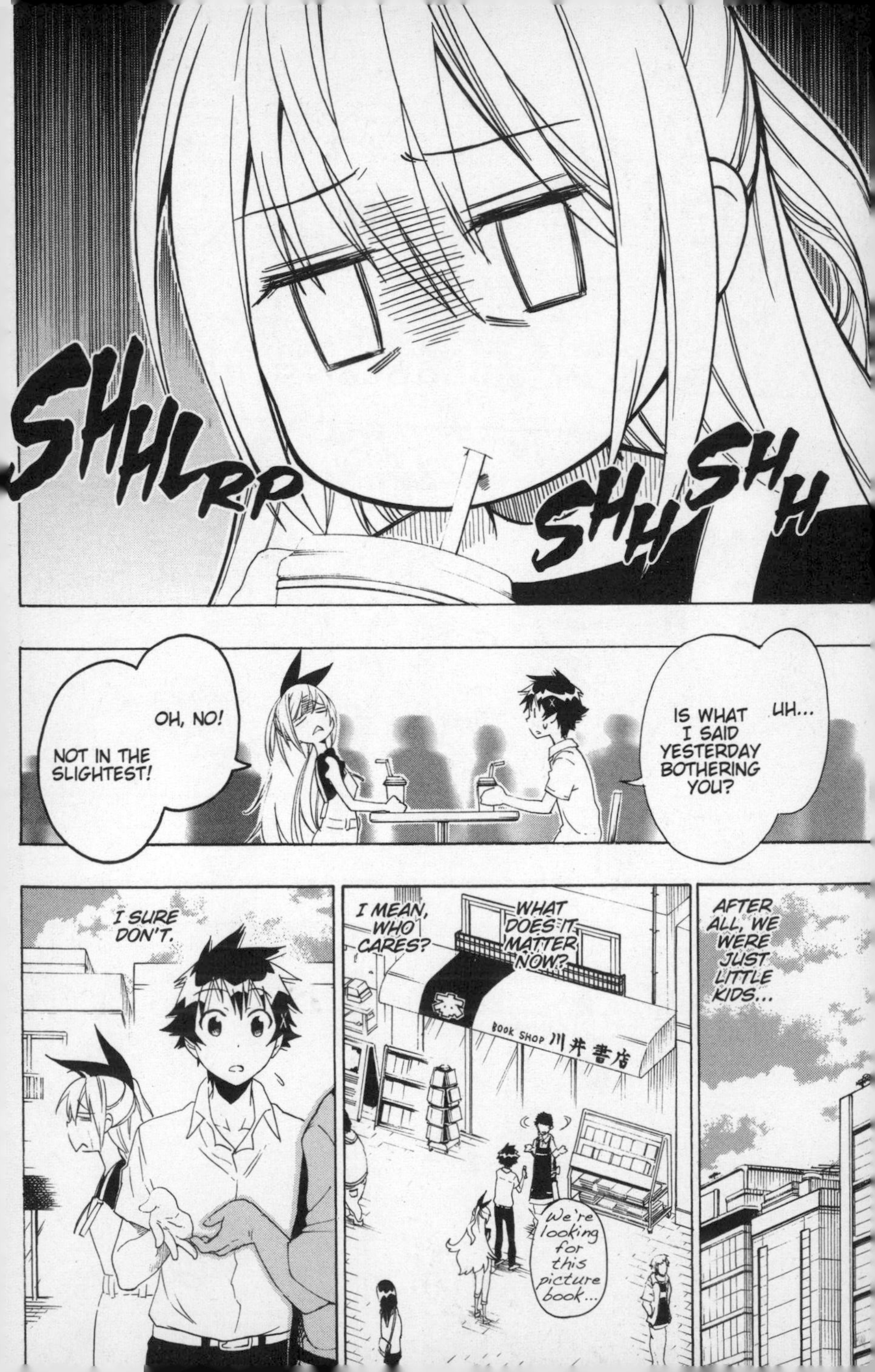
SHHLRP
SHH SHH
UH...
IS WHAT I SAID YESTERDAY BOTHERING YOU?
OH, NO!
NOT IN THE SLIGHTEST!
AFTER ALL, WE WERE JUST LITTLE KIDS...
WHAT DOES IT MATTER NOW?
I MEAN, WHO CARES?
BOOK SHOP 川井書店
We're looking for this picture book...
I SURE DON'T.

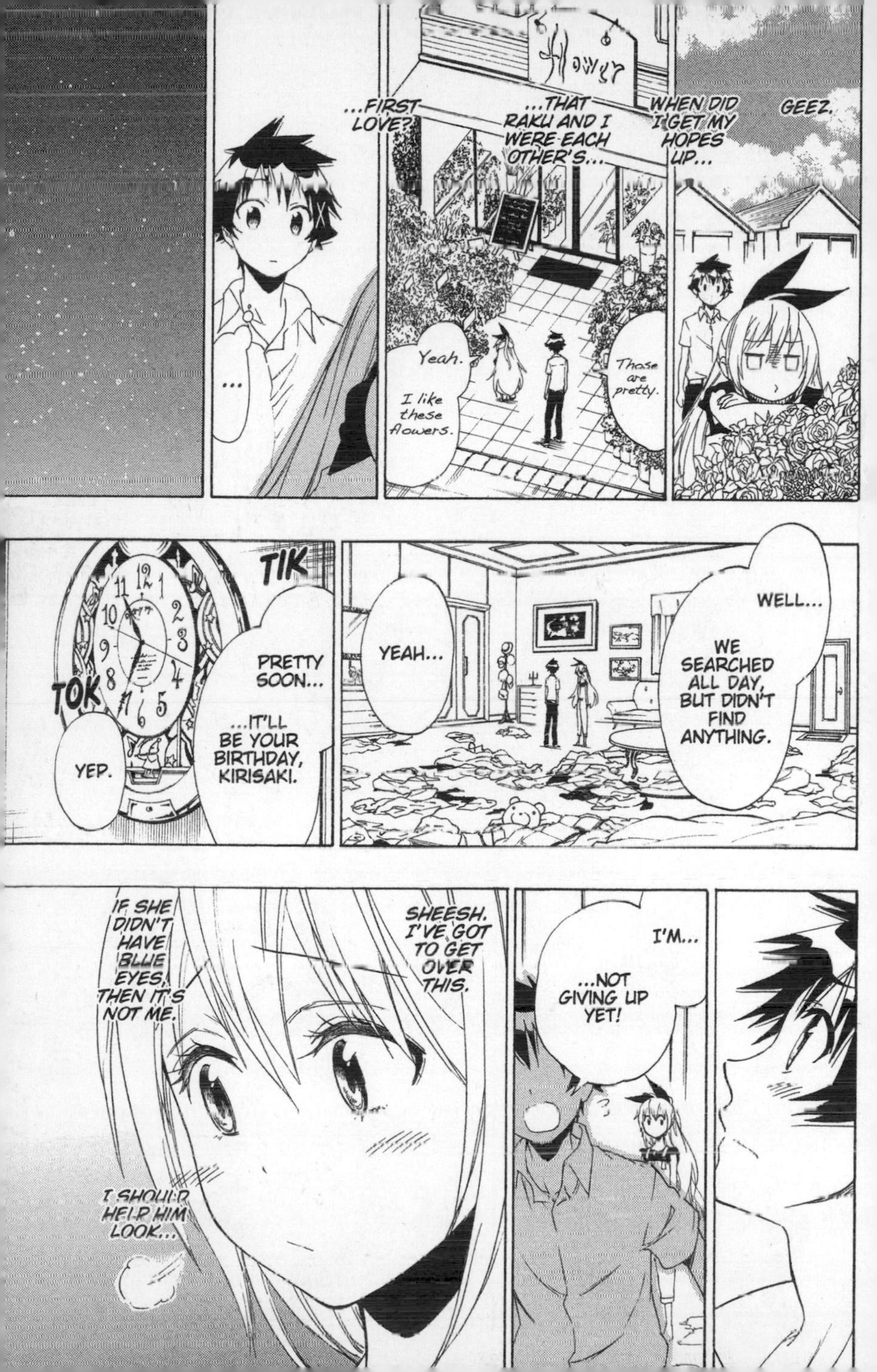
GEEZ.
WHEN DID I GET MY HOPES UP...
...THAT RAKU AND I WERE EACH OTHER'S...
...FIRST LOVE?
Those are pretty.
Yeah.
I like these flowers.
...
WELL...
WE SEARCHED ALL DAY, BUT DIDN'T FIND ANYTHING.
YEAH...
TIK
PRETTY SOON...
...IT'LL BE YOUR BIRTHDAY, KIRISAKI.
TOK
YEP.
I'M...
...NOT GIVING UP YET!
SHEESH. I'VE GOT TO GET OVER THIS.
IF SHE DIDN'T HAVE BLUE EYES, THEN IT'S NOT ME.
I SHOULD HELP HIM LOOK...

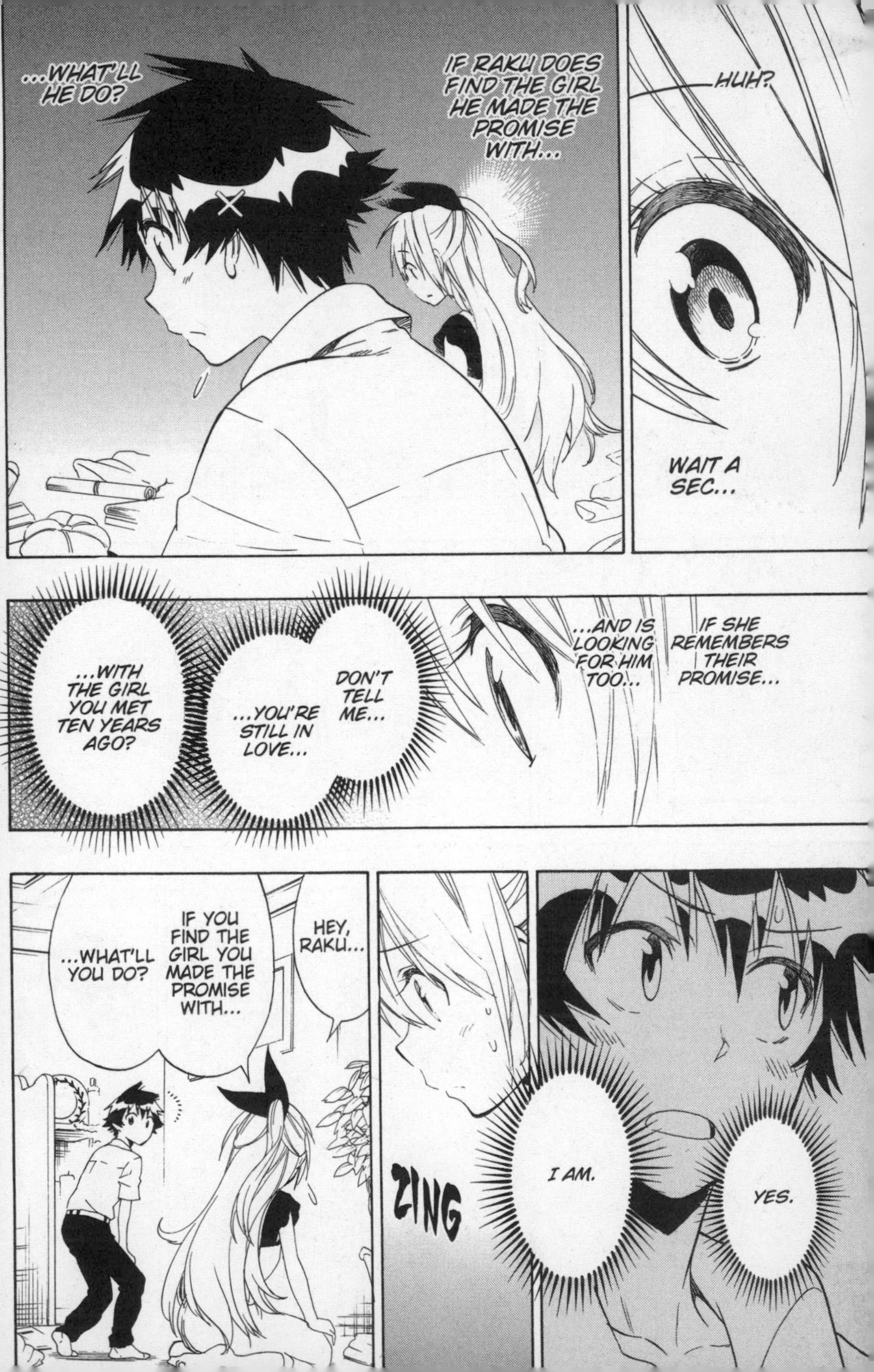
HUH?
WAIT A SEC...
IF RAKU DOES FIND THE GIRL HE MADE THE PROMISE WITH...
...WHAT'LL HE DO?
IF SHE REMEMBERS THEIR PROMISE...
...AND IS LOOKING FOR HIM TOO...
DON'T TELL ME...
...YOU'RE STILL IN LOVE...
...WITH THE GIRL YOU MET TEN YEARS AGO?
YES.
I AM.
ZING
HEY, RAKU...
IF YOU FIND THE GIRL YOU MADE THE PROMISE WITH...
...WHAT'LL YOU DO?

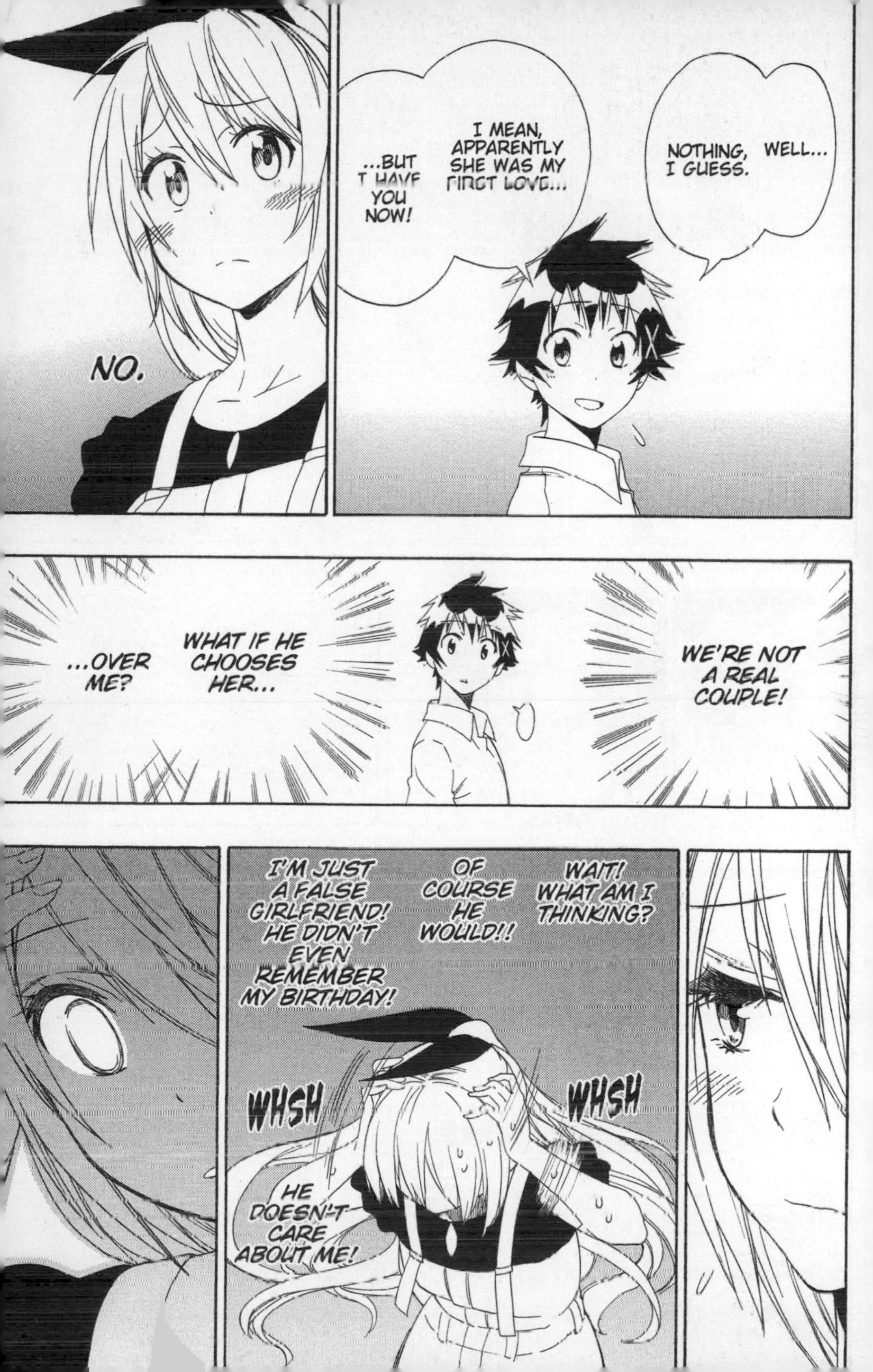
WELL...
NOTHING, I GUESS.
I MEAN, APPARENTLY SHE WAS MY FIRST LOVE...
...BUT I HAVE YOU NOW!
NO.
WE'RE NOT A REAL COUPLE!
WHAT IF HE CHOOSES HER...
...OVER ME?
WAIT! WHAT AM I THINKING?
OF COURSE HE WOULD!!
I'M JUST A FALSE GIRLFRIEND! HE DIDN'T EVEN REMEMBER MY BIRTHDAY!
WHSH
WHSH
HE DOESN'T CARE ABOUT ME!

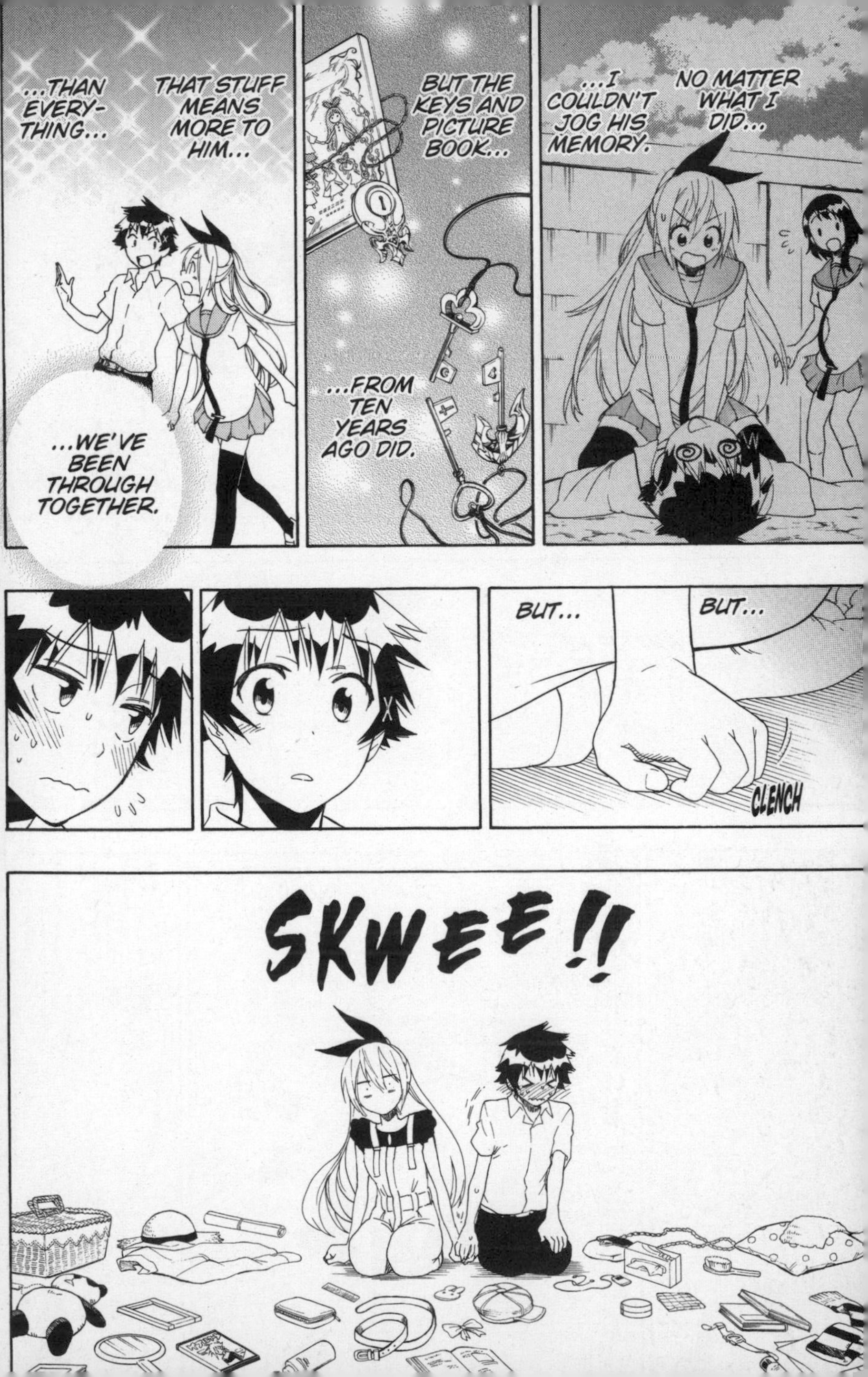
NO MATTER WHAT I DID...
...I COULDN'T JOG HIS MEMORY.
BUT THE KEYS AND PICTURE BOOK...
...FROM TEN YEARS AGO DID.
THAT STUFF MEANS MORE TO HIM...
...THAN EVERY-THING...
...WE'VE BEEN THROUGH TOGETHER.
BUT...
BUT...
CLENCH
SKWEE!!

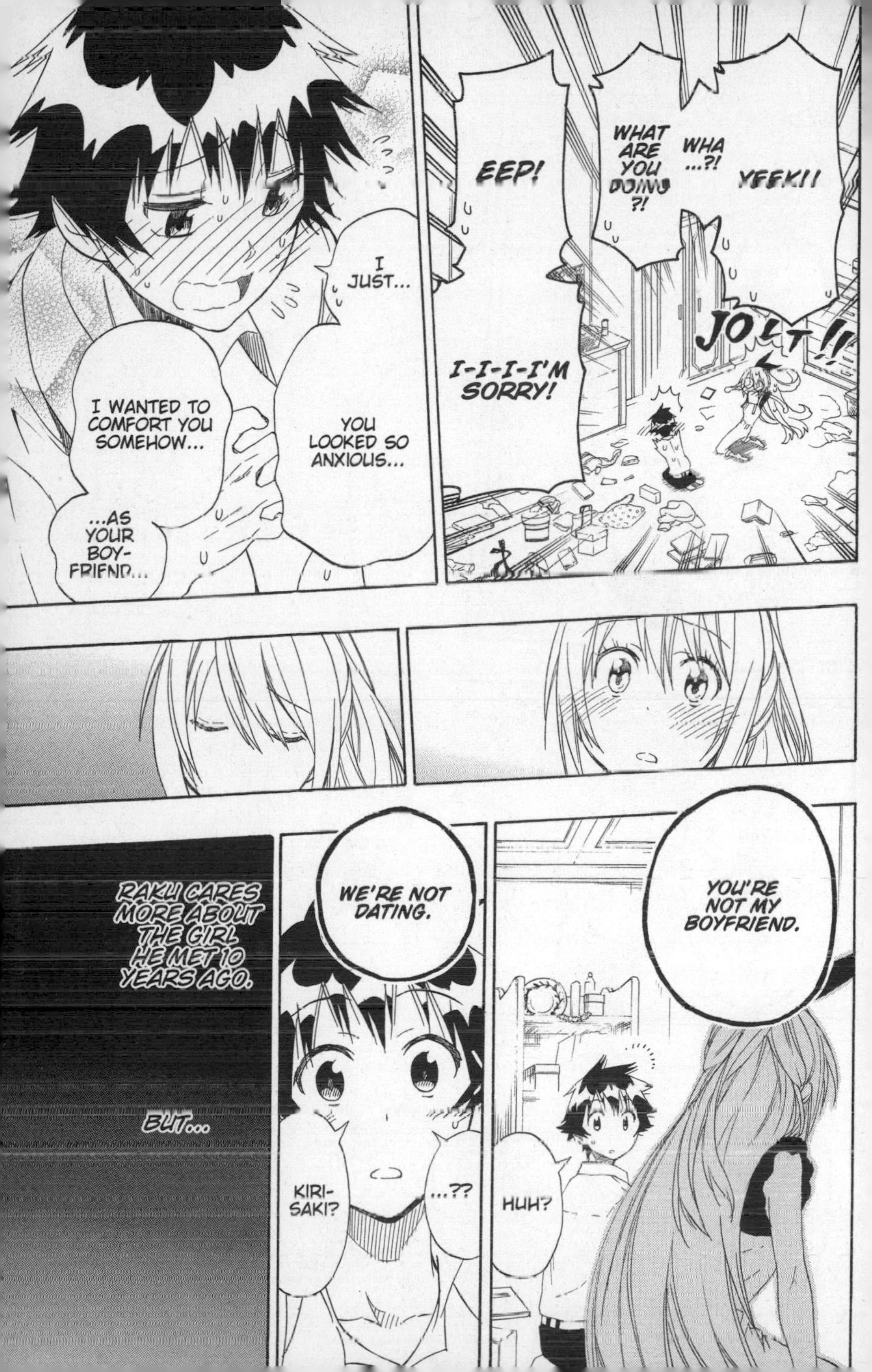
YEEK!!
WHA ...?!
WHAT ARE YOU DOING ?!
EEP!
JOLT!!
I-I-I-I'M SORRY!
I JUST...
YOU LOOKED SO ANXIOUS...
I WANTED TO COMFORT YOU SOMEHOW...
...AS YOUR BOY-FRIEND...
YOU'RE NOT MY BOYFRIEND.
HUH?
WE'RE NOT DATING.
...??
KIRI-SAKI?
RAKU CARES MORE ABOUT THE GIRL HE MET 10 YEARS AGO.
BUT...

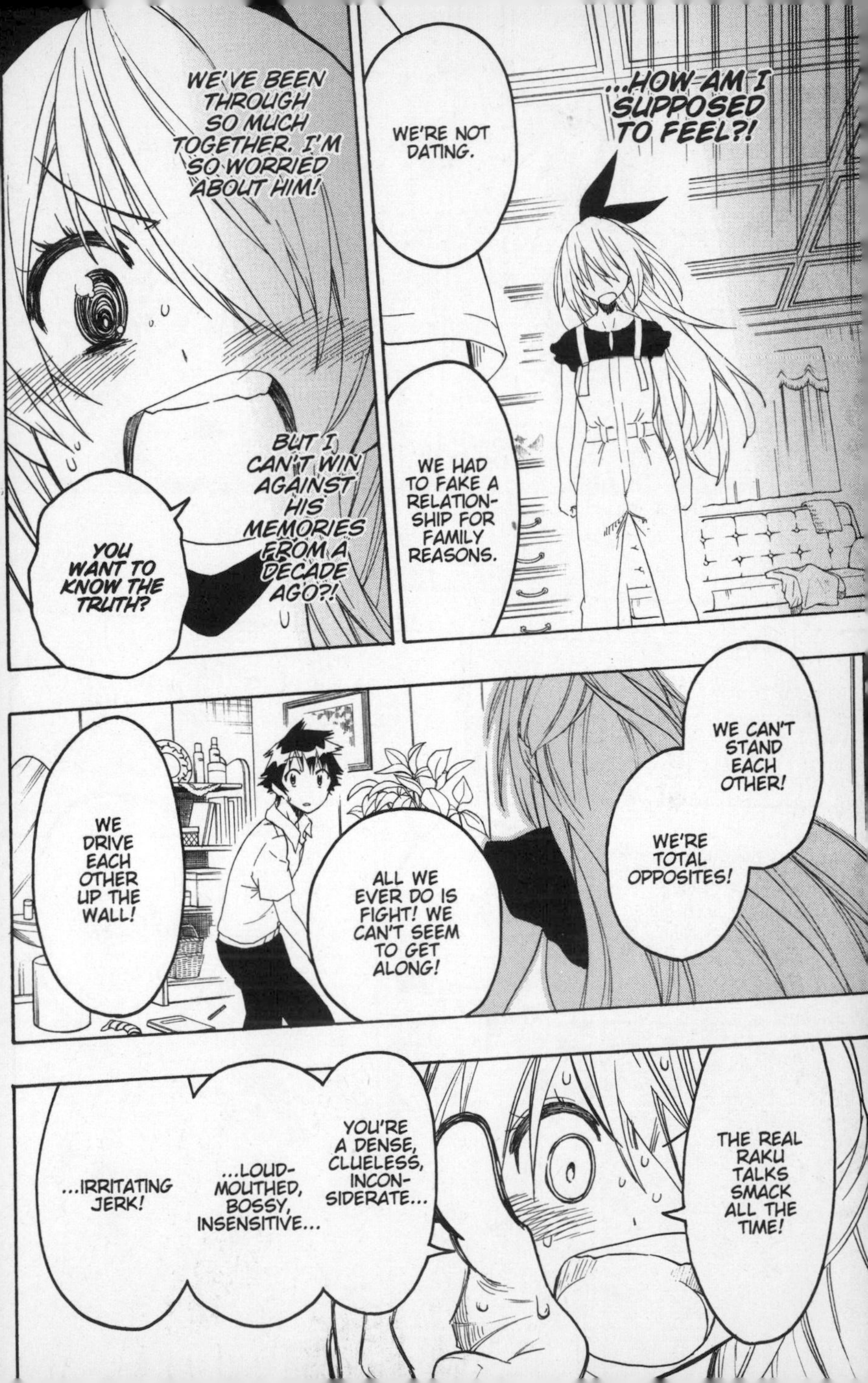
...HOW AM I SUPPOSED TO FEEL?!
WE'RE NOT DATING.
WE HAD TO FAKE A RELATIONSHIP FOR FAMILY REASONS.
WE'VE BEEN THROUGH SO MUCH TOGETHER. I'M SO WORRIED ABOUT HIM!
BUT I CAN'T WIN AGAINST HIS MEMORIES FROM A DECADE AGO?!
YOU WANT TO KNOW THE TRUTH?
WE CAN'T STAND EACH OTHER!
WE'RE TOTAL OPPOSITES!
ALL WE EVER DO IS FIGHT! WE CAN'T SEEM TO GET ALONG!
WE DRIVE EACH OTHER UP THE WALL!
THE REAL RAKU TALKS SMACK ALL THE TIME!
YOU'RE A DENSE, CLUELESS, INCONSIDERATE...
...LOUD-MOUTHED, BOSSY, INSENSITIVE...
...IRRITATING JERK!

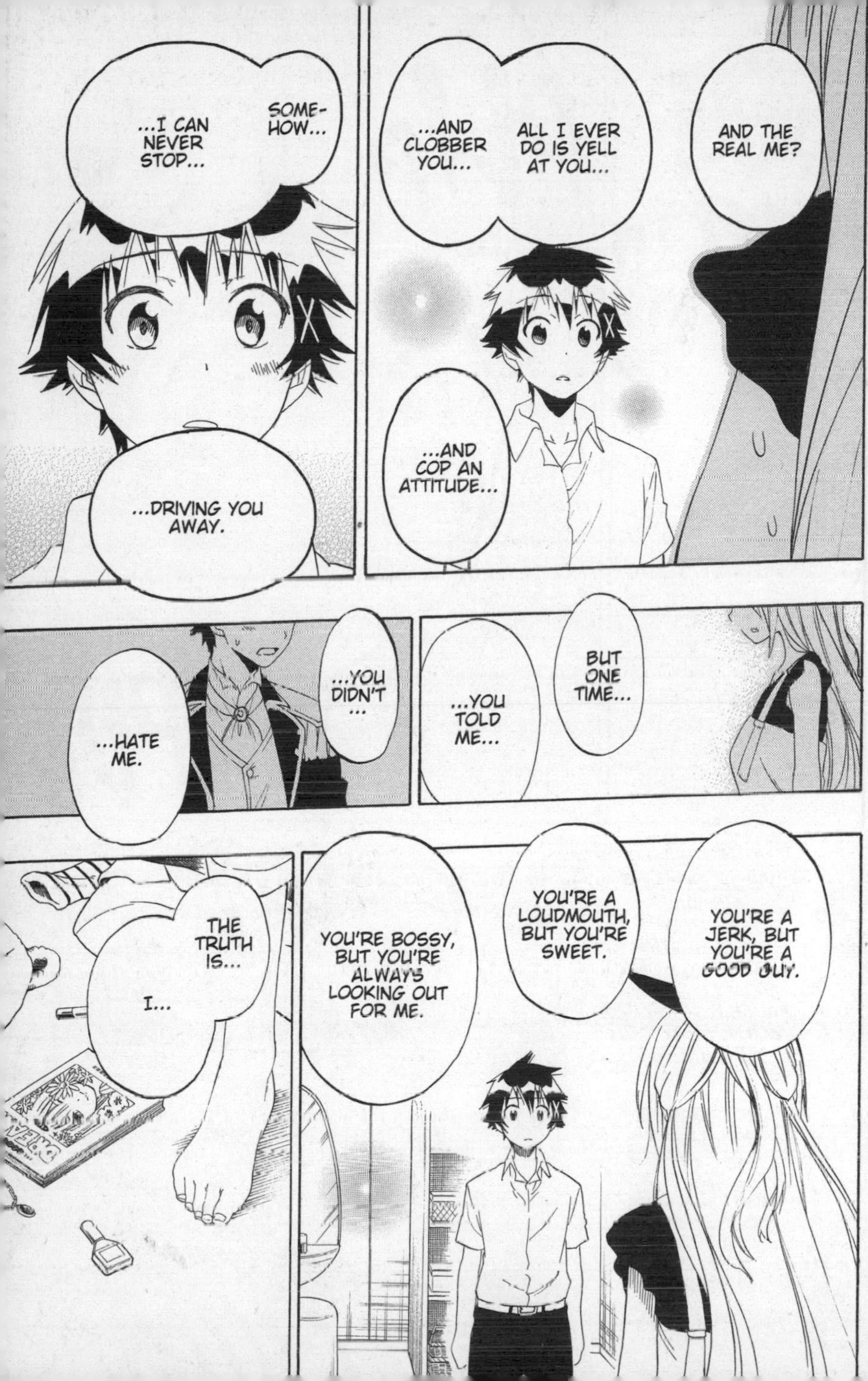

AND THE REAL ME?
ALL I EVER DO IS YELL AT YOU...
...AND CLOBBER YOU...
...AND COP AN ATTITUDE...
SOME-HOW...
...I CAN NEVER STOP...
...DRIVING YOU AWAY.
BUT ONE TIME...
...YOU TOLD ME...
...YOU DIDN'T ...
...HATE ME.
YOU'RE A JERK, BUT YOU'RE A GOOD GUY.
YOU'RE A LOUDMOUTH, BUT YOU'RE SWEET.
YOU'RE BOSSY, BUT YOU'RE ALWAYS LOOKING OUT FOR ME.
THE TRUTH IS...
I...

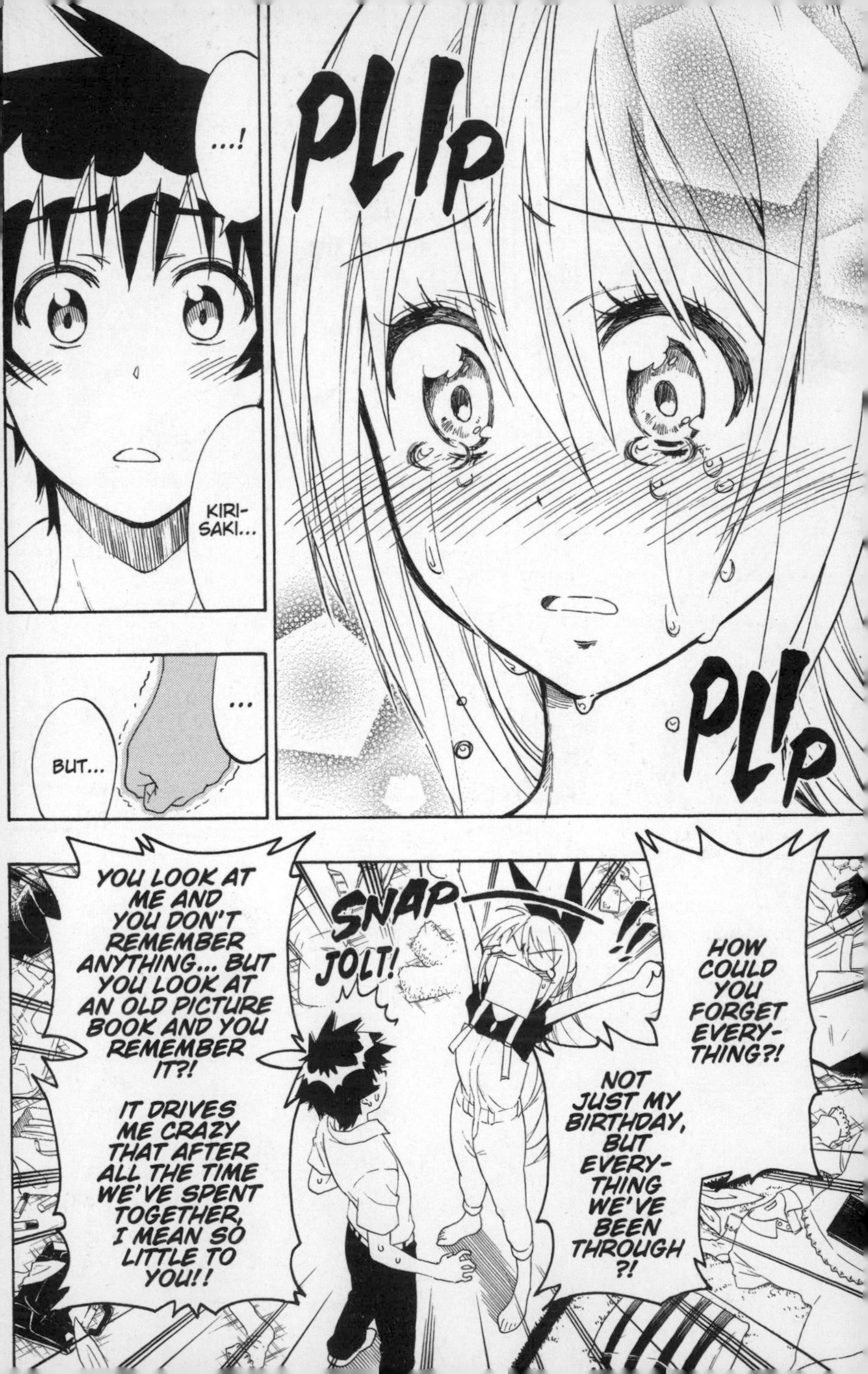
PLIP
PLIP
...!
KIRI-SAKI...
...
BUT...
HOW COULD YOU FORGET EVERYTHING?!
SNAP
!!
JOLT!
NOT JUST MY BIRTHDAY, BUT EVERYTHING WE'VE BEEN THROUGH?!
YOU LOOK AT ME AND YOU DON'T REMEMBER ANYTHING... BUT YOU LOOK AT AN OLD PICTURE BOOK AND YOU REMEMBER IT?!
IT DRIVES ME CRAZY THAT AFTER ALL THE TIME WE'VE SPENT TOGETHER, I MEAN SO LITTLE TO YOU!!

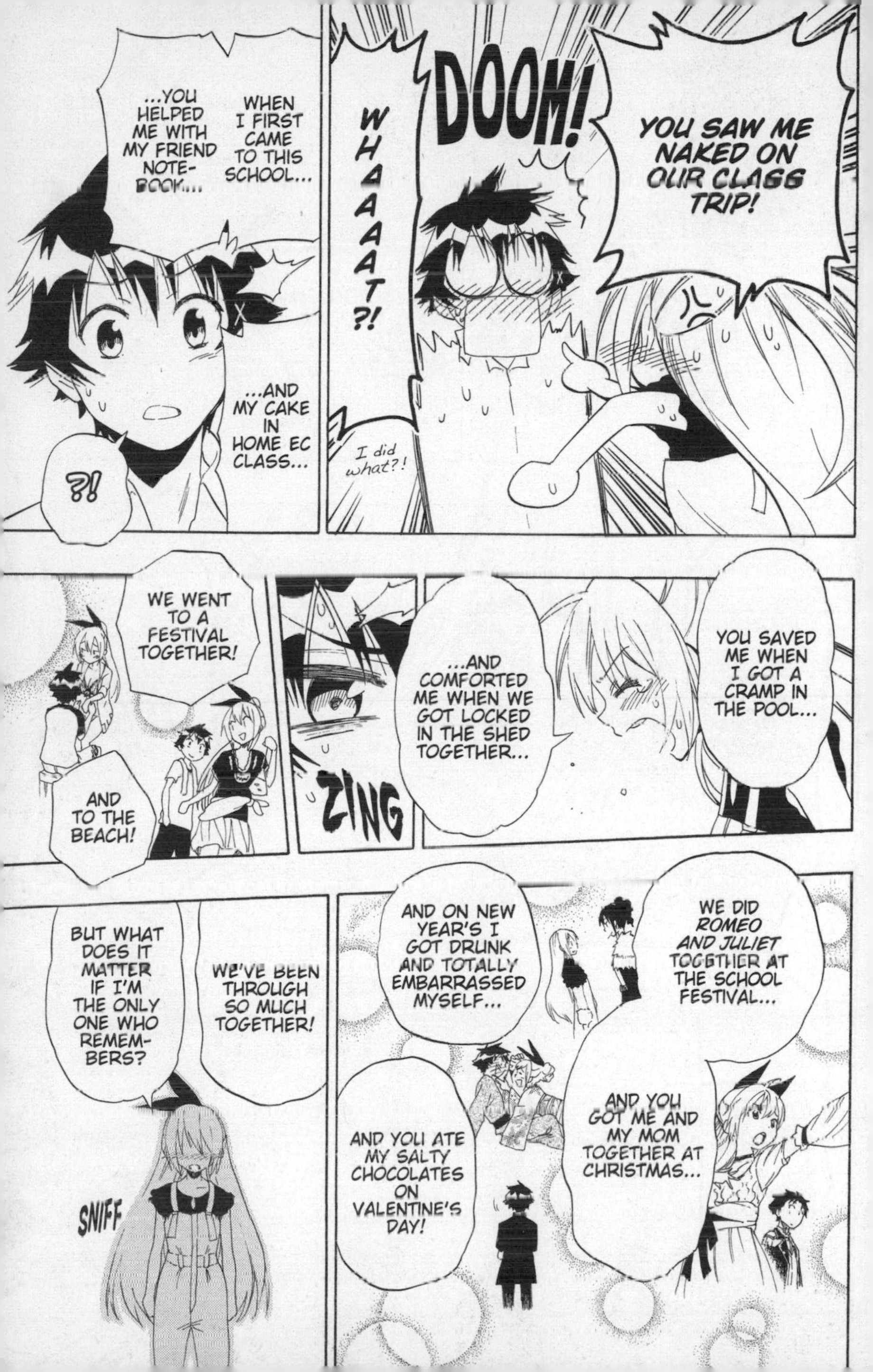
YOU SAW ME NAKED ON OUR CLASS TRIP!
DOOM!
WHAAAAAT?!
I did what?!
WHEN I FIRST CAME TO THIS SCHOOL...
...YOU HELPED ME WITH MY FRIEND NOTE-BOOK...
...AND MY CAKE IN HOME EC CLASS...
?!
YOU SAVED ME WHEN I GOT A CRAMP IN THE POOL...
...AND COMFORTED ME WHEN WE GOT LOCKED IN THE SHED TOGETHER...
ZING
WE WENT TO A FESTIVAL TOGETHER!
AND TO THE BEACH!
WE DID ROMEO AND JULIET TOGETHER AT THE SCHOOL FESTIVAL...
AND ON NEW YEAR'S I GOT DRUNK AND TOTALLY EMBARRASSED MYSELF...
AND YOU GOT ME AND MY MOM TOGETHER AT CHRISTMAS...
AND YOU ATE MY SALTY CHOCOLATES ON VALENTINE'S DAY!
WE'VE BEEN THROUGH SO MUCH TOGETHER!
BUT WHAT DOES IT MATTER IF I'M THE ONLY ONE WHO REMEMBERS?
SNIFF

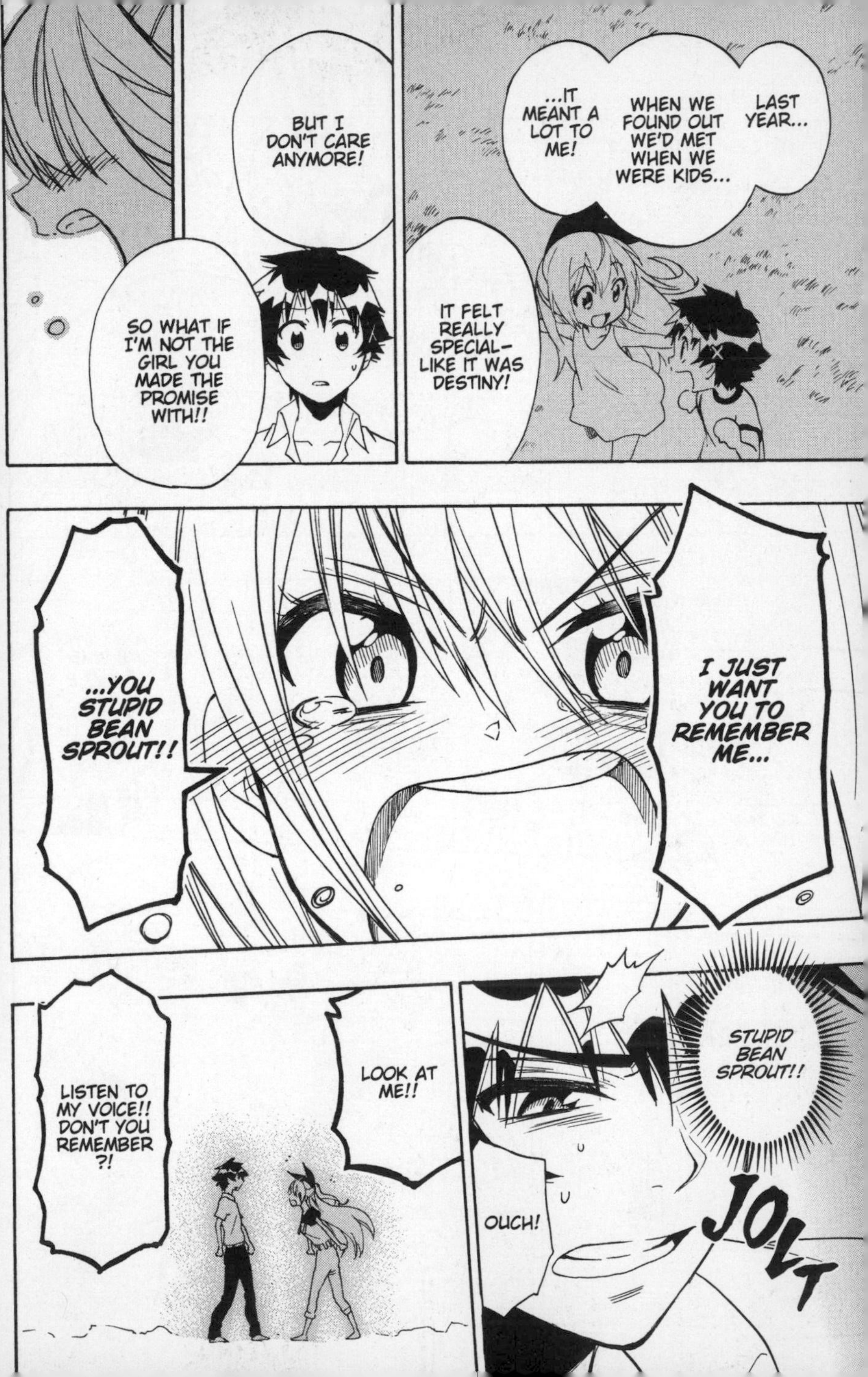
LAST YEAR...
WHEN WE FOUND OUT WE'D MET WHEN WE WERE KIDS...
...IT MEANT A LOT TO ME!
IT FELT REALLY SPECIAL—LIKE IT WAS DESTINY!
BUT I DON'T CARE ANYMORE!
SO WHAT IF I'M NOT THE GIRL YOU MADE THE PROMISE WITH!!
I JUST WANT YOU TO REMEMBER ME...
...YOU STUPID BEAN SPROUT!!
STUPID BEAN SPROUT!!
JOLT
OUCH!
LOOK AT ME!!
LISTEN TO MY VOICE!! DON'T YOU REMEMBER?!

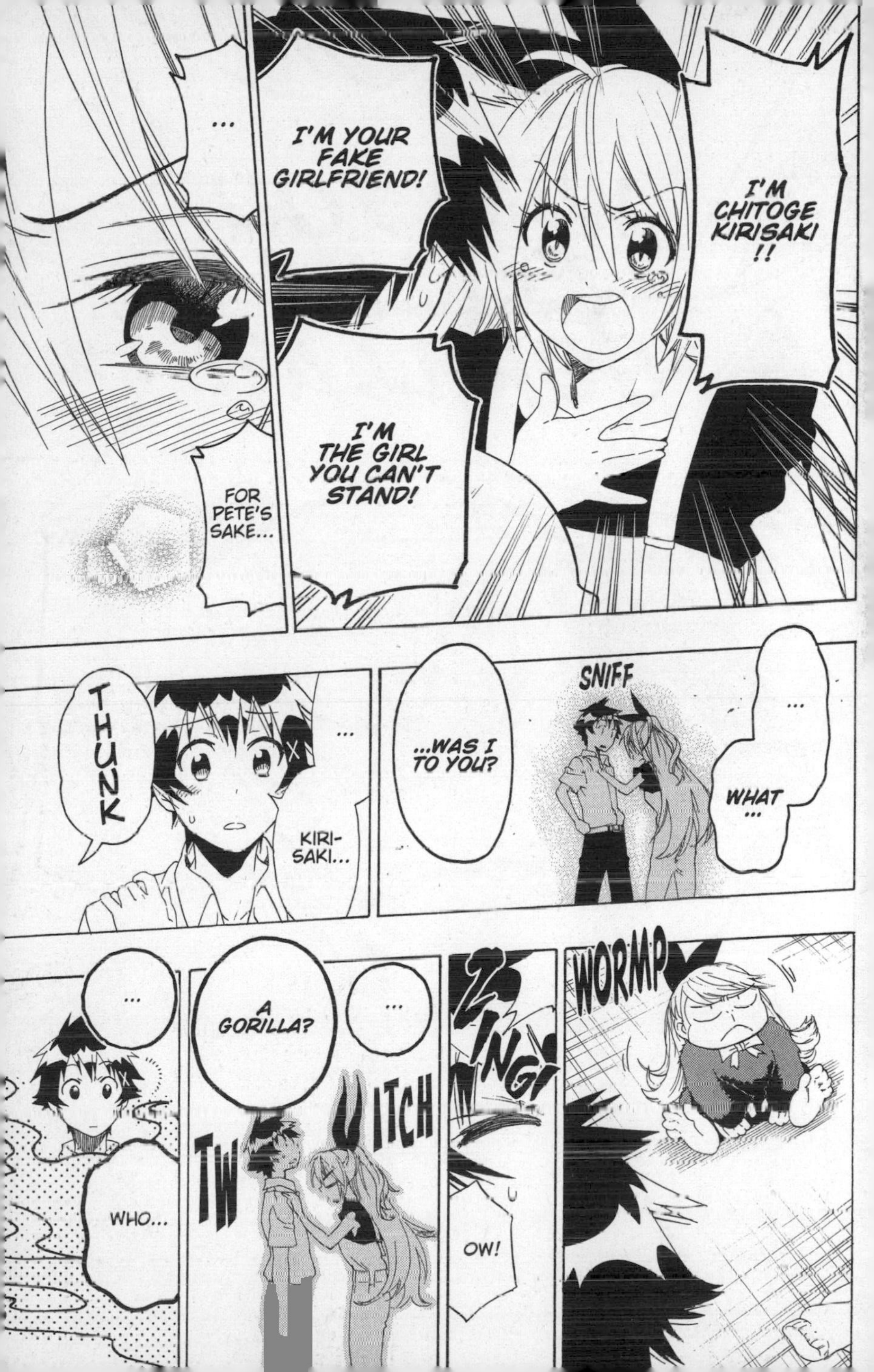
I'M CHITOGE KIRISAKI!!
I'M YOUR FAKE GIRLFRIEND!
I'M THE GIRL YOU CAN'T STAND!
...
FOR PETE'S SAKE...
...
WHAT ...
SNIFF
...WAS I TO YOU?
...
KIRI-SAKI...
THUNK
WORMP
ZING!
OW!
...
A GORILLA?
TWITCH
...
WHO...

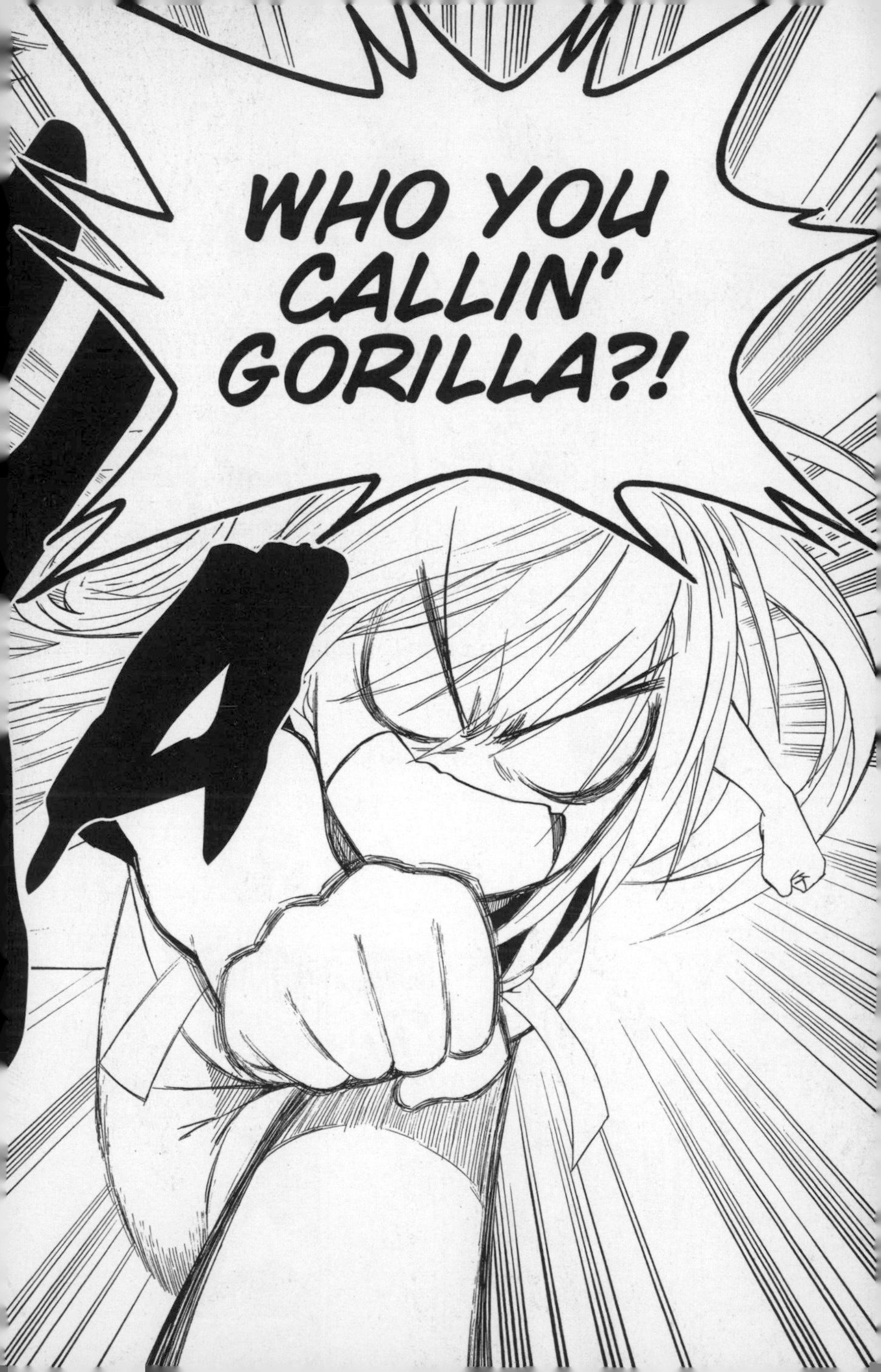
WHO YOU CALLIN' GORILLA?!

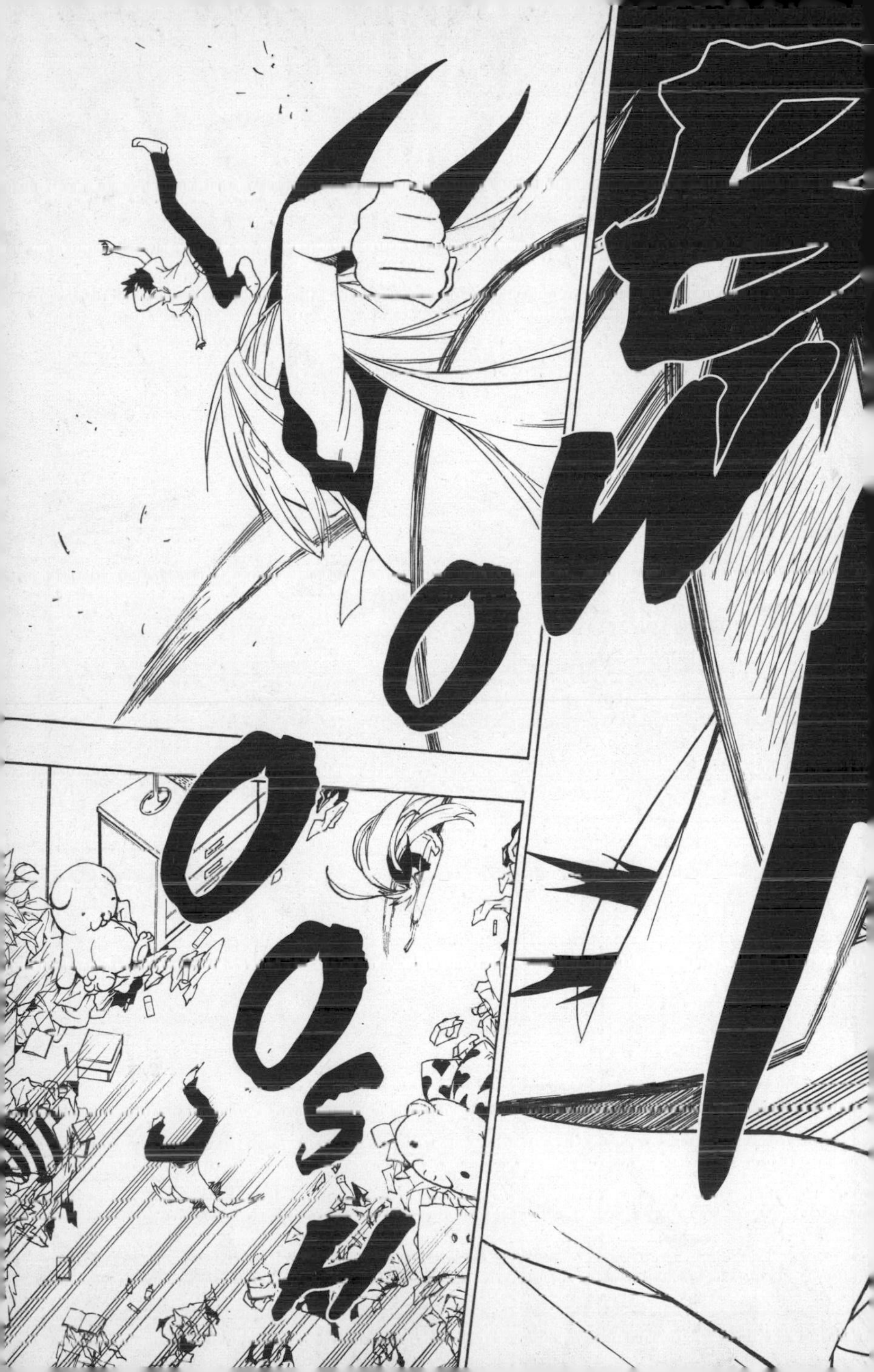
WOOOSH

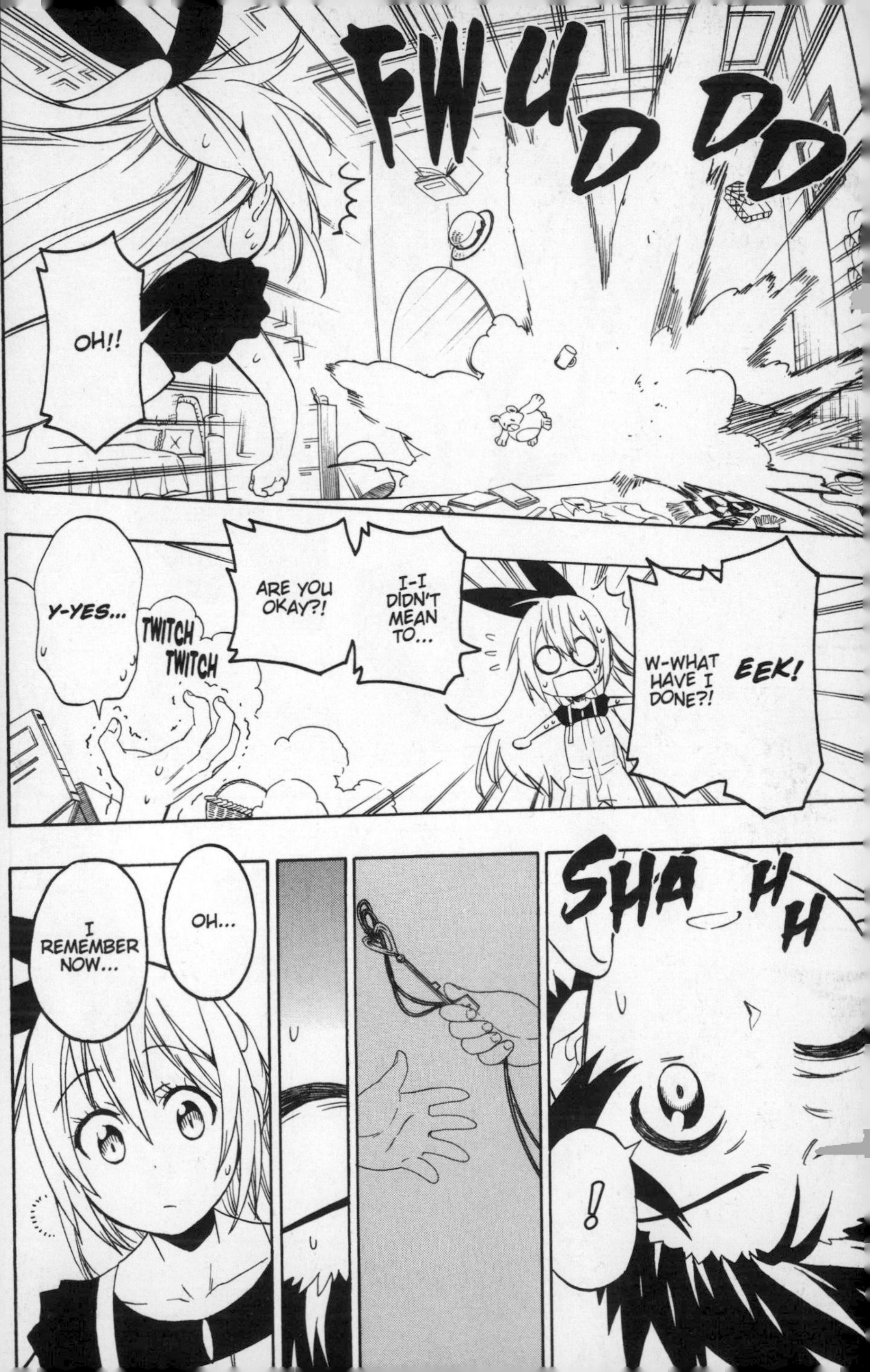
FWUDDD
OH!!
EEK!
W-WHAT HAVE I DONE?!
I-I DIDN'T MEAN TO...
ARE YOU OKAY?!
TWITCH TWITCH
Y-YES...
SHAHH
OH...
I REMEMBER NOW...

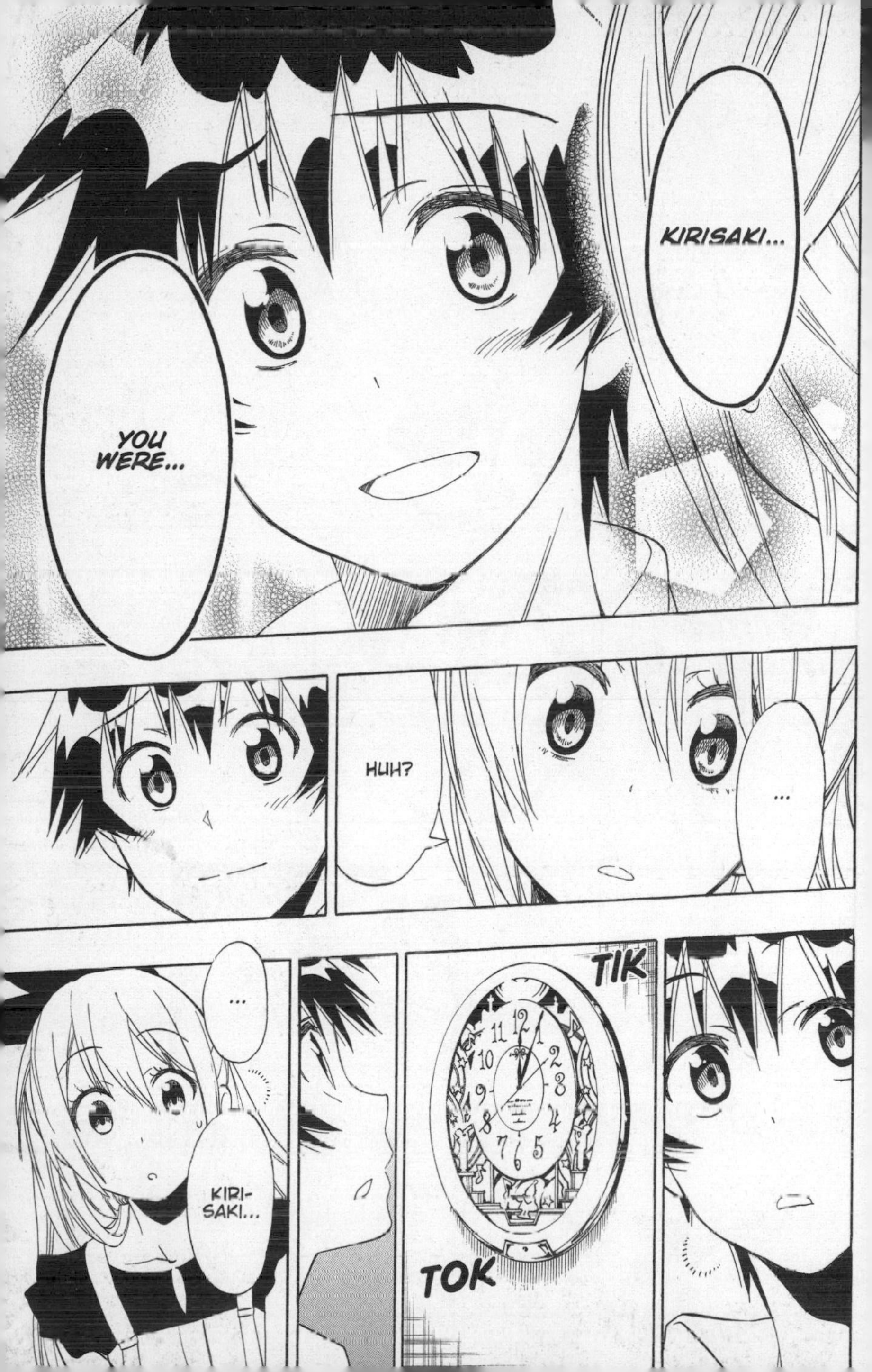
KIRISAKI...
YOU WERE...
...
HUH?
TIK
TOK
...
KIRI-SAKI...

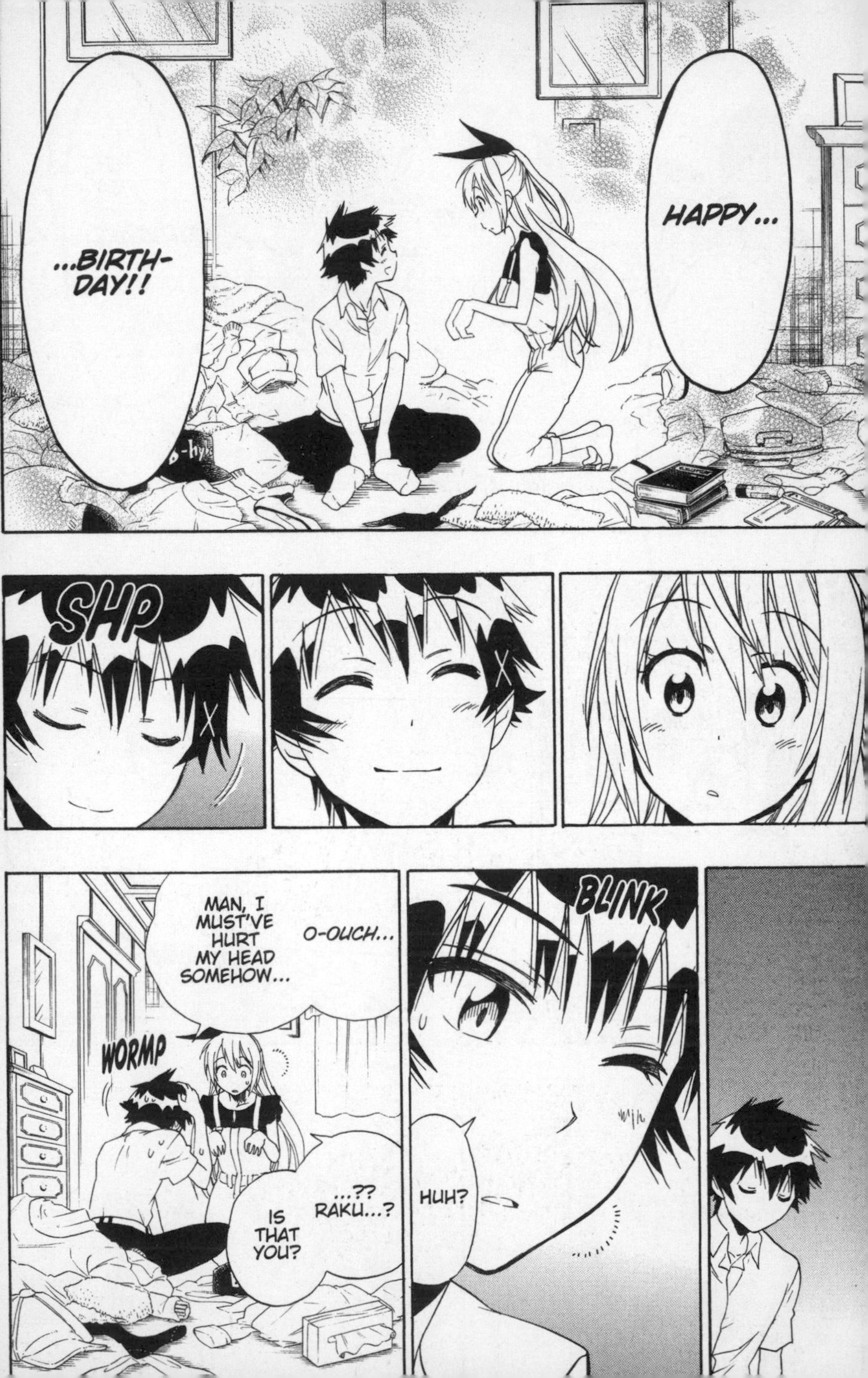
HAPPY...
...BIRTH-DAY!!
SHP
BLINK
HUH?
O-OUCH...
MAN, I MUST'VE HURT MY HEAD SOMEHOW...
WORMP
...?? RAKU...? IS THAT YOU?

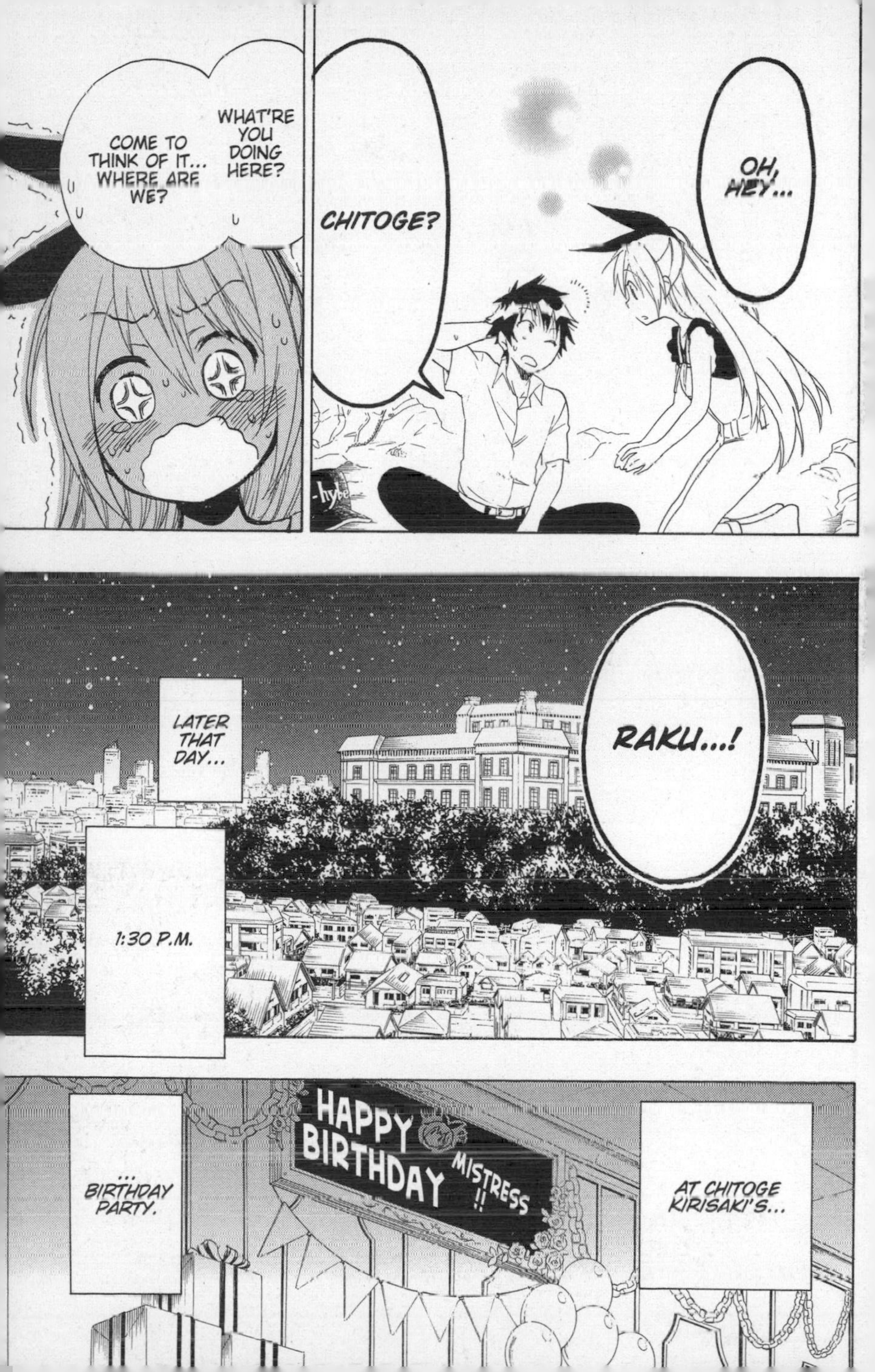
OH, HEY...
CHITOGE?
WHAT'RE YOU DOING HERE?
COME TO THINK OF IT... WHERE ARE WE?
RAKU...!
LATER THAT DAY...
1:30 P.M.
AT CHITOGE KIRISAKI'S...
HAPPY BIRTHDAY MISTRESS!!
...BIRTHDAY PARTY.

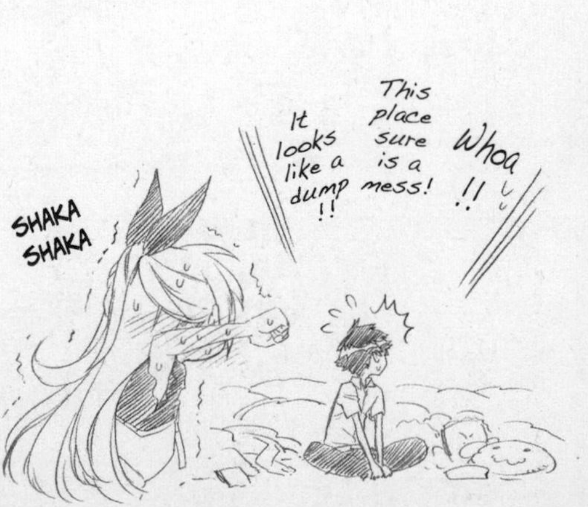
Whoa!!
This place sure is a mess!
It looks like a dump!!
SHAKA SHAKA

Chapter 92: Bouquet

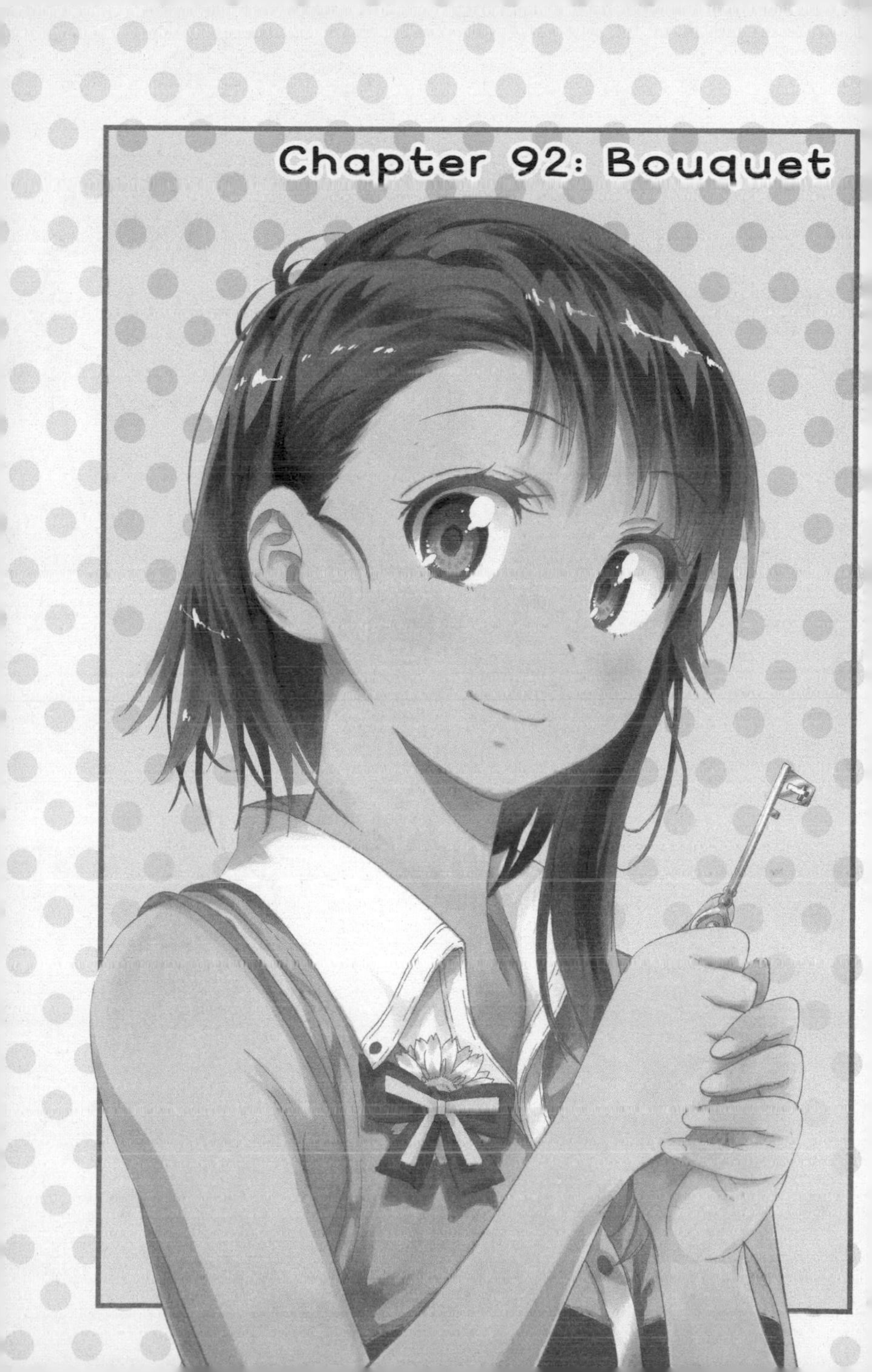

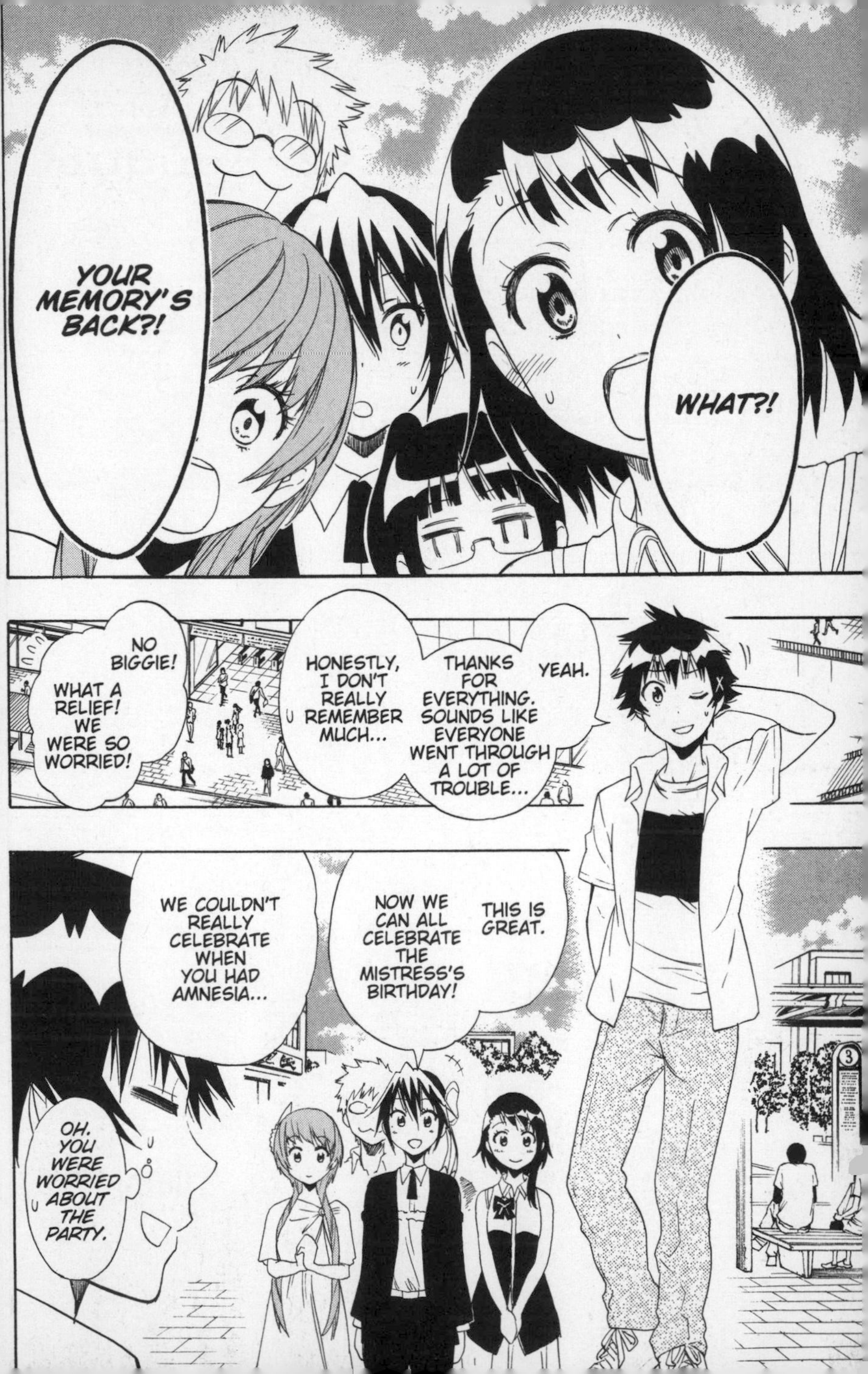
WHAT?!
YOUR MEMORY'S BACK?!
YEAH.
THANKS FOR EVERYTHING. SOUNDS LIKE EVERYONE WENT THROUGH A LOT OF TROUBLE...
HONESTLY, I DON'T REALLY REMEMBER MUCH...
NO BIGGIE! WHAT A RELIEF! WE WERE SO WORRIED!
THIS IS GREAT.
NOW WE CAN ALL CELEBRATE THE MISTRESS'S BIRTHDAY!
WE COULDN'T REALLY CELEBRATE WHEN YOU HAD AMNESIA...
OH. YOU WERE WORRIED ABOUT THE PARTY.

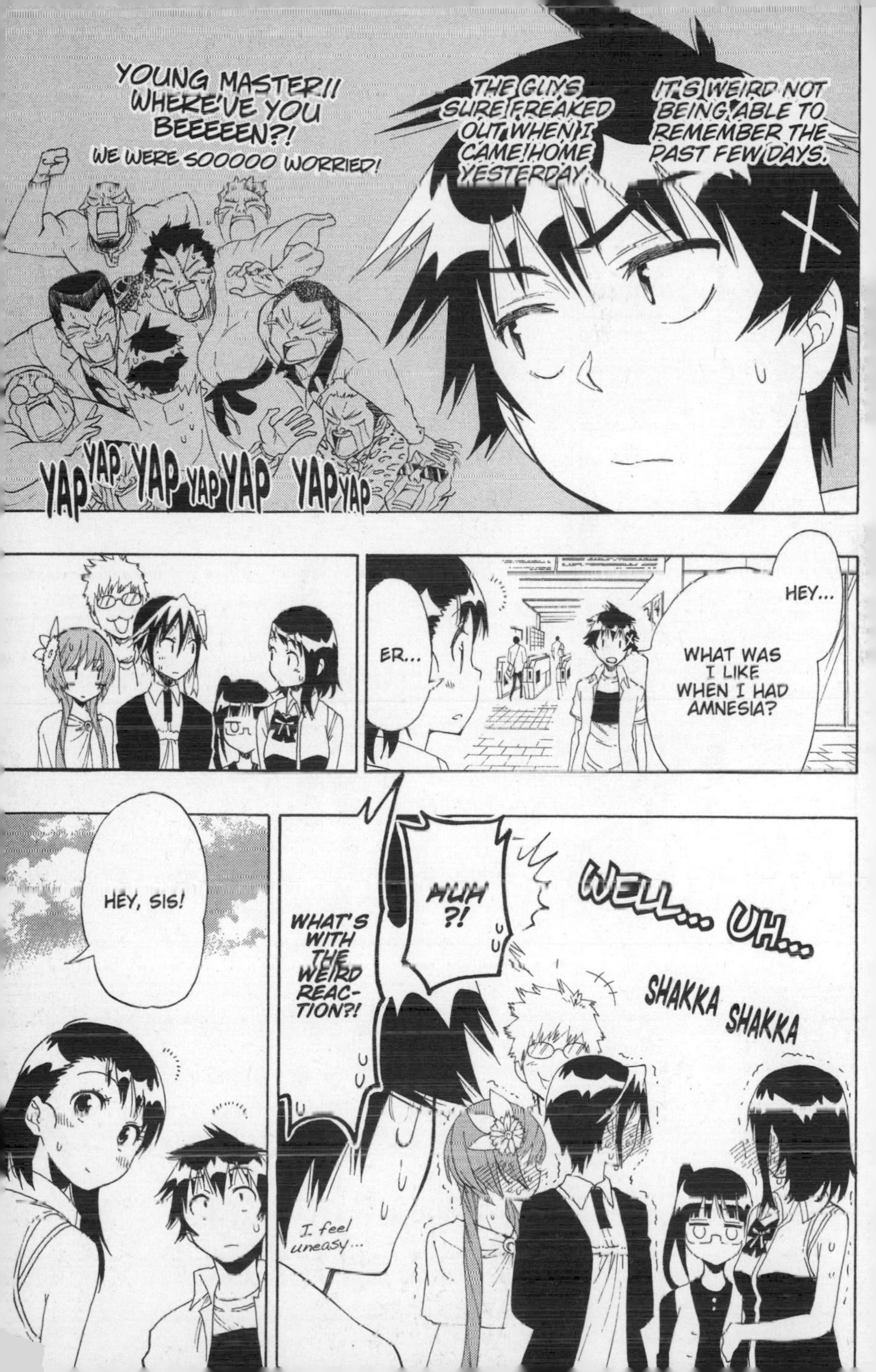
IT'S WEIRD NOT BEING ABLE TO REMEMBER THE PAST FEW DAYS.
THE GUYS SURE FREAKED OUT WHEN I CAME HOME YESTERDAY.
YOUNG MASTER!! WHERE'VE YOU BEEEEEN?!
WE WERE SOOOOO WORRIED!
YAP YAP YAP YAP YAP YAP YAP
HEY...
WHAT WAS I LIKE WHEN I HAD AMNESIA?
ER...
WELL... UH...
SHAKKA SHAKKA
HUH?!
WHAT'S WITH THE WEIRD REACTION?!
I feel uneasy...
HEY, SIS!

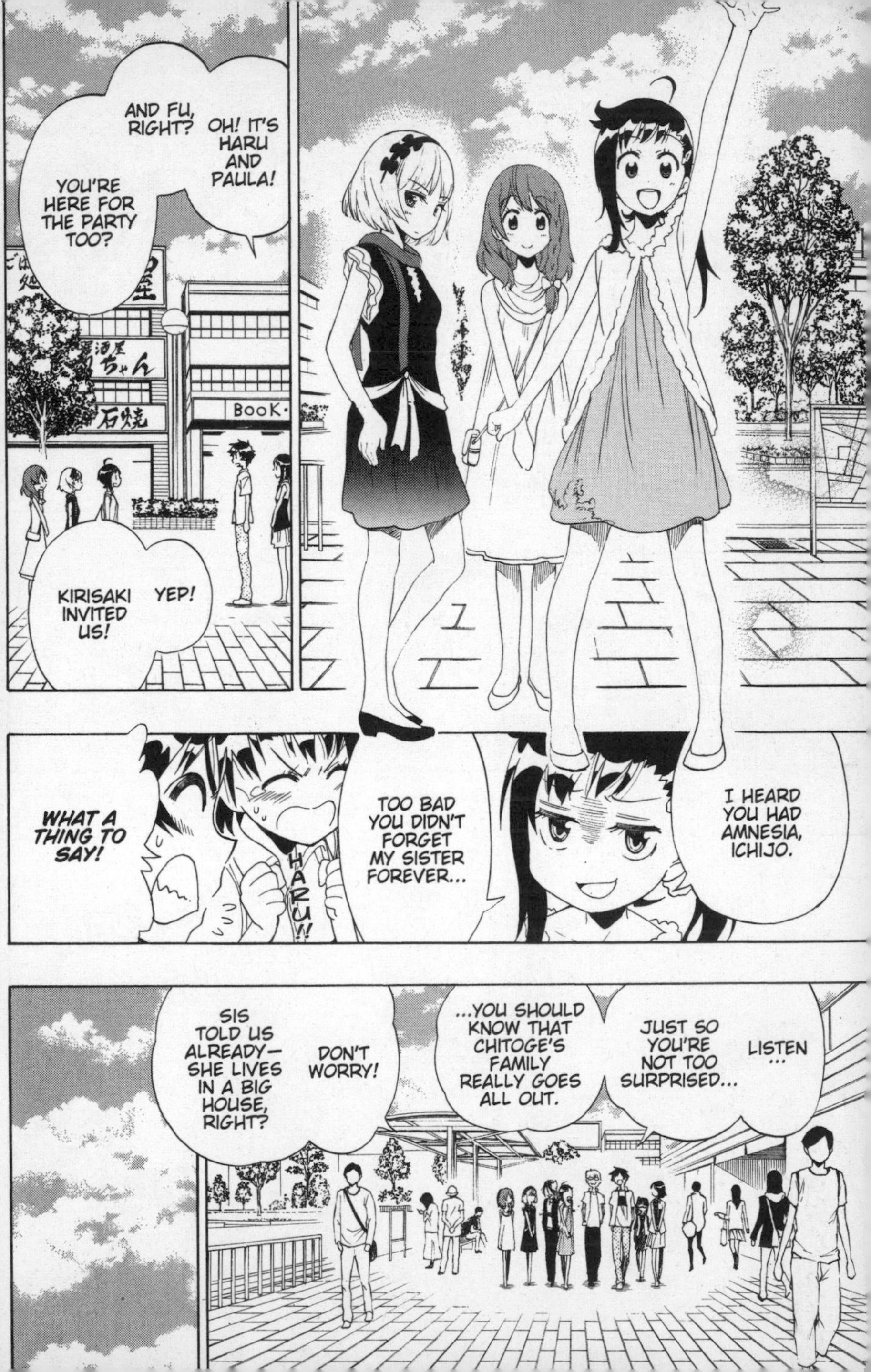
OH! IT'S HARU AND PAULA!
AND FU, RIGHT?
YOU'RE HERE FOR THE PARTY TOO?
BOOK.
YEP!
KIRISAKI INVITED US!
I HEARD YOU HAD AMNESIA, ICHIJO.
TOO BAD YOU DIDN'T FORGET MY SISTER FOREVER...
HARU!!
WHAT A THING TO SAY!
LISTEN...
JUST SO YOU'RE NOT TOO SURPRISED...
...YOU SHOULD KNOW THAT CHITOGE'S FAMILY REALLY GOES ALL OUT.
DON'T WORRY!
SIS TOLD US ALREADY— SHE LIVES IN A BIG HOUSE, RIGHT?

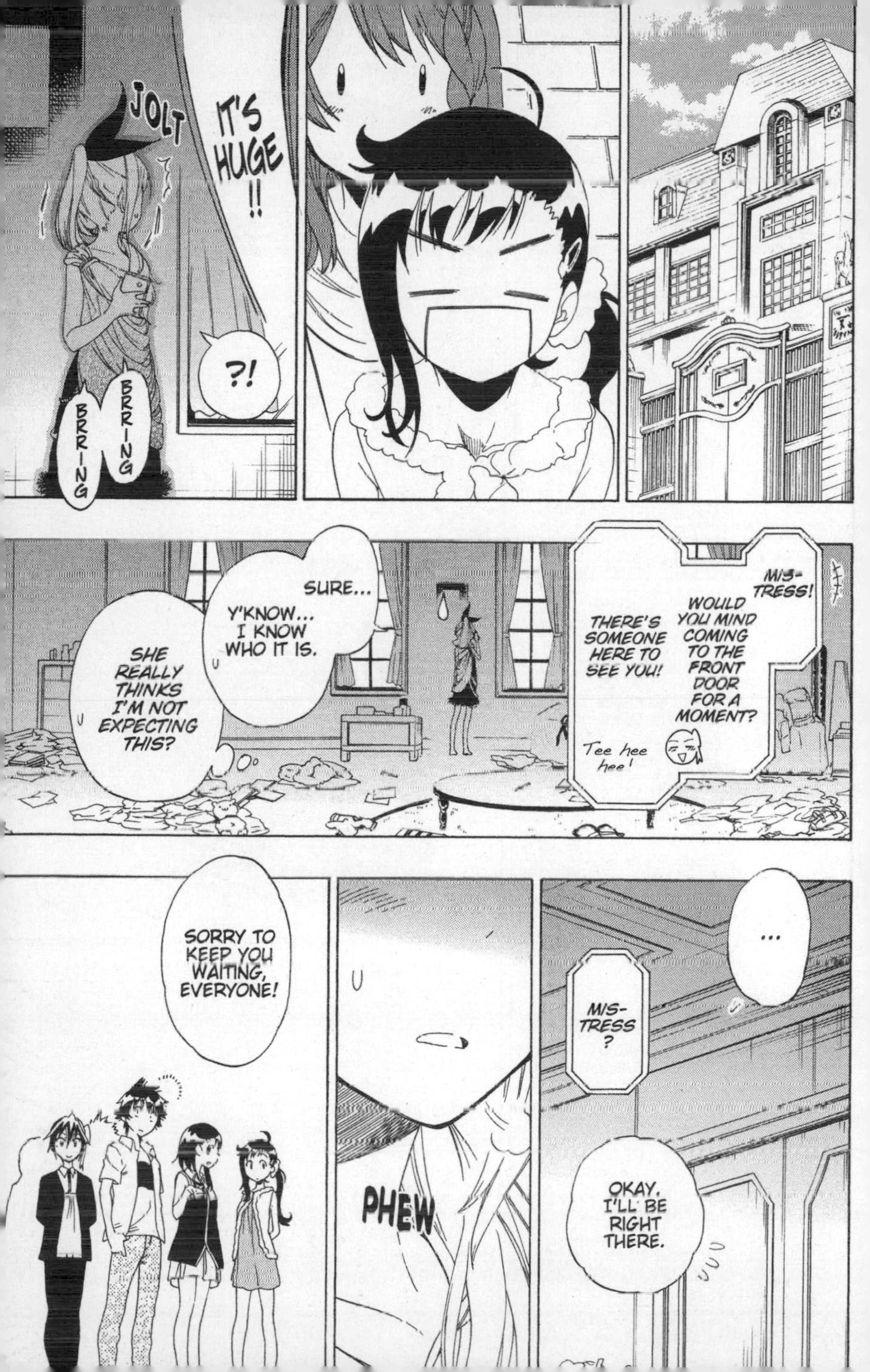
IT'S HUGE!!
JOLT
?!
BRRING BRRING
MIS-TRESS!
WOULD YOU MIND COMING TO THE FRONT DOOR FOR A MOMENT?
THERE'S SOMEONE HERE TO SEE YOU!
Tee hee hee!
SURE...
Y'KNOW... I KNOW WHO IT IS.
SHE REALLY THINKS I'M NOT EXPECTING THIS?
...
MIS-TRESS?
OKAY. I'LL BE RIGHT THERE.
PHEW
SORRY TO KEEP YOU WAITING, EVERYONE!

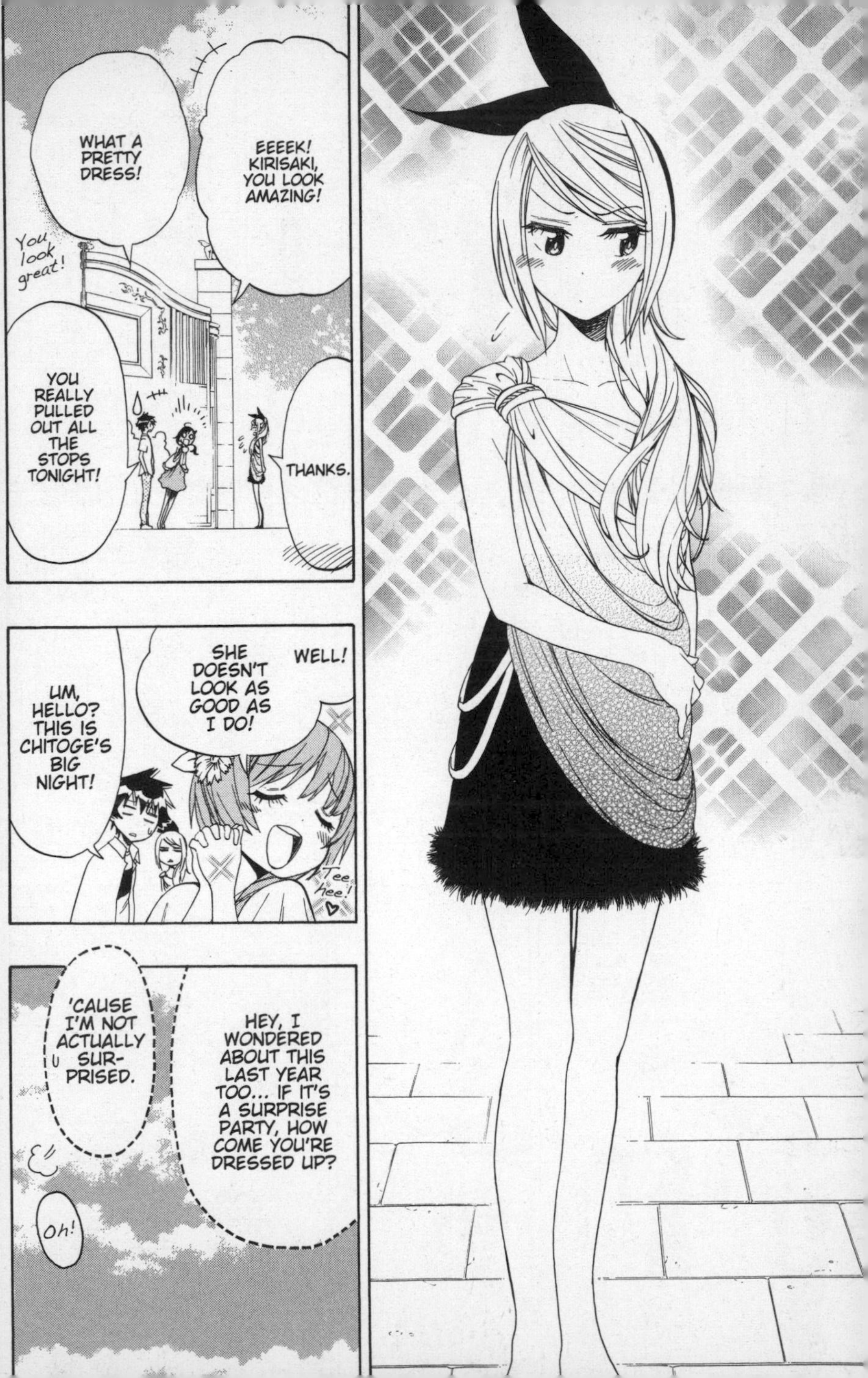
EEEEK! KIRISAKI, YOU LOOK AMAZING!
WHAT A PRETTY DRESS!
You look great!
THANKS.
YOU REALLY PULLED OUT ALL THE STOPS TONIGHT!
WELL!
SHE DOESN'T LOOK AS GOOD AS I DO!
Tee hee!
UM, HELLO? THIS IS CHITOGE'S BIG NIGHT!
HEY, I WONDERED ABOUT THIS LAST YEAR TOO... IF IT'S A SURPRISE PARTY, HOW COME YOU'RE DRESSED UP?
'CAUSE I'M NOT ACTUALLY SUR-PRISED.
Oh!

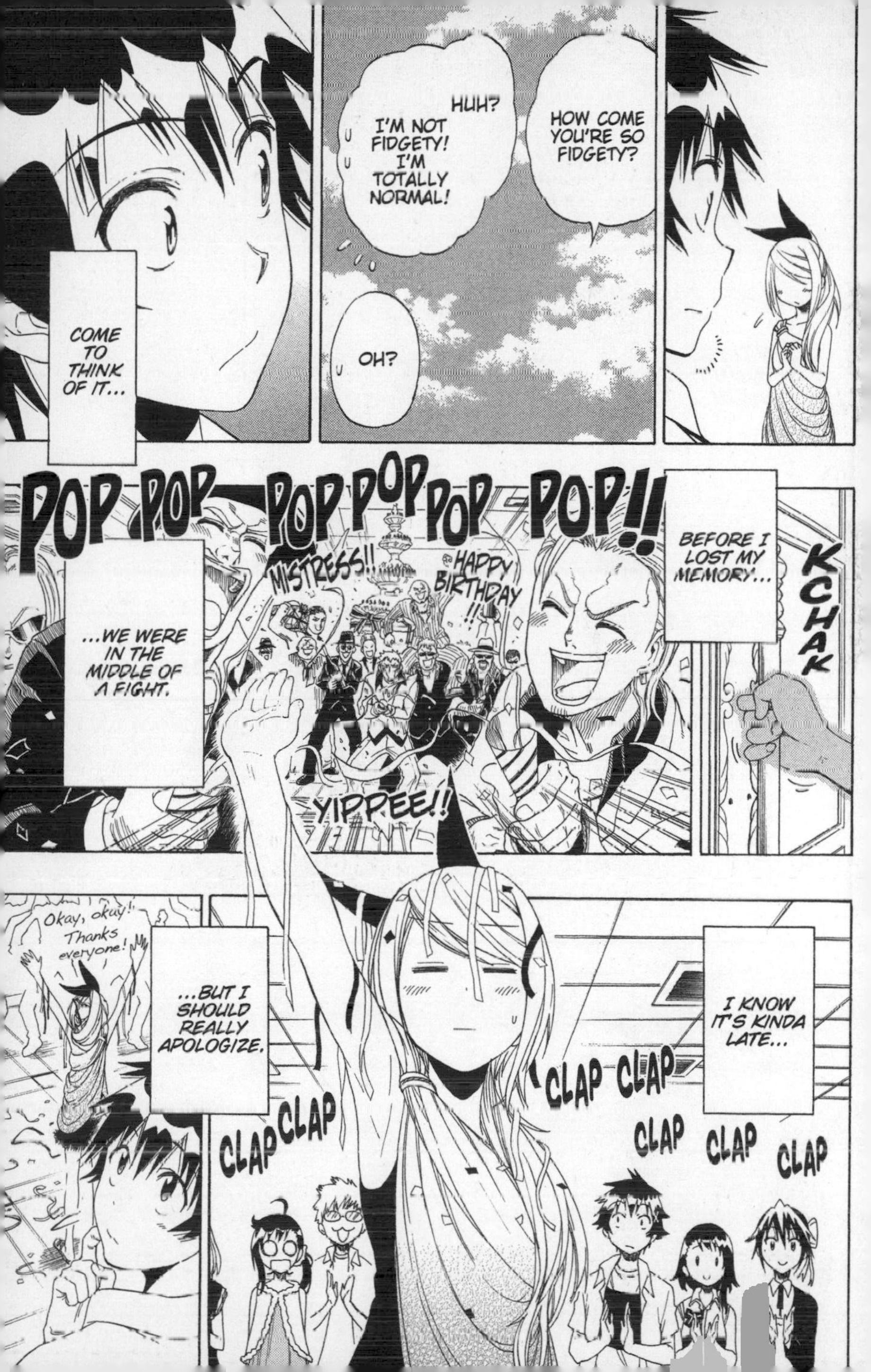
HOW COME YOU'RE SO FIDGETY?
HUH?
I'M NOT FIDGETY! I'M TOTALLY NORMAL!
OH?
COME TO THINK OF IT...
BEFORE I LOST MY MEMORY...
KCHAK
POP POP POP POP POP POP!!
HAPPY BIRTHDAY!!
MISTRESS!!
...WE WERE IN THE MIDDLE OF A FIGHT.
YIPPEE!!
I KNOW IT'S KINDA LATE...
CLAP CLAP
CLAP CLAP CLAP
CLAP CLAP
...BUT I SHOULD REALLY APOLOGIZE.
Okay, okay! Thanks everyone!

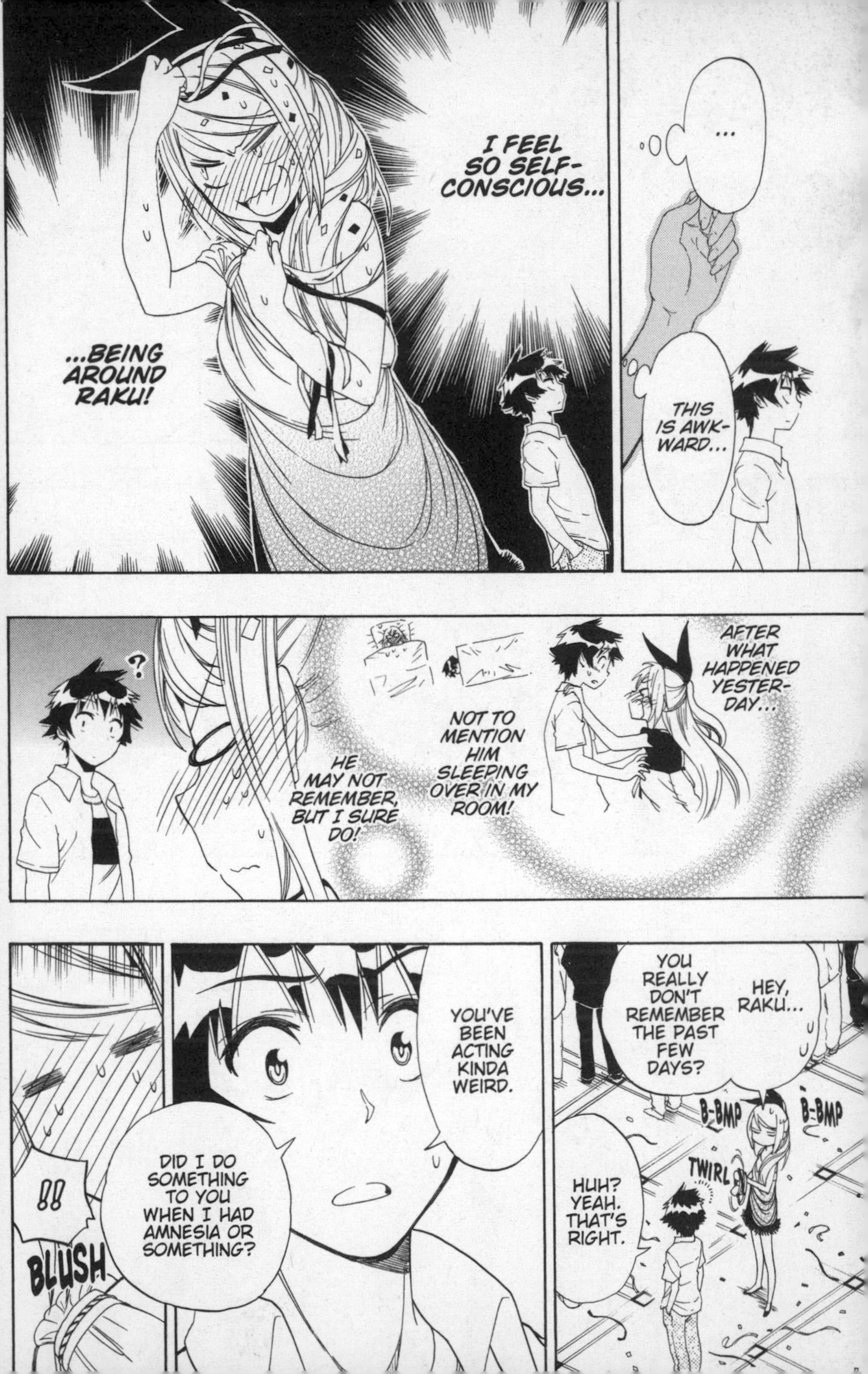
...
THIS IS AWKWARD...
I FEEL SO SELF-CONSCIOUS...
...BEING AROUND RAKU!
AFTER WHAT HAPPENED YESTERDAY...
NOT TO MENTION HIM SLEEPING OVER IN MY ROOM!
HE MAY NOT REMEMBER, BUT I SURE DO!
HEY, RAKU...
YOU REALLY DON'T REMEMBER THE PAST FEW DAYS?
B-BMP
B-BMP
TWIRL
HUH? YEAH. THAT'S RIGHT.
YOU'VE BEEN ACTING KINDA WEIRD.
DID I DO SOMETHING TO YOU WHEN I HAD AMNESIA OR SOMETHING?
!!
BLUSH

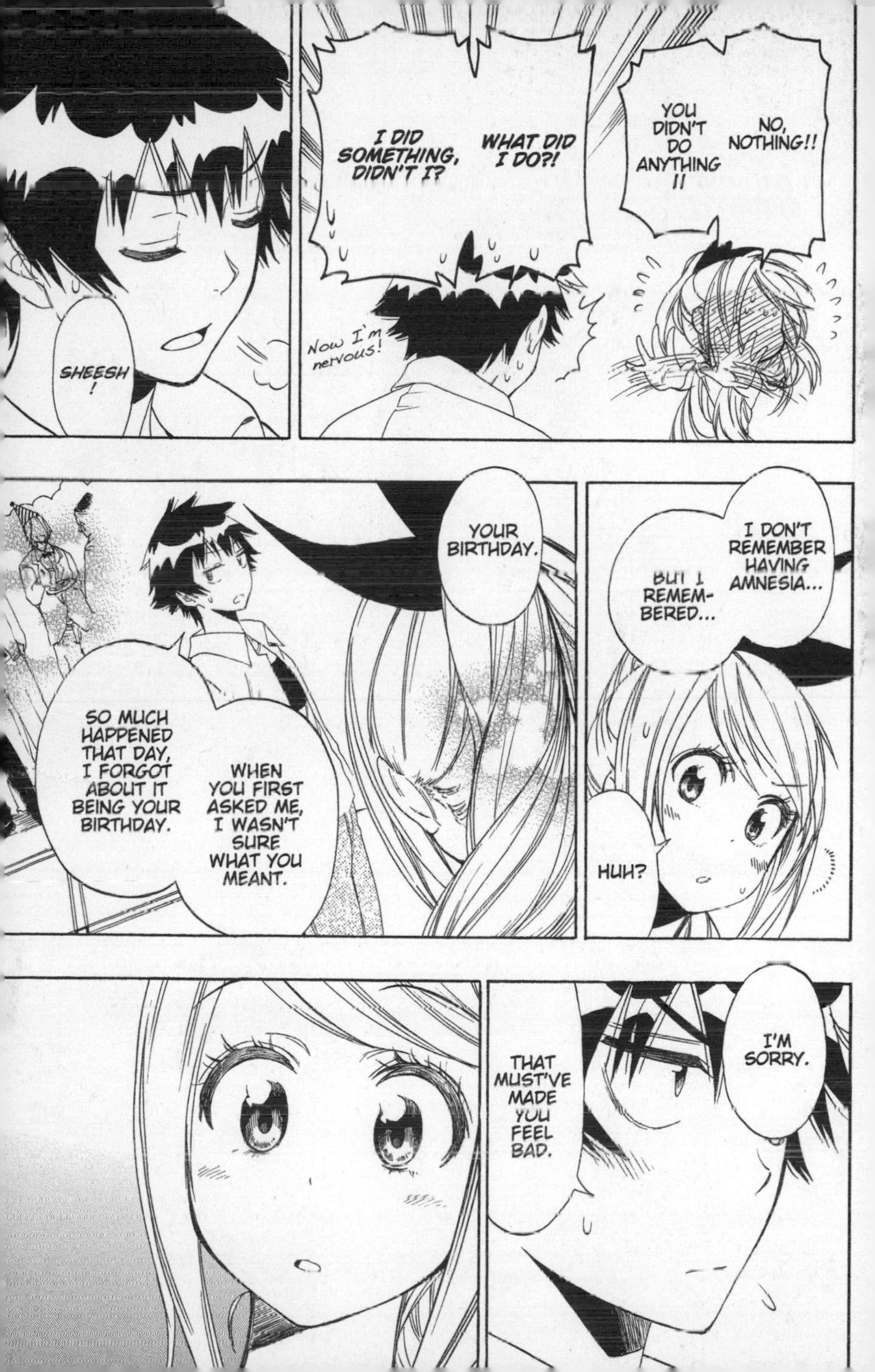
NO, NOTHING!!
YOU DIDN'T DO ANYTHING !!
WHAT DID I DO?!
I DID SOMETHING, DIDN'T I?
Now I'm nervous!
SHEESH !
I DON'T REMEMBER HAVING AMNESIA...
BUT I REMEMBERED...
HUH?
YOUR BIRTHDAY.
WHEN YOU FIRST ASKED ME, I WASN'T SURE WHAT YOU MEANT.
SO MUCH HAPPENED THAT DAY, I FORGOT ABOUT IT BEING YOUR BIRTHDAY.
I'M SORRY.
THAT MUST'VE MADE YOU FEEL BAD.

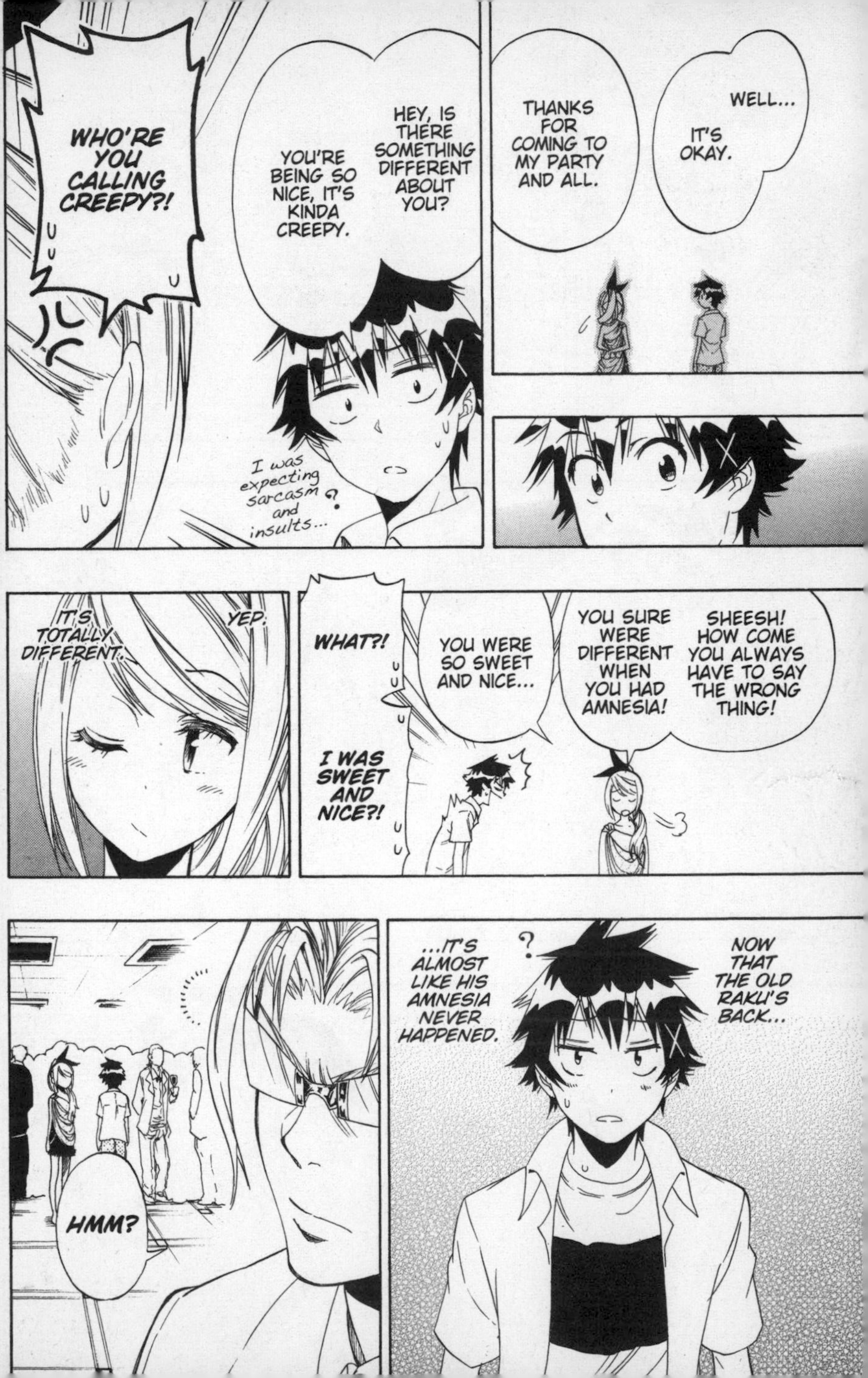
WELL... IT'S OKAY.
THANKS FOR COMING TO MY PARTY AND ALL.
HEY, IS THERE SOMETHING DIFFERENT ABOUT YOU?
YOU'RE BEING SO NICE, IT'S KINDA CREEPY.
I was expecting sarcasm and insults...?
WHO'RE YOU CALLING CREEPY?!
SHEESH! HOW COME YOU ALWAYS HAVE TO SAY THE WRONG THING!
YOU SURE WERE DIFFERENT WHEN YOU HAD AMNESIA!
YOU WERE SO SWEET AND NICE...
WHAT?!
I WAS SWEET AND NICE?!
YEP.
IT'S TOTALLY DIFFERENT.
NOW THAT THE OLD RAKU'S BACK...
...IT'S ALMOST LIKE HIS AMNESIA NEVER HAPPENED.
?
HMM?

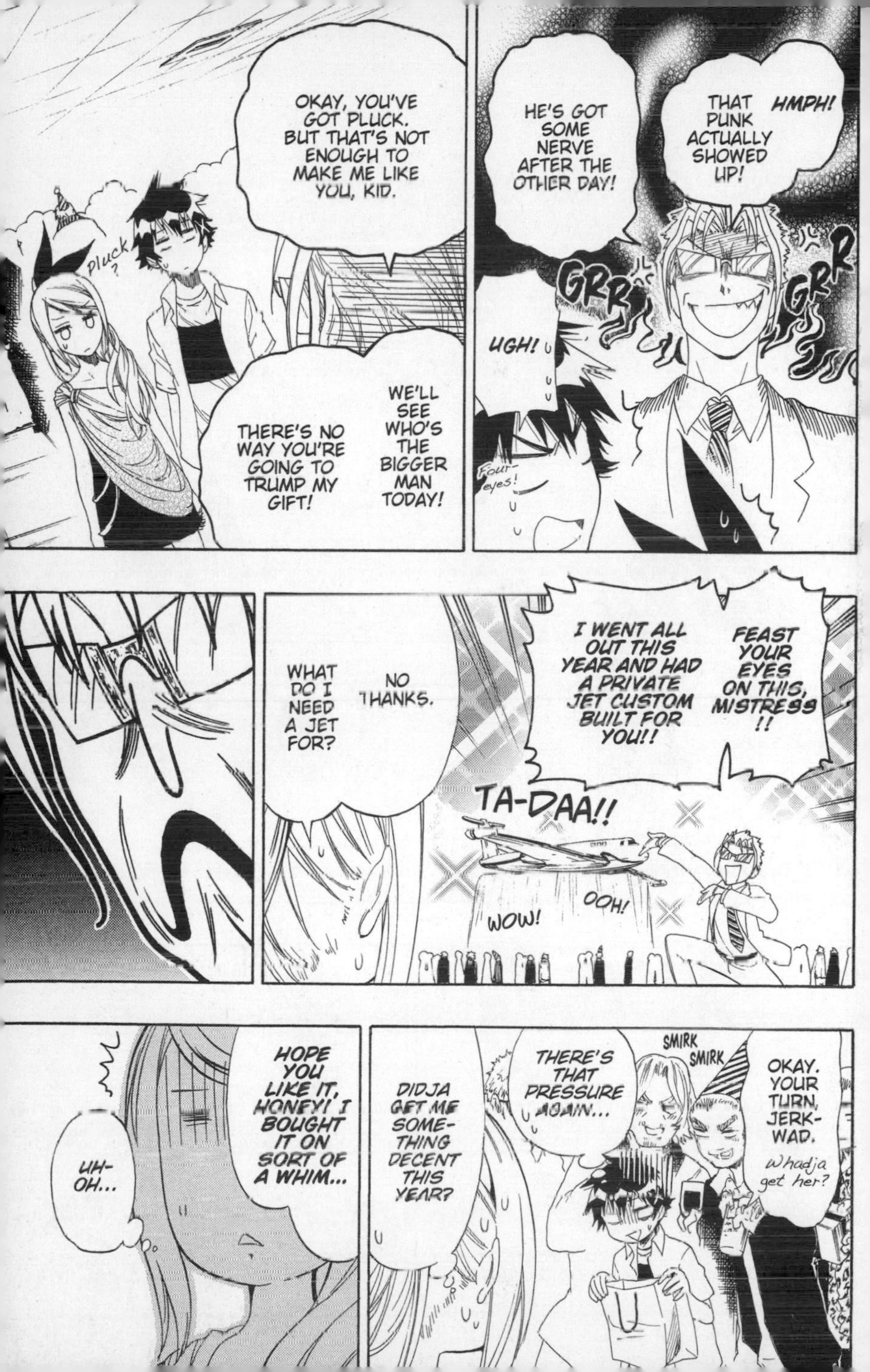
HMPH!
THAT PUNK ACTUALLY SHOWED UP!
HE'S GOT SOME NERVE AFTER THE OTHER DAY!
GRR
GRR
UGH!
Four-eyes!
OKAY, YOU'VE GOT PLUCK. BUT THAT'S NOT ENOUGH TO MAKE ME LIKE YOU, KID.
WE'LL SEE WHO'S THE BIGGER MAN TODAY!
THERE'S NO WAY YOU'RE GOING TO TRUMP MY GIFT!
Pluck?
FEAST YOUR EYES ON THIS, MISTRESS!!
I WENT ALL OUT THIS YEAR AND HAD A PRIVATE JET CUSTOM BUILT FOR YOU!!
NO THANKS.
WHAT DO I NEED A JET FOR?
TA-DAA!!
OOH!
WOW!
OKAY. YOUR TURN, JERKWAD.
SMIRK
SMIRK
Whadja get her?
THERE'S THAT PRESSURE AGAIN...
DIDJA GET ME SOMETHING DECENT THIS YEAR?
HOPE YOU LIKE IT, HONEY! I BOUGHT IT ON SORT OF A WHIM...
UH-OH...

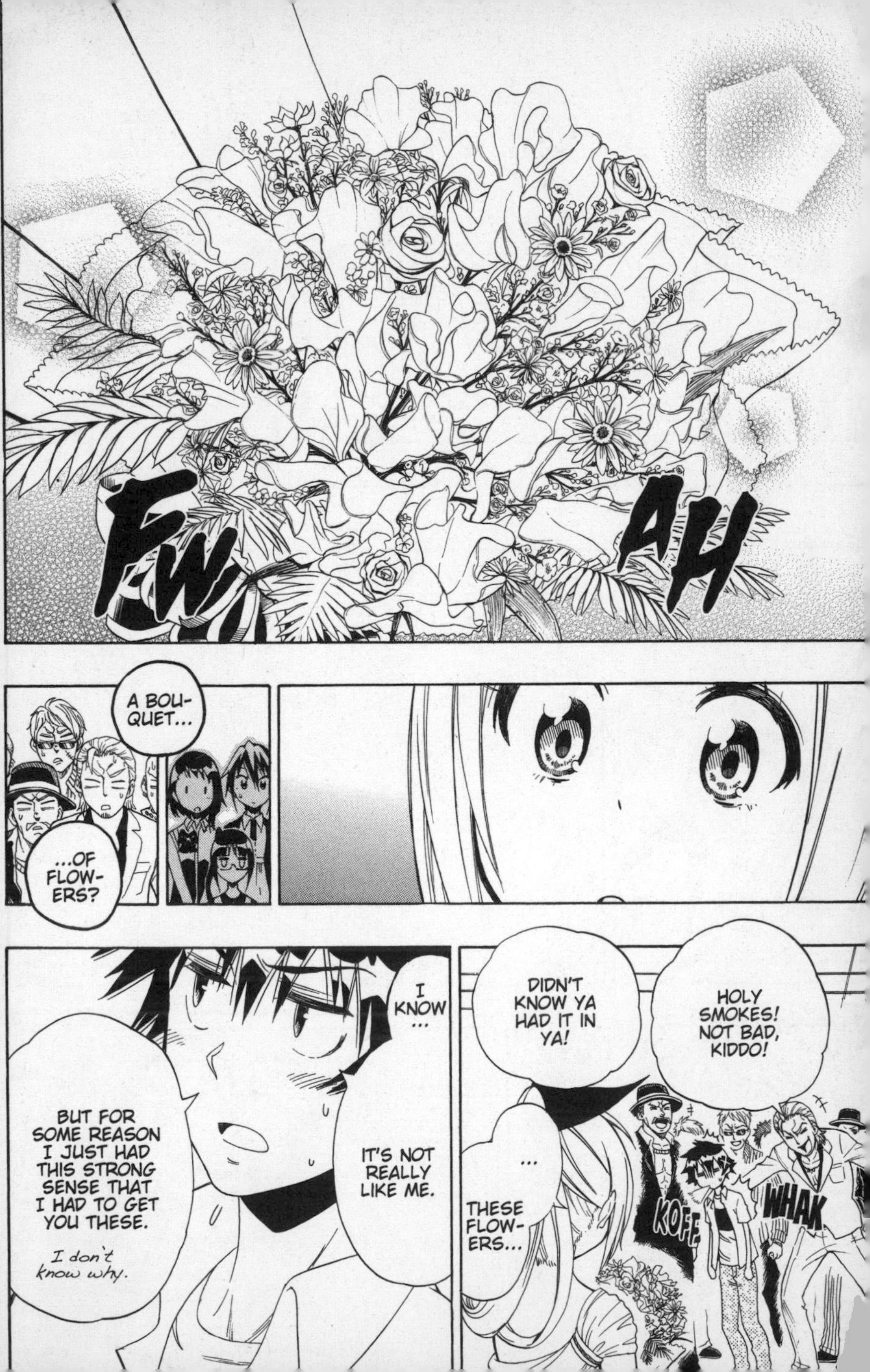
FWAH
A BOUQUET...
...OF FLOWERS?
HOLY SMOKES! NOT BAD, KIDDO!
DIDN'T KNOW YA HAD IT IN YA!
WHAK
KOFF
... THESE FLOWERS...
I KNOW...
IT'S NOT REALLY LIKE ME.
BUT FOR SOME REASON I JUST HAD THIS STRONG SENSE THAT I HAD TO GET YOU THESE.
I don't know why.

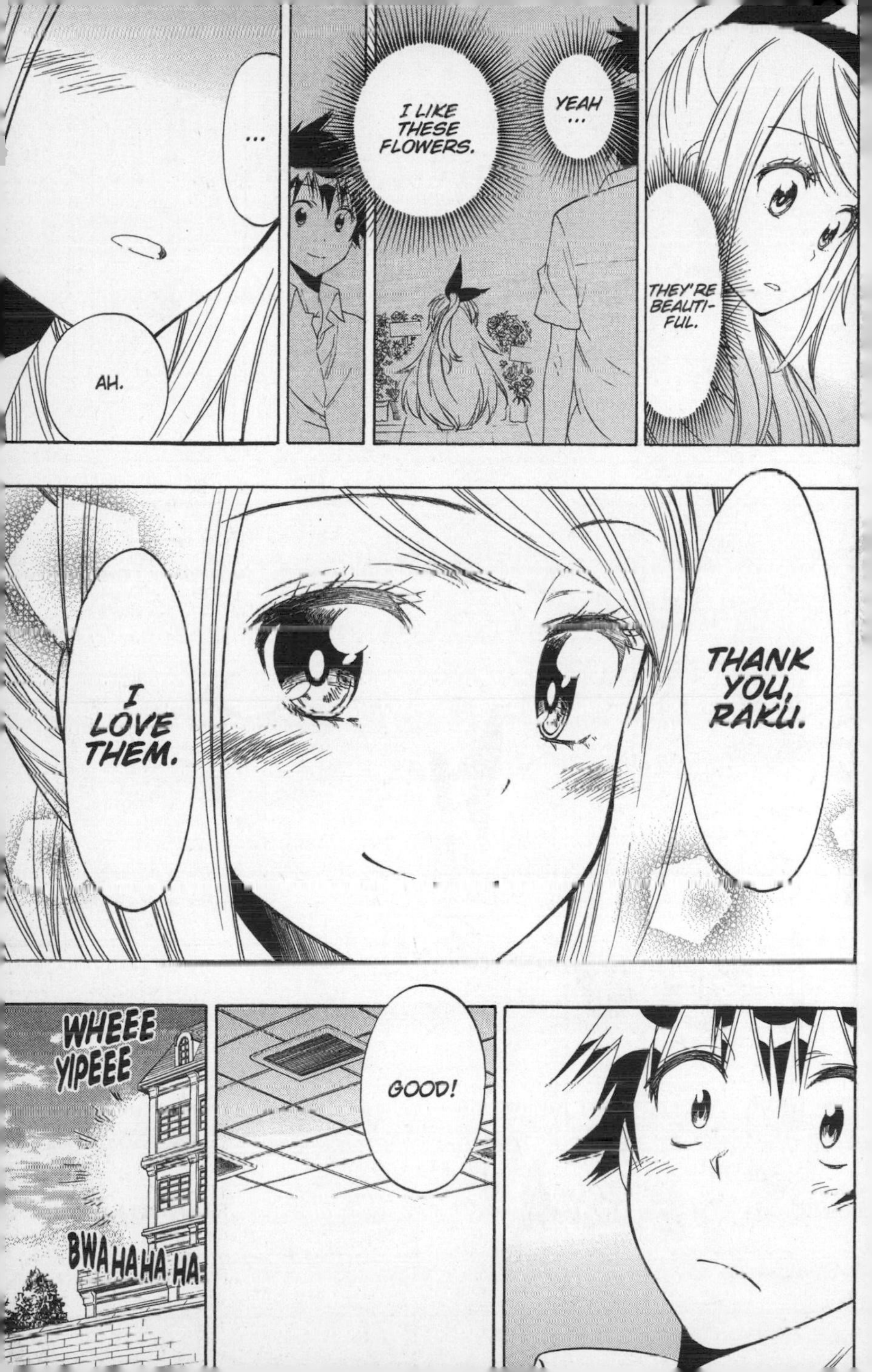
THEY'RE BEAUTIFUL.
YEAH ...
I LIKE THESE FLOWERS.
...
AH.
THANK YOU, RAKU.
I LOVE THEM.
GOOD!
WHEEE
YIPEEE
BWAHAHAHA

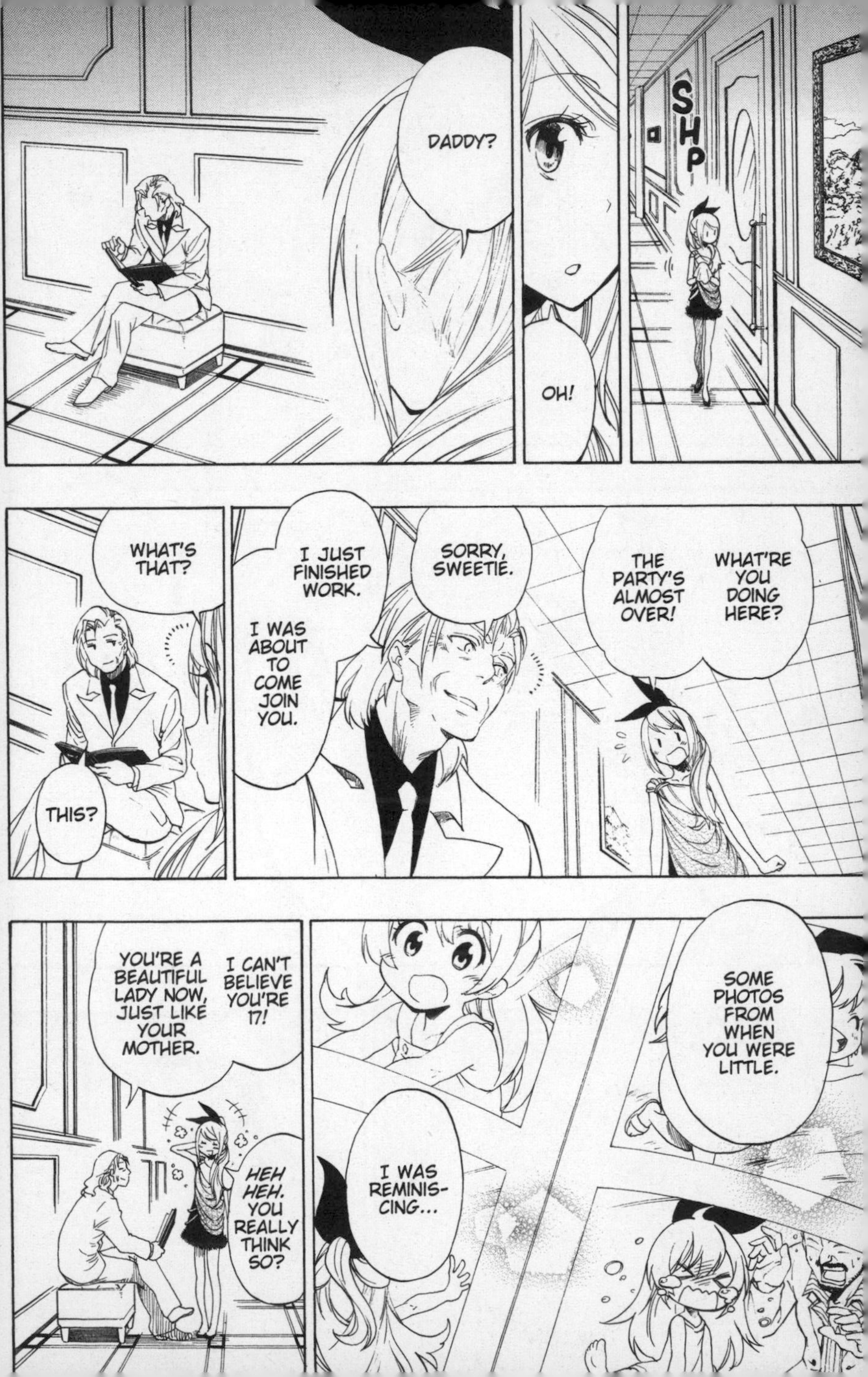
SHP
OH!
DADDY?
WHAT'RE YOU DOING HERE?
THE PARTY'S ALMOST OVER!
SORRY, SWEETIE.
I JUST FINISHED WORK.
I WAS ABOUT TO COME JOIN YOU.
WHAT'S THAT?
THIS?
SOME PHOTOS FROM WHEN YOU WERE LITTLE.
I WAS REMINIS-CING...
I CAN'T BELIEVE YOU'RE 17!
YOU'RE A BEAUTIFUL LADY NOW, JUST LIKE YOUR MOTHER.
HEH HEH. YOU REALLY THINK SO?

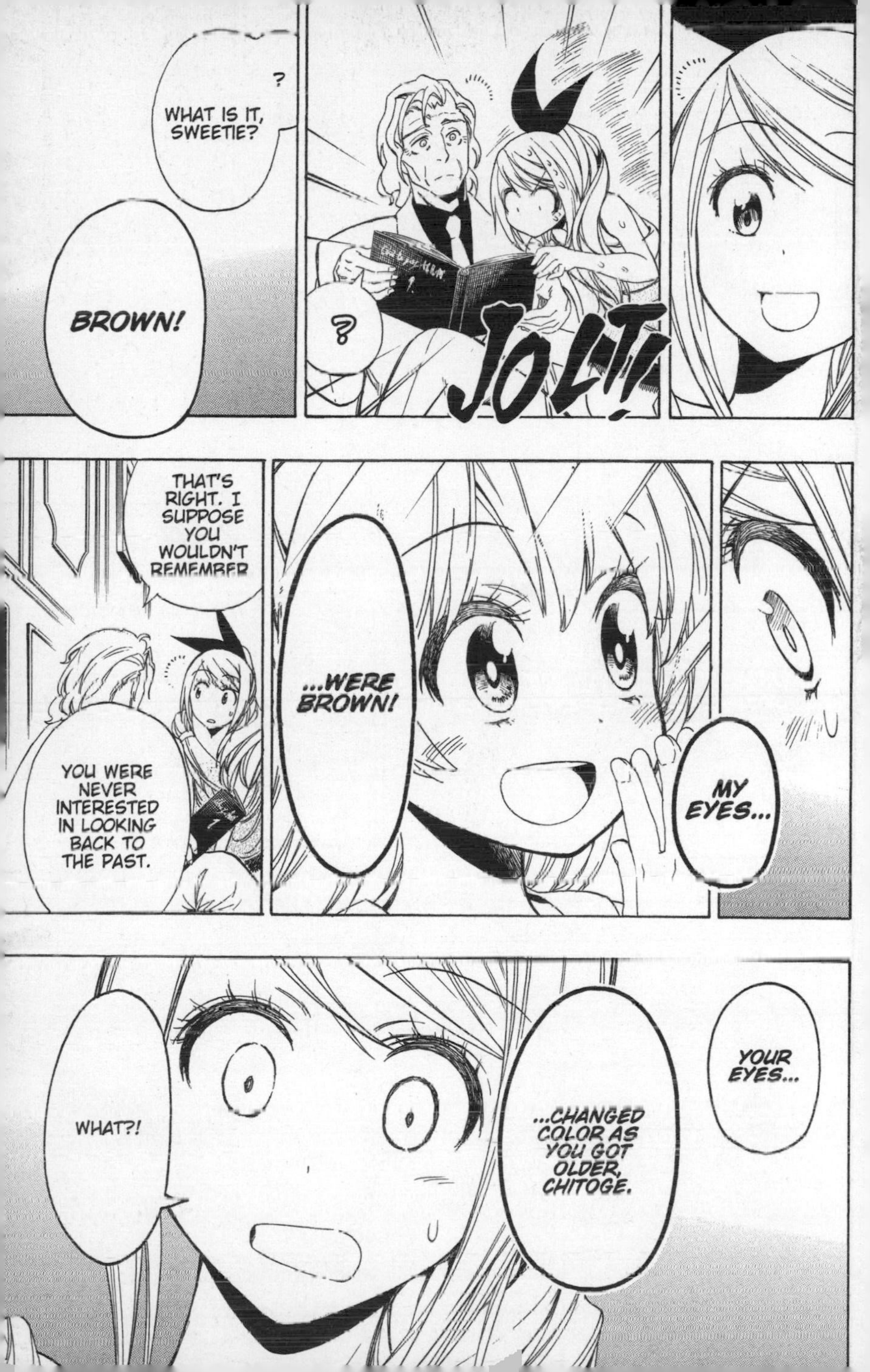
?
JOLT!
?
WHAT IS IT, SWEETIE?
BROWN!
MY EYES...
...WERE BROWN!
THAT'S RIGHT. I SUPPOSE YOU WOULDN'T REMEMBER
YOU WERE NEVER INTERESTED IN LOOKING BACK TO THE PAST.
YOUR EYES...
...CHANGED COLOR AS YOU GOT OLDER, CHITOGE.
WHAT?!

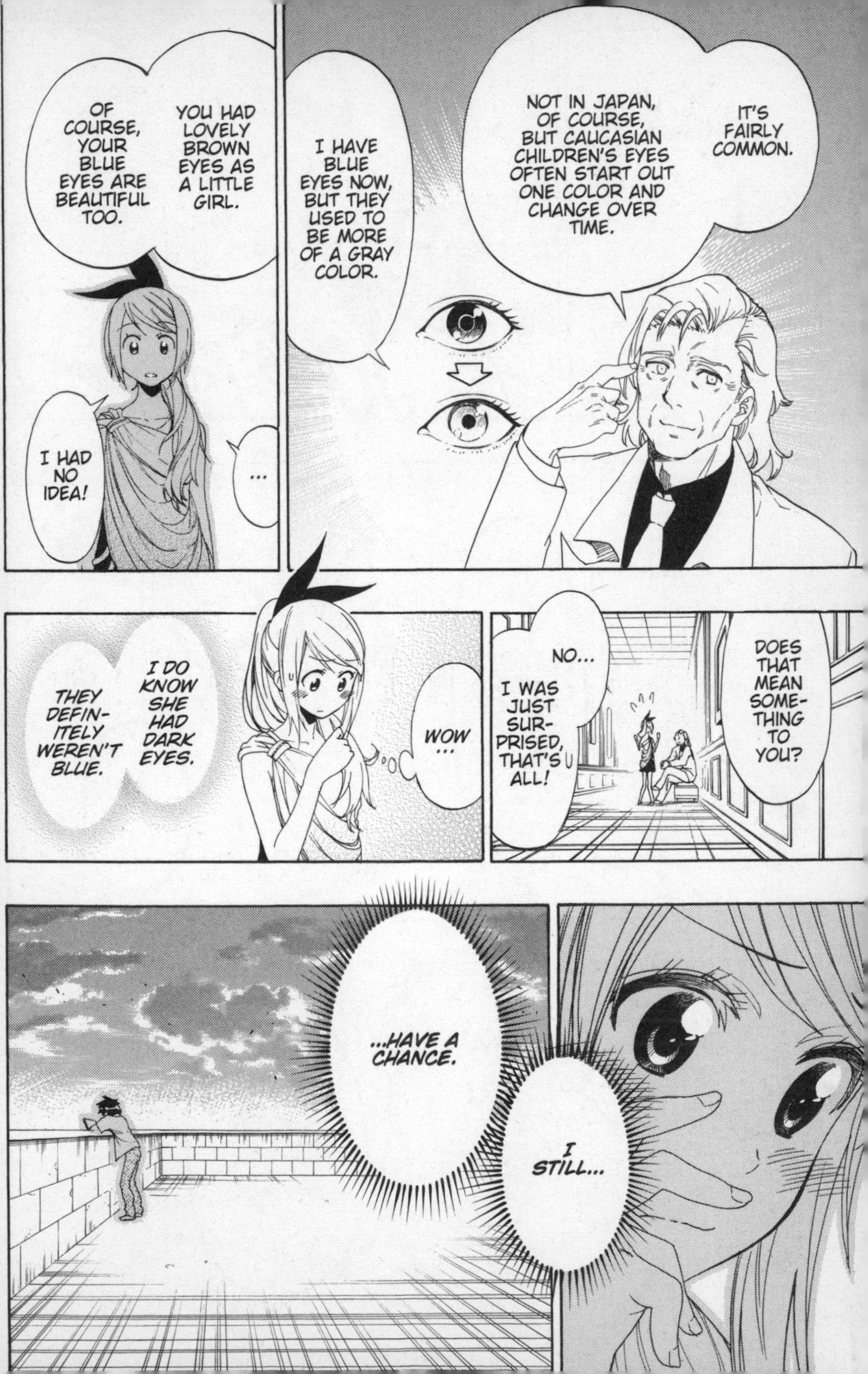
IT'S FAIRLY COMMON.
NOT IN JAPAN, OF COURSE, BUT CAUCASIAN CHILDREN'S EYES OFTEN START OUT ONE COLOR AND CHANGE OVER TIME.
I HAVE BLUE EYES NOW, BUT THEY USED TO BE MORE OF A GRAY COLOR.
YOU HAD LOVELY BROWN EYES AS A LITTLE GIRL.
OF COURSE, YOUR BLUE EYES ARE BEAUTIFUL TOO.
...
I HAD NO IDEA!
DOES THAT MEAN SOMETHING TO YOU?
NO...
I WAS JUST SURPRISED, THAT'S ALL!
WOW...
I DO KNOW SHE HAD DARK EYES.
THEY DEFINITELY WEREN'T BLUE.
I STILL...
...HAVE A CHANCE.

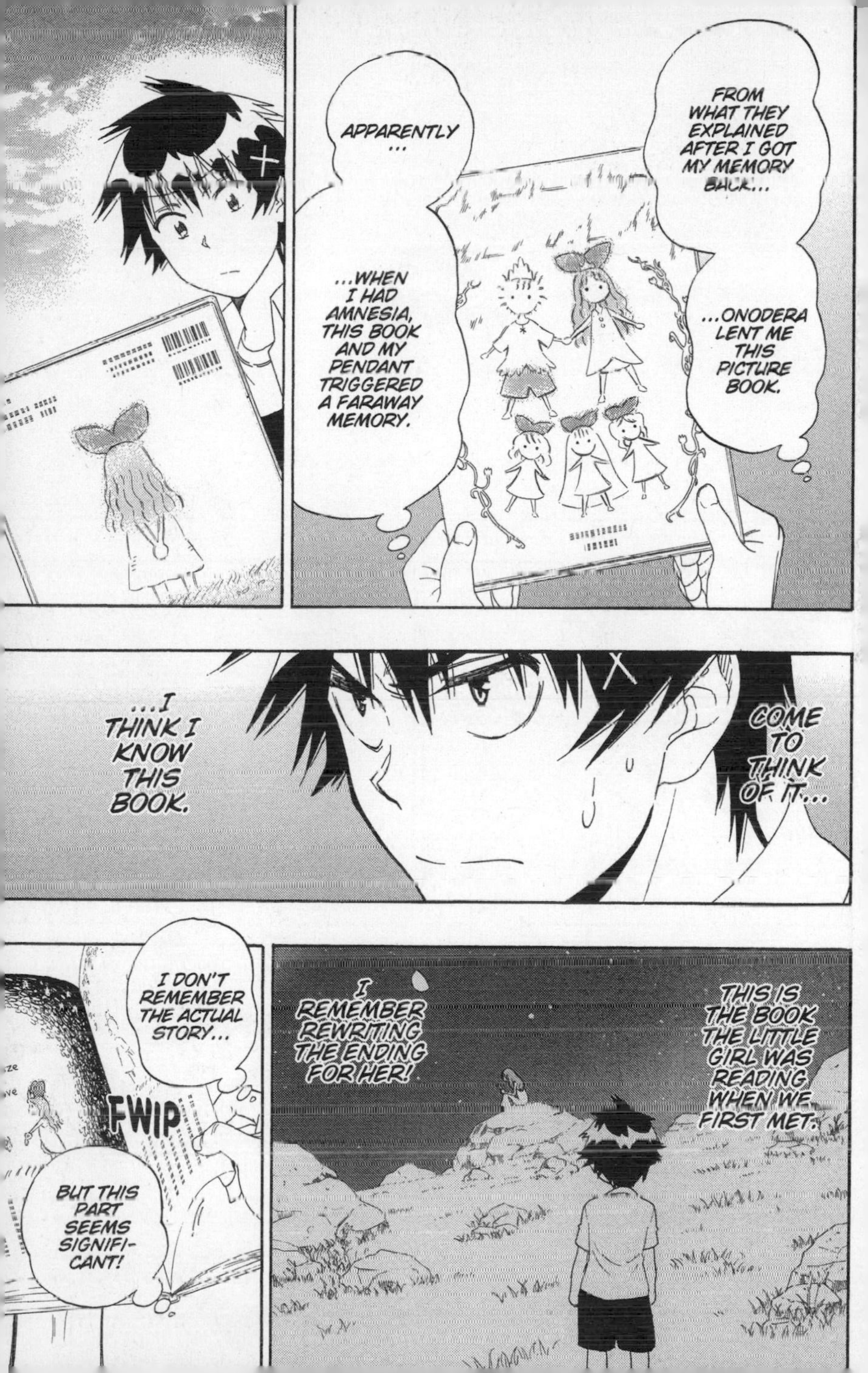
FROM WHAT THEY EXPLAINED AFTER I GOT MY MEMORY BACK...
...ONODERA LENT ME THIS PICTURE BOOK.
APPARENTLY...
...WHEN I HAD AMNESIA, THIS BOOK AND MY PENDANT TRIGGERED A FARAWAY MEMORY.
COME TO THINK OF IT...
...I THINK I KNOW THIS BOOK.
THIS IS THE BOOK THE LITTLE GIRL WAS READING WHEN WE FIRST MET.
I REMEMBER REWRITING THE ENDING FOR HER!
I DON'T REMEMBER THE ACTUAL STORY...
FWIP
BUT THIS PART SEEMS SIGNIFICANT!

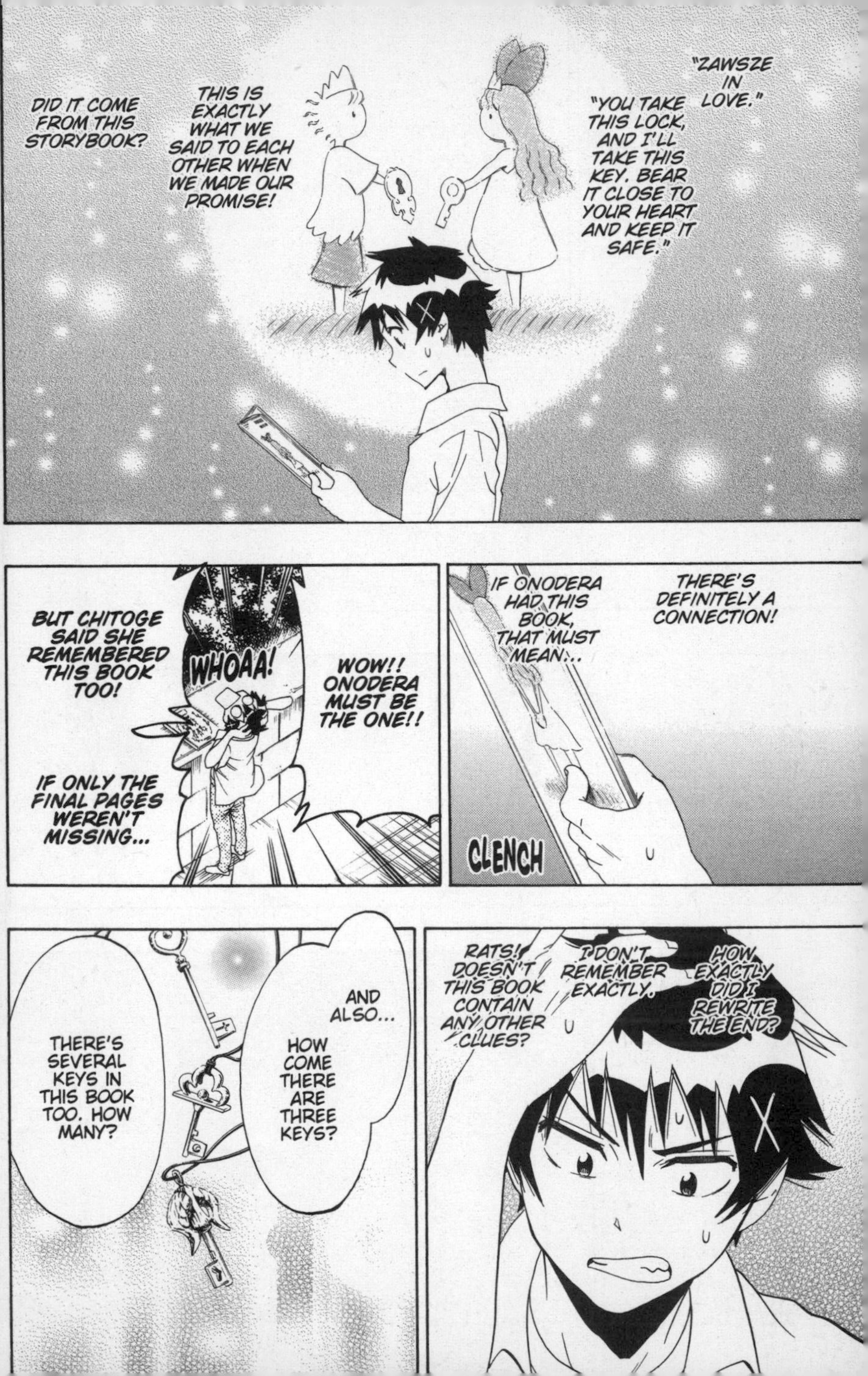
"ZAWSZE IN LOVE."
"YOU TAKE THIS LOCK, AND I'LL TAKE THIS KEY. BEAR IT CLOSE TO YOUR HEART AND KEEP IT SAFE."
THIS IS EXACTLY WHAT WE SAID TO EACH OTHER WHEN WE MADE OUR PROMISE!
DID IT COME FROM THIS STORYBOOK?
THERE'S DEFINITELY A CONNECTION!
IF ONODERA HAD THIS BOOK, THAT MUST MEAN...
CLENCH
WOW!! ONODERA MUST BE THE ONE!!
WHOAA!
BUT CHITOGE SAID SHE REMEMBERED THIS BOOK TOO!
IF ONLY THE FINAL PAGES WEREN'T MISSING...
HOW EXACTLY DID I REWRITE THE END?
I DON'T REMEMBER EXACTLY.
RATS! DOESN'T THIS BOOK CONTAIN ANY OTHER CLUES?
AND ALSO... HOW COME THERE ARE THREE KEYS?
THERE'S SEVERAL KEYS IN THIS BOOK TOO. HOW MANY?

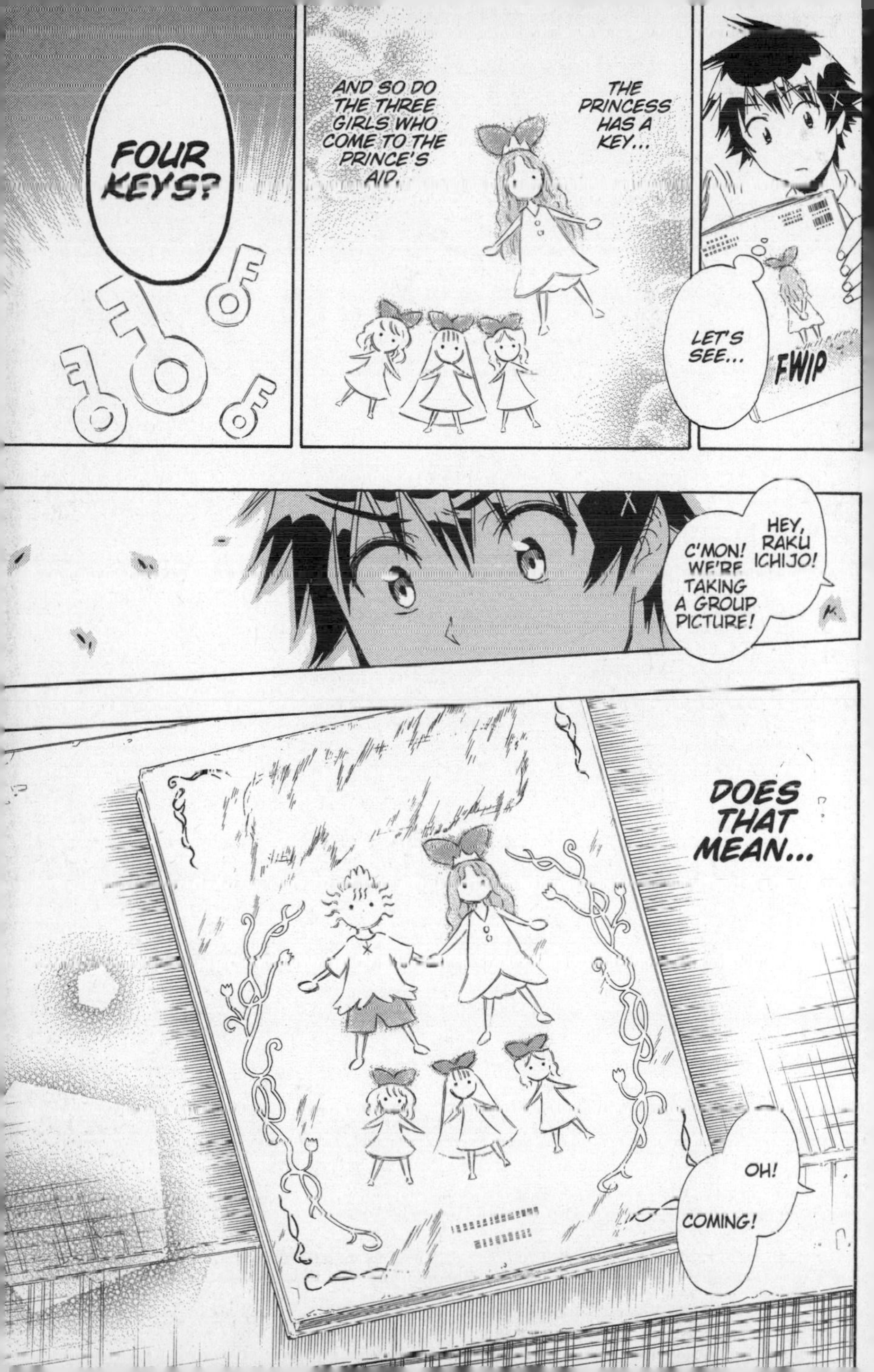
LET'S SEE...
FWIP
THE PRINCESS HAS A KEY...
AND SO DO THE THREE GIRLS WHO COME TO THE PRINCE'S AID.
FOUR KEYS?
HEY, RAKU ICHIJO!
C'MON! WE'RE TAKING A GROUP PICTURE!
DOES THAT MEAN...
OH!
COMING!

☆ Chitoge's Favorite Flower ☆

《 Sweet Peas 》

Said to symbolize
sweet memories

Super time-consuming
to draw...

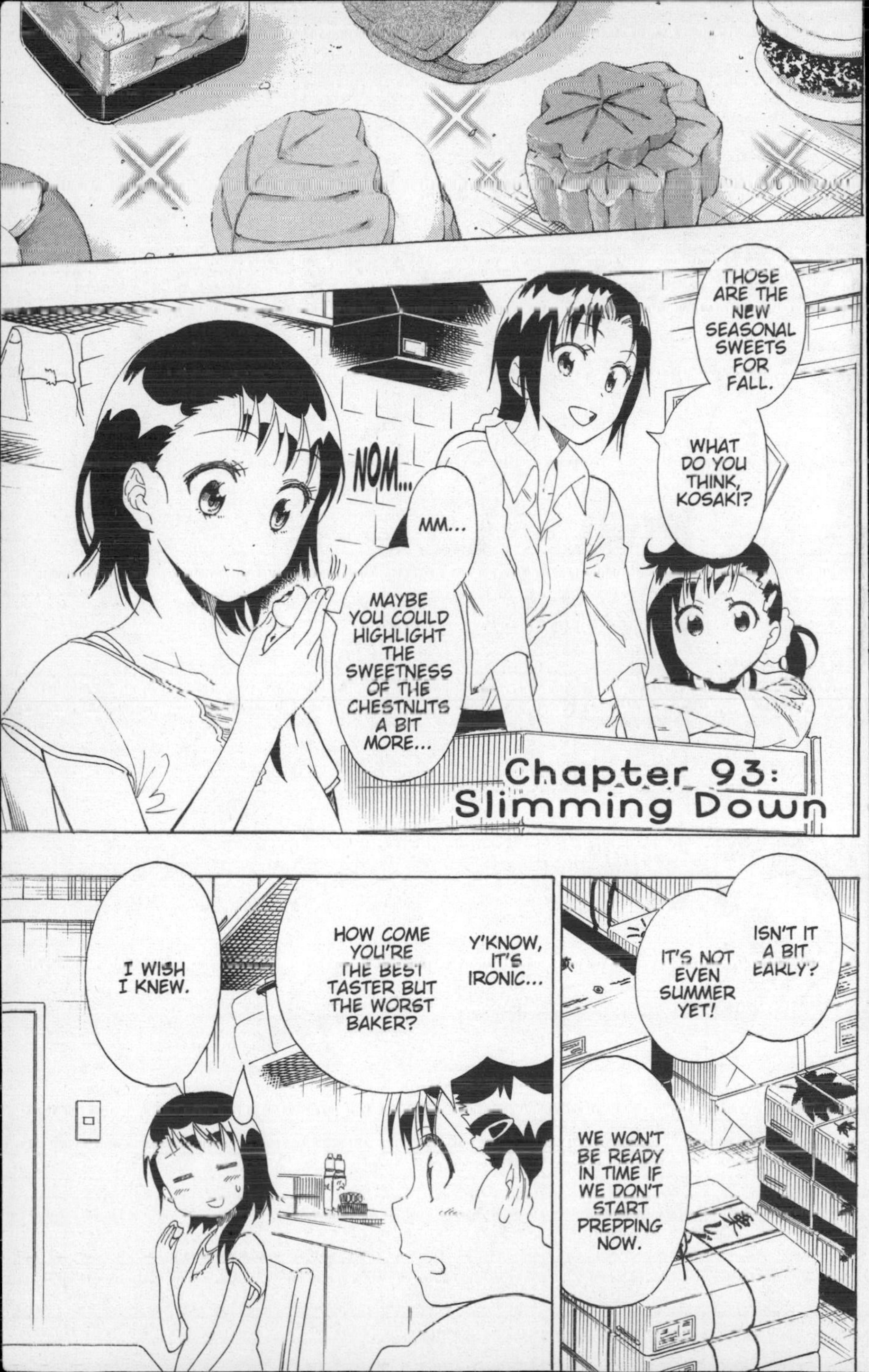
THOSE ARE THE NEW SEASONAL SWEETS FOR FALL.
WHAT DO YOU THINK, KOSAKI?
NOM...
MM...
MAYBE YOU COULD HIGHLIGHT THE SWEETNESS OF THE CHESTNUTS A BIT MORE...
Chapter 93: Slimming Down
ISN'T IT A BIT EARLY?
IT'S NOT EVEN SUMMER YET!
WE WON'T BE READY IN TIME IF WE DON'T START PREPPING NOW.
Y'KNOW, IT'S IRONIC...
HOW COME YOU'RE THE BEST TASTER BUT THE WORST BAKER?
I WISH I KNEW.

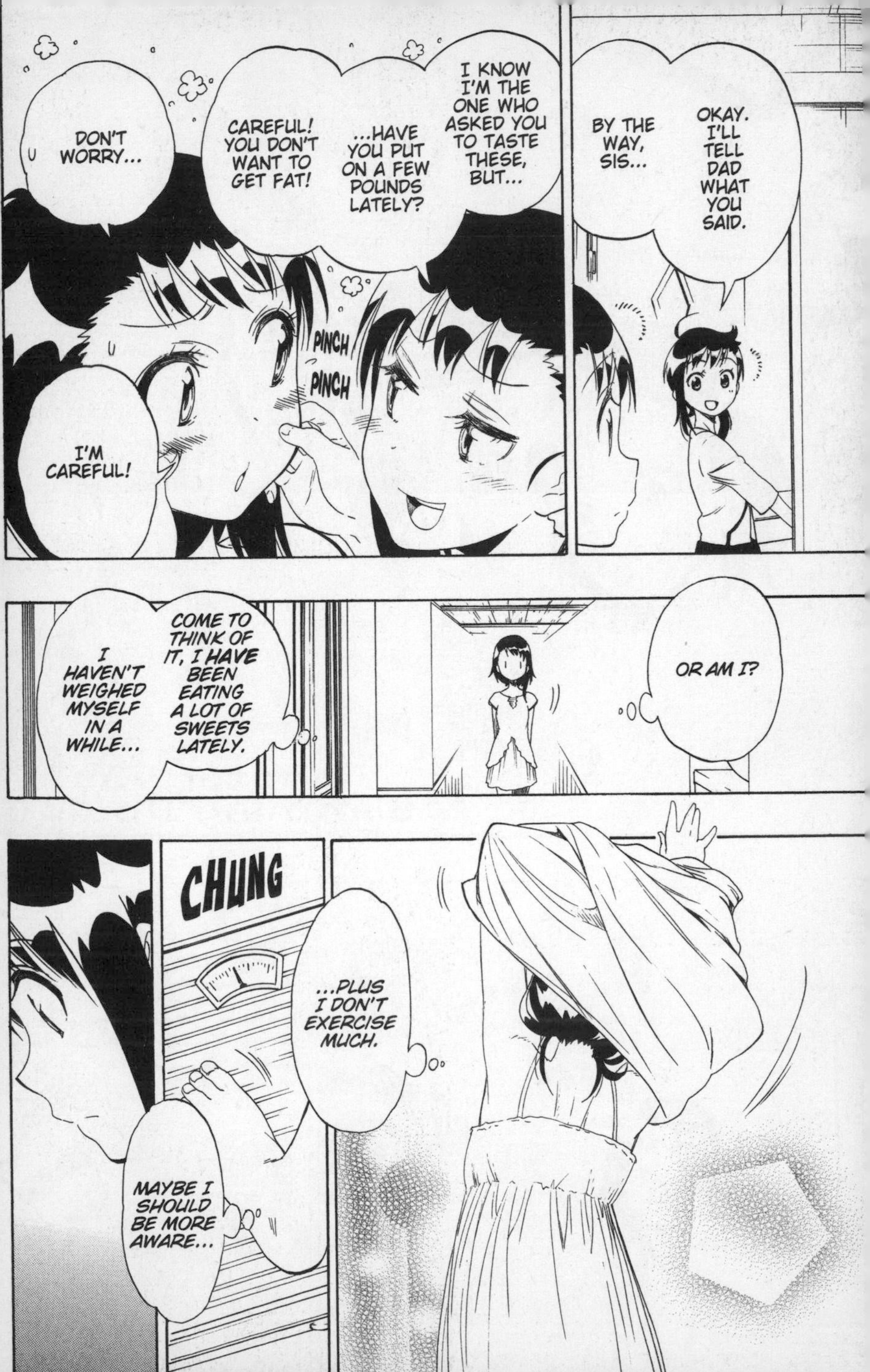
OKAY. I'LL TELL DAD WHAT YOU SAID.
BY THE WAY, SIS...
I KNOW I'M THE ONE WHO ASKED YOU TO TASTE THESE, BUT...
...HAVE YOU PUT ON A FEW POUNDS LATELY?
CAREFUL! YOU DON'T WANT TO GET FAT!
PINCH
PINCH
DON'T WORRY...
I'M CAREFUL!
OR AM I?
COME TO THINK OF IT, I HAVE BEEN EATING A LOT OF SWEETS LATELY.
I HAVEN'T WEIGHED MYSELF IN A WHILE...
...PLUS I DON'T EXERCISE MUCH.
CHUNG
MAYBE I SHOULD BE MORE AWARE...

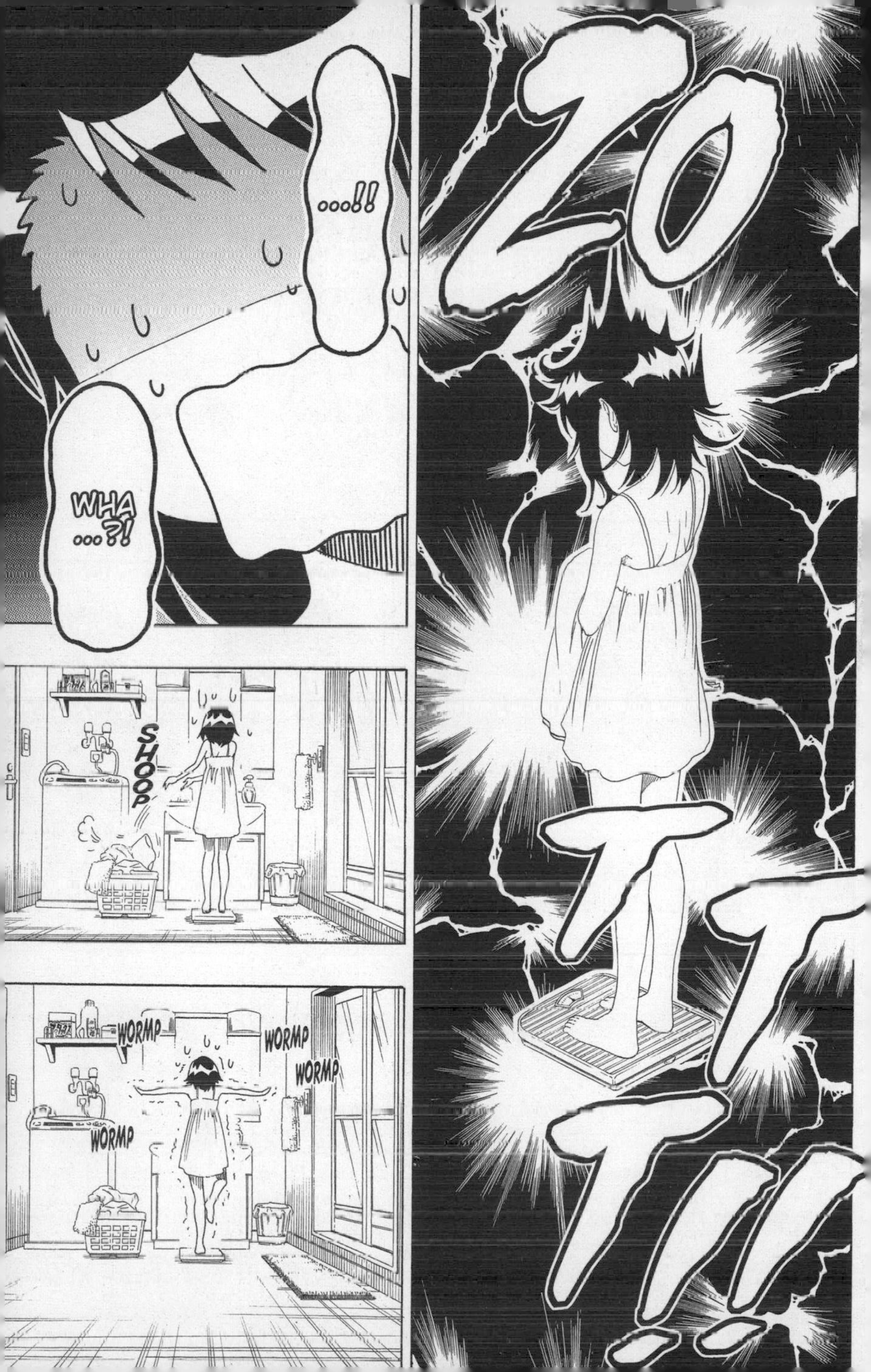
ZOTTTT!!
OOO!!
WHA...?!
SHOOP
WORMP
WORMP
WORMP
WORMP

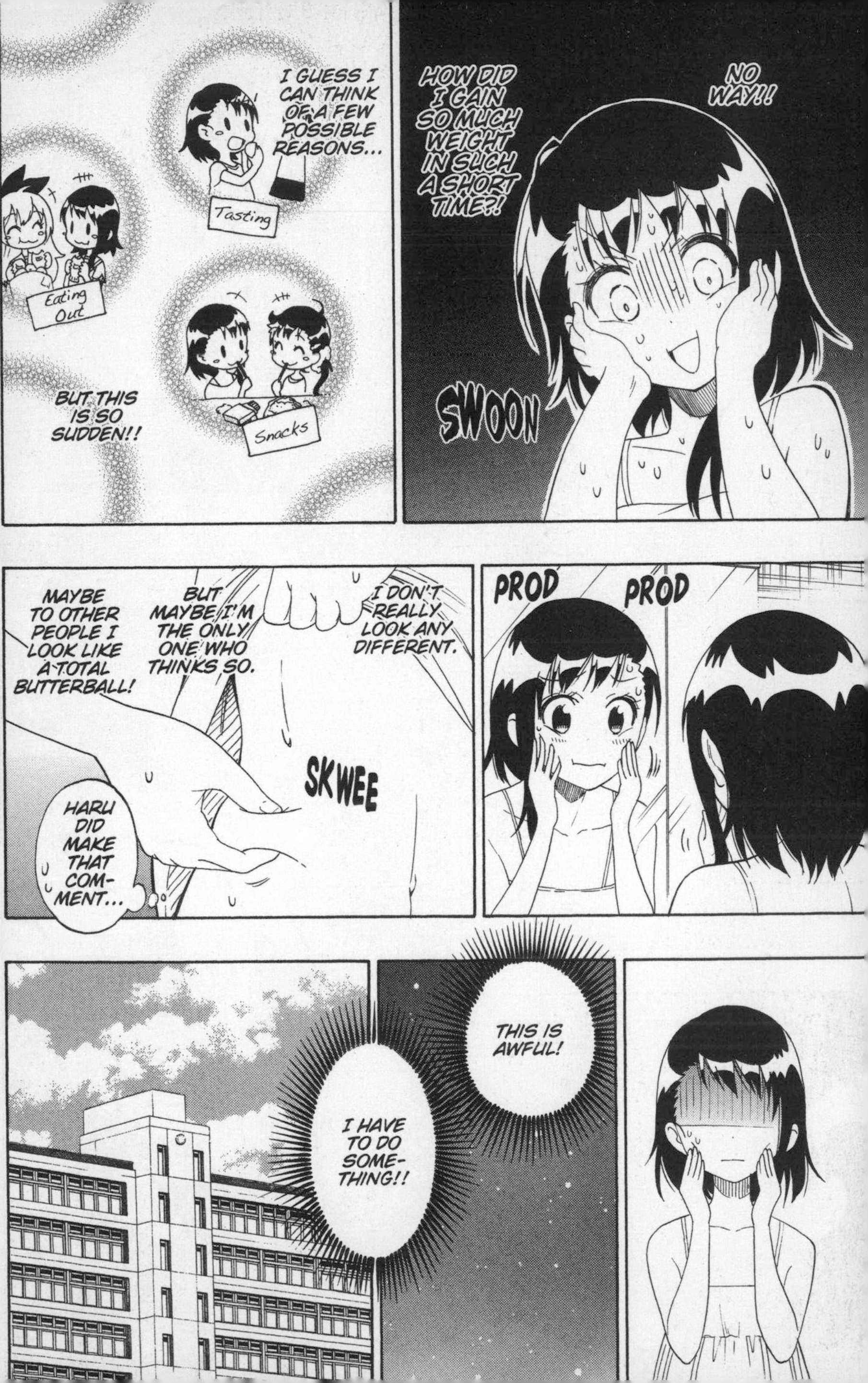
NO WAY!!
HOW DID I GAIN SO MUCH WEIGHT IN SUCH A SHORT TIME?!
SWOON
I GUESS I CAN THINK OF A FEW POSSIBLE REASONS...
Tasting
Eating Out
Snacks
BUT THIS IS SO SUDDEN!!
PROD
PROD
I DON'T REALLY LOOK ANY DIFFERENT.
BUT MAYBE I'M THE ONLY ONE WHO THINKS SO.
MAYBE TO OTHER PEOPLE I LOOK LIKE A TOTAL BUTTERBALL!
SKWEE
HARU DID MAKE THAT COM-MENT...
THIS IS AWFUL!
I HAVE TO DO SOME-THING!!

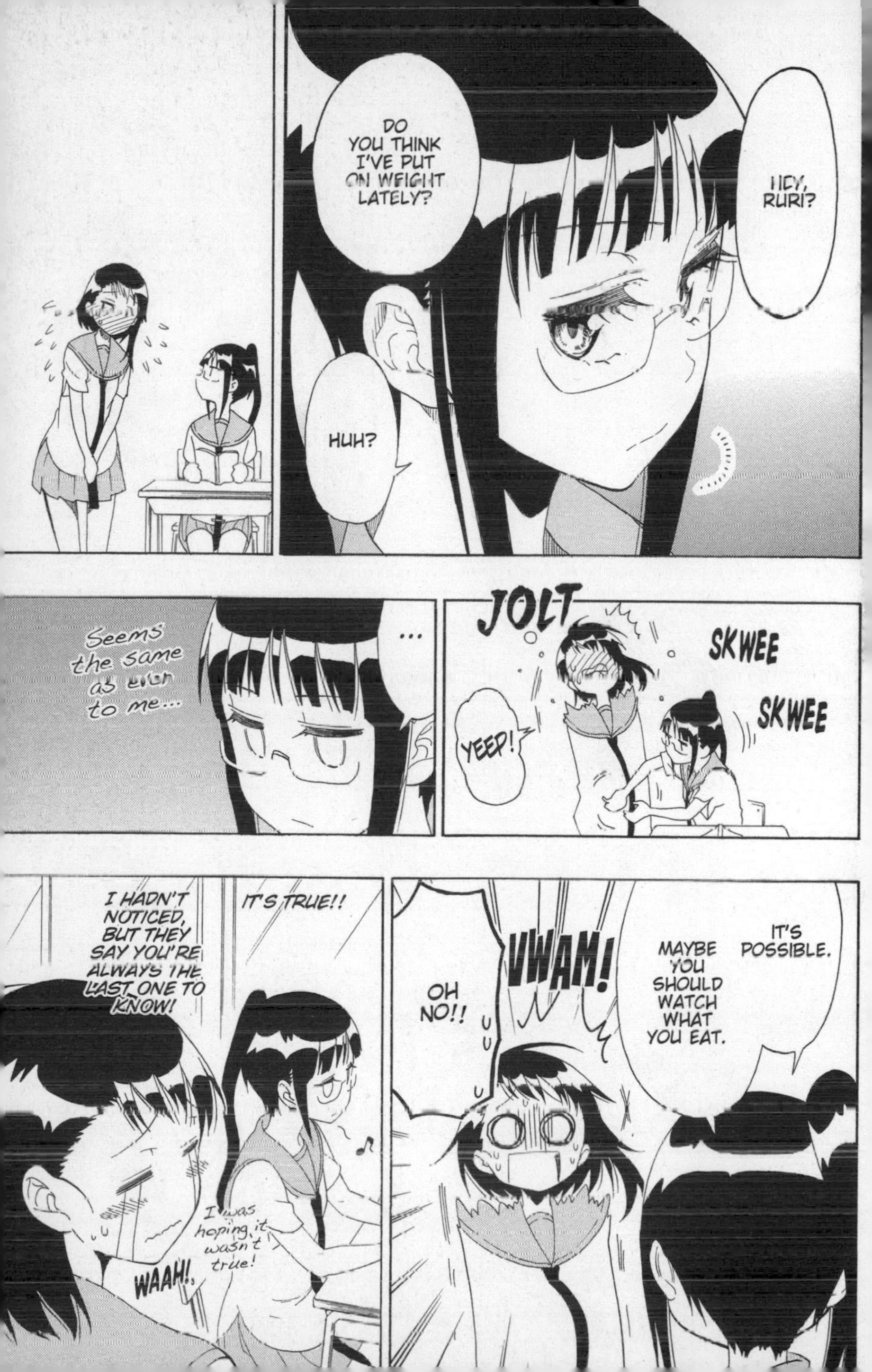
HEY, RURI?
DO YOU THINK I'VE PUT ON WEIGHT LATELY?
HUH?
JOLT
YEEP!
SKWEE
SKWEE
...
Seems the same as ever to me...
IT'S POSSIBLE.
MAYBE YOU SHOULD WATCH WHAT YOU EAT.
VWAM!
OH NO!!
IT'S TRUE!!
I HADN'T NOTICED, BUT THEY SAY YOU'RE ALWAYS THE LAST ONE TO KNOW!
I was hoping it wasn't true!
WAAH!

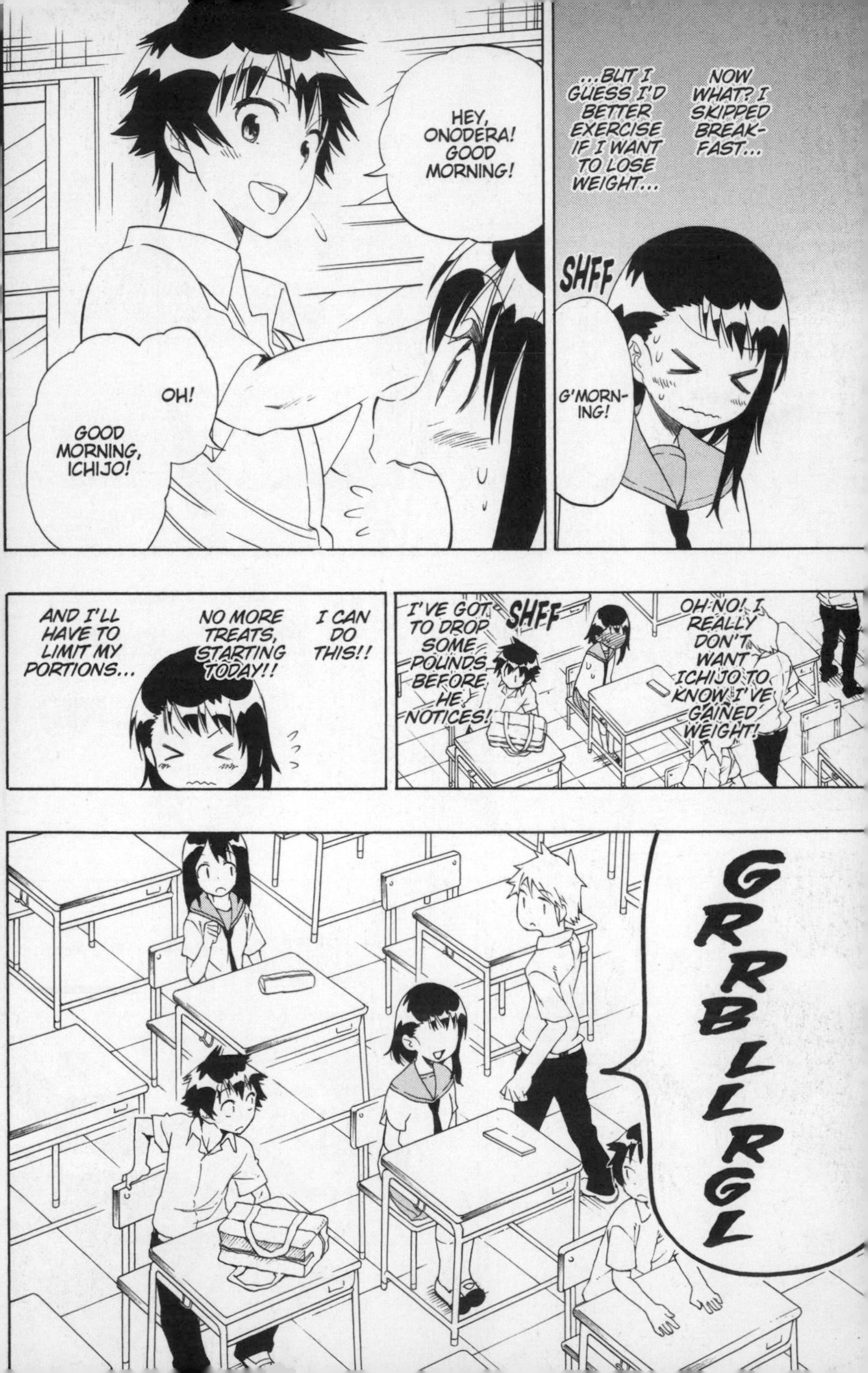
NOW WHAT? I SKIPPED BREAK-FAST...
...BUT I GUESS I'D BETTER EXERCISE IF I WANT TO LOSE WEIGHT...
SHFF
G'MORN-ING!
HEY, ONODERA! GOOD MORNING!
OH!
GOOD MORNING, ICHIJO!
OH NO! I REALLY DON'T WANT ICHIJO TO KNOW I'VE GAINED WEIGHT!
SHFF
I'VE GOT TO DROP SOME POUNDS BEFORE HE NOTICES!
I CAN DO THIS!!
NO MORE TREATS, STARTING TODAY!!
AND I'LL HAVE TO LIMIT MY PORTIONS...
GRRBLLRGL

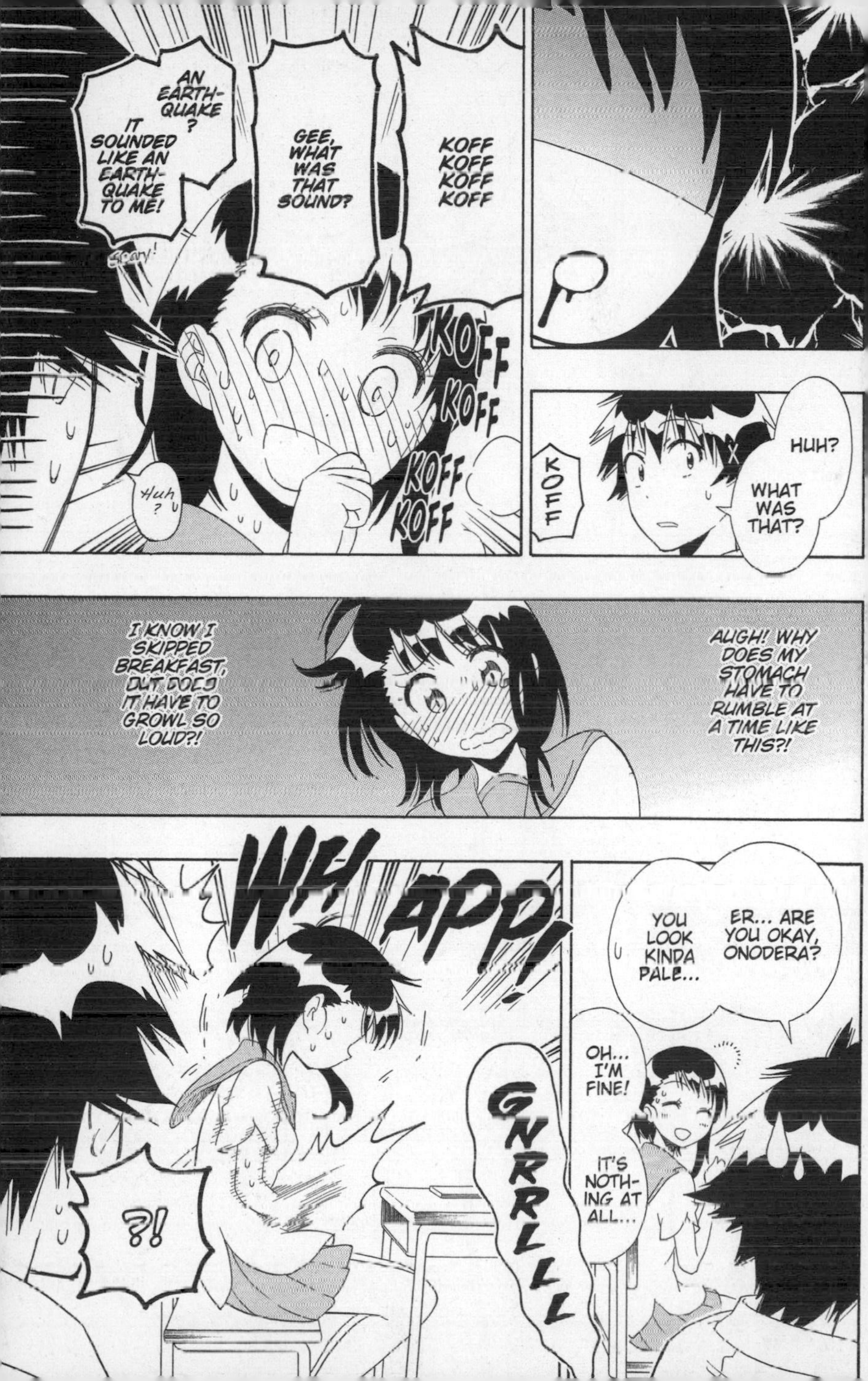
HUH?
WHAT WAS THAT?
KOFF
KOFF KOFF KOFF KOFF
GEE, WHAT WAS THAT SOUND?
AN EARTHQUAKE?
IT SOUNDED LIKE AN EARTHQUAKE TO ME!
KOFF KOFF KOFF KOFF
Huh?
AUGH! WHY DOES MY STOMACH HAVE TO RUMBLE AT A TIME LIKE THIS?!
I KNOW I SKIPPED BREAKFAST, BUT DOES IT HAVE TO GROWL SO LOUD?!
ER... ARE YOU OKAY, ONODERA?
YOU LOOK KINDA PALE...
OH... I'M FINE!
IT'S NOTHING AT ALL...
GNRRLLL
WHAPP!
?!

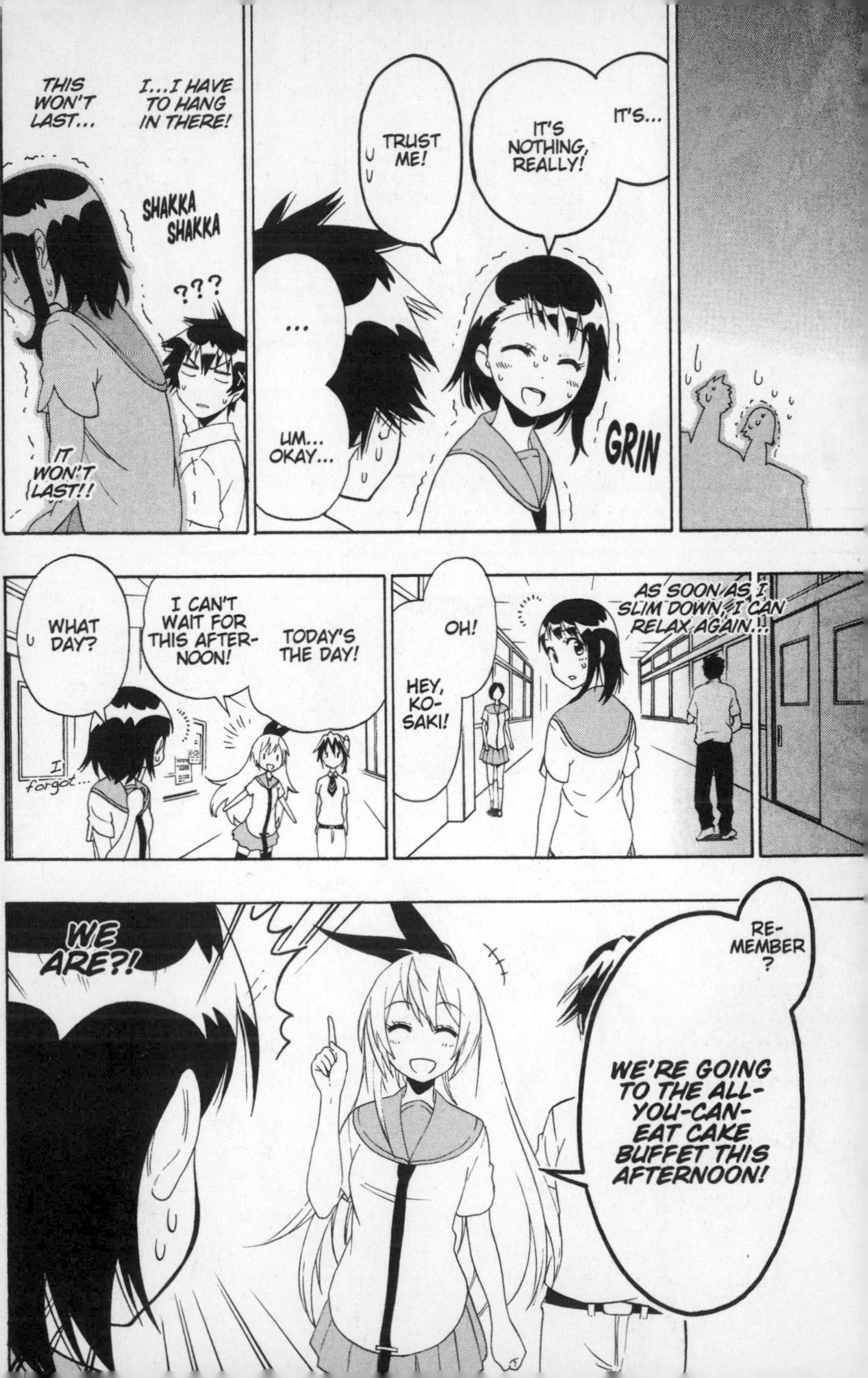
IT'S... IT'S NOTHING, REALLY!
TRUST ME!
GRIN
...
UM... OKAY...
I...I HAVE TO HANG IN THERE!
THIS WON'T LAST...
SHAKKA SHAKKA
???
IT WON'T LAST!!
AS SOON AS I SLIM DOWN, I CAN RELAX AGAIN...
OH!
HEY, KO-SAKI!
TODAY'S THE DAY!
I CAN'T WAIT FOR THIS AFTER-NOON!
WHAT DAY?
I forgot...
RE-MEMBER?
WE'RE GOING TO THE ALL-YOU-CAN-EAT CAKE BUFFET THIS AFTERNOON!
WE ARE?!

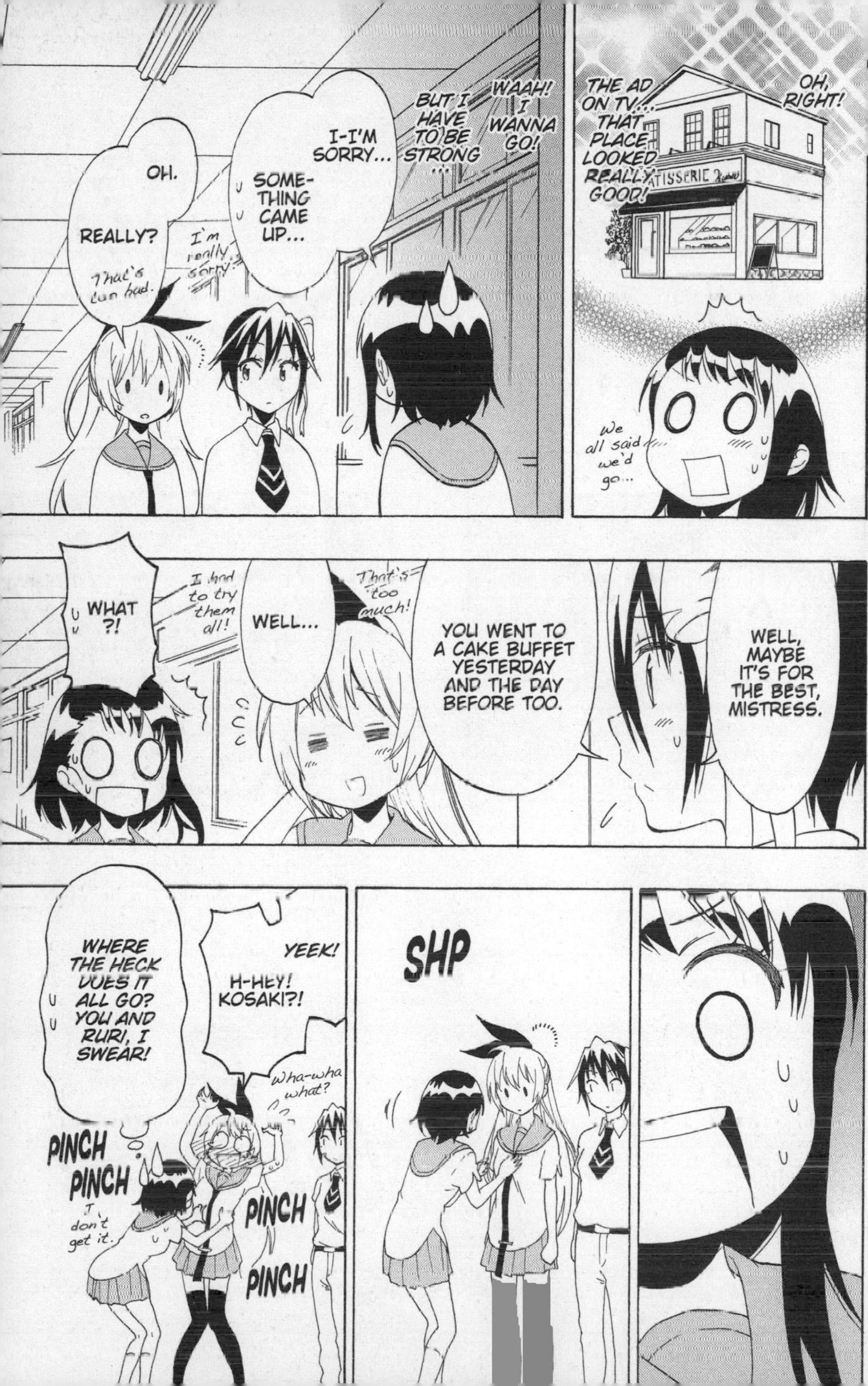
OH, RIGHT!
THE AD ON TV... THAT PLACE LOOKED REALLY GOOD!
We all said we'd go...
WAAH! I WANNA GO!
BUT I HAVE TO BE STRONG...
I-I'M SORRY... SOMETHING CAME UP...
I'm really sorry!
OH. REALLY?
That's too bad.
WELL, MAYBE IT'S FOR THE BEST, MISTRESS.
YOU WENT TO A CAKE BUFFET YESTERDAY AND THE DAY BEFORE TOO.
That's too much!
WELL...
I had to try them all!
WHAT?!
SHP
YEEK! H-HEY! KOSAKI?!
WHERE THE HECK DOES IT ALL GO? YOU AND RURI, I SWEAR!
Wha-wha what?
PINCH PINCH
I don't get it.
PINCH PINCH

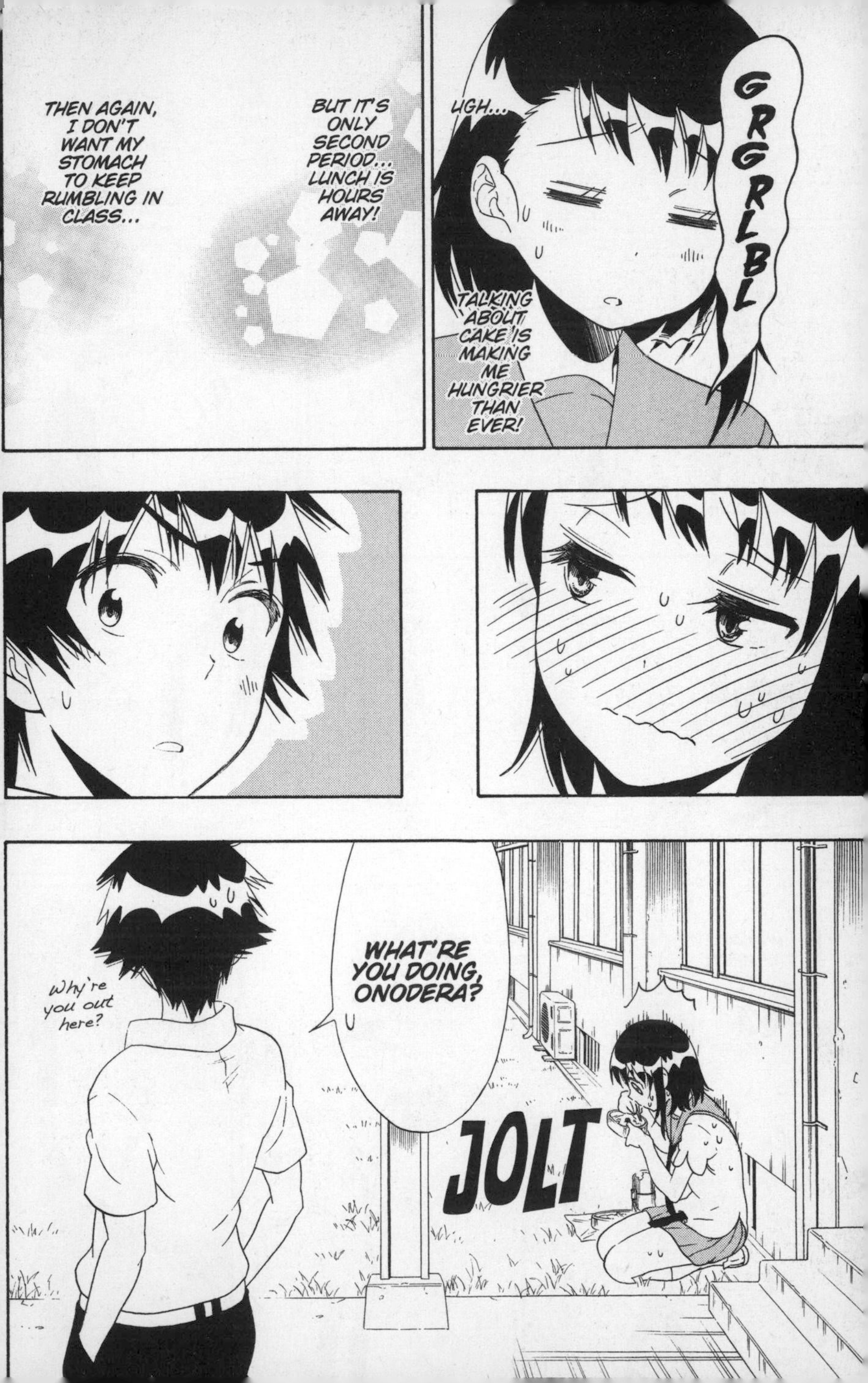
GRGRLBL
UGH...
TALKING ABOUT CAKE IS MAKING ME HUNGRIER THAN EVER!
BUT IT'S ONLY SECOND PERIOD... LUNCH IS HOURS AWAY!
THEN AGAIN, I DON'T WANT MY STOMACH TO KEEP RUMBLING IN CLASS...
WHAT'RE YOU DOING, ONODERA?
Why're you out here?
JOLT

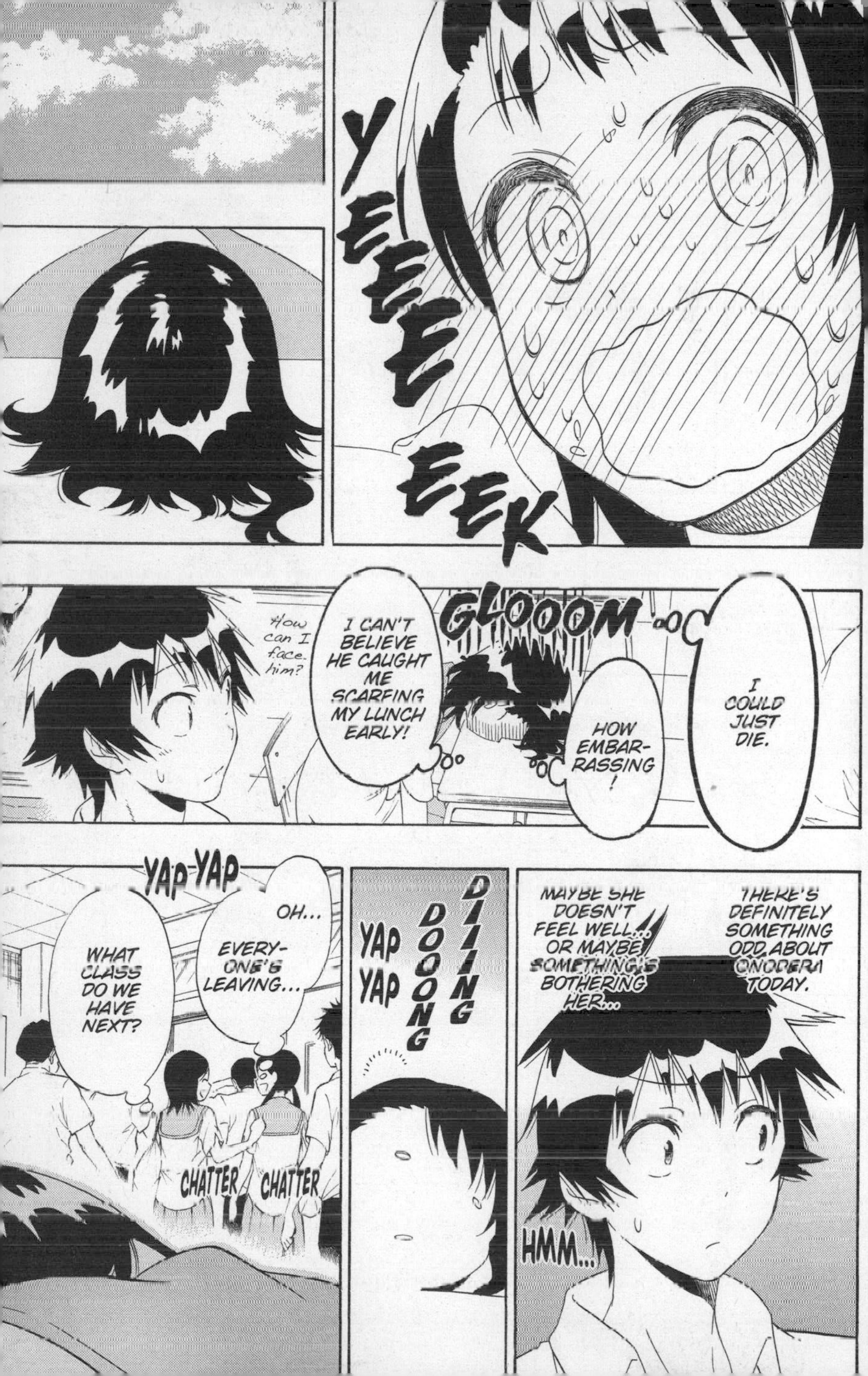
YEEEEEEK
I COULD JUST DIE.
HOW EMBARRASSING!
GLOOOM
I CAN'T BELIEVE HE CAUGHT ME SCARFING MY LUNCH EARLY!
How can I face him?
THERE'S DEFINITELY SOMETHING ODD ABOUT ONODERA TODAY.
MAYBE SHE DOESN'T FEEL WELL... OR MAYBE SOMETHING'S BOTHERING HER...
HMM...
DIIING DOOOONG
YAP YAP
YAP-YAP
OH... EVERYONE'S LEAVING...
WHAT CLASS DO WE HAVE NEXT?
CHATTER CHATTER

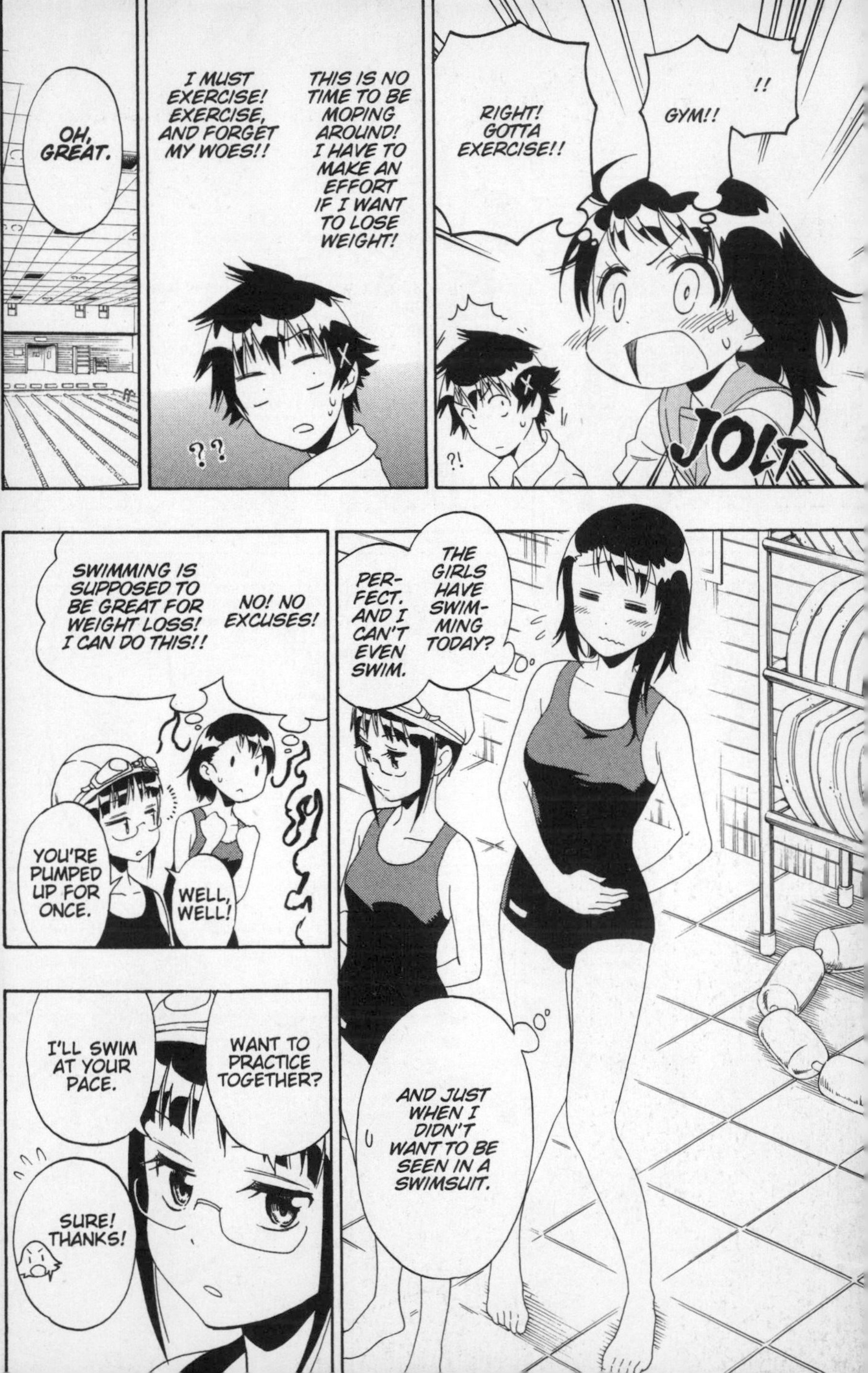
!!
GYM!!
RIGHT! GOTTA EXERCISE!!
JOLT
?!
THIS IS NO TIME TO BE MOPING AROUND! I HAVE TO MAKE AN EFFORT IF I WANT TO LOSE WEIGHT!
I MUST EXERCISE! EXERCISE, AND FORGET MY WOES!!
??
OH, GREAT.
THE GIRLS HAVE SWIM-MING TODAY?
PER-FECT. AND I CAN'T EVEN SWIM.
AND JUST WHEN I DIDN'T WANT TO BE SEEN IN A SWIMSUIT.
NO! NO EXCUSES!
SWIMMING IS SUPPOSED TO BE GREAT FOR WEIGHT LOSS! I CAN DO THIS!!
WELL, WELL!
YOU'RE PUMPED UP FOR ONCE.
WANT TO PRACTICE TOGETHER?
I'LL SWIM AT YOUR PACE.
SURE! THANKS!

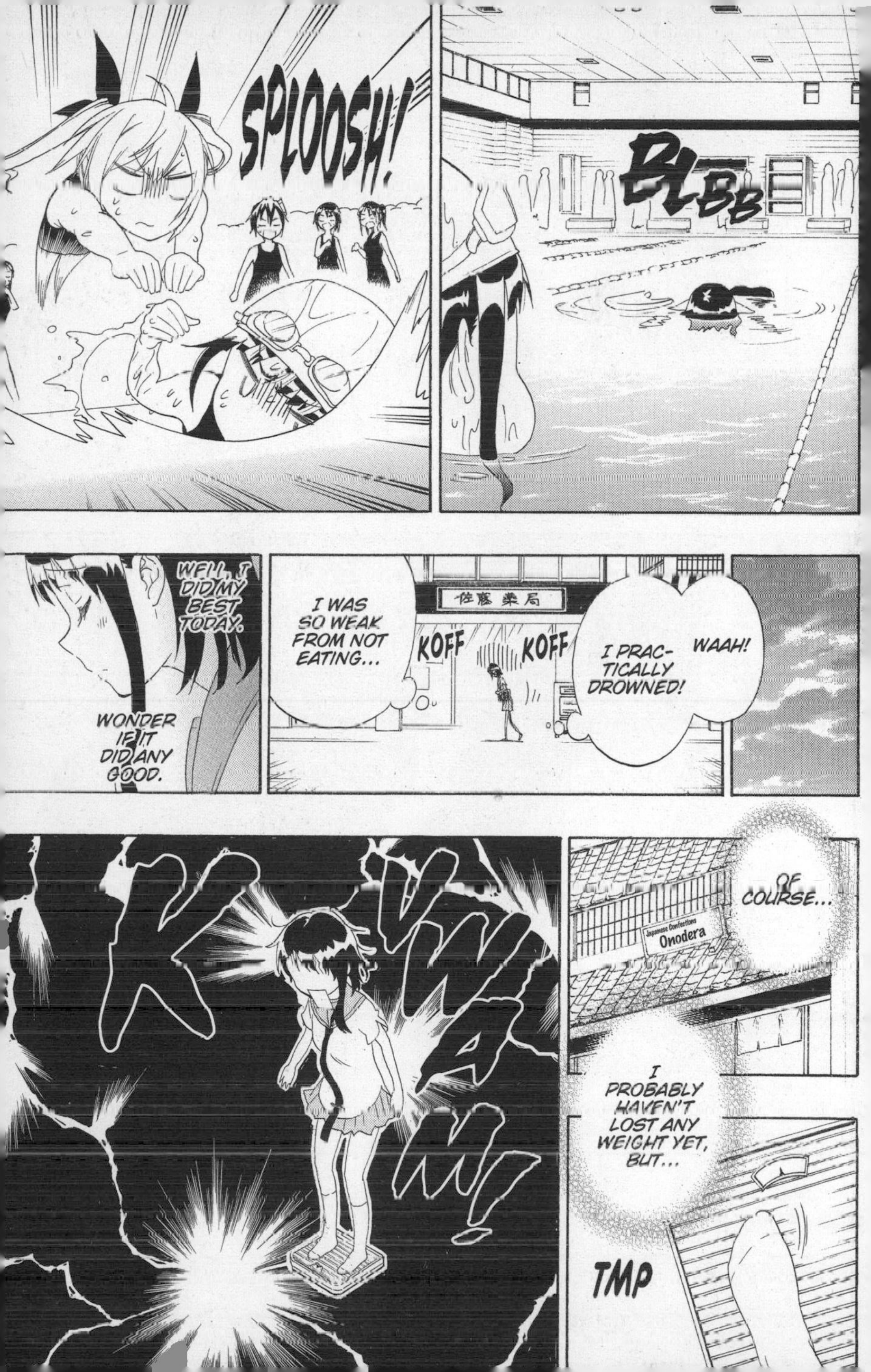
BLBB
SPLOOSH!
WAAH!
I PRAC-TICALLY DROWNED!
KOFF
KOFF
I WAS SO WEAK FROM NOT EATING...
佐藤薬局
WELL, I DID MY BEST TODAY.
WONDER IF IT DID ANY GOOD.
OF COURSE...
Japanese Confections
Onodera
I PROBABLY HAVEN'T LOST ANY WEIGHT YET, BUT...
TMP
KVWAM!

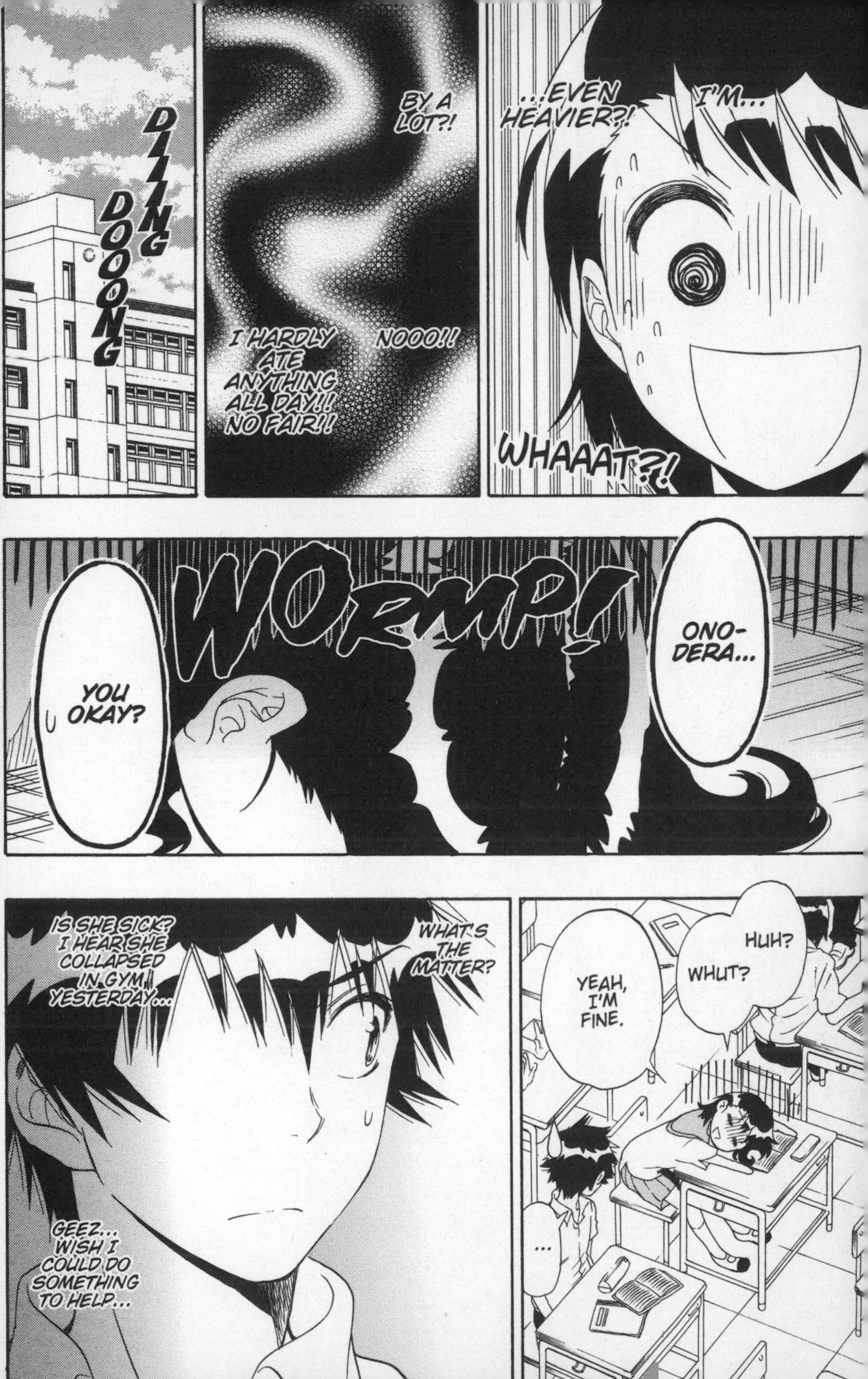
I'M...
...EVEN HEAVIER?!
WHAAAT?!
BY A LOT?!
NOOO!!
I HARDLY ATE ANYTHING ALL DAY!! NO FAIR!!
DIIING
DOOOONG
ONO-DERA...
WORMP!
YOU OKAY?
HUH?
WHUT?
YEAH, I'M FINE.
...
WHAT'S THE MATTER?
IS SHE SICK? I HEAR SHE COLLAPSED IN GYM YESTERDAY...
GEEZ... WISH I COULD DO SOMETHING TO HELP...

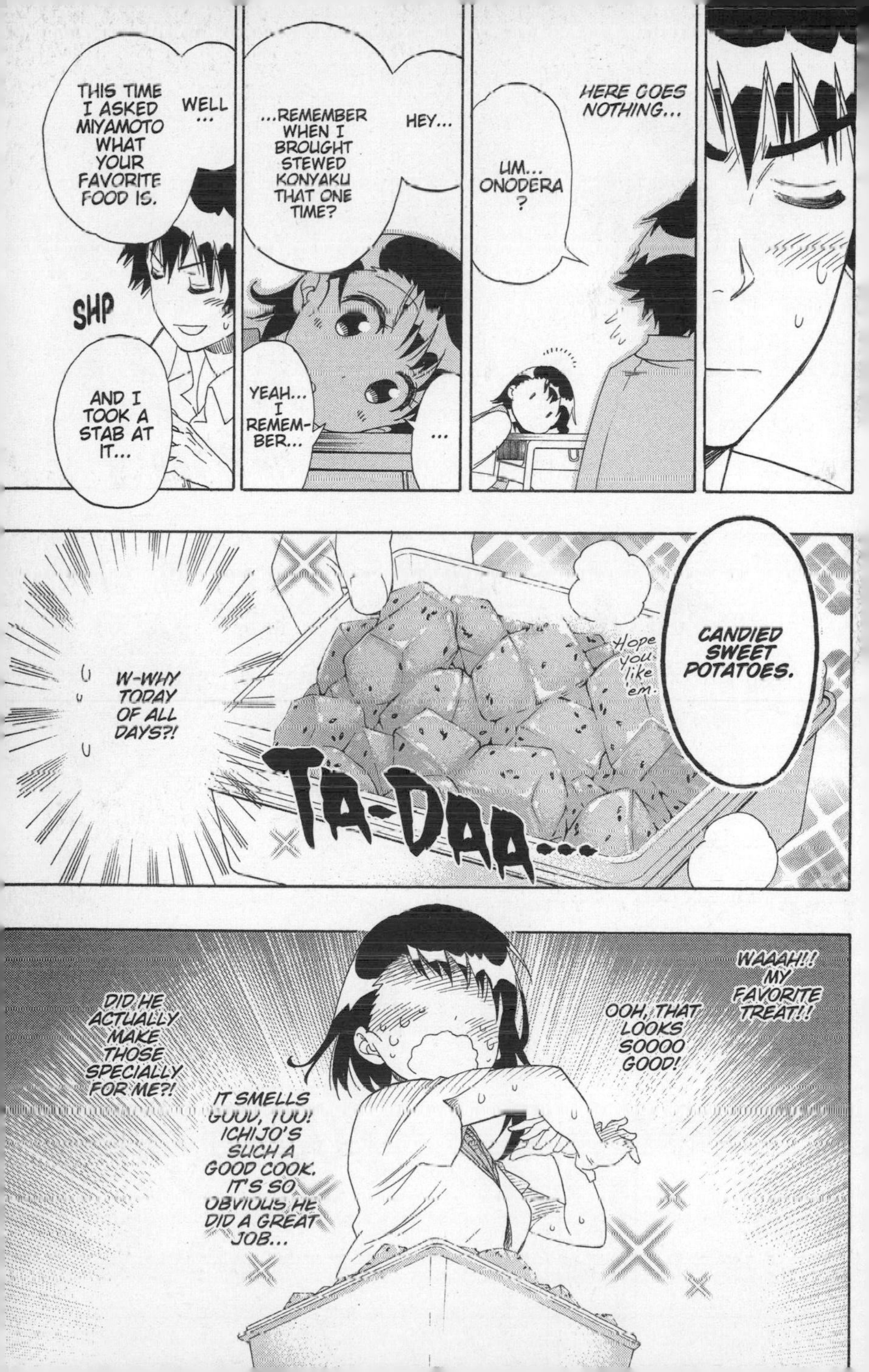
HERE GOES NOTHING...
UM... ONODERA ?
HEY...
...REMEMBER WHEN I BROUGHT STEWED KONYAKU THAT ONE TIME?
YEAH... I REMEMBER...
...
WELL...
THIS TIME I ASKED MIYAMOTO WHAT YOUR FAVORITE FOOD IS.
SHP
AND I TOOK A STAB AT IT...
CANDIED SWEET POTATOES.
Hope you like 'em.
TA-DAA...
W-WHY TODAY OF ALL DAYS?!
WAAAH!! MY FAVORITE TREAT!!
OOH, THAT LOOKS SOOOO GOOD!
DID HE ACTUALLY MAKE THOSE SPECIALLY FOR ME?!
IT SMELLS GOOD, TOO! ICHIJO'S SUCH A GOOD COOK. IT'S SO OBVIOUS HE DID A GREAT JOB...

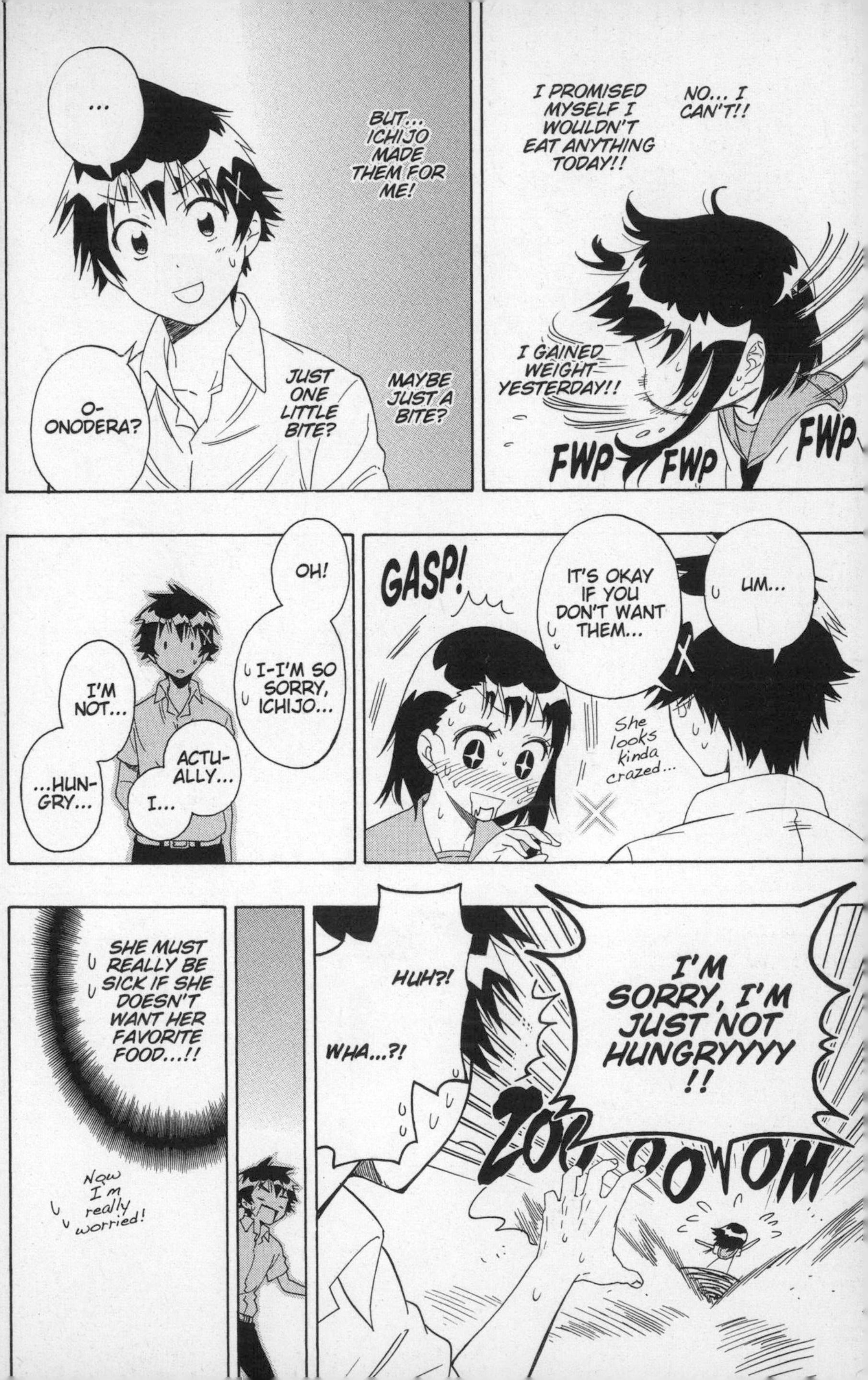
NO... I CAN'T!!
I PROMISED MYSELF I WOULDN'T EAT ANYTHING TODAY!!
I GAINED WEIGHT YESTERDAY!!
FWP
FWP
FWP
BUT... ICHIJO MADE THEM FOR ME!
...
MAYBE JUST A BITE?
JUST ONE LITTLE BITE?
O-ONODERA?
UM...
IT'S OKAY IF YOU DON'T WANT THEM...
GASP!
She looks kinda crazed...
OH!
I-I'M SO SORRY, ICHIJO...
ACTU-ALLY... I...
I'M NOT...
...HUN-GRY...
I'M SORRY, I'M JUST NOT HUNGRYYYY!!
HUH?!
WHA...?!
ZOOOOOOM
SHE MUST REALLY BE SICK IF SHE DOESN'T WANT HER FAVORITE FOOD...!!
Now I'm really worried!

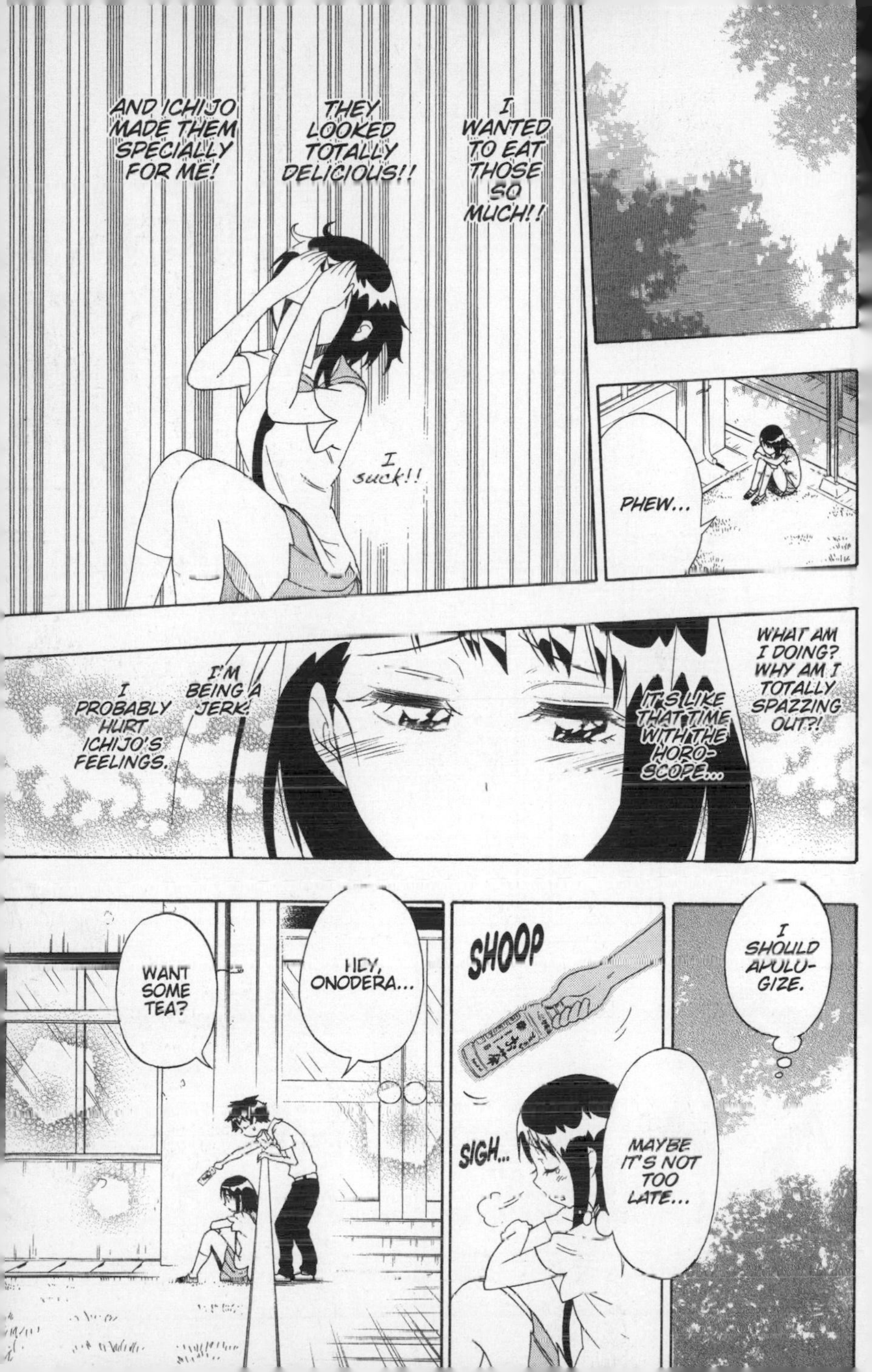
PHEW...
I WANTED TO EAT THOSE SO MUCH!!
THEY LOOKED TOTALLY DELICIOUS!!
AND ICHIJO MADE THEM SPECIALLY FOR ME!
I suck!!
WHAT AM I DOING? WHY AM I TOTALLY SPAZZING OUT?!
IT'S LIKE THAT TIME WITH THE HORO-SCOPE...
I'M BEING A JERK.
I PROBABLY HURT ICHIJO'S FEELINGS.
I SHOULD APOLO-GIZE.
MAYBE IT'S NOT TOO LATE...
SIGH...
SHOOP
HEY, ONODERA...
WANT SOME TEA?

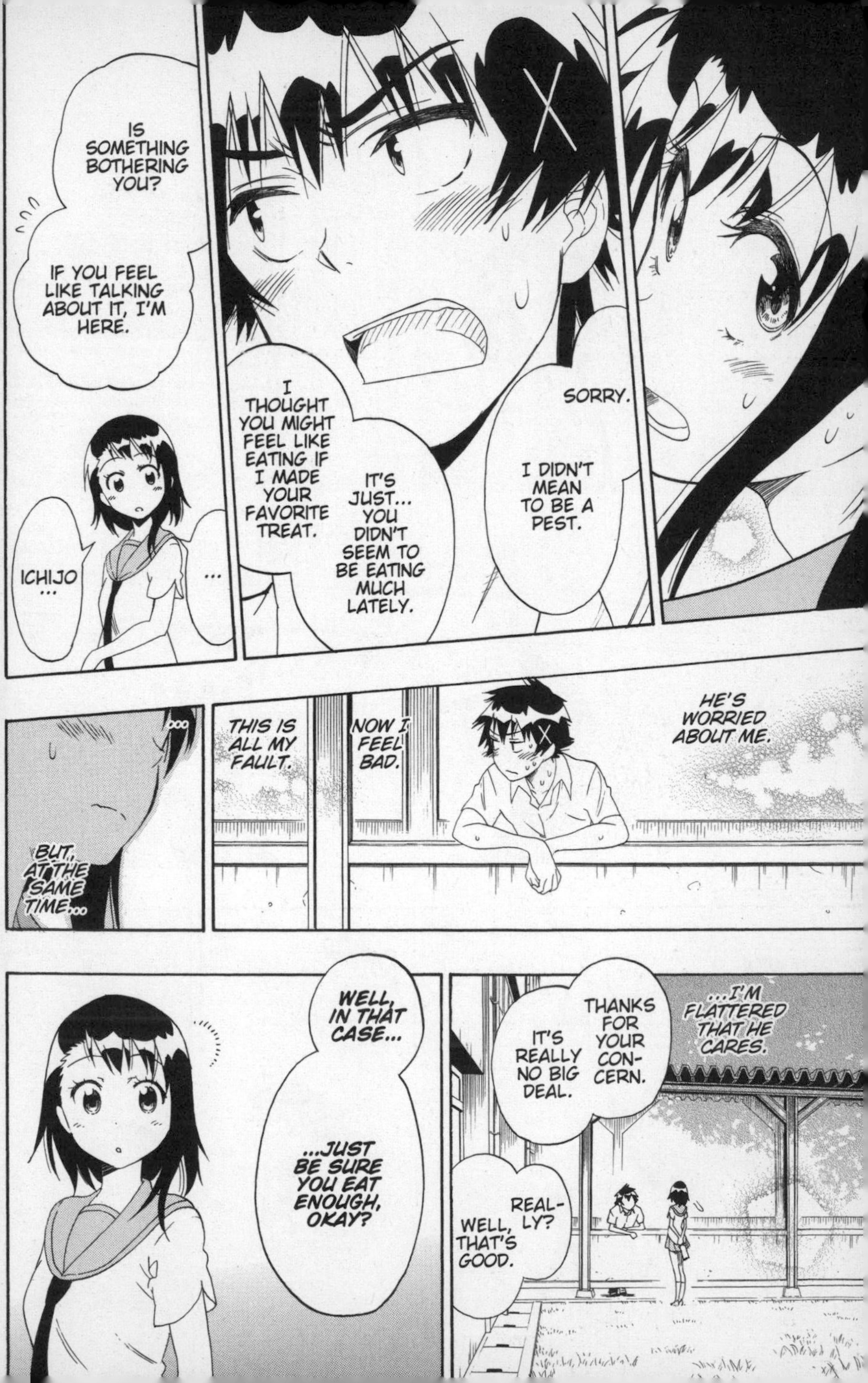
SORRY.
I DIDN'T MEAN TO BE A PEST.
IT'S JUST... YOU DIDN'T SEEM TO BE EATING MUCH LATELY.
I THOUGHT YOU MIGHT FEEL LIKE EATING IF I MADE YOUR FAVORITE TREAT.
...
ICHIJO ...
IS SOMETHING BOTHERING YOU?
IF YOU FEEL LIKE TALKING ABOUT IT, I'M HERE.
HE'S WORRIED ABOUT ME.
NOW I FEEL BAD.
THIS IS ALL MY FAULT.
...
BUT, AT THE SAME TIME...
...I'M FLATTERED THAT HE CARES.
THANKS FOR YOUR CONCERN.
IT'S REALLY NO BIG DEAL.
REAL-LY?
WELL, THAT'S GOOD.
WELL, IN THAT CASE...
...JUST BE SURE YOU EAT ENOUGH, OKAY?

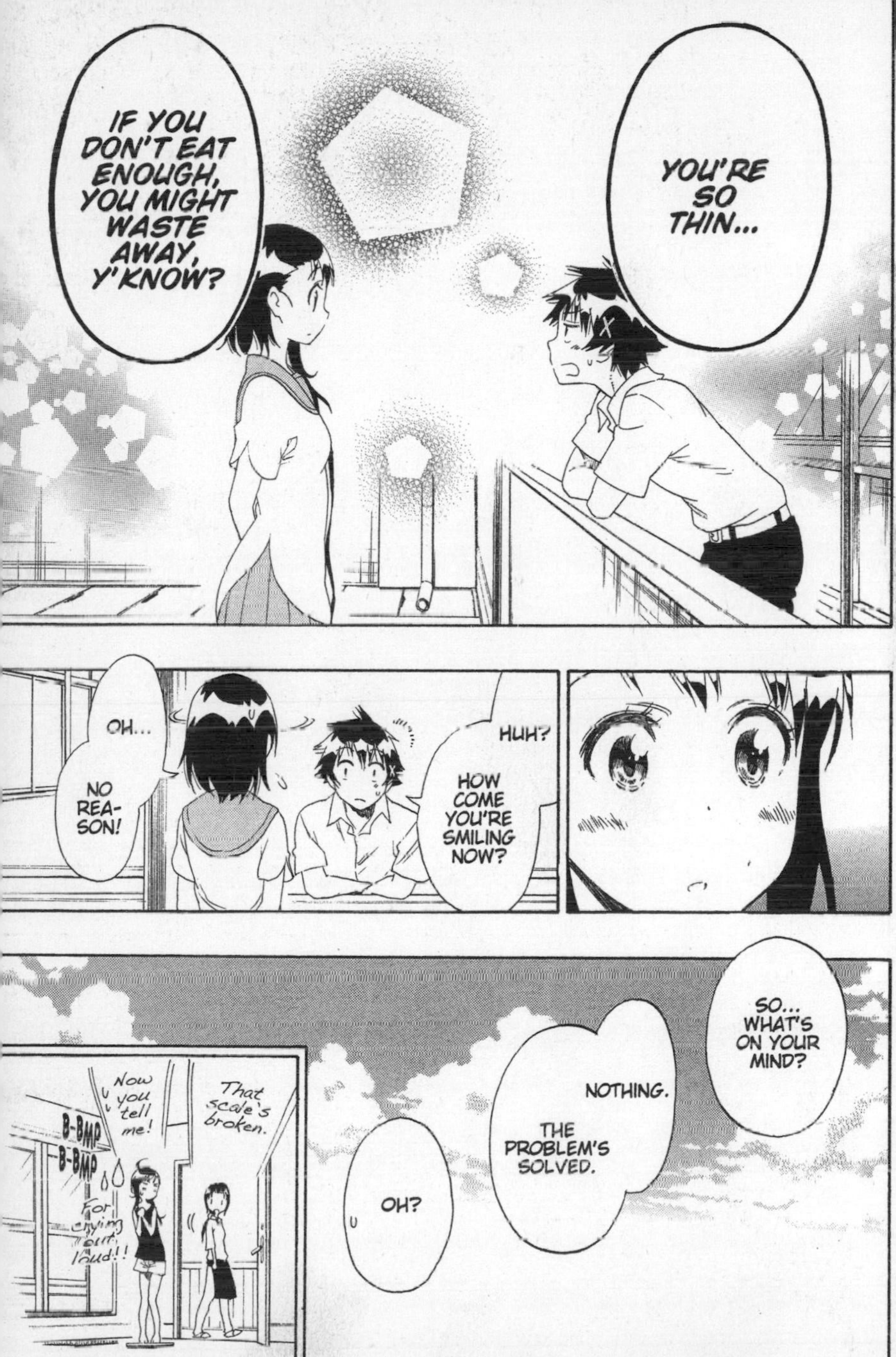
YOU'RE SO THIN...
IF YOU DON'T EAT ENOUGH, YOU MIGHT WASTE AWAY, Y'KNOW?
HUH?
HOW COME YOU'RE SMILING NOW?
OH...
NO REA-SON!
SO... WHAT'S ON YOUR MIND?
NOTHING.
THE PROBLEM'S SOLVED.
OH?
That scale's broken.
Now you tell me!
B-BMP
B-BMP
For crying out loud!!

Oooh!! So delicious ...!!!
Crispy, with a silkiness to the sauce, piping hot on the inside, and just the right amount of oil. The sweetness of the honey complements the subtle flavor of the potato without over-whelming it, and yada yada yada...
So happy!!
BLUSH
Wow, this is awe-some!
She really likes it!

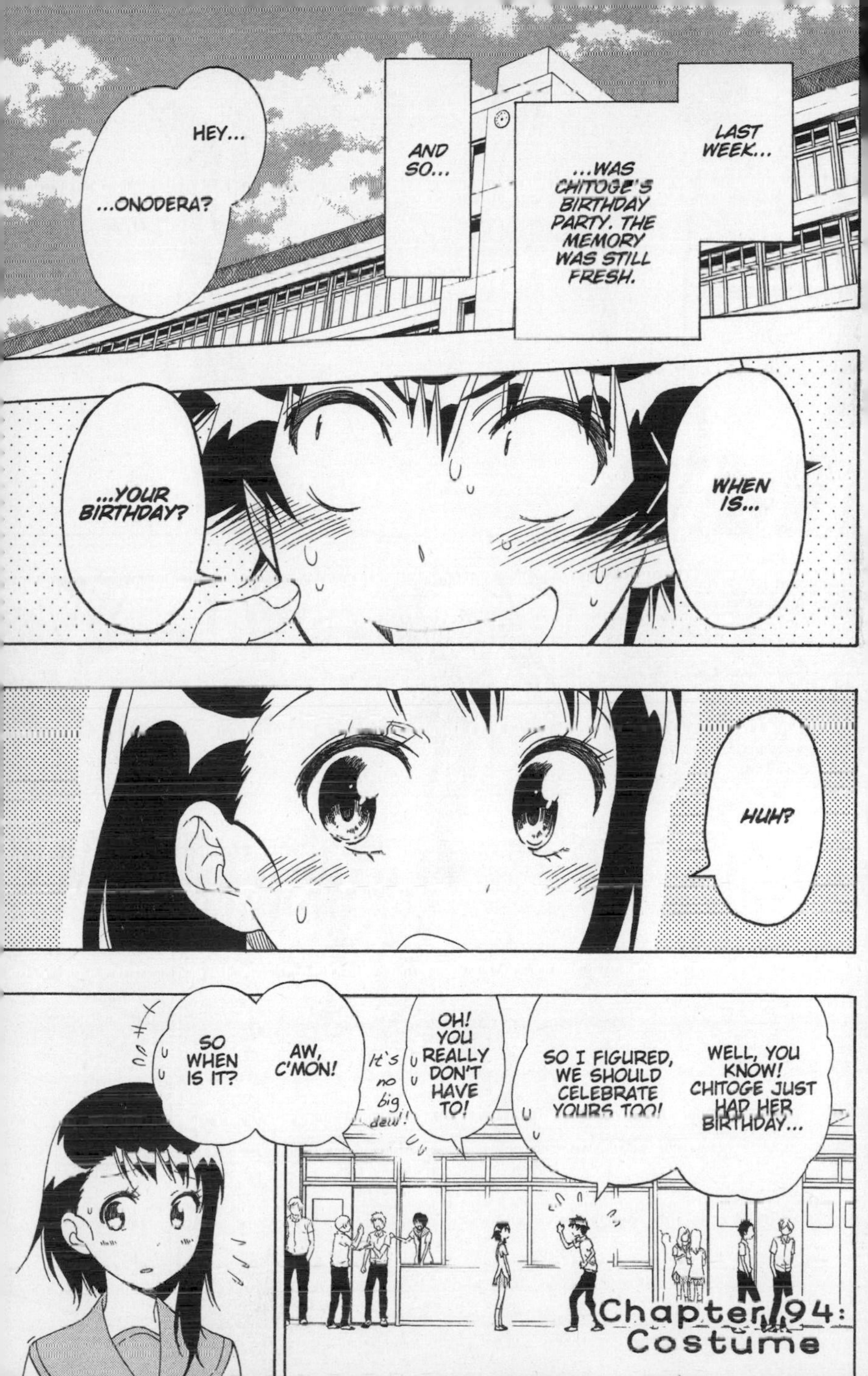
LAST WEEK...
...WAS CHITOGE'S BIRTHDAY PARTY. THE MEMORY WAS STILL FRESH.
AND SO...
HEY...
...ONODERA?
WHEN IS...
...YOUR BIRTHDAY?
HUH?
WELL, YOU KNOW! CHITOGE JUST HAD HER BIRTHDAY...
SO I FIGURED, WE SHOULD CELEBRATE YOURS TOO!
OH! YOU REALLY DON'T HAVE TO!
It's no big deal!
AW, C'MON!
SO WHEN IS IT?

Chapter 94: Costume

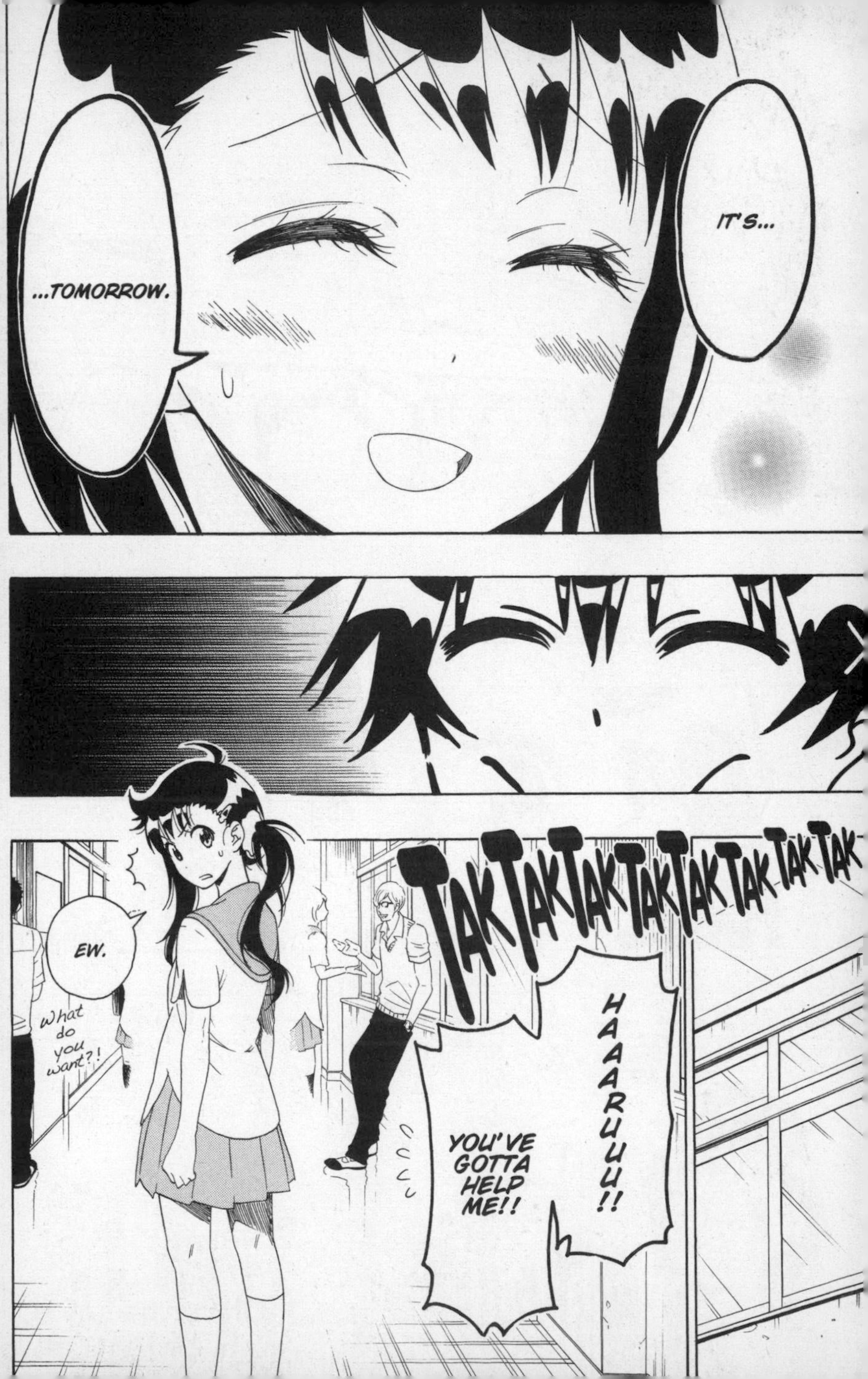
IT'S...
...TOMORROW.
TAK TAK TAK TAK TAK TAK TAK TAK
HAAARUUUU!!
YOU'VE GOTTA HELP ME!!
EW.
What do you want?!

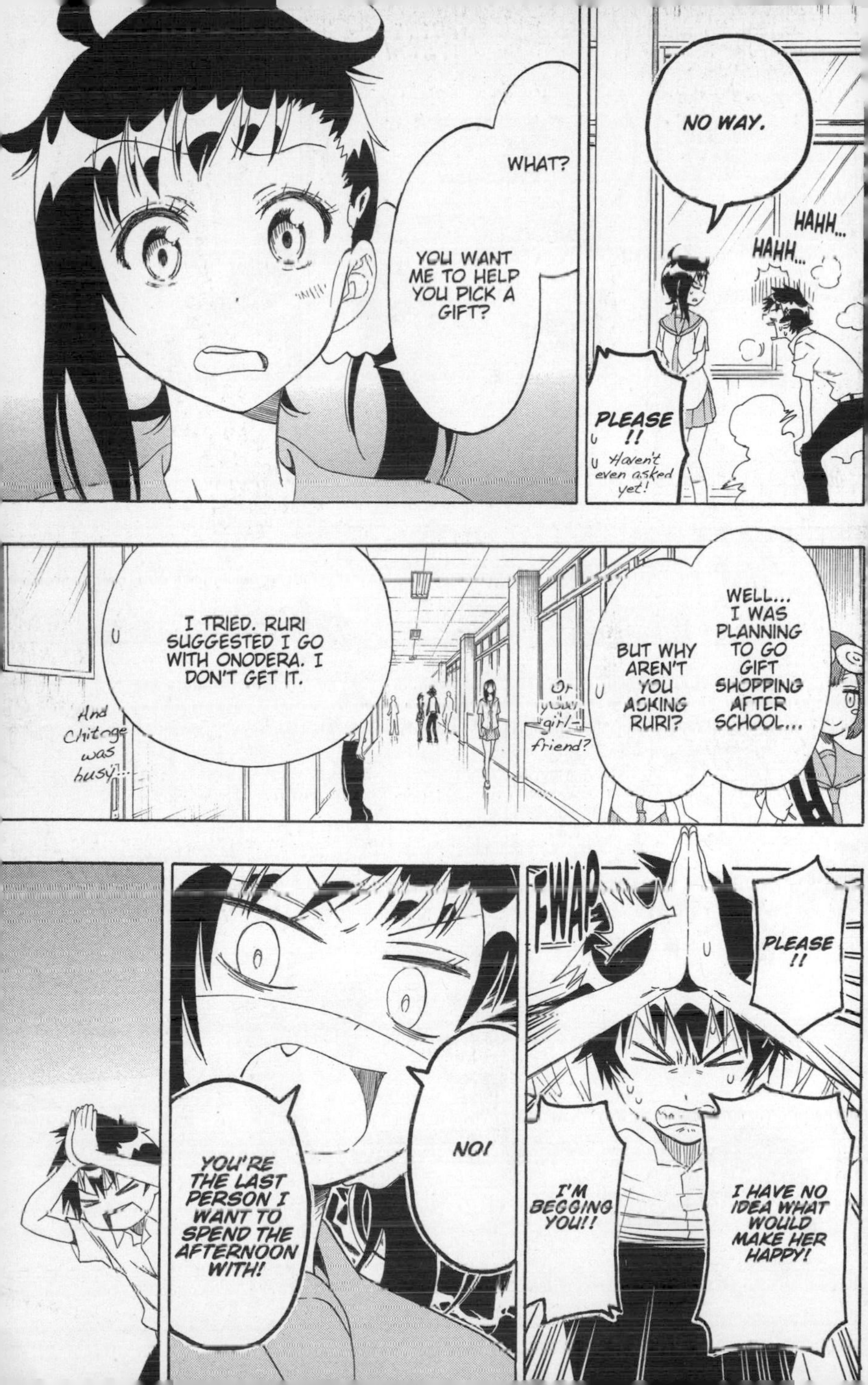
NO WAY.
HAHH... HAHH...
PLEASE !!
Haven't even asked yet!
WHAT?
YOU WANT ME TO HELP YOU PICK A GIFT?
WELL... I WAS PLANNING TO GO GIFT SHOPPING AFTER SCHOOL...
BUT WHY AREN'T YOU ASKING RURI?
Or your girl-friend?
I TRIED. RURI SUGGESTED I GO WITH ONODERA. I DON'T GET IT.
And Chitoge was busy...
FWAP
PLEASE !!
I HAVE NO IDEA WHAT WOULD MAKE HER HAPPY!
I'M BEGGING YOU!!
NO!
YOU'RE THE LAST PERSON I WANT TO SPEND THE AFTERNOON WITH!

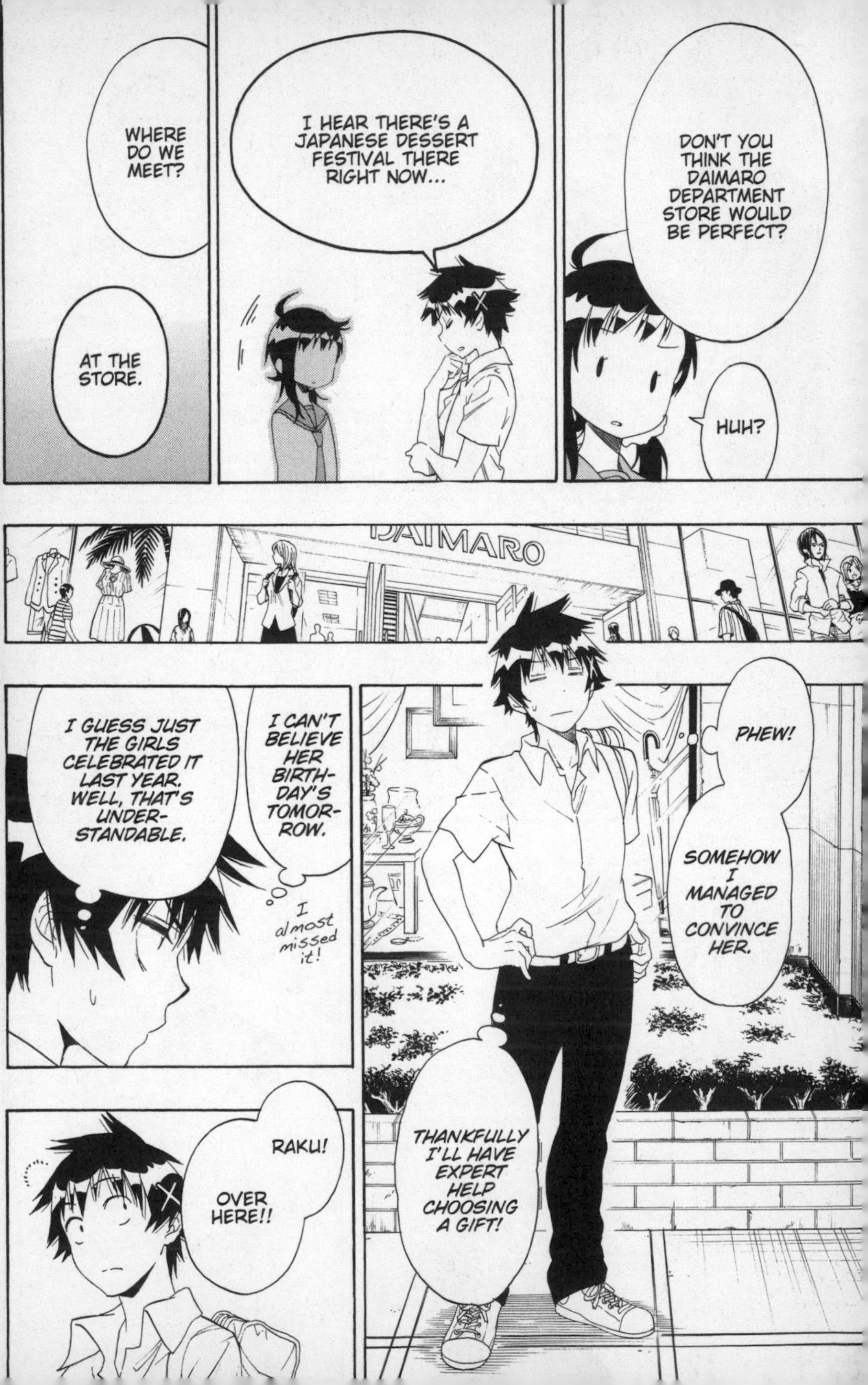
DON'T YOU THINK THE DAIMARO DEPARTMENT STORE WOULD BE PERFECT?
HUH?
I HEAR THERE'S A JAPANESE DESSERT FESTIVAL THERE RIGHT NOW...
WHERE DO WE MEET?
AT THE STORE.
DAIMARO
PHEW!
SOMEHOW I MANAGED TO CONVINCE HER.
THANKFULLY I'LL HAVE EXPERT HELP CHOOSING A GIFT!
I CAN'T BELIEVE HER BIRTHDAY'S TOMORROW.
I almost missed it!
I GUESS JUST THE GIRLS CELEBRATED IT LAST YEAR. WELL, THAT'S UNDERSTANDABLE.
RAKU!
OVER HERE!!

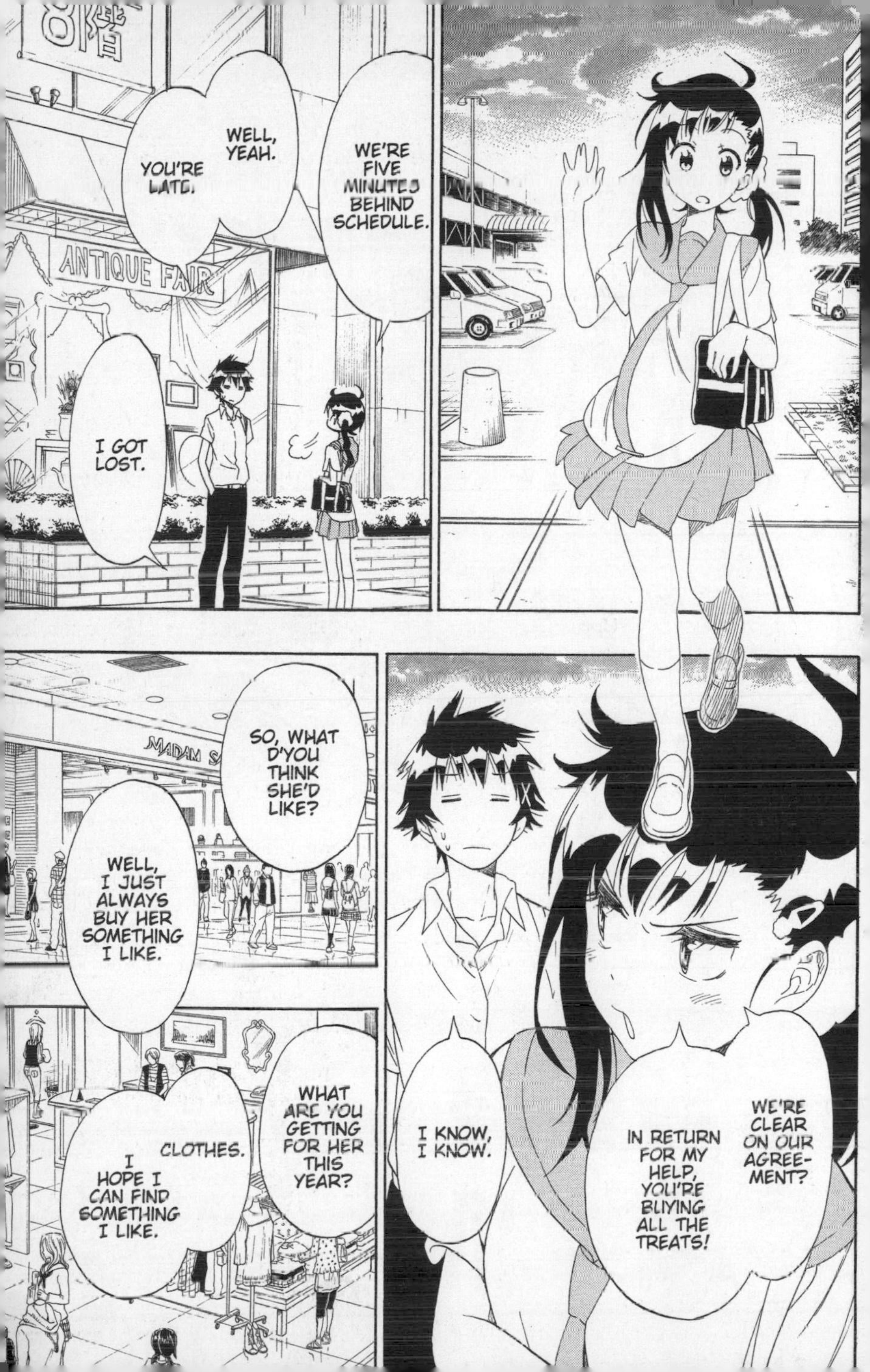
8階
ANTIQUE FAIR
WE'RE FIVE MINUTES BEHIND SCHEDULE.
WELL, YEAH.
YOU'RE LATE.
I GOT LOST.
WE'RE CLEAR ON OUR AGREE-MENT?
IN RETURN FOR MY HELP, YOU'RE BUYING ALL THE TREATS!
I KNOW, I KNOW.
SO, WHAT D'YOU THINK SHE'D LIKE?
WELL, I JUST ALWAYS BUY HER SOMETHING I LIKE.
WHAT ARE YOU GETTING FOR HER THIS YEAR?
CLOTHES.
I HOPE I CAN FIND SOMETHING I LIKE.

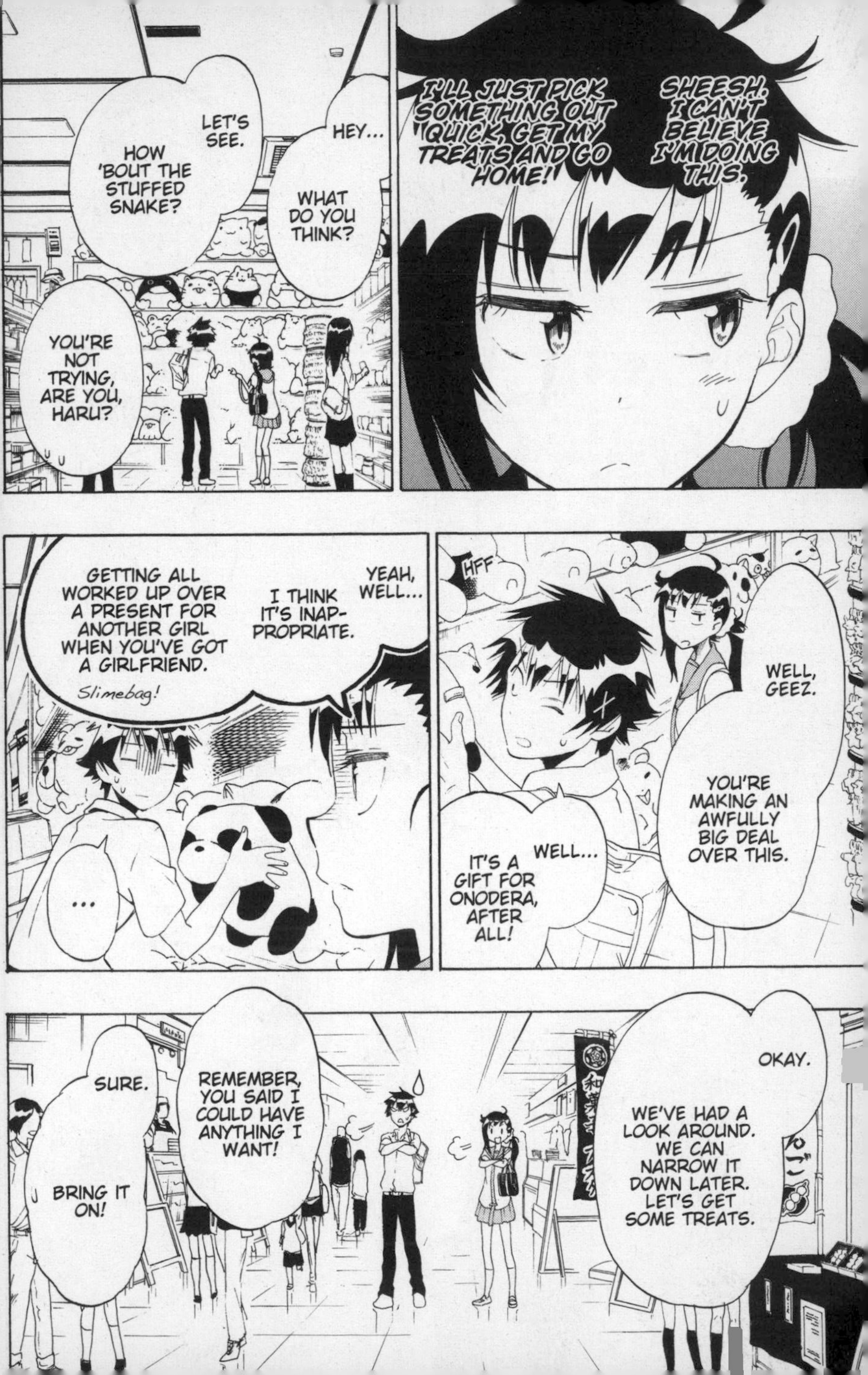
SHEESH. I CAN'T BELIEVE I'M DOING THIS.
I'LL JUST PICK SOMETHING OUT QUICK, GET MY TREATS AND GO HOME!!
HEY... WHAT DO YOU THINK?
LET'S SEE. HOW 'BOUT THE STUFFED SNAKE?
YOU'RE NOT TRYING, ARE YOU, HARU?
HFF
WELL, GEEZ. YOU'RE MAKING AN AWFULLY BIG DEAL OVER THIS.
WELL... IT'S A GIFT FOR ONODERA, AFTER ALL!
YEAH, WELL... I THINK IT'S INAP-PROPRIATE.
GETTING ALL WORKED UP OVER A PRESENT FOR ANOTHER GIRL WHEN YOU'VE GOT A GIRLFRIEND.
Slimebag!
...
OKAY. WE'VE HAD A LOOK AROUND. WE CAN NARROW IT DOWN LATER. LET'S GET SOME TREATS.
REMEMBER, YOU SAID I COULD HAVE ANYTHING I WANT!
SURE. BRING IT ON!

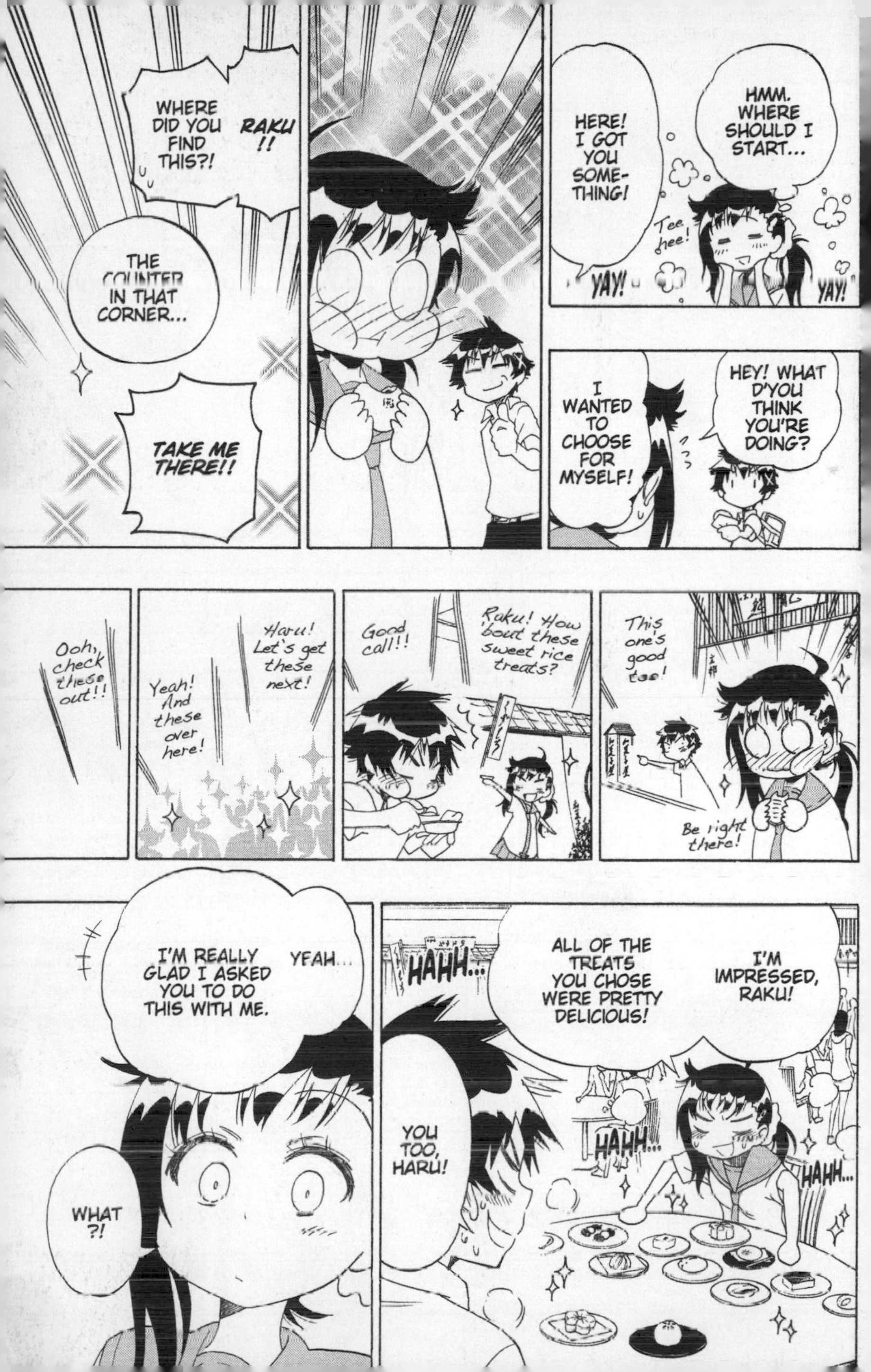
HMM. WHERE SHOULD I START...
HERE! I GOT YOU SOME-THING!
Tee hee!
YAY!
YAY!
HEY! WHAT D'YOU THINK YOU'RE DOING?
I WANTED TO CHOOSE FOR MYSELF!
RAKU!!
WHERE DID YOU FIND THIS?!
THE COUNTER IN THAT CORNER...
TAKE ME THERE!!
This one's good too!
Be right there!
Raku! How 'bout these sweet rice treats?
Good call!!
Haru! Let's get these next!
Yeah! And these over here!
Ooh, check these out!!
I'M IMPRESSED, RAKU!
ALL OF THE TREATS YOU CHOSE WERE PRETTY DELICIOUS!
HAHH...
YOU TOO, HARU!
HAHH...
HAHH...
YEAH...
I'M REALLY GLAD I ASKED YOU TO DO THIS WITH ME.
WHAT ?!

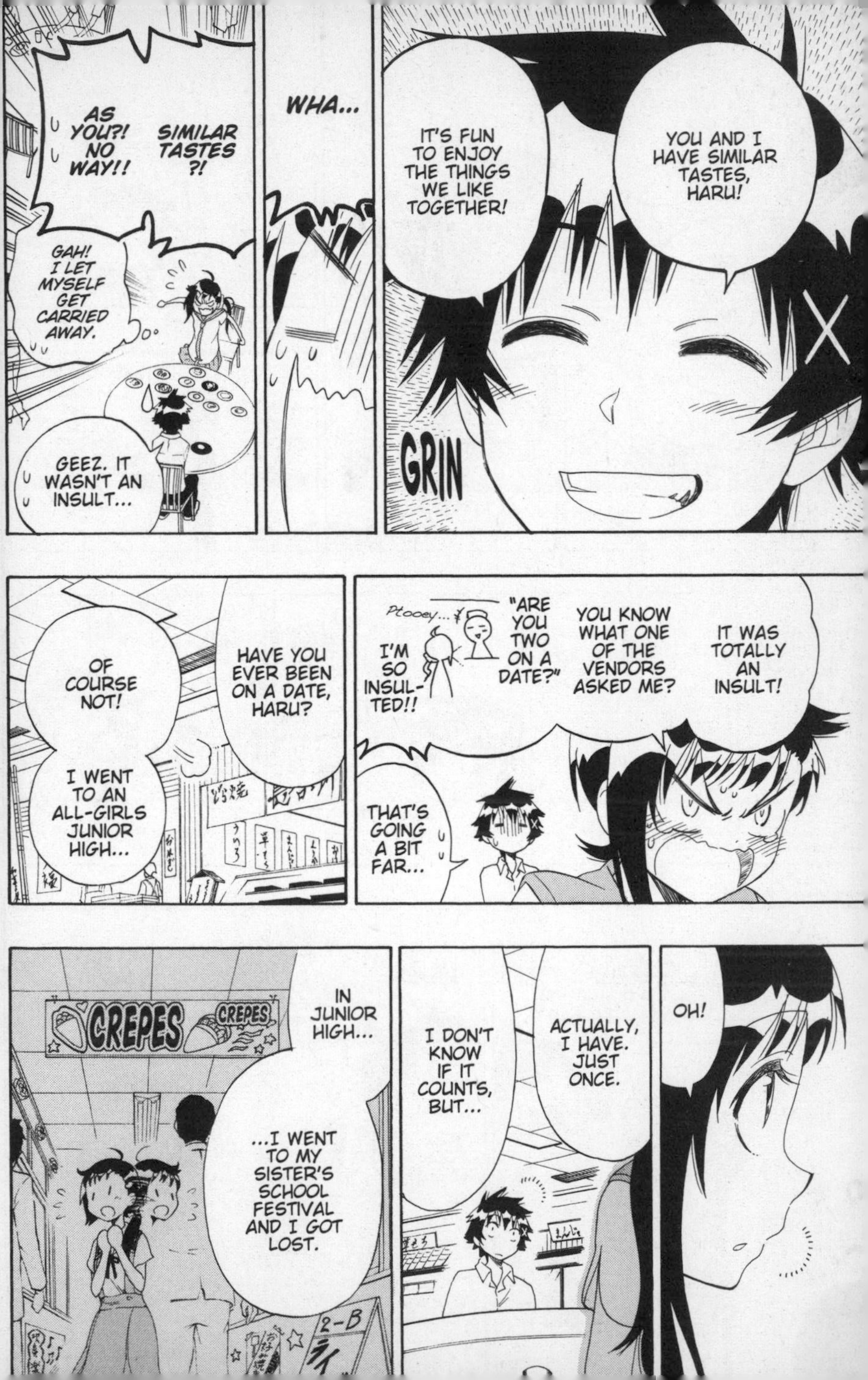
YOU AND I HAVE SIMILAR TASTES, HARU!
IT'S FUN TO ENJOY THE THINGS WE LIKE TOGETHER!
GRIN
WHA...
SIMILAR TASTES ?!
AS YOU?! NO WAY!!
GAH! I LET MYSELF GET CARRIED AWAY.
GEEZ. IT WASN'T AN INSULT...
IT WAS TOTALLY AN INSULT!
YOU KNOW WHAT ONE OF THE VENDORS ASKED ME?
"ARE YOU TWO ON A DATE?"
Ptooey...
I'M SO INSUL-TED!!
THAT'S GOING A BIT FAR...
HAVE YOU EVER BEEN ON A DATE, HARU?
OF COURSE NOT!
I WENT TO AN ALL-GIRLS JUNIOR HIGH...
OH!
ACTUALLY, I HAVE. JUST ONCE.
I DON'T KNOW IF IT COUNTS, BUT...
IN JUNIOR HIGH...
...I WENT TO MY SISTER'S SCHOOL FESTIVAL AND I GOT LOST.
CREPES
CREPES
2-B

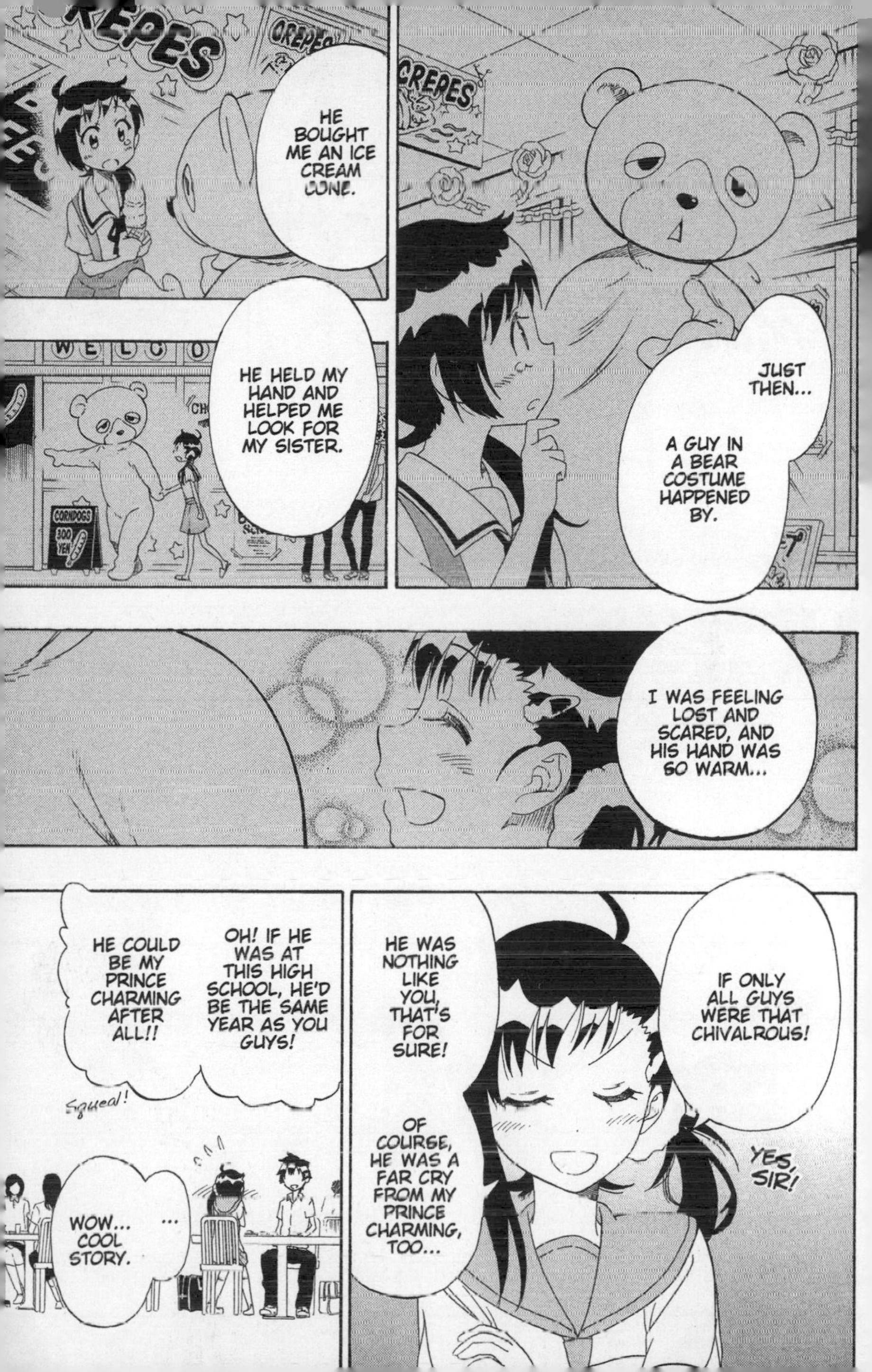
JUST THEN...
A GUY IN A BEAR COSTUME HAPPENED BY.
CREPES
CREPES
HE BOUGHT ME AN ICE CREAM CONE.
HE HELD MY HAND AND HELPED ME LOOK FOR MY SISTER.
CORNDOGS 300 YEN
I WAS FEELING LOST AND SCARED, AND HIS HAND WAS SO WARM...
IF ONLY ALL GUYS WERE THAT CHIVALROUS!
YES, SIR!
HE WAS NOTHING LIKE YOU, THAT'S FOR SURE!
OF COURSE, HE WAS A FAR CRY FROM MY PRINCE CHARMING, TOO...
OH! IF HE WAS AT THIS HIGH SCHOOL, HE'D BE THE SAME YEAR AS YOU GUYS!
HE COULD BE MY PRINCE CHARMING AFTER ALL!!
Squeal!
...
WOW... COOL STORY.

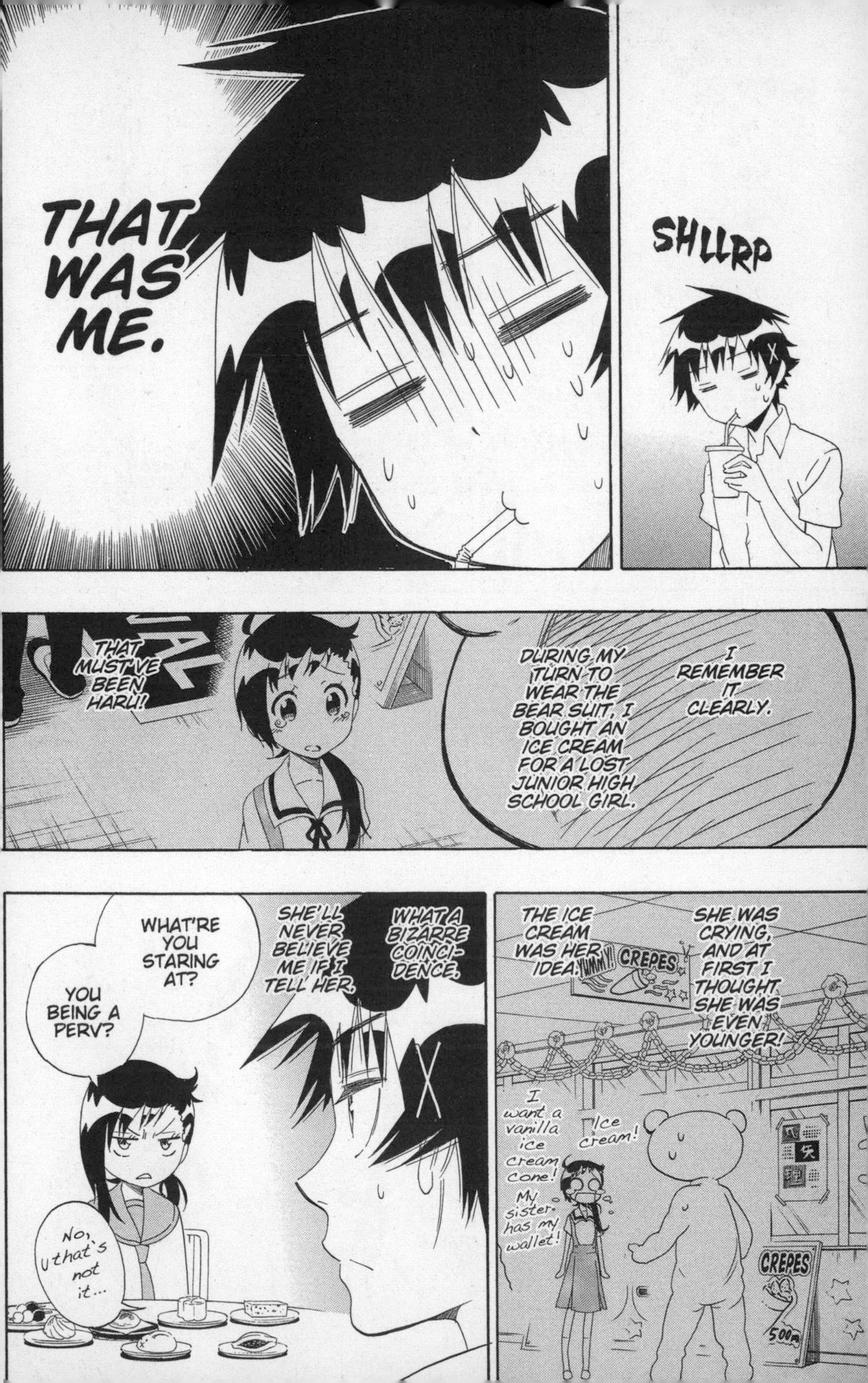
SHLLRP
THAT WAS ME.
I REMEMBER IT CLEARLY.
DURING MY TURN TO WEAR THE BEAR SUIT, I BOUGHT AN ICE CREAM FOR A LOST JUNIOR HIGH SCHOOL GIRL.
THAT MUST'VE BEEN HARU!
SHE WAS CRYING, AND AT FIRST I THOUGHT SHE WAS EVEN YOUNGER!
THE ICE CREAM WAS HER IDEA.
YUMMY! CREPES
Ice cream!
I want a vanilla ice cream cone!
My sister has my wallet!
CREPES
WHAT A BIZARRE COINCIDENCE.
SHE'LL NEVER BELIEVE ME IF I TELL HER.
WHAT'RE YOU STARING AT?
YOU BEING A PERV?
No, that's not it...

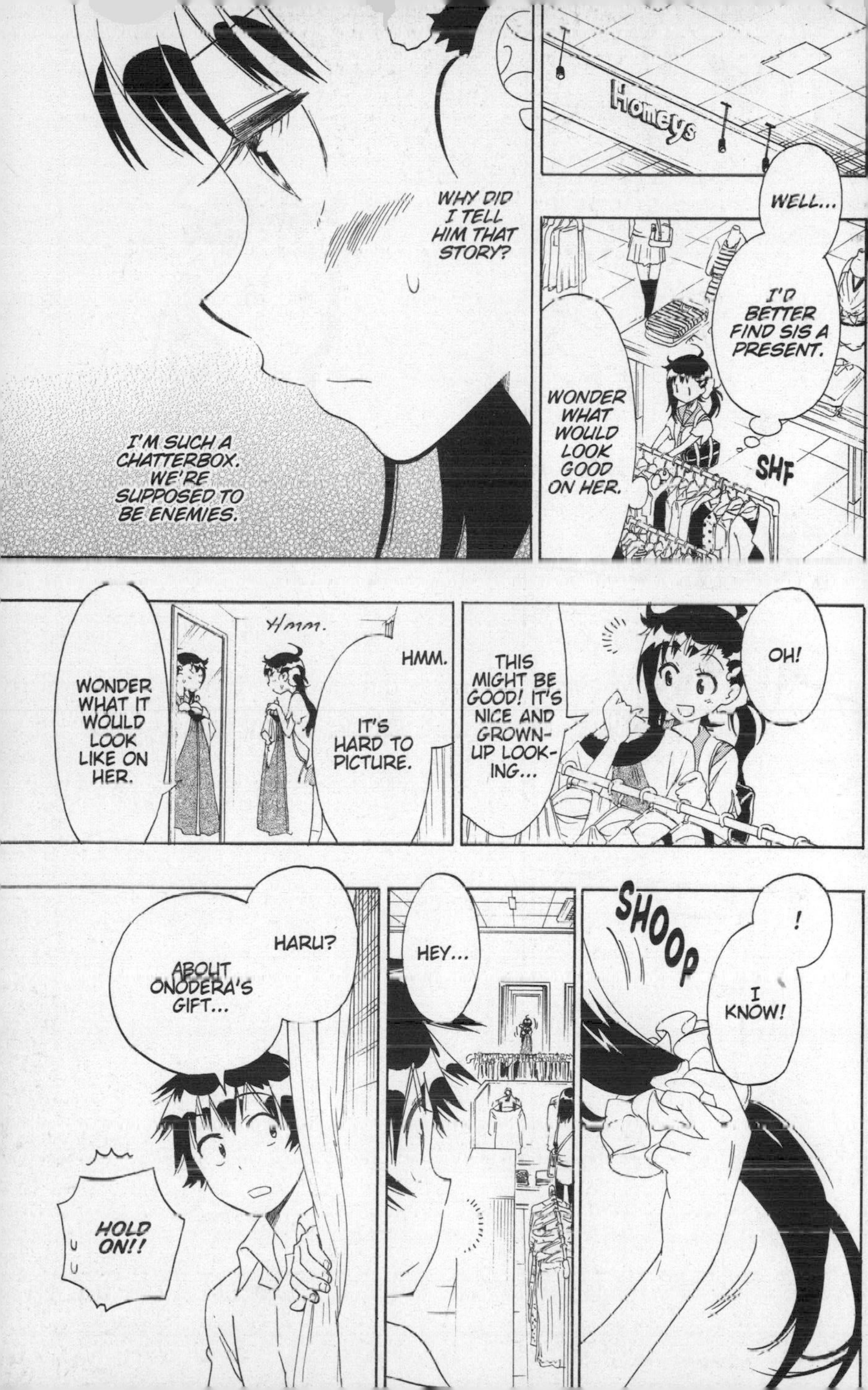
Homeys
WELL...
I'D BETTER FIND SIS A PRESENT.
WONDER WHAT WOULD LOOK GOOD ON HER.
SHF
WHY DID I TELL HIM THAT STORY?
I'M SUCH A CHATTERBOX. WE'RE SUPPOSED TO BE ENEMIES.
OH!
THIS MIGHT BE GOOD! IT'S NICE AND GROWN-UP LOOKING...
HMM.
Hmm.
IT'S HARD TO PICTURE.
WONDER WHAT IT WOULD LOOK LIKE ON HER.
SHOOP
!
I KNOW!
HEY...
HARU?
ABOUT ONODERA'S GIFT...
HOLD ON!!

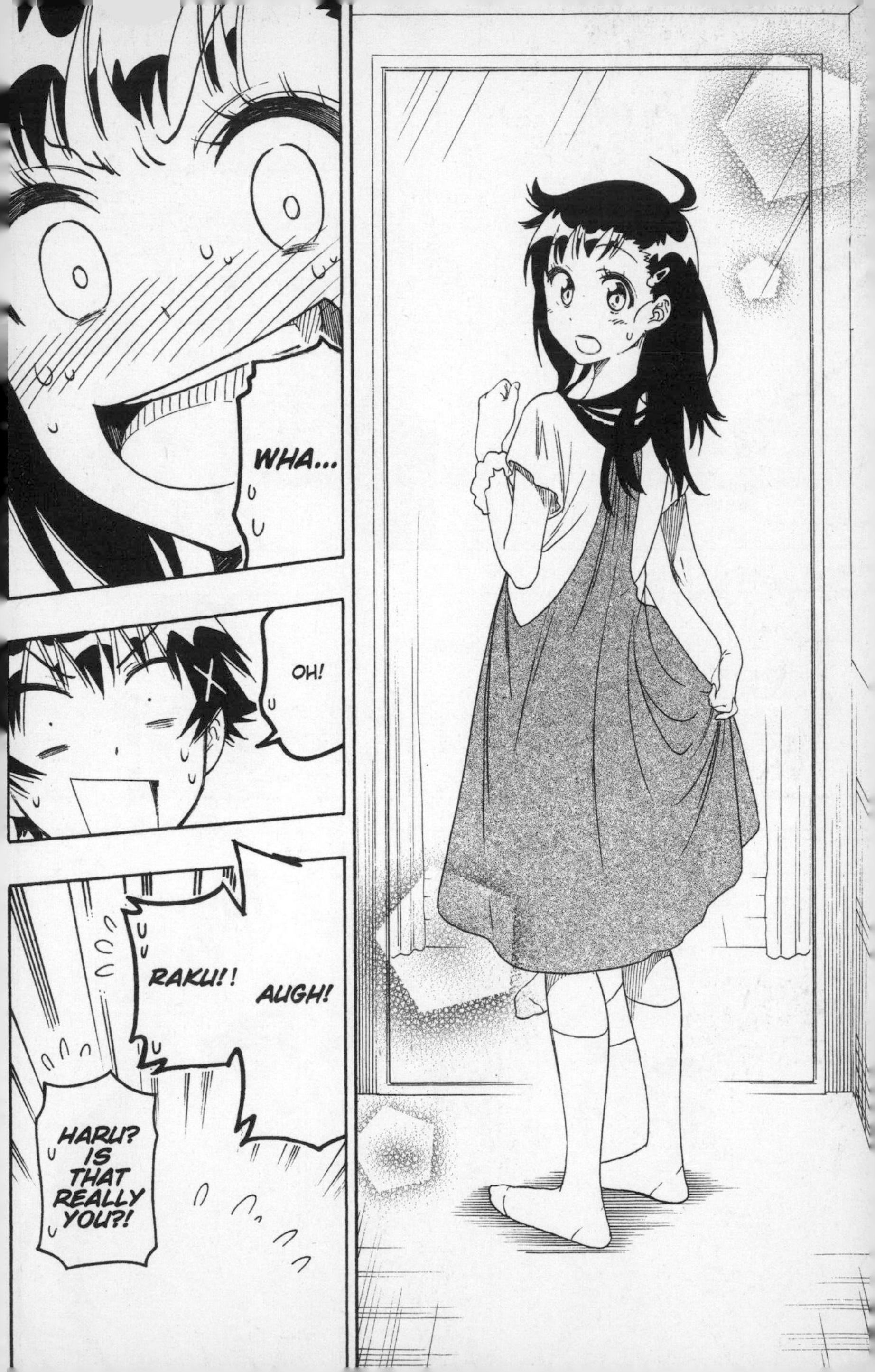
WHA...
OH!
RAKU!!
AUGH!
HARU? IS THAT REALLY YOU?!

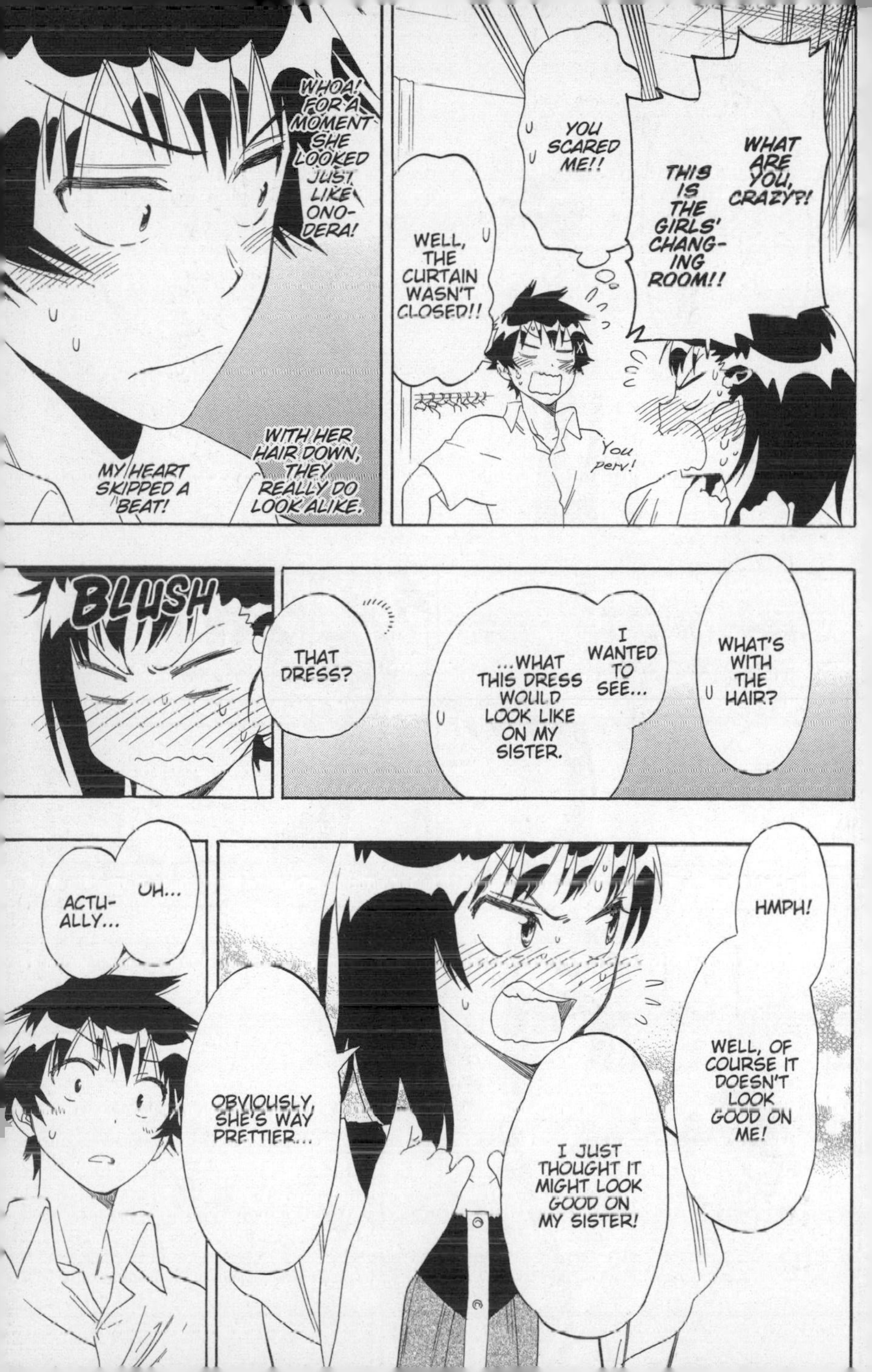
WHAT ARE YOU, CRAZY?!
THIS IS THE GIRLS' CHANGING ROOM!!
YOU SCARED ME!!
WELL, THE CURTAIN WASN'T CLOSED!!
You perv!
WHOA! FOR A MOMENT SHE LOOKED JUST LIKE ONODERA!
WITH HER HAIR DOWN, THEY REALLY DO LOOK ALIKE.
MY HEART SKIPPED A BEAT!
WHAT'S WITH THE HAIR?
I WANTED TO SEE...
...WHAT THIS DRESS WOULD LOOK LIKE ON MY SISTER.
THAT DRESS?
BLUSH
HMPH!
WELL, OF COURSE IT DOESN'T LOOK GOOD ON ME!
I JUST THOUGHT IT MIGHT LOOK GOOD ON MY SISTER!
OBVIOUSLY, SHE'S WAY PRETTIER...
UH...
ACTUALLY...

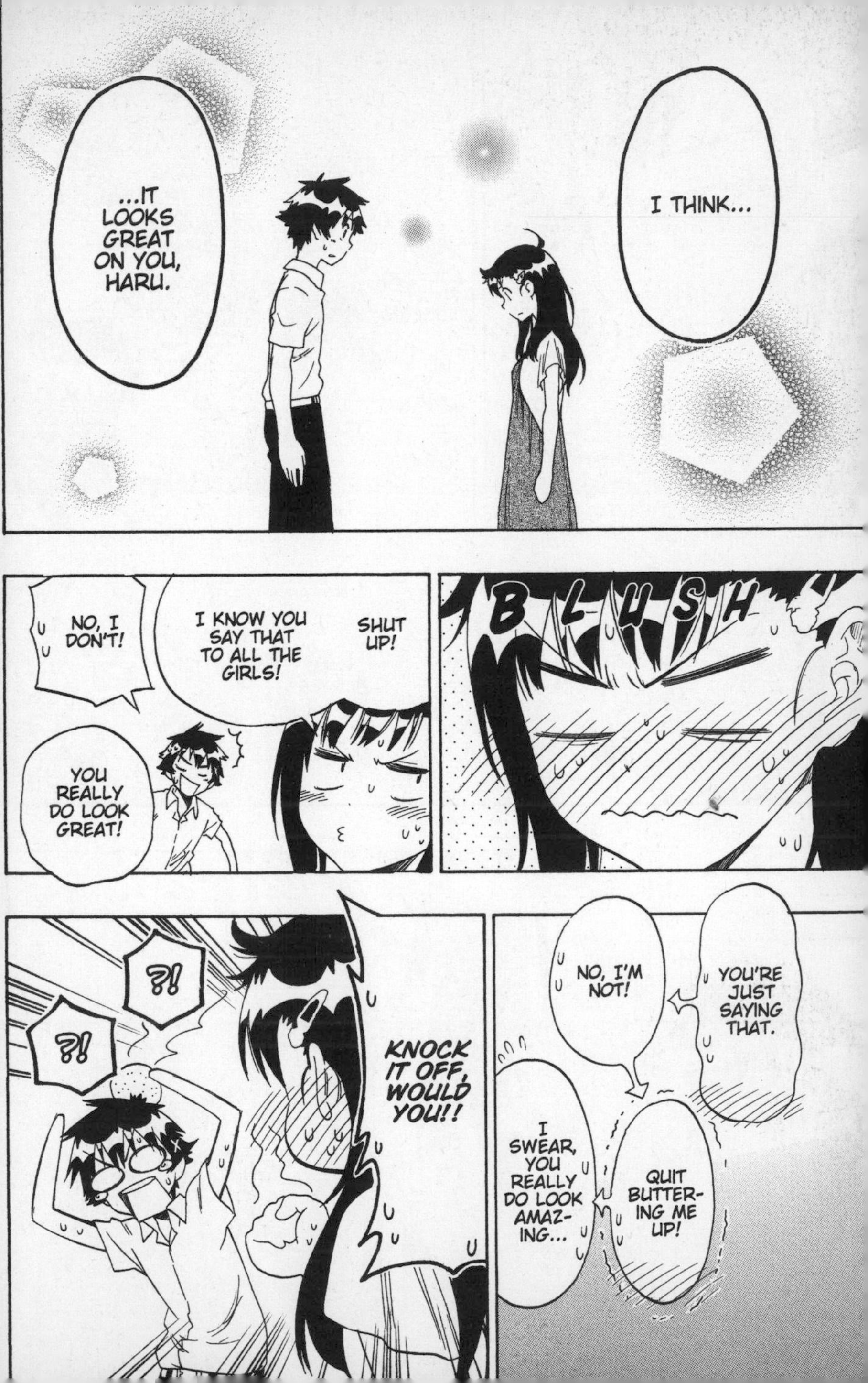
I THINK...
...IT LOOKS GREAT ON YOU, HARU.
BLUSH
SHUT UP!
I KNOW YOU SAY THAT TO ALL THE GIRLS!
NO, I DON'T!
YOU REALLY DO LOOK GREAT!
YOU'RE JUST SAYING THAT.
NO, I'M NOT!
QUIT BUTTERING ME UP!
I SWEAR, YOU REALLY DO LOOK AMAZING...
KNOCK IT OFF, WOULD YOU!!
?!
?!

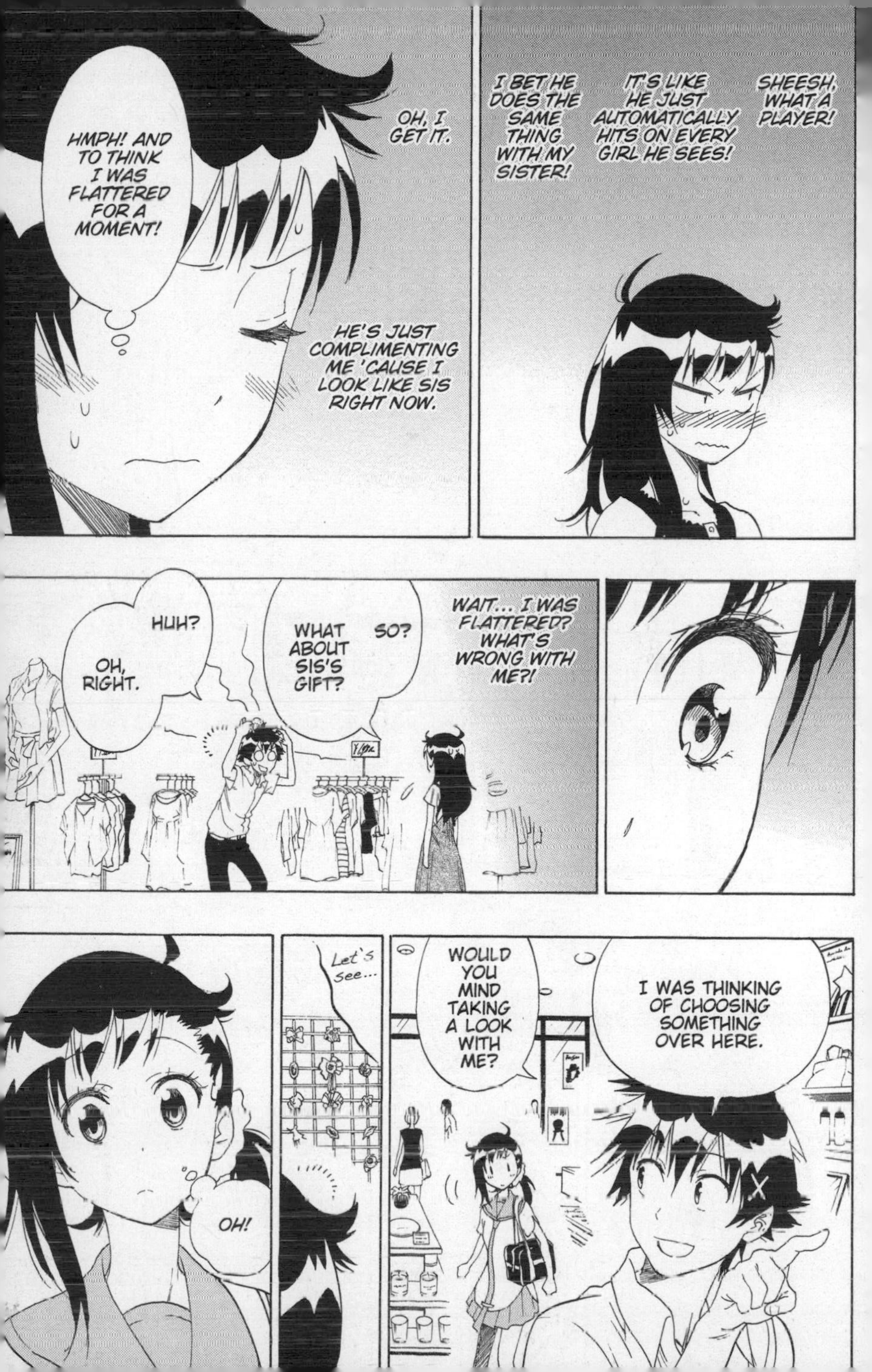
SHEESH, WHAT A PLAYER!
IT'S LIKE HE JUST AUTOMATICALLY HITS ON EVERY GIRL HE SEES!
I BET HE DOES THE SAME THING WITH MY SISTER!
OH, I GET IT.
HE'S JUST COMPLIMENTING ME 'CAUSE I LOOK LIKE SIS RIGHT NOW.
HMPH! AND TO THINK I WAS FLATTERED FOR A MOMENT!
WAIT... I WAS FLATTERED? WHAT'S WRONG WITH ME?!
SO? WHAT ABOUT SIS'S GIFT?
HUH? OH, RIGHT.
I WAS THINKING OF CHOOSING SOMETHING OVER HERE.
WOULD YOU MIND TAKING A LOOK WITH ME?
Let's see...
OH!

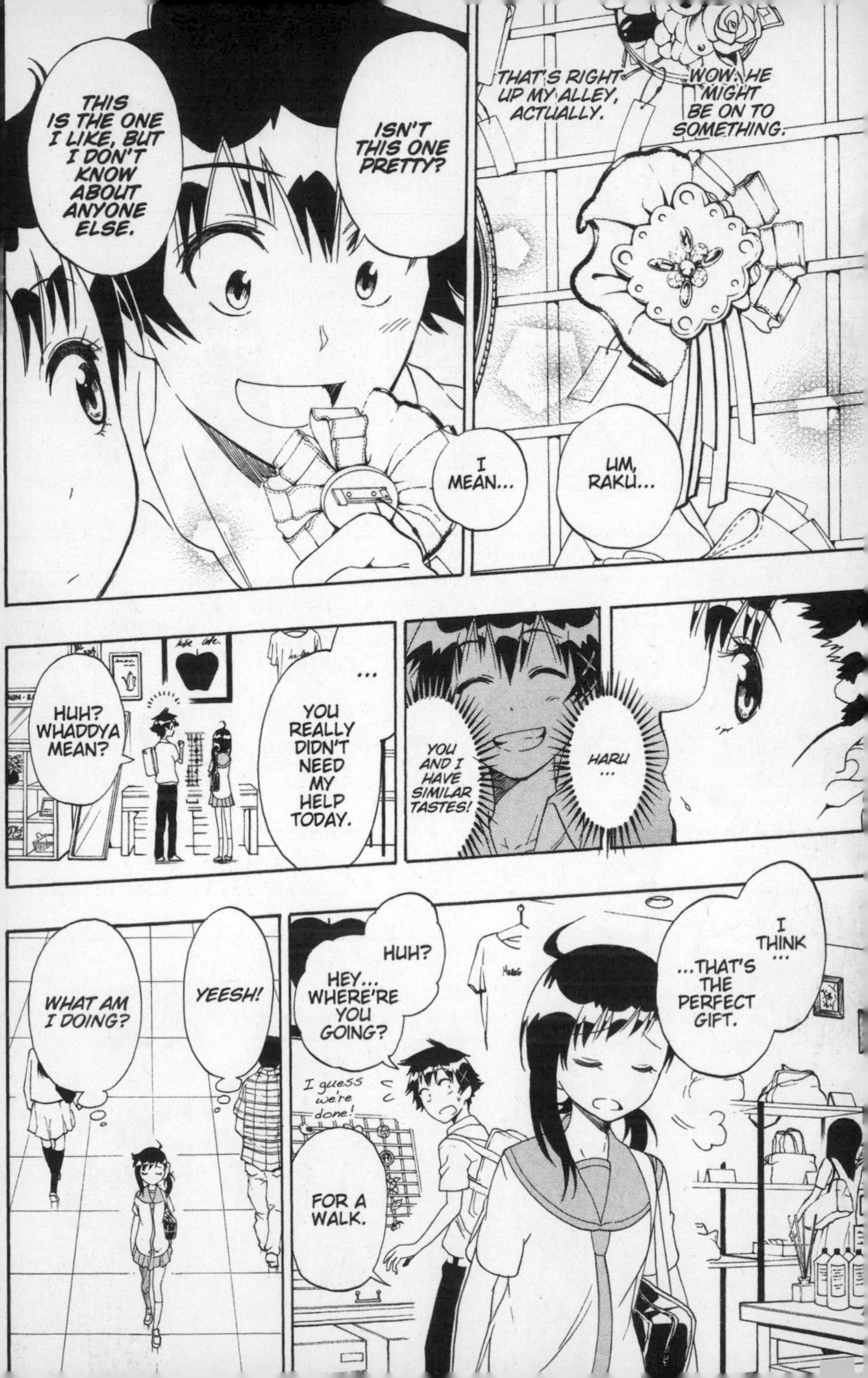
WOW. HE MIGHT BE ON TO SOMETHING.
THAT'S RIGHT UP MY ALLEY, ACTUALLY.
UM, RAKU...
I MEAN...
ISN'T THIS ONE PRETTY?
THIS IS THE ONE I LIKE, BUT I DON'T KNOW ABOUT ANYONE ELSE.
HARU...
YOU AND I HAVE SIMILAR TASTES!
...
YOU REALLY DIDN'T NEED MY HELP TODAY.
HUH? WHADDYA MEAN?
I THINK...
...THAT'S THE PERFECT GIFT.
HUH?
HEY... WHERE'RE YOU GOING?
I guess we're done!
FOR A WALK.
YEESH!
WHAT AM I DOING?

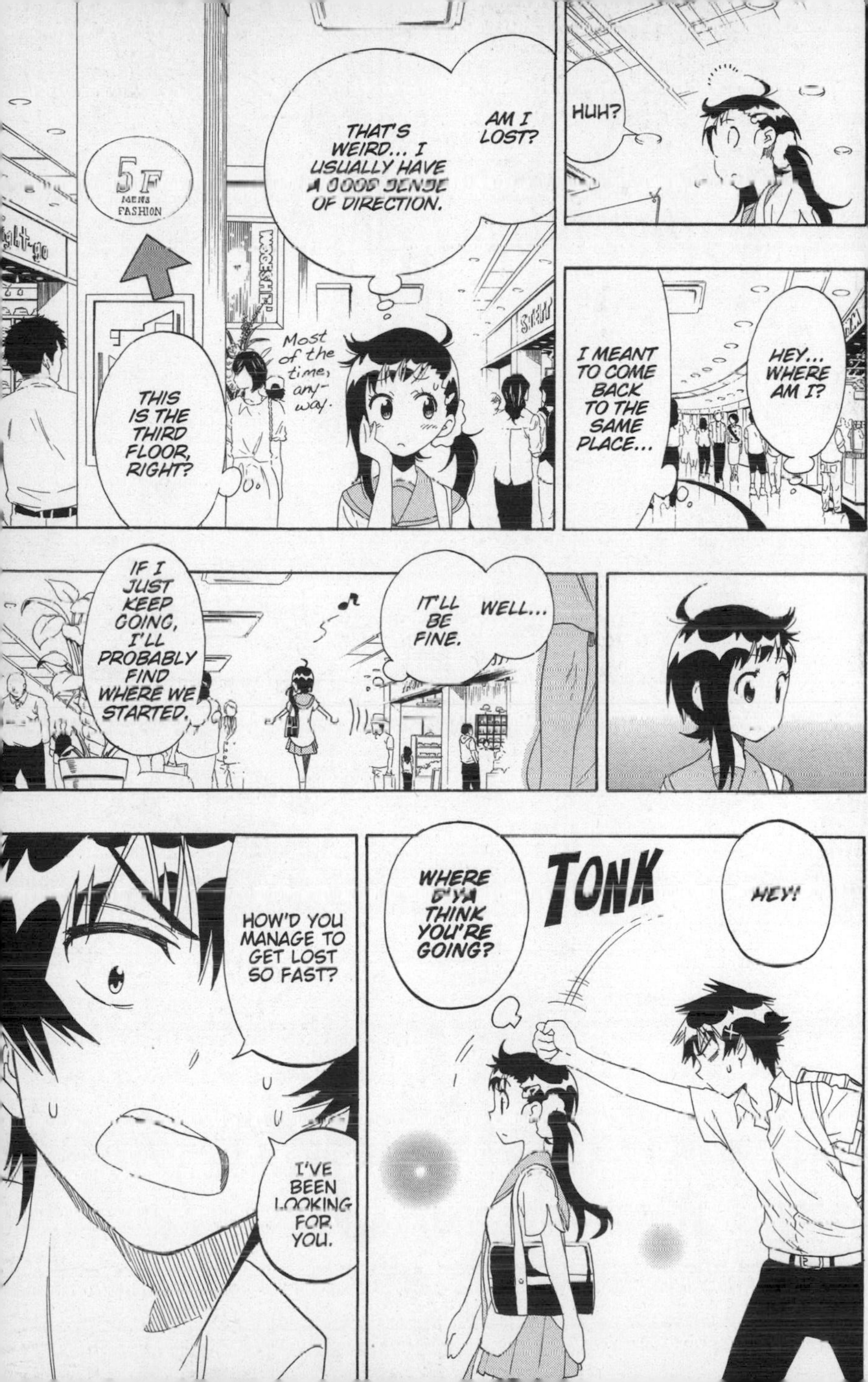
HUH?
HEY... WHERE AM I?
I MEANT TO COME BACK TO THE SAME PLACE...
AM I LOST?
THAT'S WEIRD... I USUALLY HAVE A GOOD SENSE OF DIRECTION.
Most of the time, anyway.
5F MENS FASHION
THIS IS THE THIRD FLOOR, RIGHT?
WELL...
IT'LL BE FINE.
IF I JUST KEEP GOING, I'LL PROBABLY FIND WHERE WE STARTED.
HEY!
TONK
WHERE D'YA THINK YOU'RE GOING?
HOW'D YOU MANAGE TO GET LOST SO FAST?
I'VE BEEN LOOKING FOR YOU.

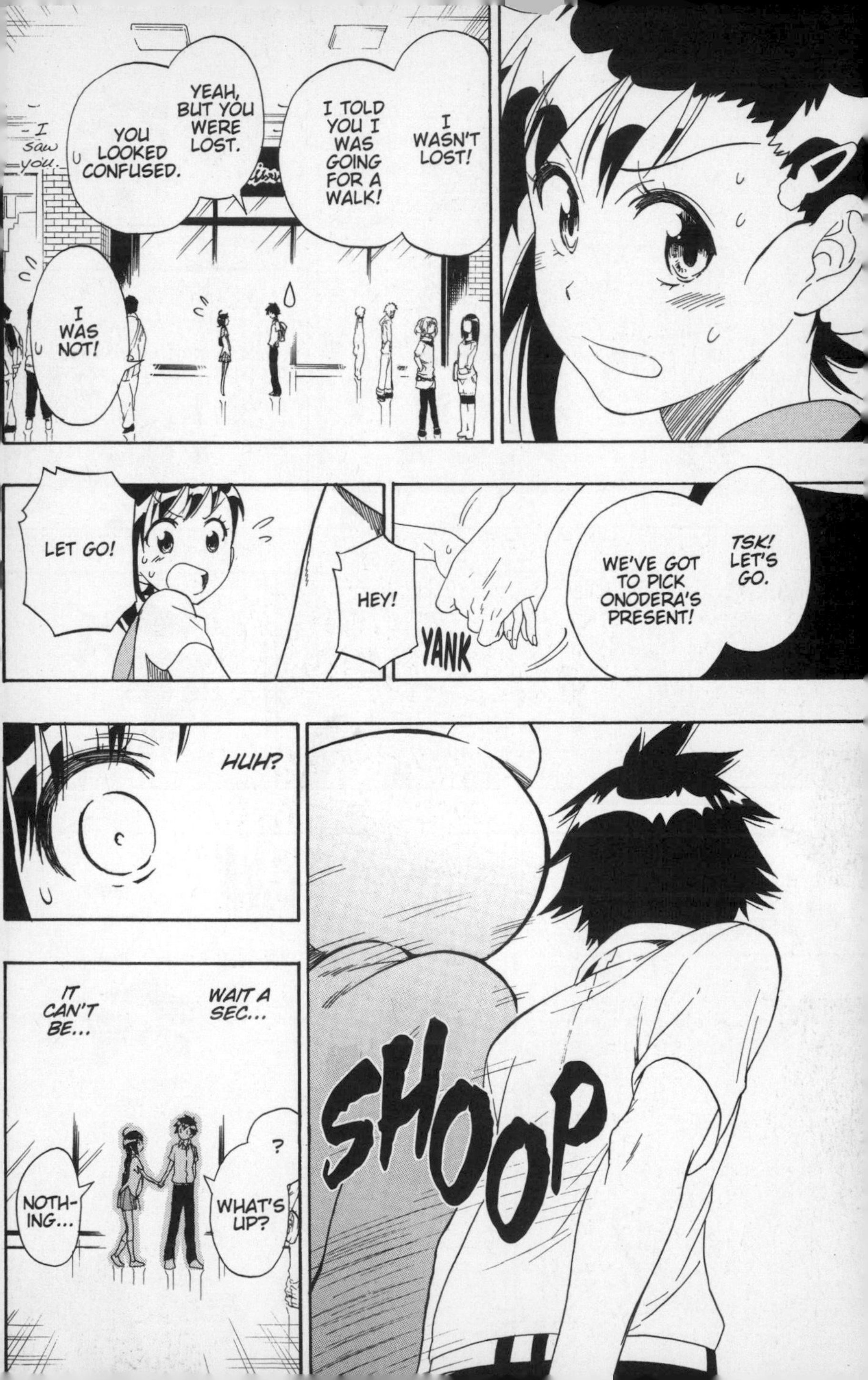
I WASN'T LOST!
I TOLD YOU I WAS GOING FOR A WALK!
YEAH, BUT YOU WERE LOST.
YOU LOOKED CONFUSED.
-I saw you...
I WAS NOT!
TSK! LET'S GO.
WE'VE GOT TO PICK ONODERA'S PRESENT!
YANK
HEY!
LET GO!
SHOOP
HUH?
WAIT A SEC...
IT CAN'T BE...
?
WHAT'S UP?
NOTHING...

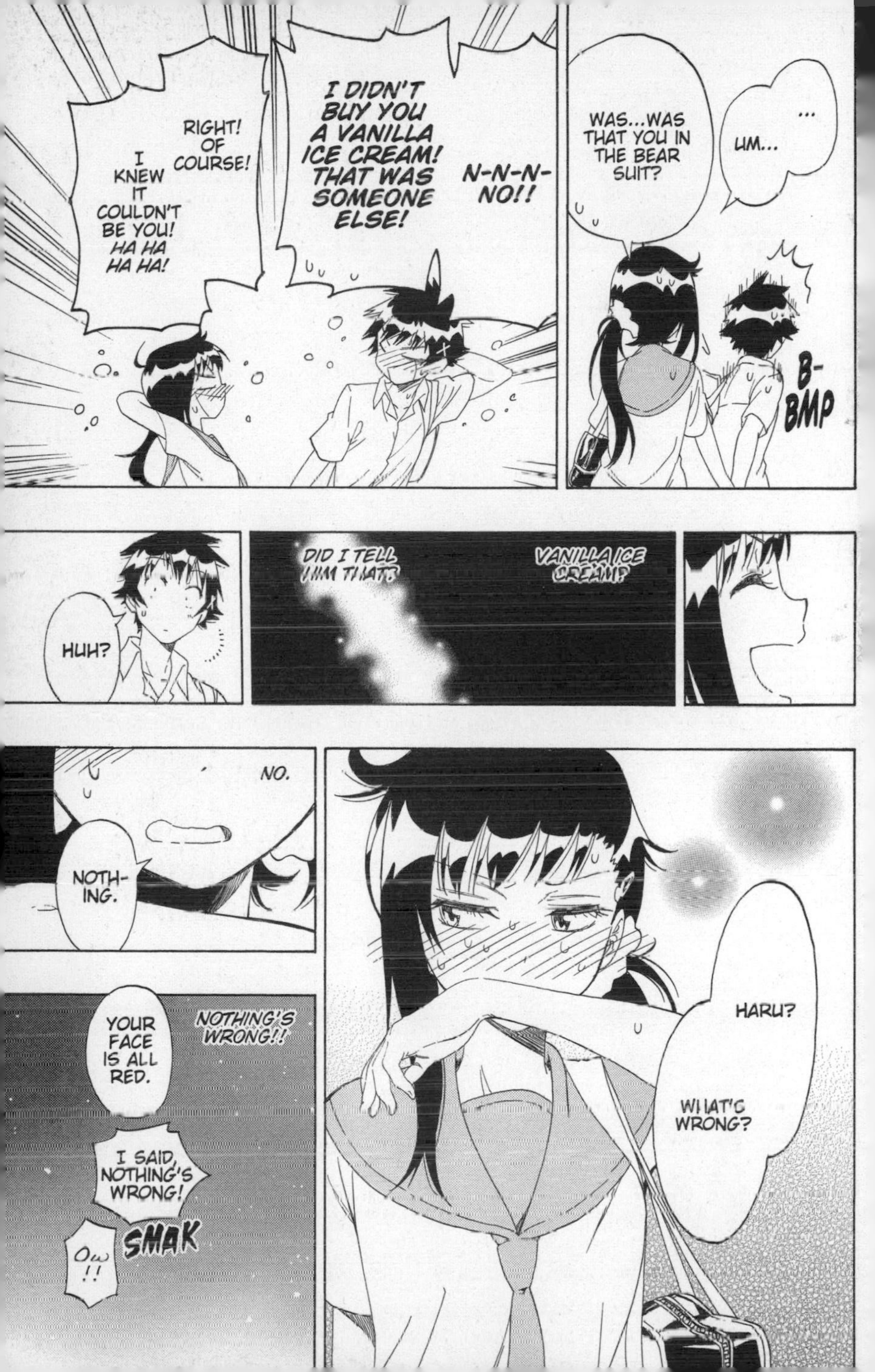
...
UM...
WAS...WAS THAT YOU IN THE BEAR SUIT?
B-BMP
N-N-N-NO!!
I DIDN'T BUY YOU A VANILLA ICE CREAM! THAT WAS SOMEONE ELSE!
RIGHT! OF COURSE!
I KNEW IT COULDN'T BE YOU! HA HA HA HA!
VANILLA ICE CREAM?
DID I TELL HIM THAT?
HUH?
HARU?
WHAT'S WRONG?
NO.
NOTH-ING.
NOTHING'S WRONG!!
YOUR FACE IS ALL RED.
I SAID, NOTHING'S WRONG!
SMAK
Ow!!

Haruuu!! I was so worried!
Thank you for bringing my sister back...
FIDGET FIDGET
What's wrong, Mr. Bear?
FIDGET FIDGET

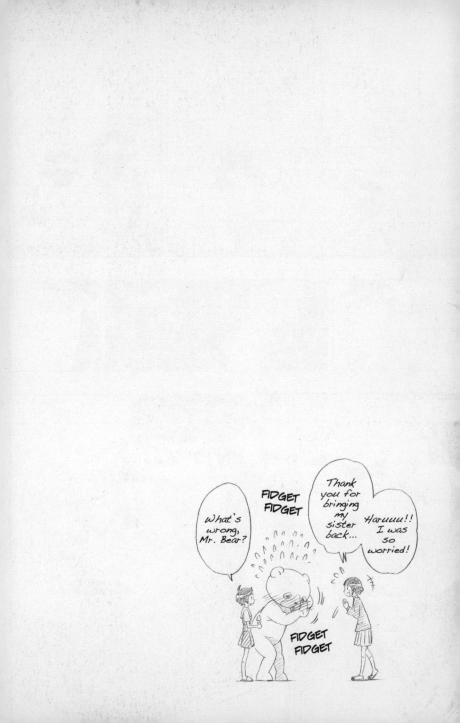

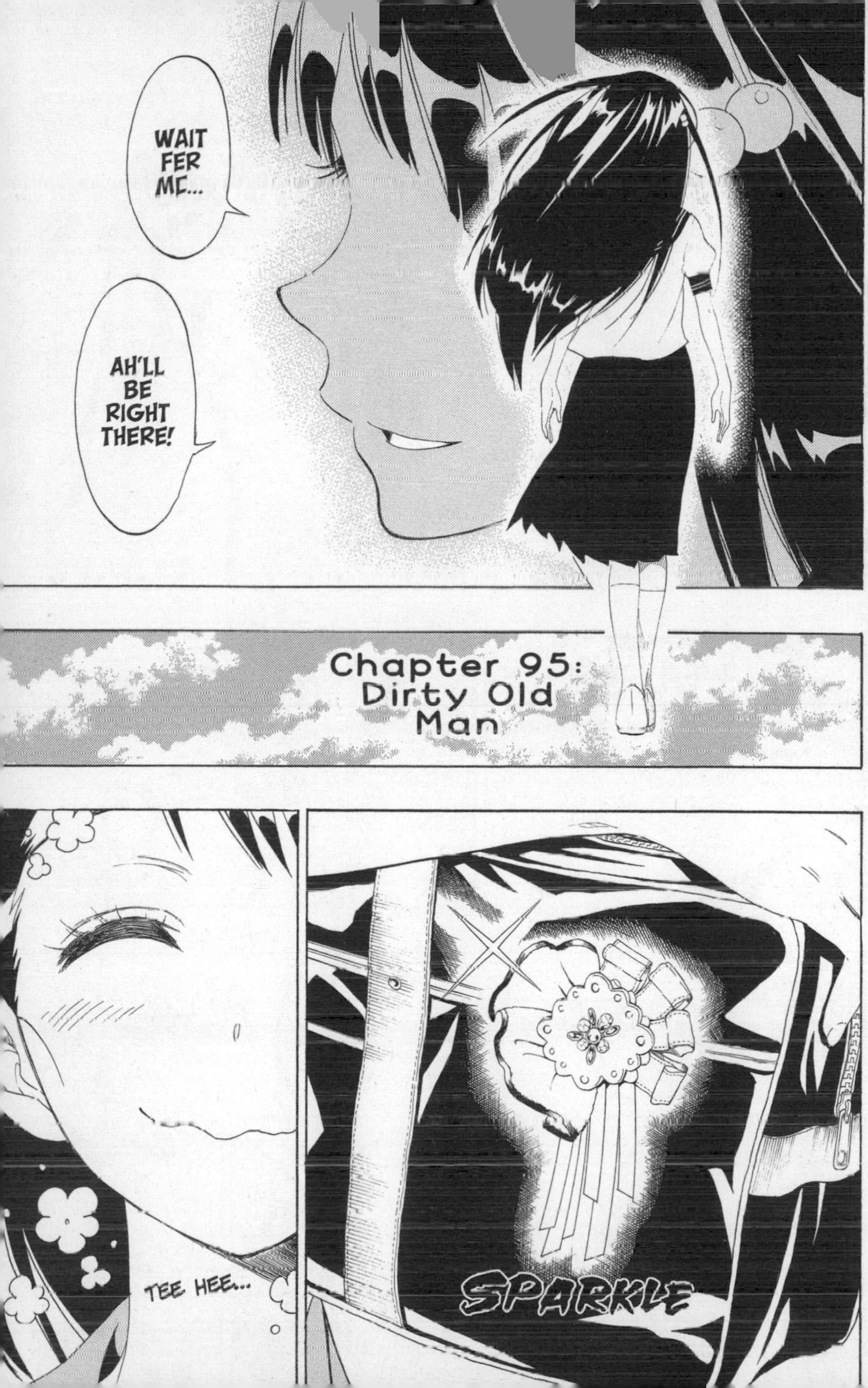
WAIT FER ME...
AH'LL BE RIGHT THERE!
Chapter 95: Dirty Old Man
SPARKLE
TEE HEE...

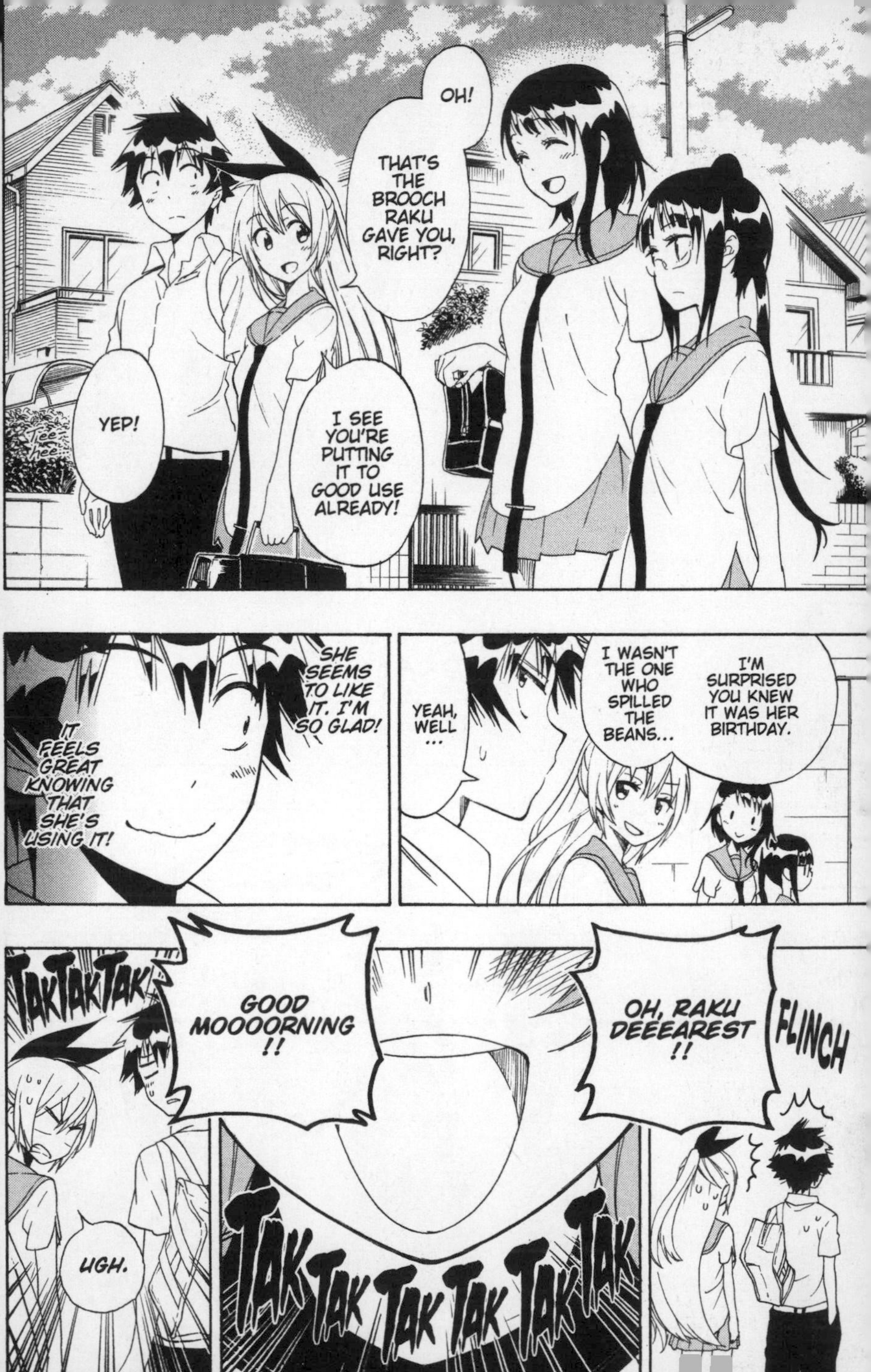
OH!
THAT'S THE BROOCH RAKU GAVE YOU, RIGHT?
I SEE YOU'RE PUTTING IT TO GOOD USE ALREADY!
YEP!
Tee-hee...
I'M SURPRISED YOU KNEW IT WAS HER BIRTHDAY.
I WASN'T THE ONE WHO SPILLED THE BEANS...
YEAH, WELL...
SHE SEEMS TO LIKE IT. I'M SO GLAD!
IT FEELS GREAT KNOWING THAT SHE'S USING IT!
FLINCH
OH, RAKU DEEEAREST!!
GOOD MOOOORNING!!
TAK TAK TAK TAK TAK TAK
TAKTAKTAK
UGH.

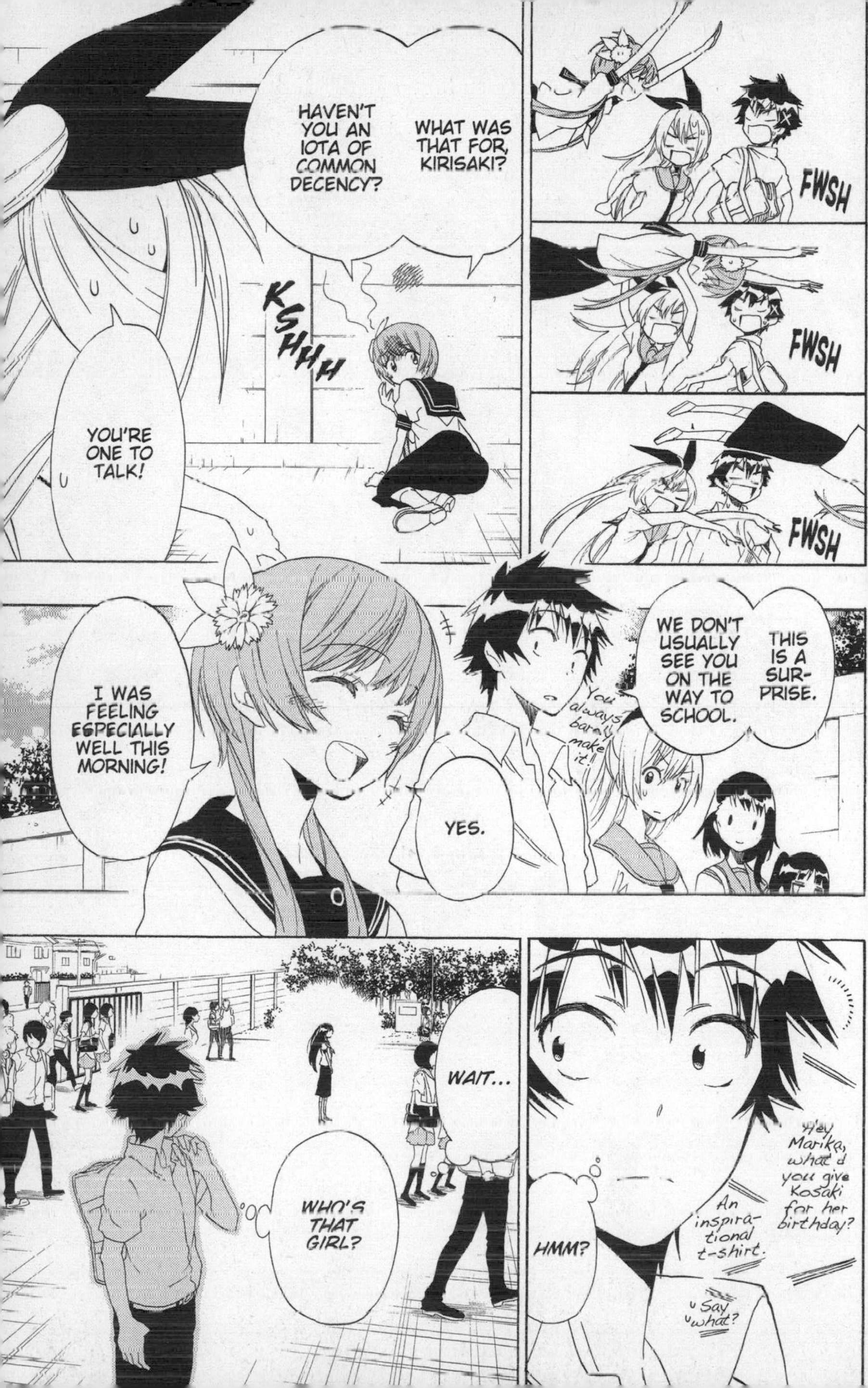
FWSH
FWSH
FWSH
WHAT WAS THAT FOR, KIRISAKI?
HAVEN'T YOU AN IOTA OF COMMON DECENCY?
KSHHH
YOU'RE ONE TO TALK!
THIS IS A SURPRISE.
WE DON'T USUALLY SEE YOU ON THE WAY TO SCHOOL.
You always barely make it!
YES.
I WAS FEELING ESPECIALLY WELL THIS MORNING!
Hey Marika, what'd you give Kosaki for her birthday?
An inspirational t-shirt.
Say what?
HMM?
WAIT...
WHO'S THAT GIRL?

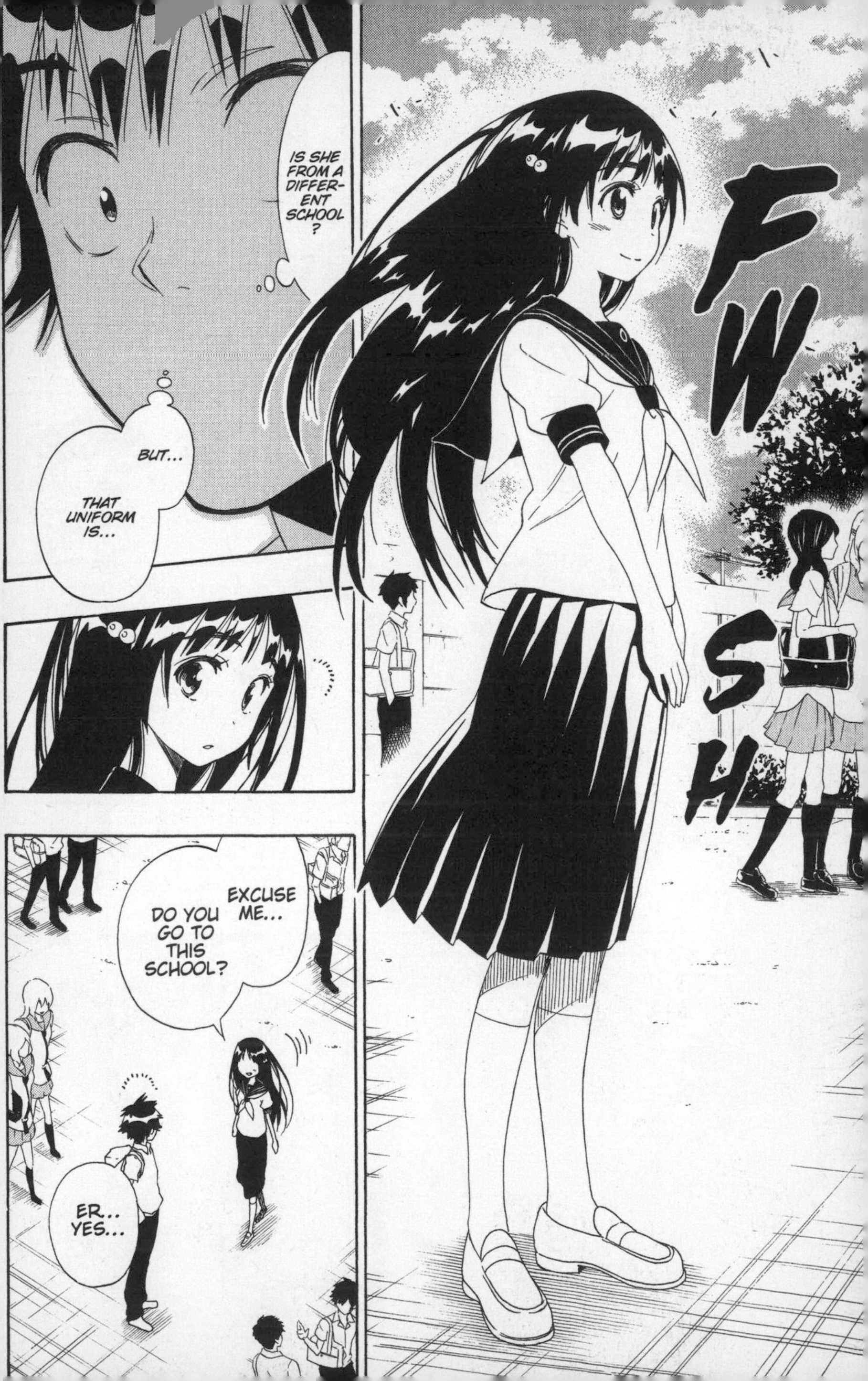
FWSSH
IS SHE FROM A DIFFERENT SCHOOL?
BUT... THAT UNIFORM IS...
EXCUSE ME... DO YOU GO TO THIS SCHOOL?
ER... YES...

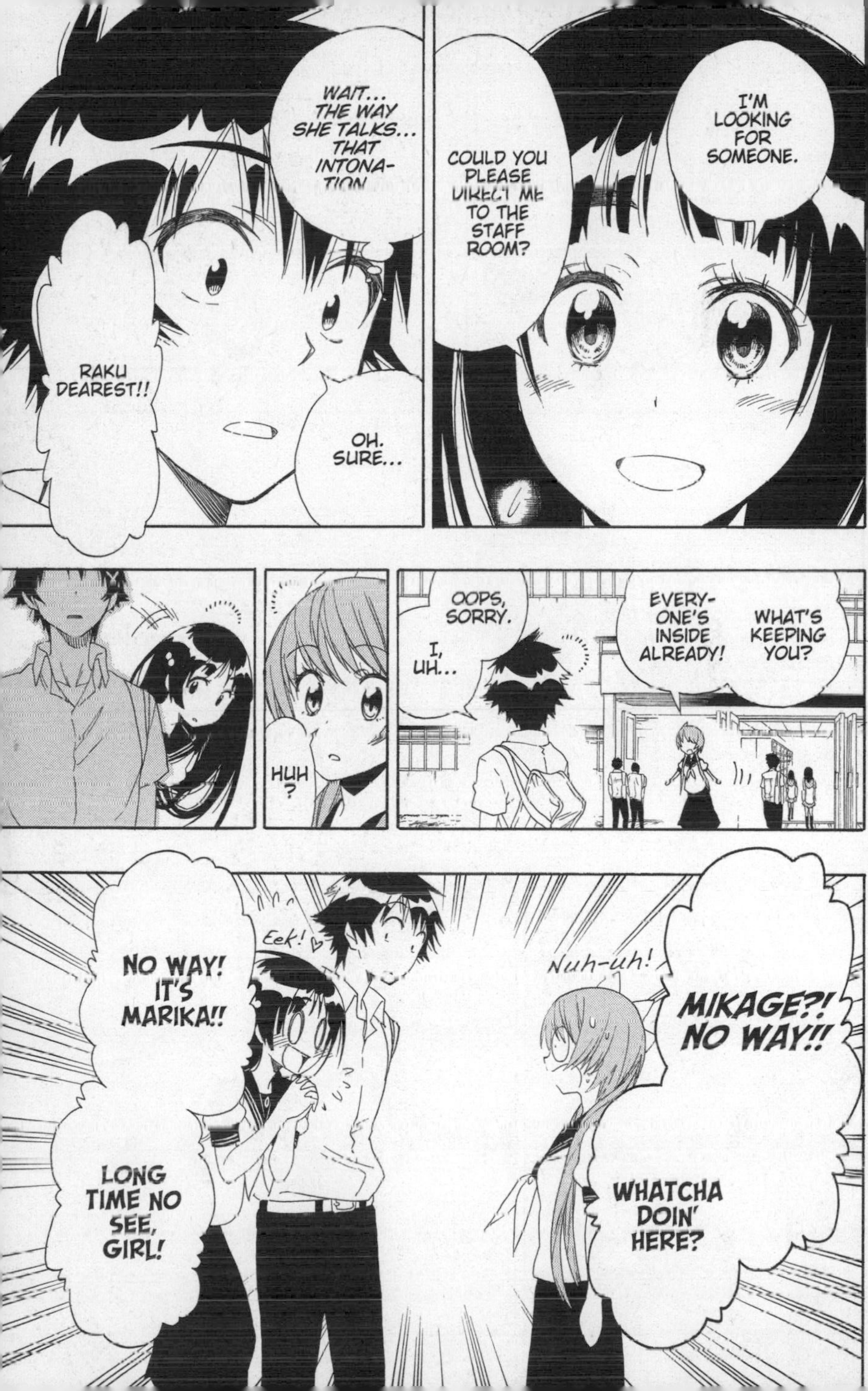
I'M LOOKING FOR SOMEONE.
COULD YOU PLEASE DIRECT ME TO THE STAFF ROOM?
WAIT... THE WAY SHE TALKS... THAT INTONA-TION
OH. SURE...
RAKU DEAREST!!
WHAT'S KEEPING YOU?
EVERY-ONE'S INSIDE ALREADY!
OOPS, SORRY.
I, UH...
HUH?
MIKAGE?! NO WAY!!
Nuh-uh!
WHATCHA DOIN' HERE?
Eek!
NO WAY! IT'S MARIKA!!
LONG TIME NO SEE, GIRL!

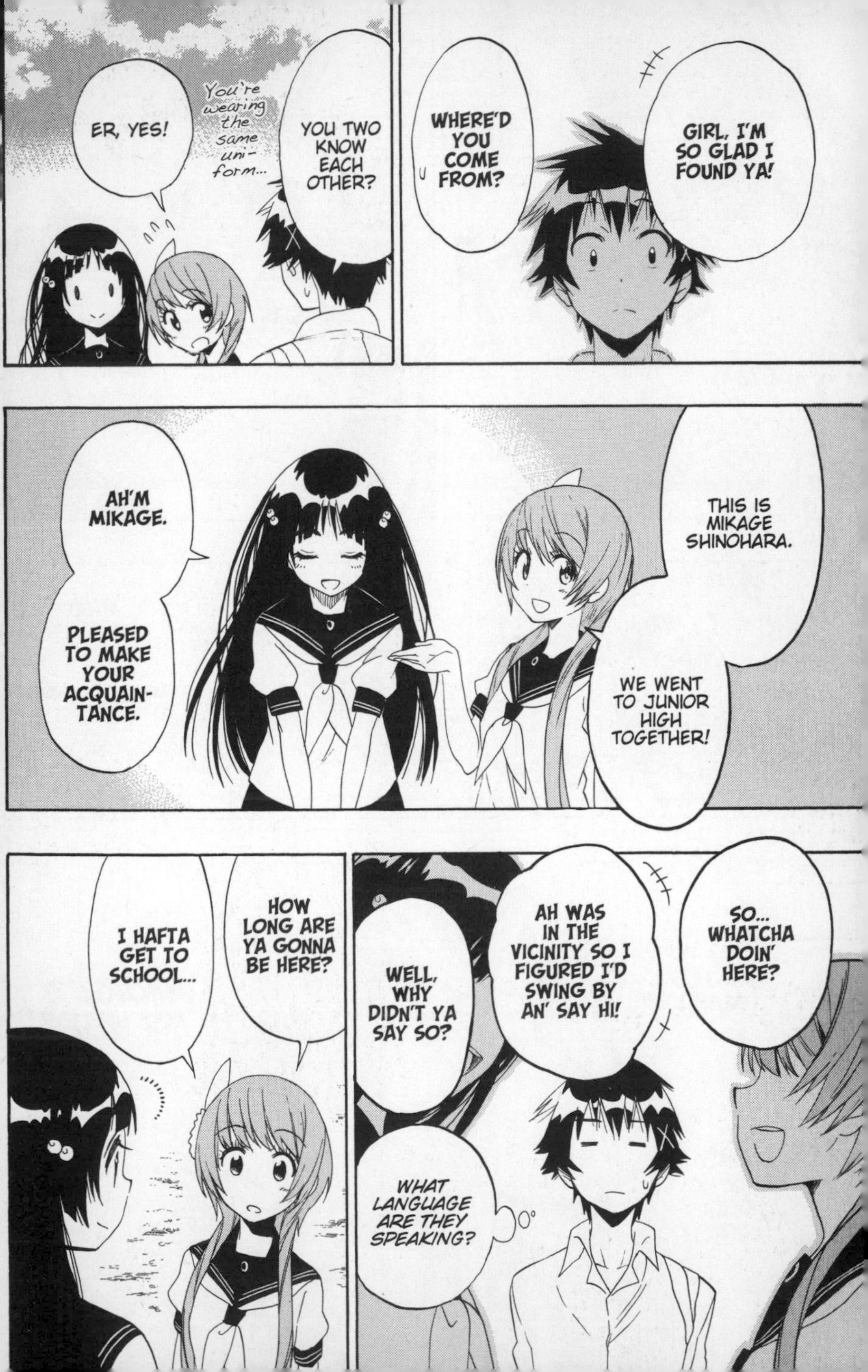
GIRL, I'M SO GLAD I FOUND YA!
WHERE'D YOU COME FROM?
YOU TWO KNOW EACH OTHER?
You're wearing the same uni-form...
ER, YES!
THIS IS MIKAGE SHINOHARA.
WE WENT TO JUNIOR HIGH TOGETHER!
AH'M MIKAGE.
PLEASED TO MAKE YOUR ACQUAIN-TANCE.
SO... WHATCHA DOIN' HERE?
AH WAS IN THE VICINITY SO I FIGURED I'D SWING BY AN' SAY HI!
WELL, WHY DIDN'T YA SAY SO?
WHAT LANGUAGE ARE THEY SPEAKING?
HOW LONG ARE YA GONNA BE HERE?
I HAFTA GET TO SCHOOL...

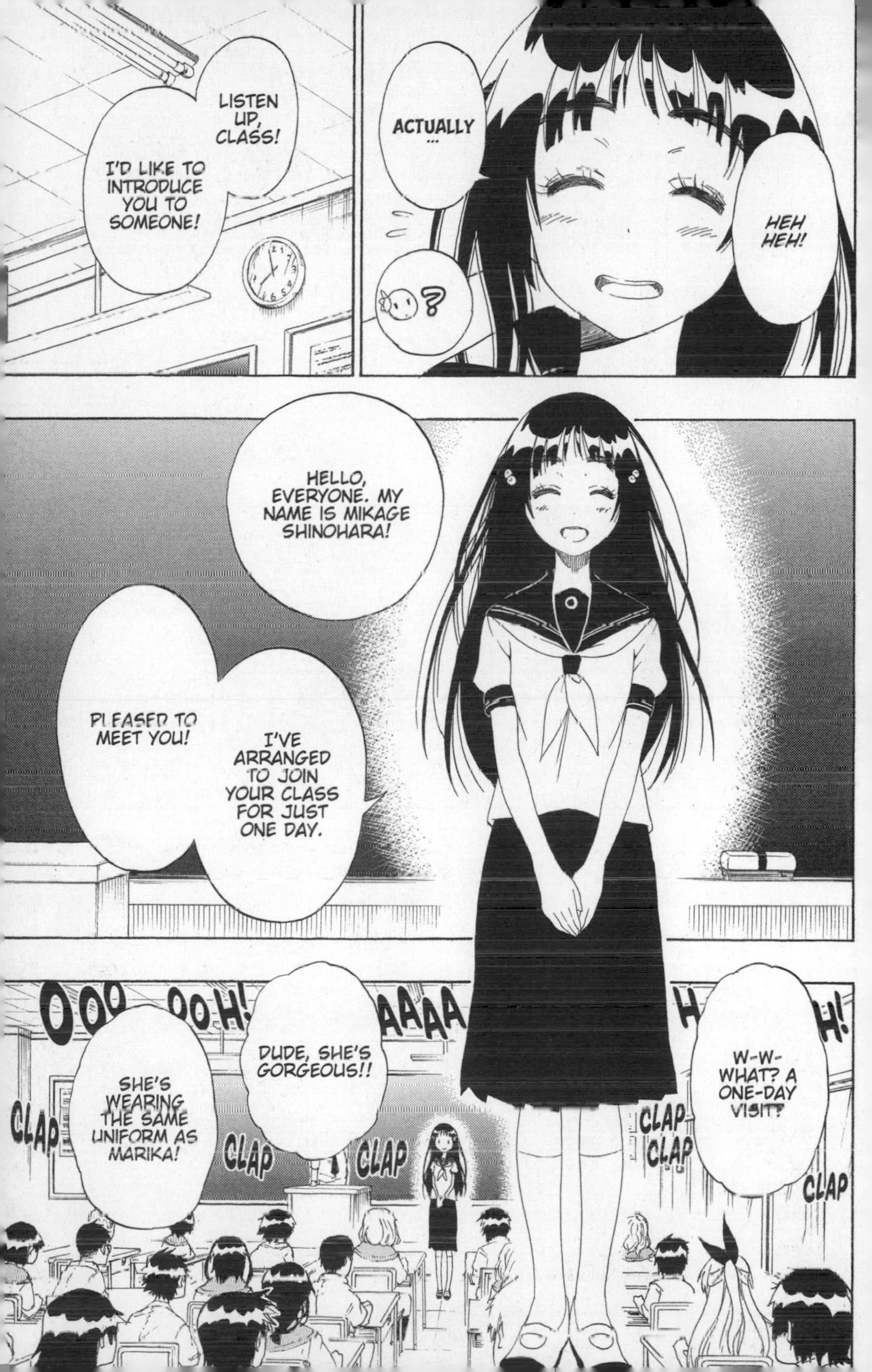

ACTUALLY ...
HEH HEH!
?
LISTEN UP, CLASS!
I'D LIKE TO INTRODUCE YOU TO SOMEONE!
HELLO, EVERYONE. MY NAME IS MIKAGE SHINOHARA!
I'VE ARRANGED TO JOIN YOUR CLASS FOR JUST ONE DAY.
PLEASED TO MEET YOU!
W-W-WHAT? A ONE-DAY VISIT?
CLAP
CLAP CLAP
CLAP
AAAA
DUDE, SHE'S GORGEOUS!!
CLAP
CLAP
SHE'S WEARING THE SAME UNIFORM AS MARIKA!
OOO OOH!
CLAP

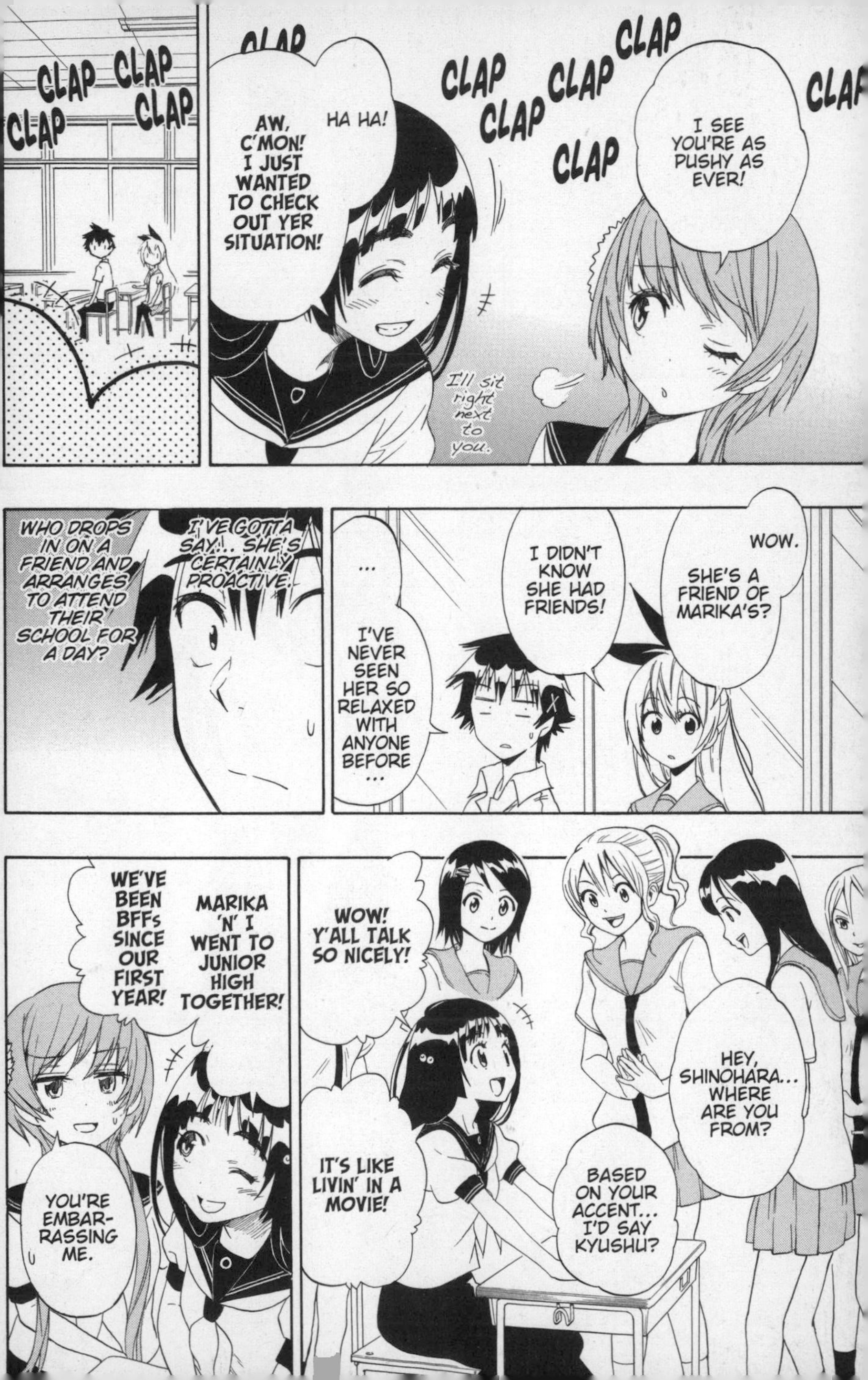
CLAP
CLAP
CLAP
CLAP
CLAP
CLAP
I SEE YOU'RE AS PUSHY AS EVER!
HA HA!
AW, C'MON! I JUST WANTED TO CHECK OUT YER SITUATION!
I'll sit right next to you.
CLAP
CLAP
CLAP
CLAP
WOW.
SHE'S A FRIEND OF MARIKA'S?
I DIDN'T KNOW SHE HAD FRIENDS!
...
I'VE NEVER SEEN HER SO RELAXED WITH ANYONE BEFORE...
I'VE GOTTA SAY... SHE'S CERTAINLY PROACTIVE.
WHO DROPS IN ON A FRIEND AND ARRANGES TO ATTEND THEIR SCHOOL FOR A DAY?
HEY, SHINOHARA... WHERE ARE YOU FROM?
BASED ON YOUR ACCENT... I'D SAY KYUSHU?
WOW! Y'ALL TALK SO NICELY!
IT'S LIKE LIVIN' IN A MOVIE!
MARIKA 'N' I WENT TO JUNIOR HIGH TOGETHER!
WE'VE BEEN BFFs SINCE OUR FIRST YEAR!
YOU'RE EMBARRASSING ME.

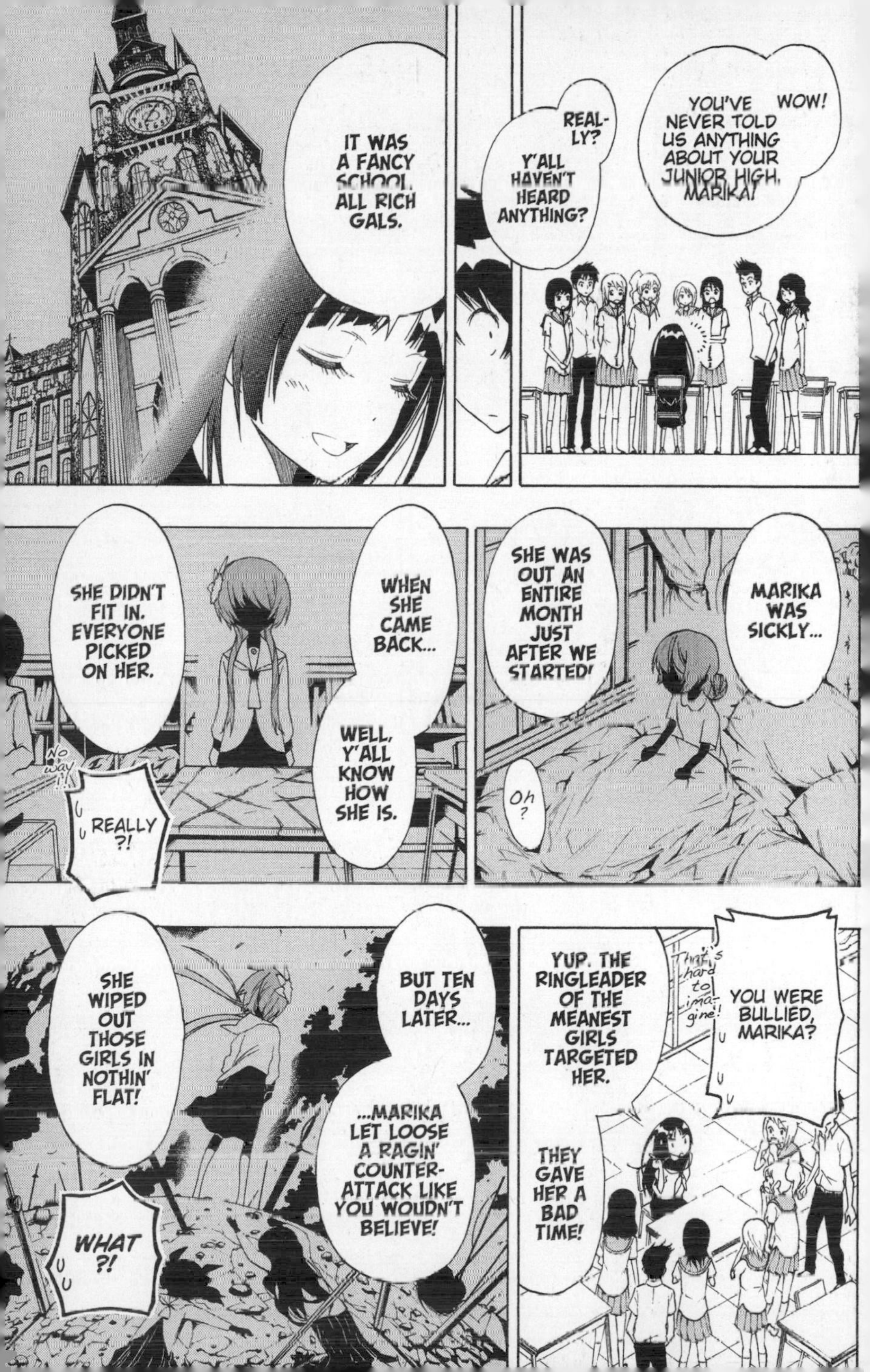
WOW!
YOU'VE NEVER TOLD US ANYTHING ABOUT YOUR JUNIOR HIGH, MARIKA!
REAL-LY?
Y'ALL HAVEN'T HEARD ANYTHING?
IT WAS A FANCY SCHOOL. ALL RICH GALS.
MARIKA WAS SICKLY...
SHE WAS OUT AN ENTIRE MONTH JUST AFTER WE STARTED!
Oh?
WHEN SHE CAME BACK...
WELL, Y'ALL KNOW HOW SHE IS.
SHE DIDN'T FIT IN. EVERYONE PICKED ON HER.
No way!!
REALLY?!
YOU WERE BULLIED, MARIKA?
That's hard to ima-gine!!
YUP. THE RINGLEADER OF THE MEANEST GIRLS TARGETED HER.
THEY GAVE HER A BAD TIME!
BUT TEN DAYS LATER...
...MARIKA LET LOOSE A RAGIN' COUNTER-ATTACK LIKE YOU WOUDN'T BELIEVE!
SHE WIPED OUT THOSE GIRLS IN NOTHIN' FLAT!
WHAT?!

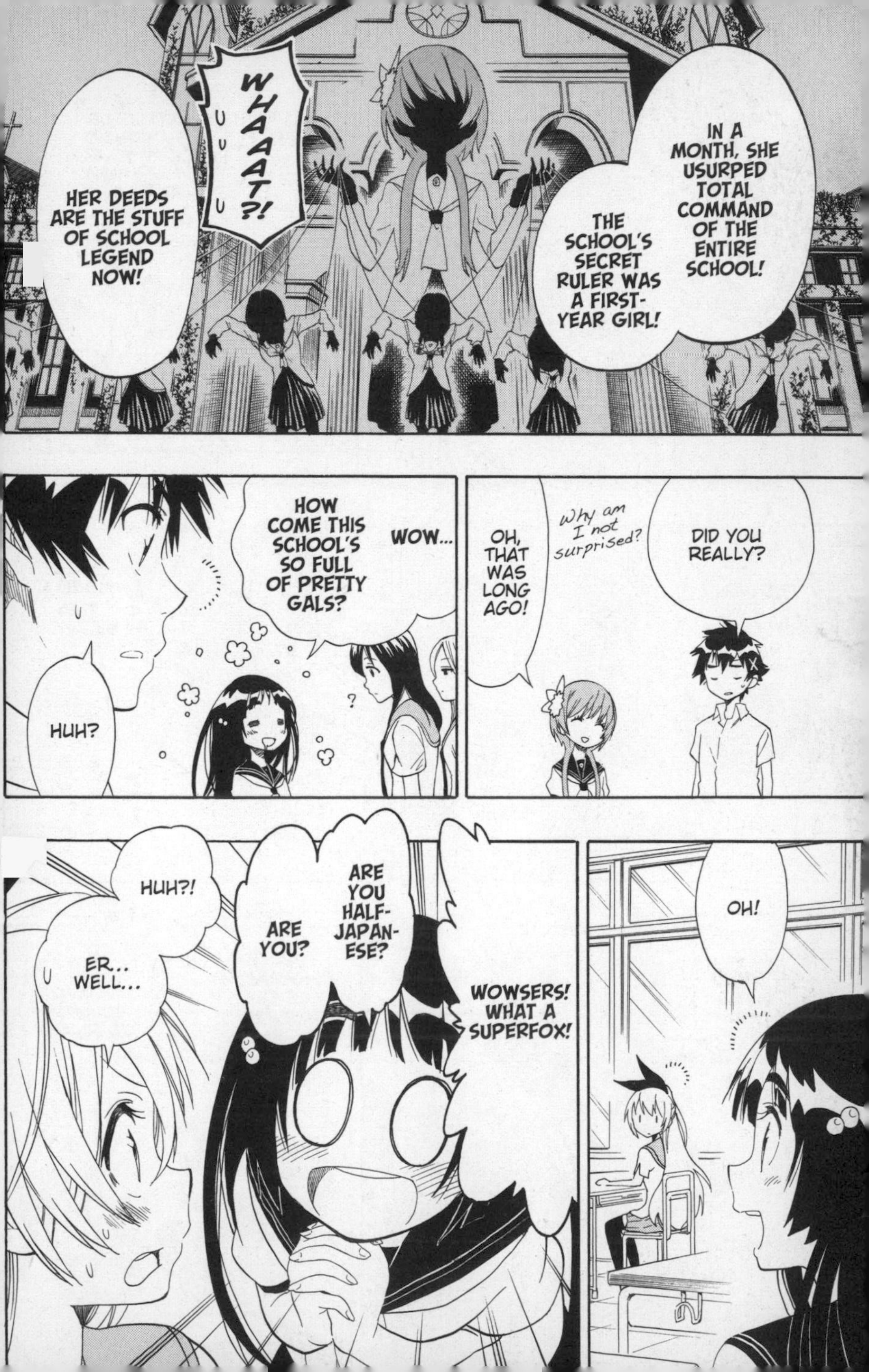
IN A MONTH, SHE USURPED TOTAL COMMAND OF THE ENTIRE SCHOOL!
THE SCHOOL'S SECRET RULER WAS A FIRST-YEAR GIRL!
WHAAAT?!
HER DEEDS ARE THE STUFF OF SCHOOL LEGEND NOW!
DID YOU REALLY?
OH, THAT WAS LONG AGO!
Why am I not surprised?
WOW...
HOW COME THIS SCHOOL'S SO FULL OF PRETTY GALS?
HUH?
OH!
WOWSERS! WHAT A SUPERFOX!
ARE YOU HALF-JAPANESE?
ARE YOU?
HUH?!
ER... WELL...

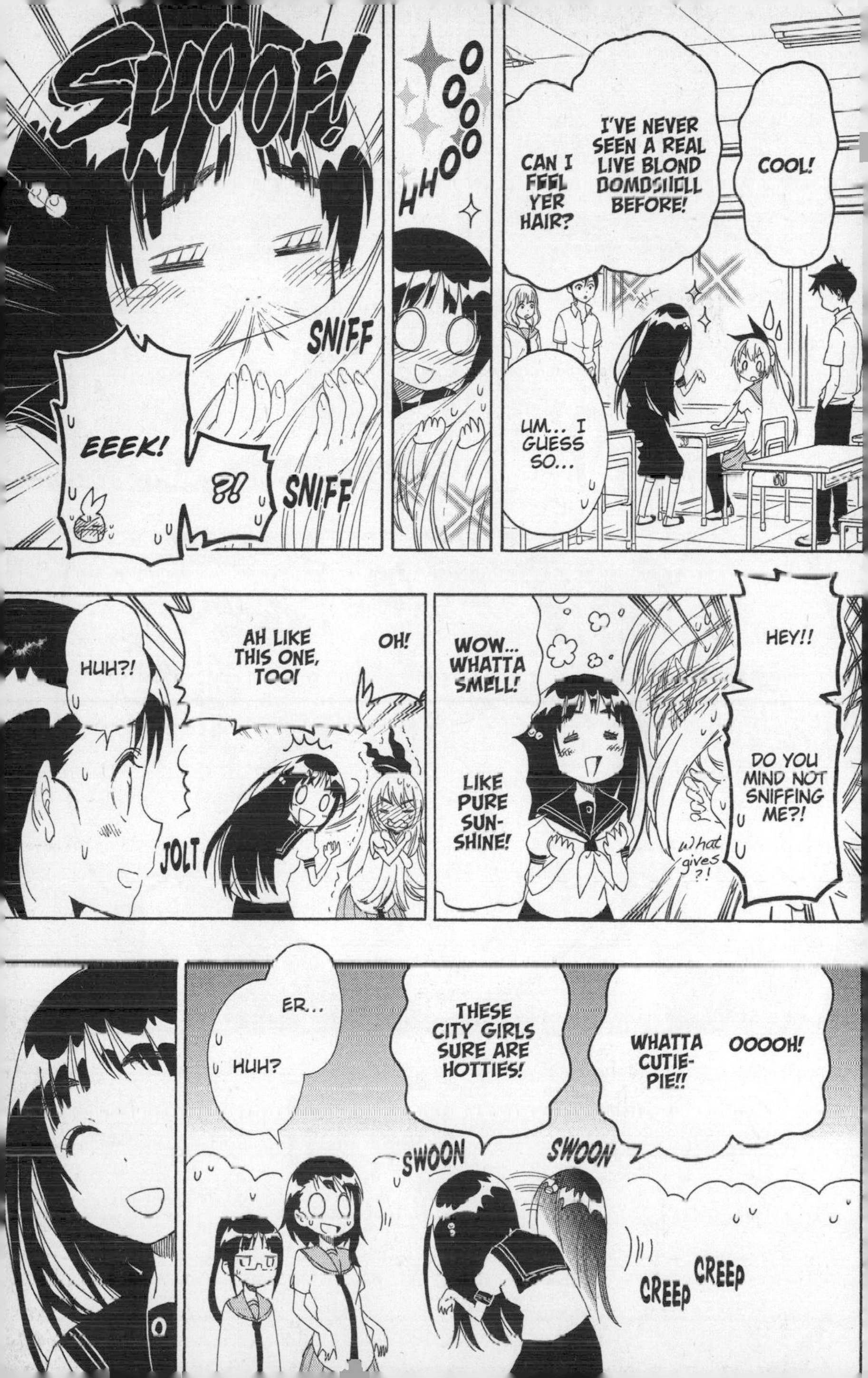
COOL!
I'VE NEVER SEEN A REAL LIVE BLOND BOMBSHELL BEFORE!
CAN I FEEL YER HAIR?
UM... I GUESS SO...
OOOOOHH
SHOOF!
SNIFF
SNIFF
EEEK!
?!
HEY!!
DO YOU MIND NOT SNIFFING ME?!
What gives?!
WOW... WHATTA SMELL!
LIKE PURE SUN-SHINE!
OH!
AH LIKE THIS ONE, TOO!
HUH?!
JOLT
OOOOH!
WHATTA CUTIE-PIE!!
SWOON
THESE CITY GIRLS SURE ARE HOTTIES!
SWOON
ER...
HUH?
CREEP
CREEP

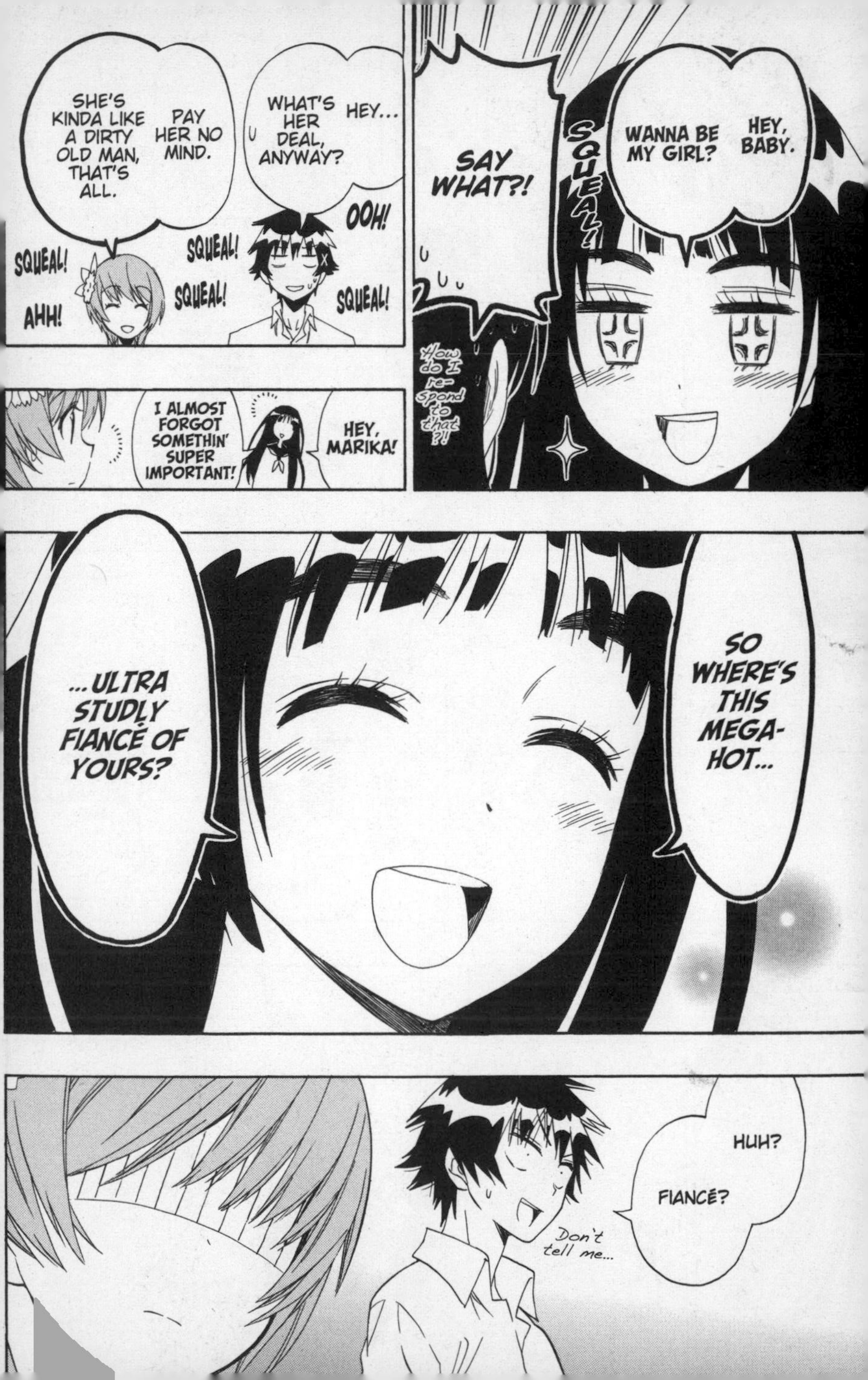
HEY, BABY.
WANNA BE MY GIRL?
SQUEAL!
SAY WHAT?!
How do I re-spond to that?!
HEY...
WHAT'S HER DEAL, ANYWAY?
OOH!
SQUEAL!
SQUEAL!
PAY HER NO MIND.
SHE'S KINDA LIKE A DIRTY OLD MAN, THAT'S ALL.
SQUEAL!
SQUEAL!
AHH!
HEY, MARIKA!
I ALMOST FORGOT SOMETHIN' SUPER IMPORTANT!
SO WHERE'S THIS MEGA-HOT...
...ULTRA STUDLY FIANCÉ OF YOURS?
HUH?
FIANCÉ?
Don't tell me...

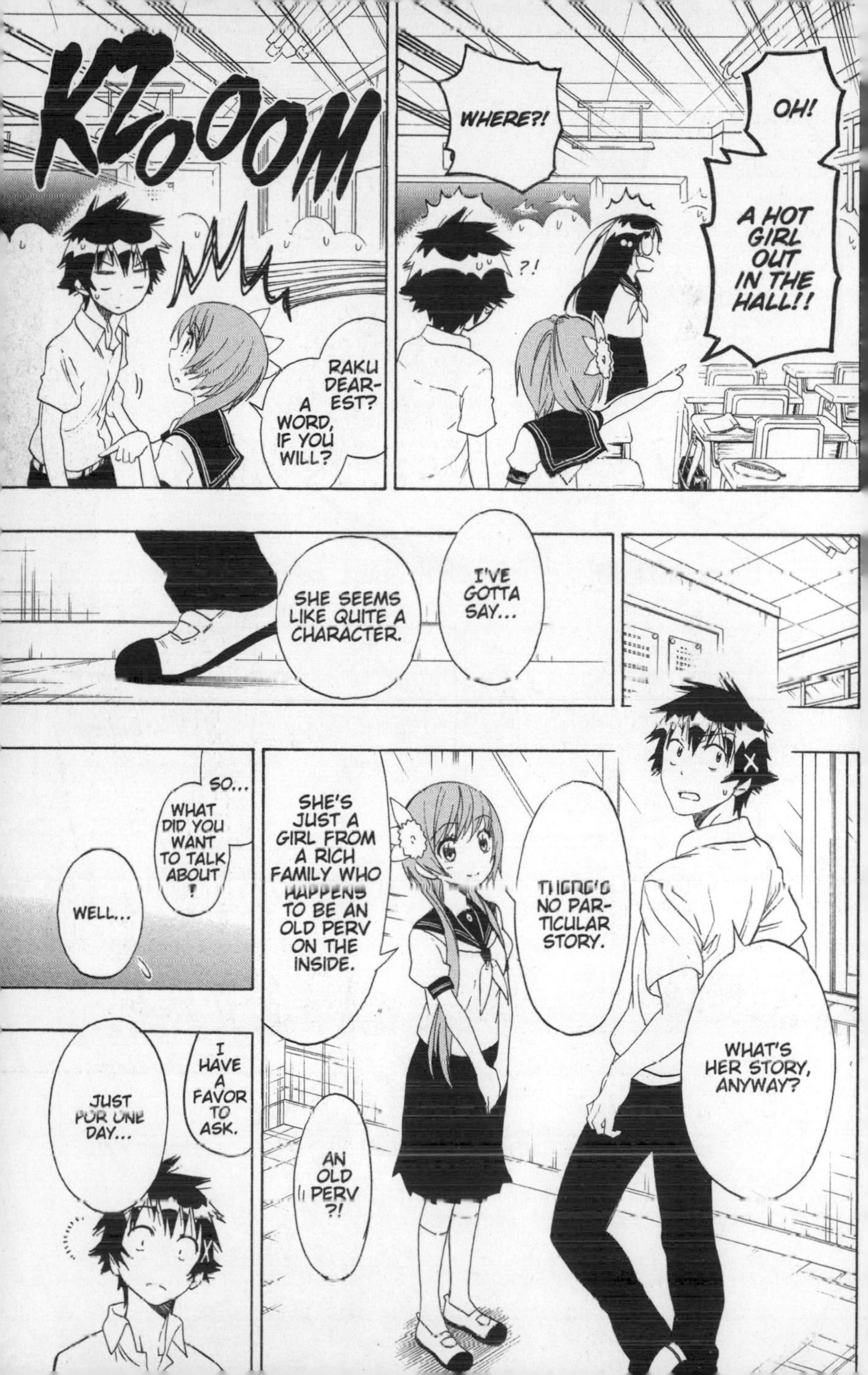
OH!
A HOT GIRL OUT IN THE HALL!!
WHERE?!
?!
KZOOOM
RAKU DEAREST? A WORD, IF YOU WILL?
I'VE GOTTA SAY...
SHE SEEMS LIKE QUITE A CHARACTER.
WHAT'S HER STORY, ANYWAY?
THERE'S NO PARTICULAR STORY.
SHE'S JUST A GIRL FROM A RICH FAMILY WHO HAPPENS TO BE AN OLD PERV ON THE INSIDE.
AN OLD PERV?!
SO... WHAT DID YOU WANT TO TALK ABOUT?
WELL...
I HAVE A FAVOR TO ASK.
JUST FOR ONE DAY...

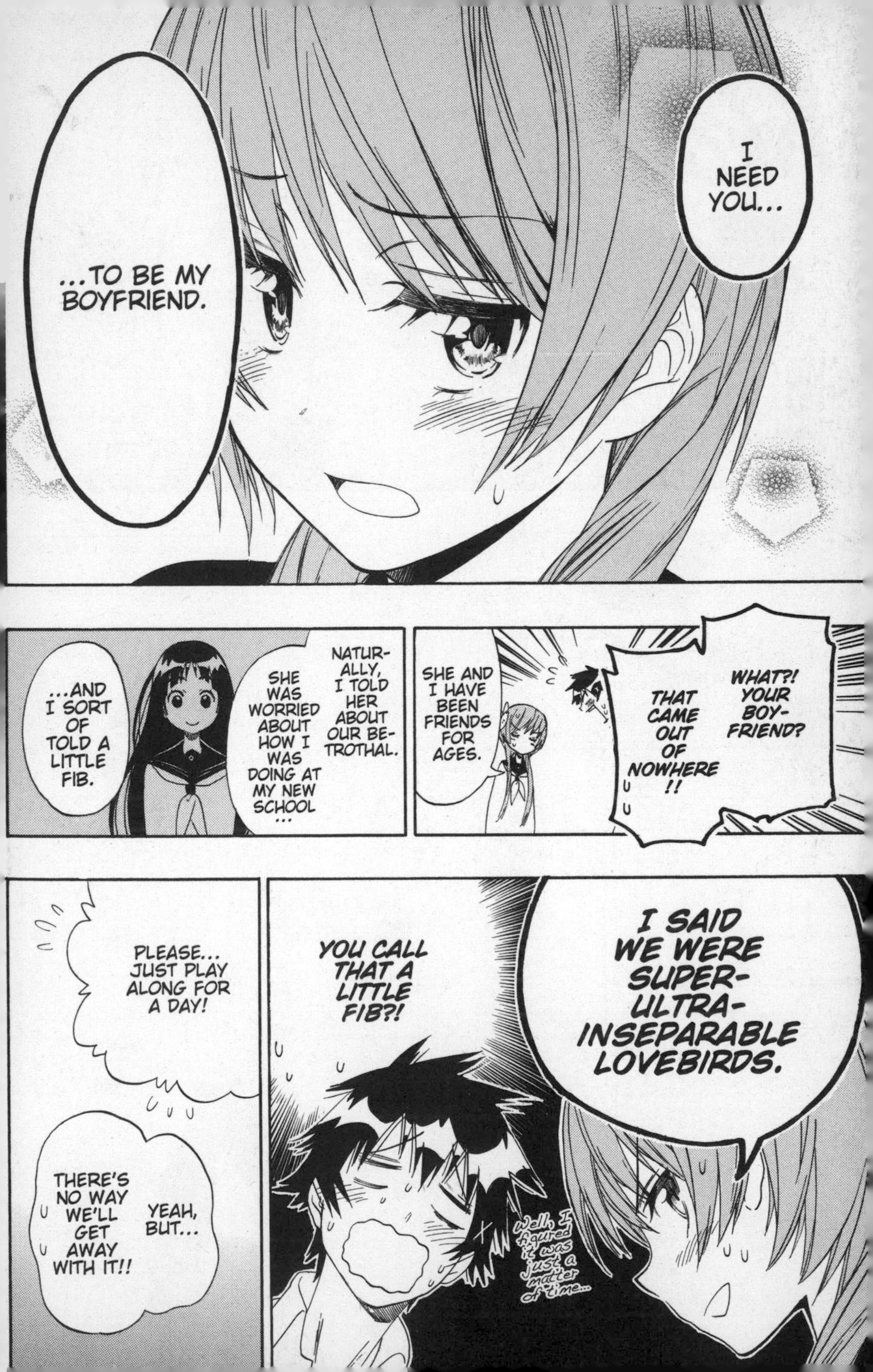
I NEED YOU...
...TO BE MY BOYFRIEND.
WHAT?! YOUR BOY-FRIEND?
THAT CAME OUT OF NOWHERE!!
SHE AND I HAVE BEEN FRIENDS FOR AGES.
NATURALLY, I TOLD HER ABOUT OUR BETROTHAL.
SHE WAS WORRIED ABOUT HOW I WAS DOING AT MY NEW SCHOOL...
...AND I SORT OF TOLD A LITTLE FIB.
I SAID WE WERE SUPER-ULTRA-INSEPARABLE LOVEBIRDS.
YOU CALL THAT A LITTLE FIB?!
Well, I figured it was just a matter of time...
PLEASE... JUST PLAY ALONG FOR A DAY!
YEAH, BUT...
THERE'S NO WAY WE'LL GET AWAY WITH IT!!

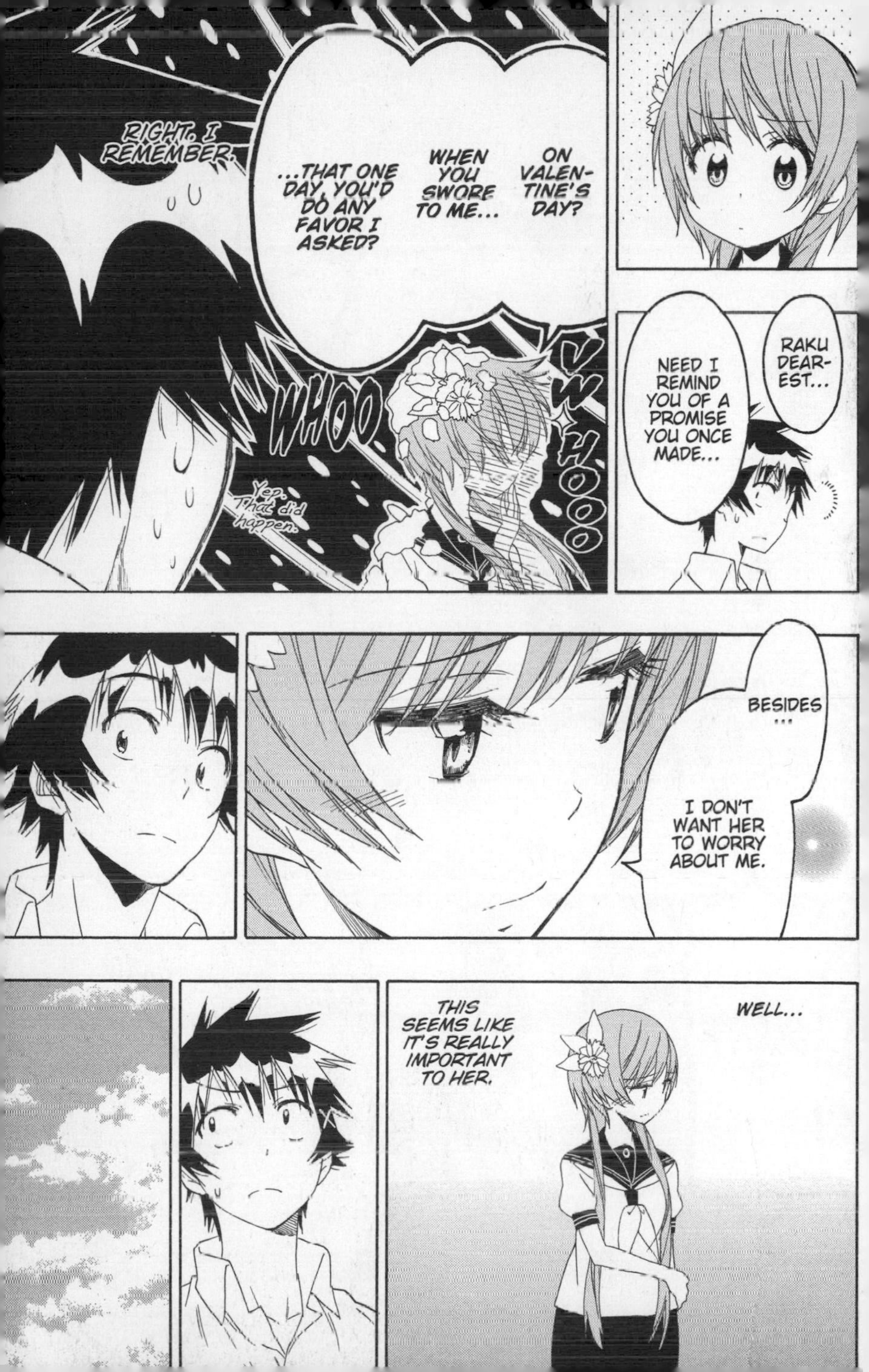
RAKU DEAREST...
NEED I REMIND YOU OF A PROMISE YOU ONCE MADE...
ON VALENTINE'S DAY?
WHEN YOU SWORE TO ME...
...THAT ONE DAY, YOU'D DO ANY FAVOR I ASKED?
VWHOOO
WHOO
RIGHT. I REMEMBER.
Yep. That did happen.
BESIDES...
I DON'T WANT HER TO WORRY ABOUT ME.
WELL...
THIS SEEMS LIKE IT'S REALLY IMPORTANT TO HER.

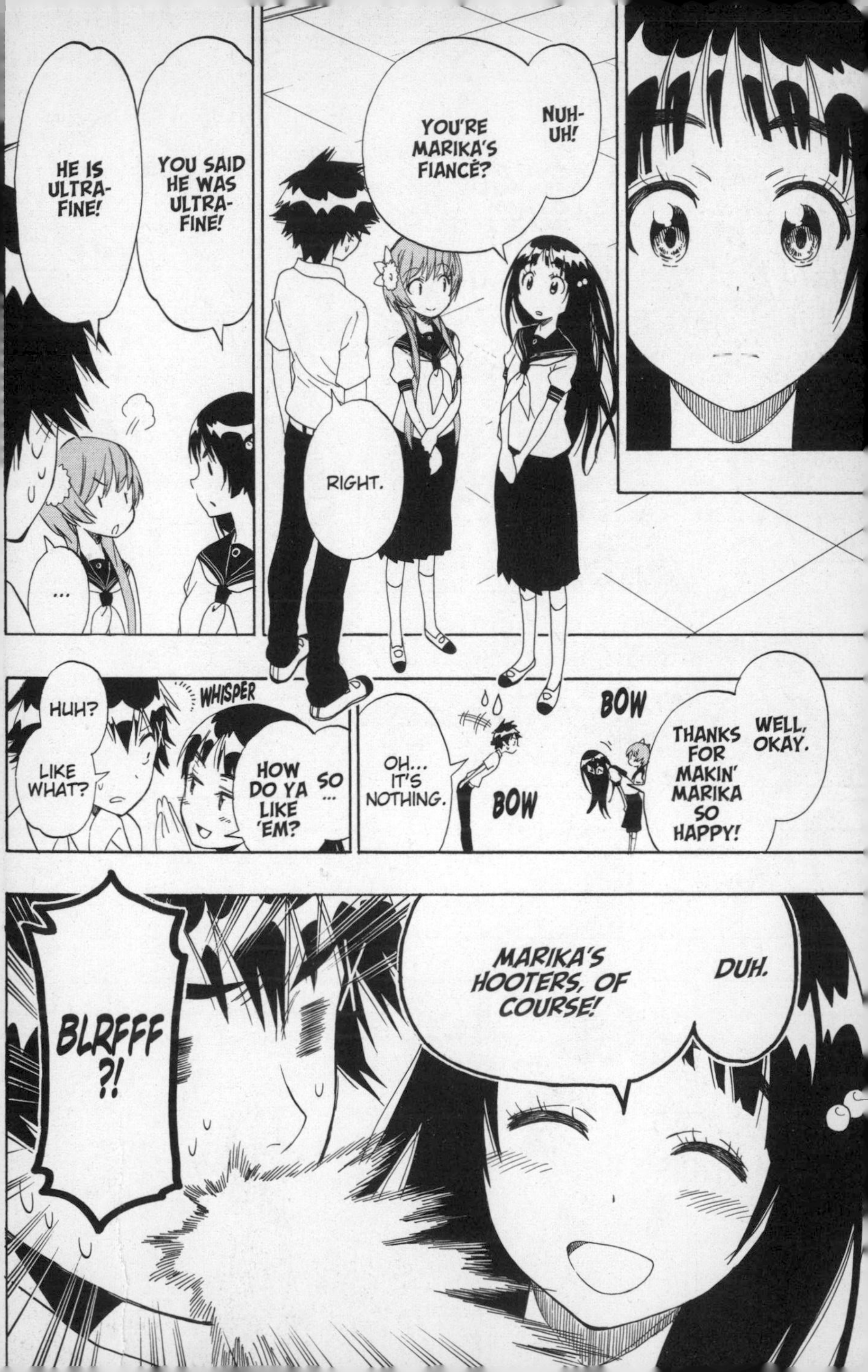
NUH-UH!
YOU'RE MARIKA'S FIANCÉ?
RIGHT.
YOU SAID HE WAS ULTRA-FINE!
HE IS ULTRA-FINE!
...
WELL, OKAY.
THANKS FOR MAKIN' MARIKA SO HAPPY!
BOW
BOW
OH... IT'S NOTHING.
SO...
HOW DO YA LIKE 'EM?
WHISPER
HUH?
LIKE WHAT?
DUH.
MARIKA'S HOOTERS, OF COURSE!
BLRFFF ?!

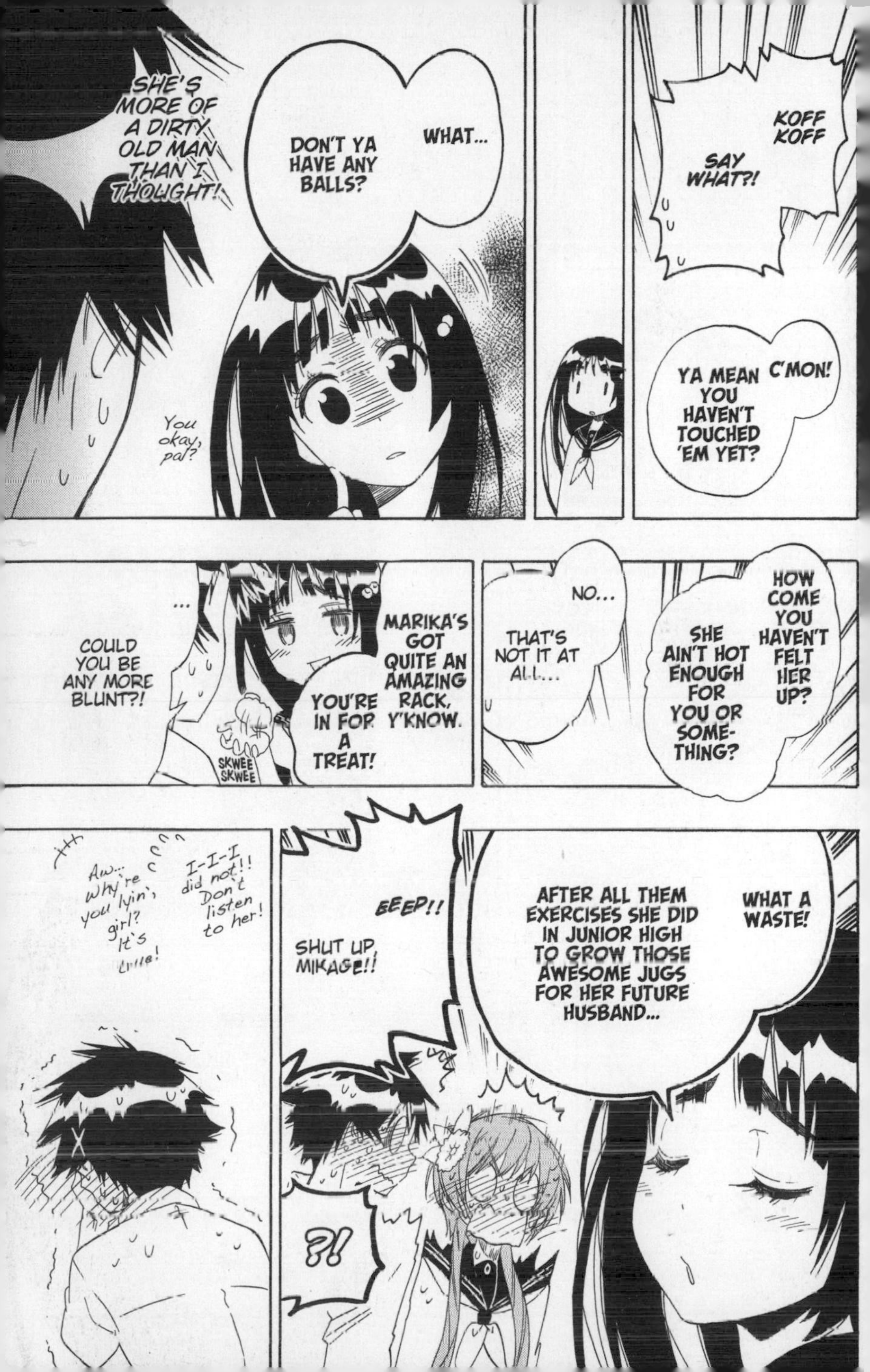
KOFF KOFF
SAY WHAT?!
C'MON!
YA MEAN YOU HAVEN'T TOUCHED 'EM YET?
WHAT...
DON'T YA HAVE ANY BALLS?
SHE'S MORE OF A DIRTY OLD MAN THAN I THOUGHT!
You okay, pal?
HOW COME YOU HAVEN'T FELT HER UP?
SHE AIN'T HOT ENOUGH FOR YOU OR SOME-THING?
NO...
THAT'S NOT IT AT ALL...
MARIKA'S GOT QUITE AN AMAZING RACK, Y'KNOW.
YOU'RE IN FOR A TREAT!
...
COULD YOU BE ANY MORE BLUNT?!
SKWEE SKWEE
WHAT A WASTE!
AFTER ALL THEM EXERCISES SHE DID IN JUNIOR HIGH TO GROW THOSE AWESOME JUGS FOR HER FUTURE HUSBAND...
BEEP!!
SHUT UP MIKAGE!!
?!
I-I-I did not!! Don't listen to her!
Aw... Why're you lyin', girl? It's cute!

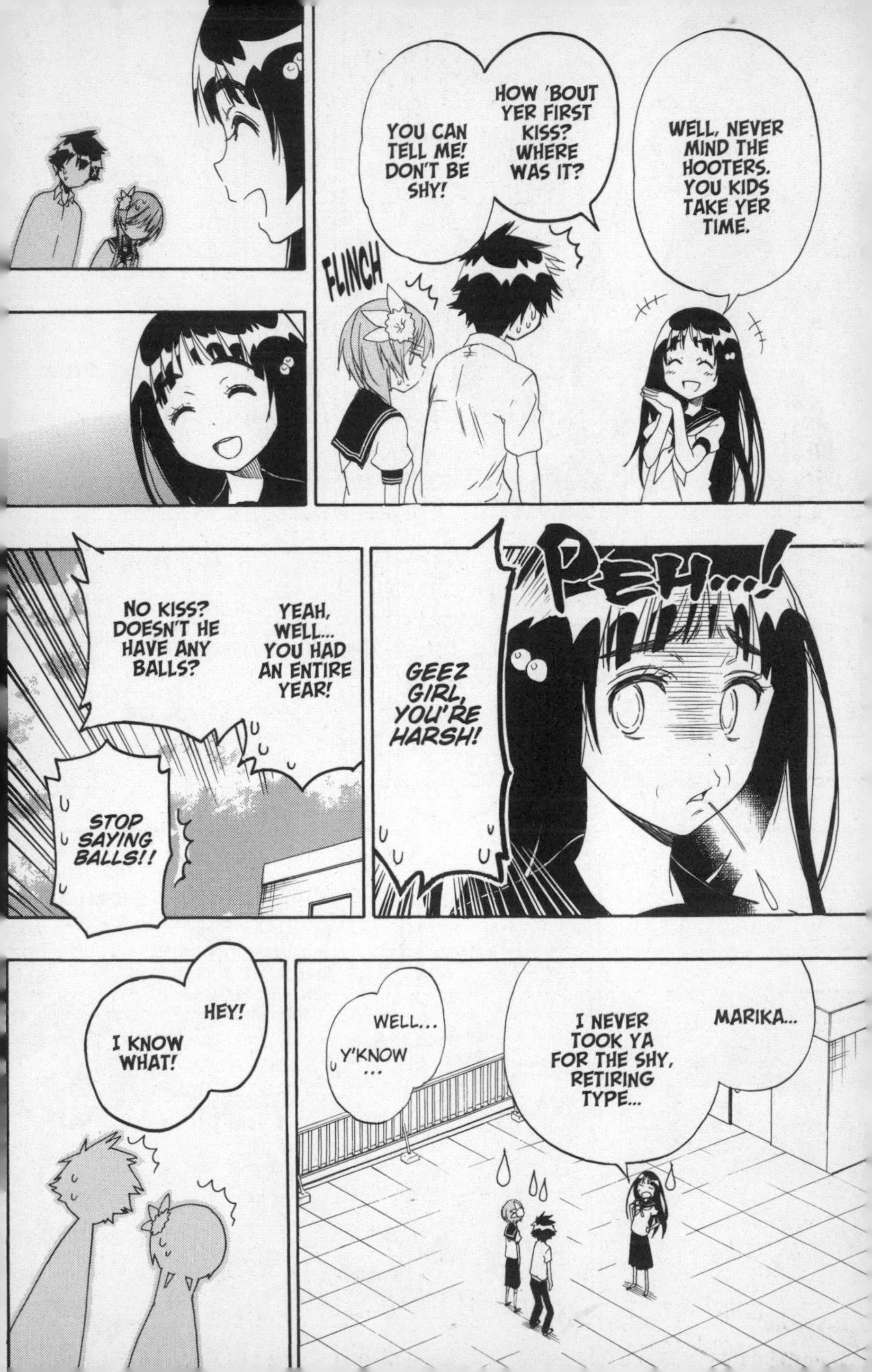
WELL, NEVER MIND THE HOOTERS. YOU KIDS TAKE YER TIME.
HOW 'BOUT YER FIRST KISS? WHERE WAS IT?
YOU CAN TELL ME! DON'T BE SHY!
FLINCH
PEH...!
GEEZ GIRL, YOU'RE HARSH!
YEAH, WELL... YOU HAD AN ENTIRE YEAR!
NO KISS? DOESN'T HE HAVE ANY BALLS?
STOP SAYING BALLS!!
MARIKA...
I NEVER TOOK YA FOR THE SHY, RETIRING TYPE...
WELL...
Y'KNOW...
HEY!
I KNOW WHAT!

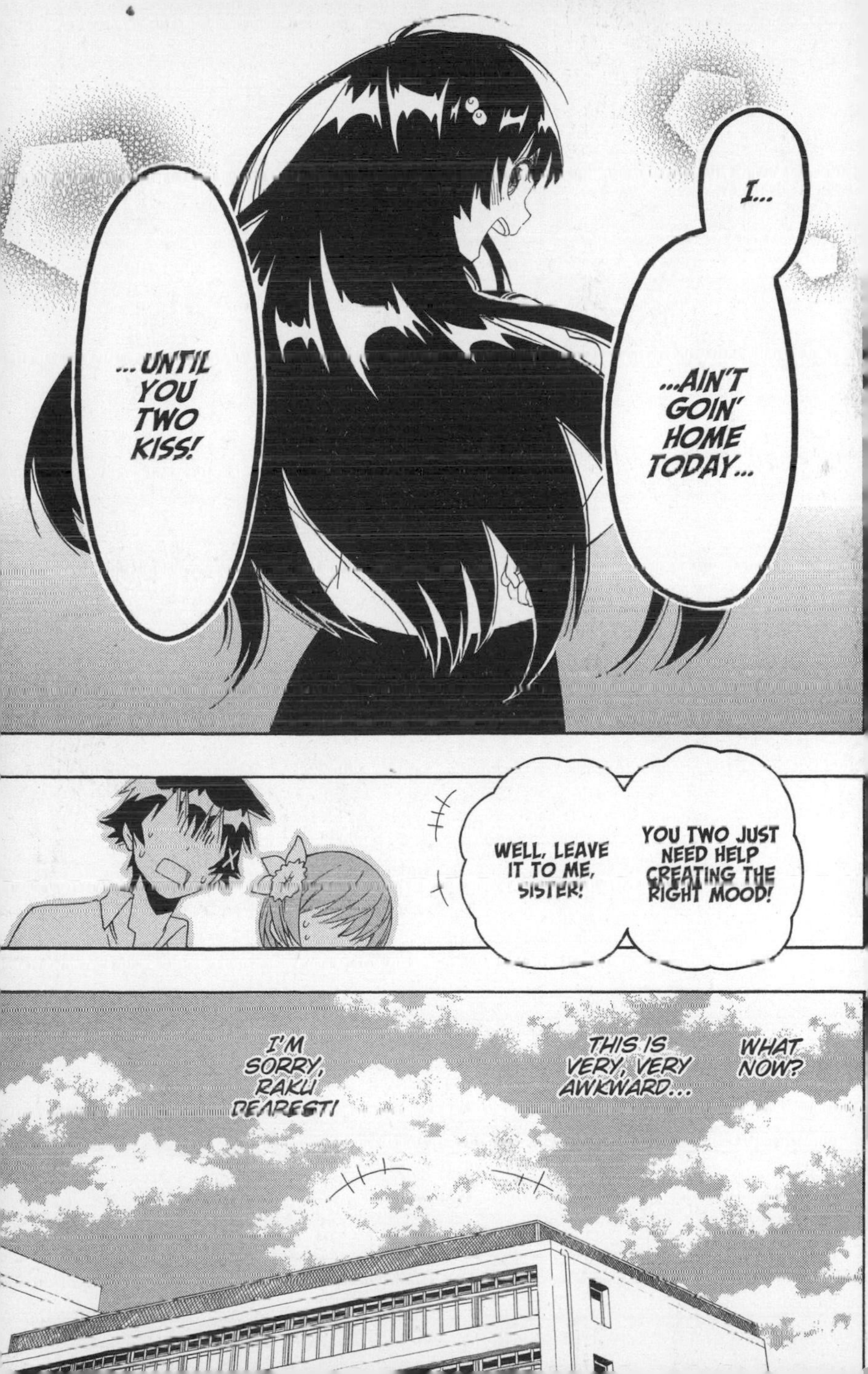
I...
...AIN'T GOIN' HOME TODAY...
...UNTIL YOU TWO KISS!
YOU TWO JUST NEED HELP CREATING THE RIGHT MOOD!
WELL, LEAVE IT TO ME, SISTER!
WHAT NOW?
THIS IS VERY, VERY AWKWARD...
I'M SORRY, RAKU DEAREST!

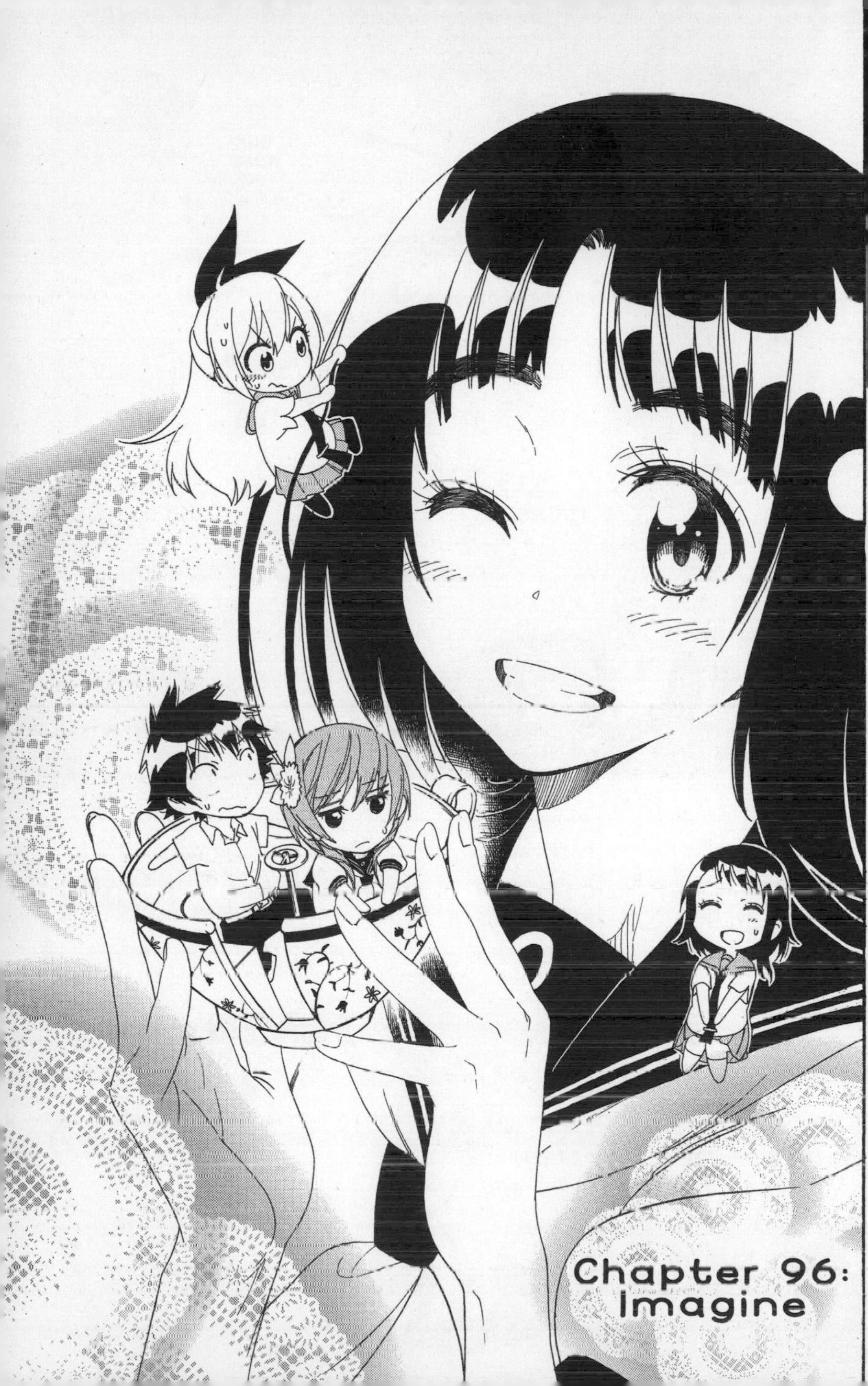
Chapter 96:
Imagine

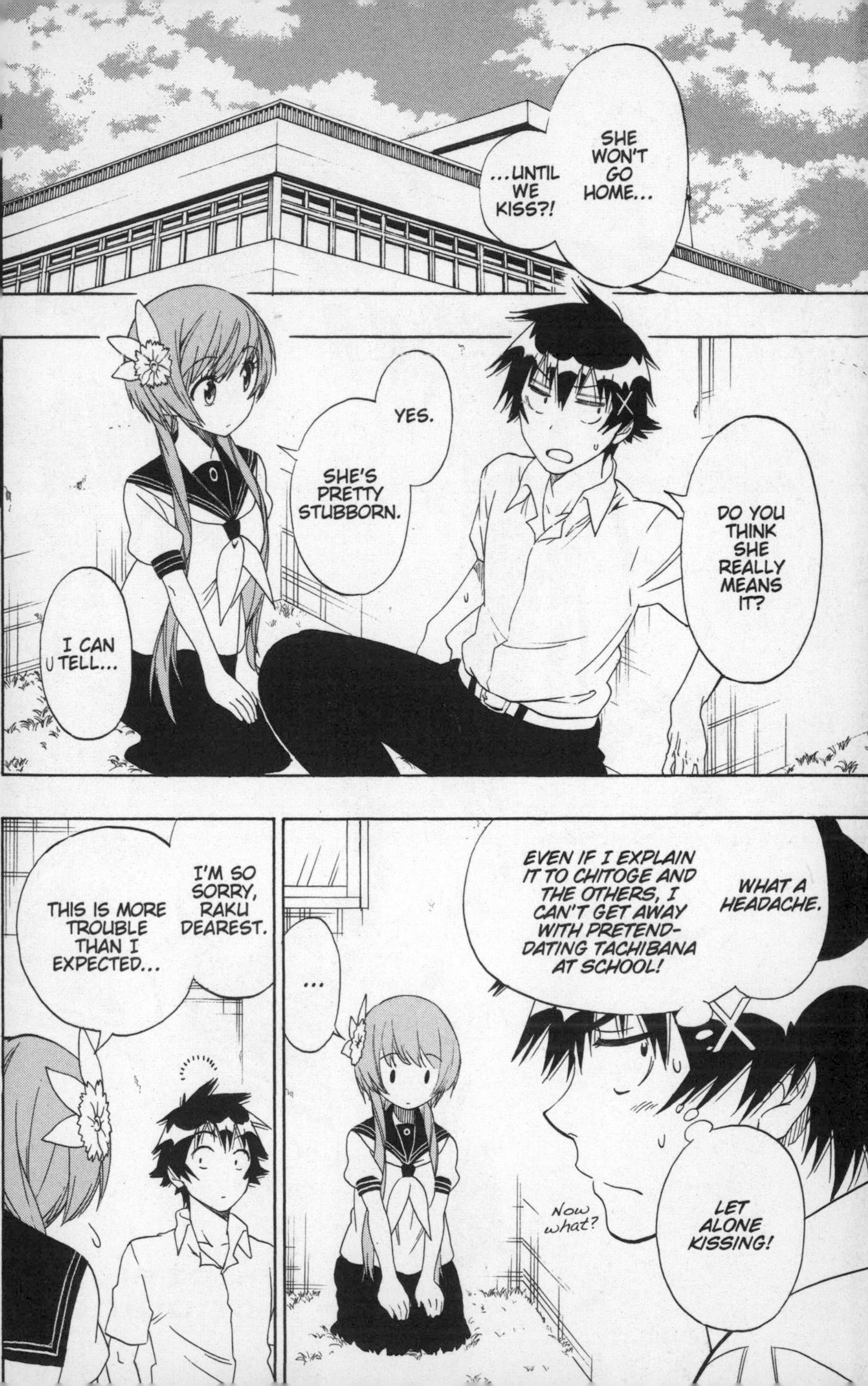
SHE WON'T GO HOME...
...UNTIL WE KISS?!
DO YOU THINK SHE REALLY MEANS IT?
YES.
SHE'S PRETTY STUBBORN.
I CAN TELL...
WHAT A HEADACHE.
EVEN IF I EXPLAIN IT TO CHITOGE AND THE OTHERS, I CAN'T GET AWAY WITH PRETEND-DATING TACHIBANA AT SCHOOL!
LET ALONE KISSING!
Now what?
...
I'M SO SORRY, RAKU DEAREST.
THIS IS MORE TROUBLE THAN I EXPECTED...

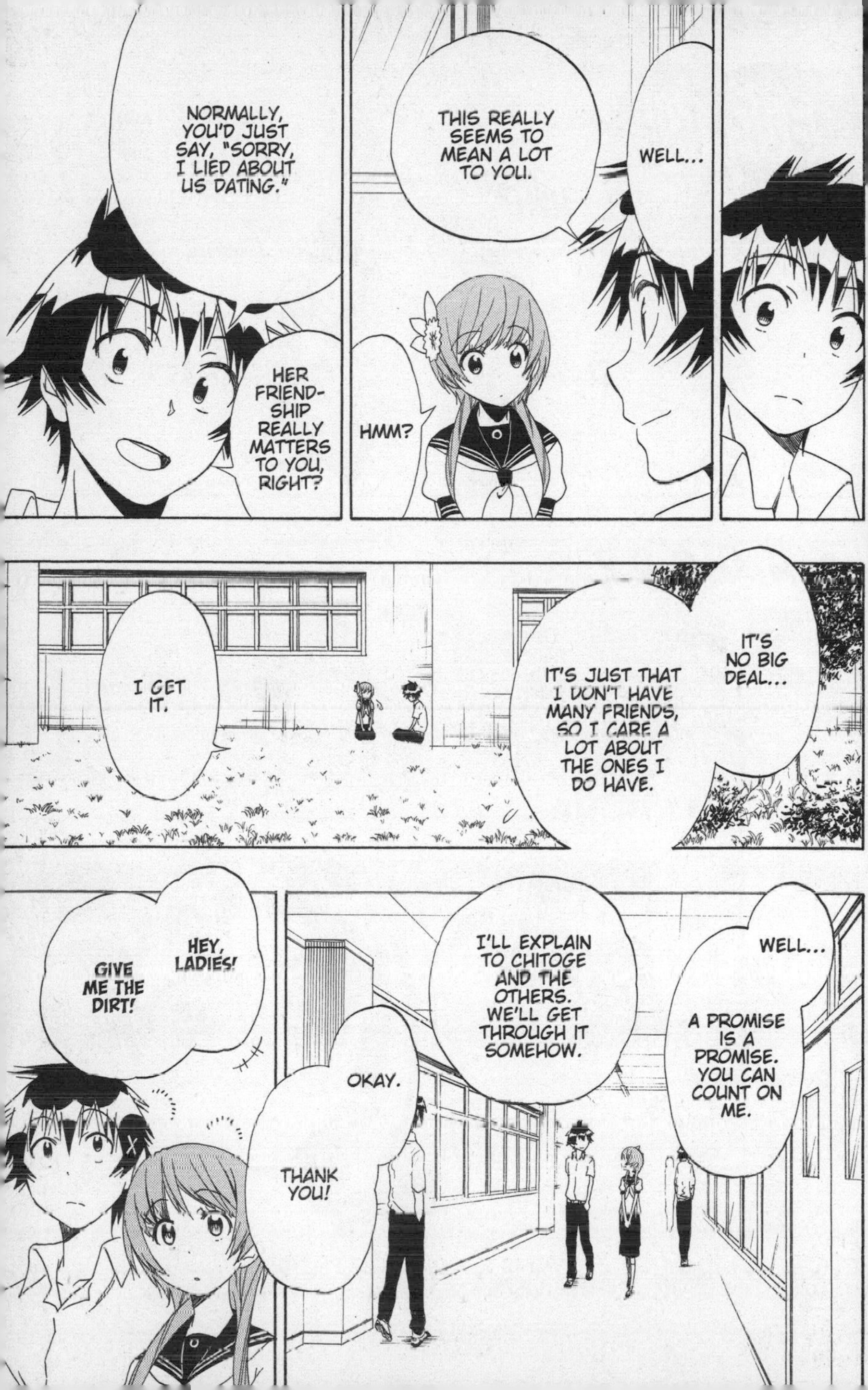
WELL...
THIS REALLY SEEMS TO MEAN A LOT TO YOU.
HMM?
NORMALLY, YOU'D JUST SAY, "SORRY, I LIED ABOUT US DATING."
HER FRIENDSHIP REALLY MATTERS TO YOU, RIGHT?
IT'S NO BIG DEAL...
IT'S JUST THAT I DON'T HAVE MANY FRIENDS, SO I CARE A LOT ABOUT THE ONES I DO HAVE.
I GET IT.
WELL...
A PROMISE IS A PROMISE. YOU CAN COUNT ON ME.
I'LL EXPLAIN TO CHITOGE AND THE OTHERS. WE'LL GET THROUGH IT SOMEHOW.
OKAY.
THANK YOU!
HEY, LADIES!
GIVE ME THE DIRT!

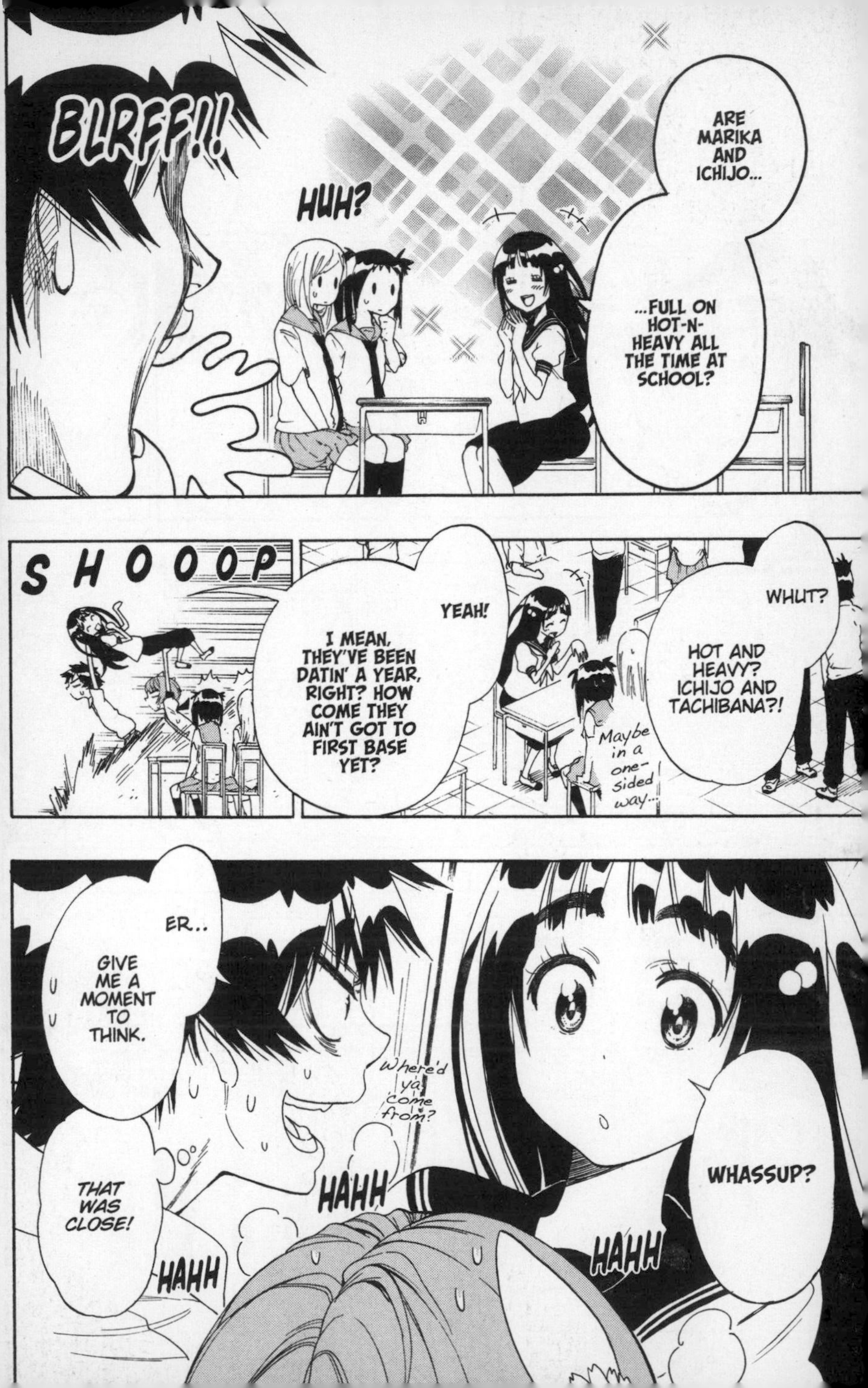
ARE MARIKA AND ICHIJO...
...FULL ON HOT-N-HEAVY ALL THE TIME AT SCHOOL?
HUH?
BLRFF!!!
WHUT?
HOT AND HEAVY? ICHIJO AND TACHIBANA?!
Maybe in a one-sided way...
YEAH!
I MEAN, THEY'VE BEEN DATIN' A YEAR, RIGHT? HOW COME THEY AIN'T GOT TO FIRST BASE YET?
SHOOOP
WHASSUP?
HAHH
Where'd ya come from?
HAHH
ER...
GIVE ME A MOMENT TO THINK.
THAT WAS CLOSE!
HAHH

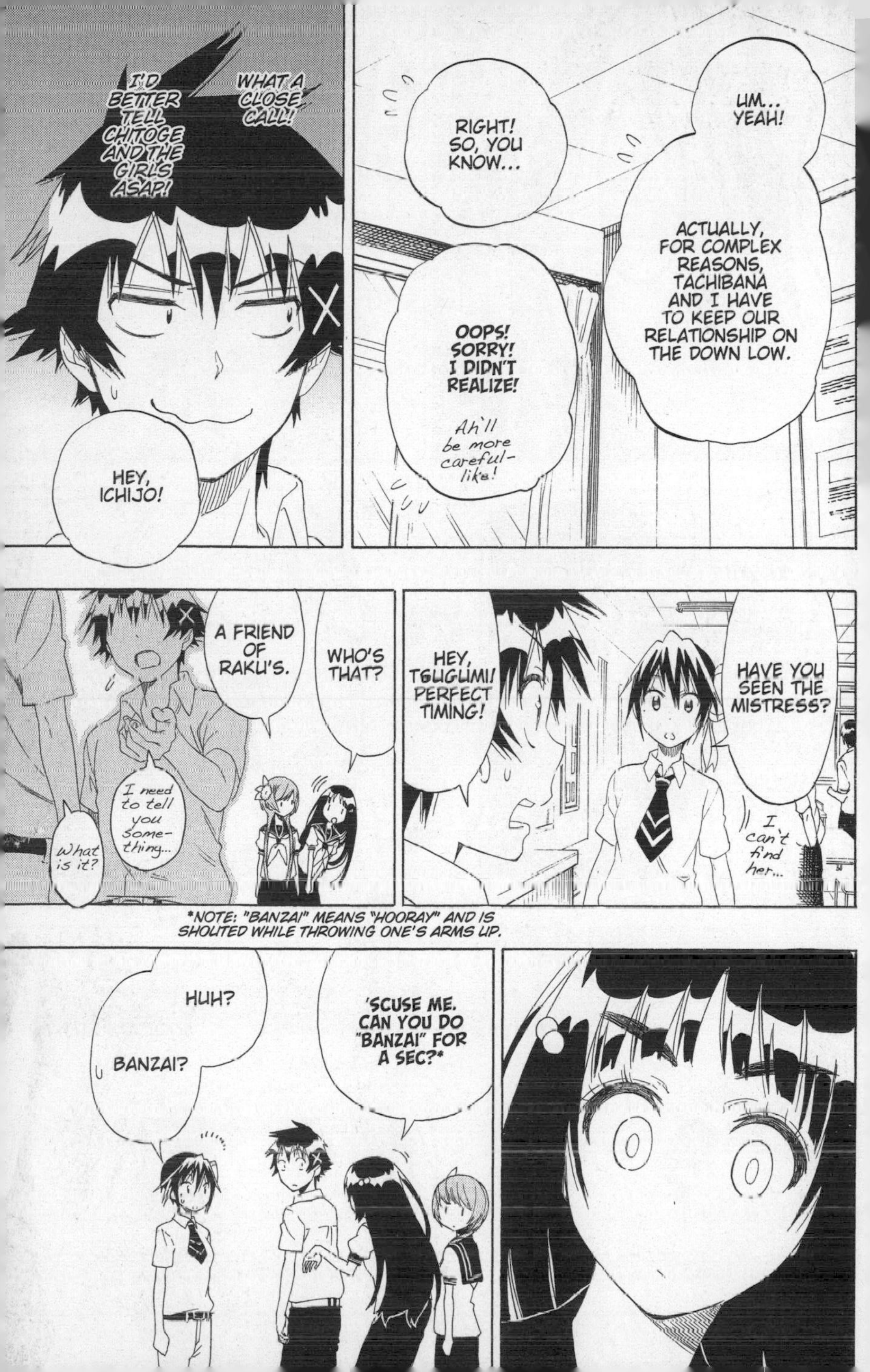
UM... YEAH!
RIGHT! SO, YOU KNOW...
ACTUALLY, FOR COMPLEX REASONS, TACHIBANA AND I HAVE TO KEEP OUR RELATIONSHIP ON THE DOWN LOW.
OOPS! SORRY! I DIDN'T REALIZE!
Ah'll be more careful-like!
WHAT A CLOSE CALL!
I'D BETTER TELL CHITOGE AND THE GIRLS ASAP!
HEY, ICHIJO!
HAVE YOU SEEN THE MISTRESS?
HEY, TSUGUMI! PERFECT TIMING!
I can't find her...
WHO'S THAT?
A FRIEND OF RAKU'S.
I need to tell you something...
What is it?
*NOTE: "BANZAI" MEANS "HOORAY" AND IS SHOUTED WHILE THROWING ONE'S ARMS UP.
'SCUSE ME. CAN YOU DO "BANZAI" FOR A SEC?*
HUH?
BANZAI?

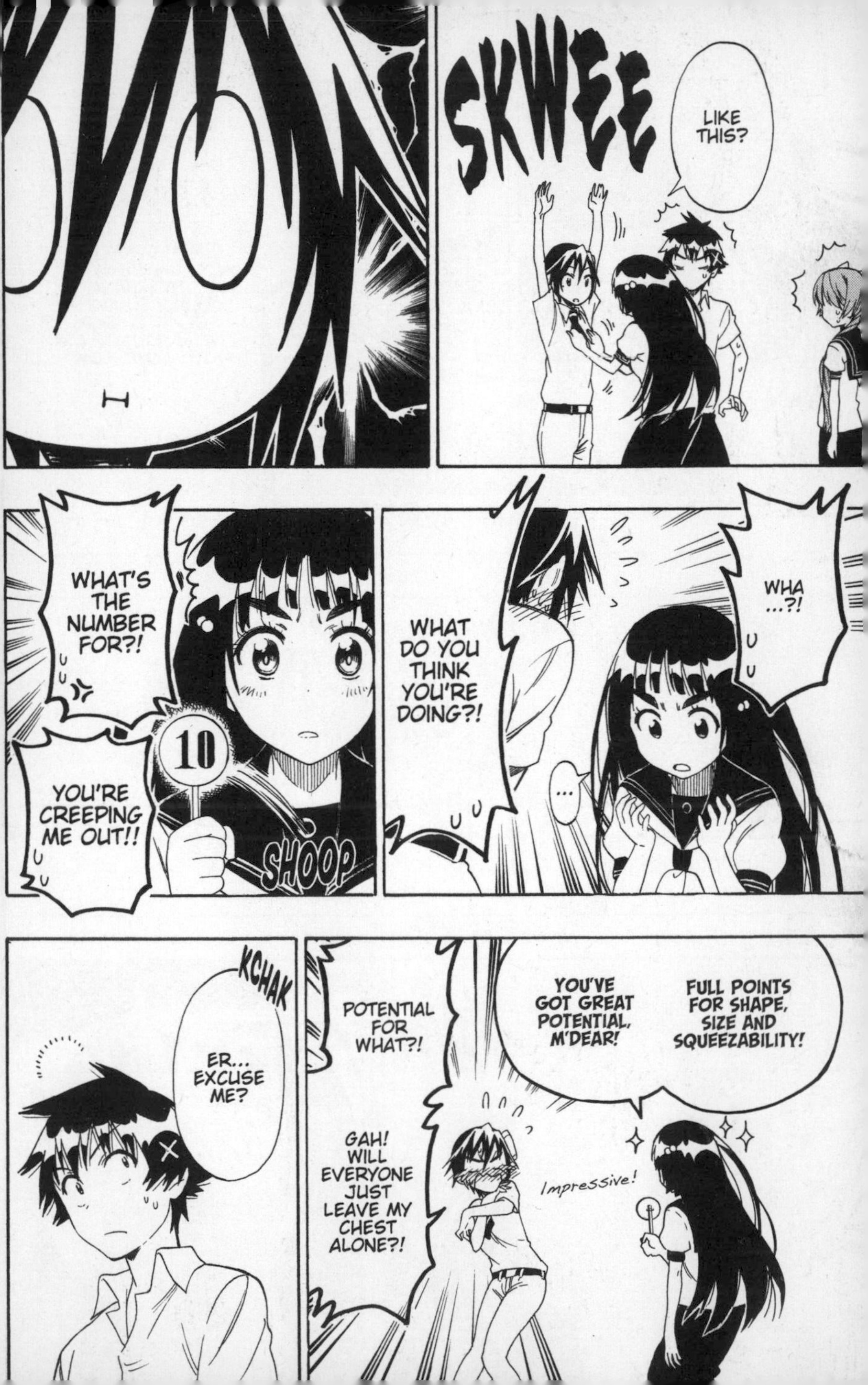
SKWEE
LIKE THIS?
WHA ...?!
WHAT DO YOU THINK YOU'RE DOING?!
...
WHAT'S THE NUMBER FOR?!
10
YOU'RE CREEPING ME OUT!!
SHOOP
FULL POINTS FOR SHAPE, SIZE AND SQUEEZABILITY!
YOU'VE GOT GREAT POTENTIAL, M'DEAR!
POTENTIAL FOR WHAT?!
Impressive!
GAH! WILL EVERYONE JUST LEAVE MY CHEST ALONE?!
KCHAK
ER... EXCUSE ME?

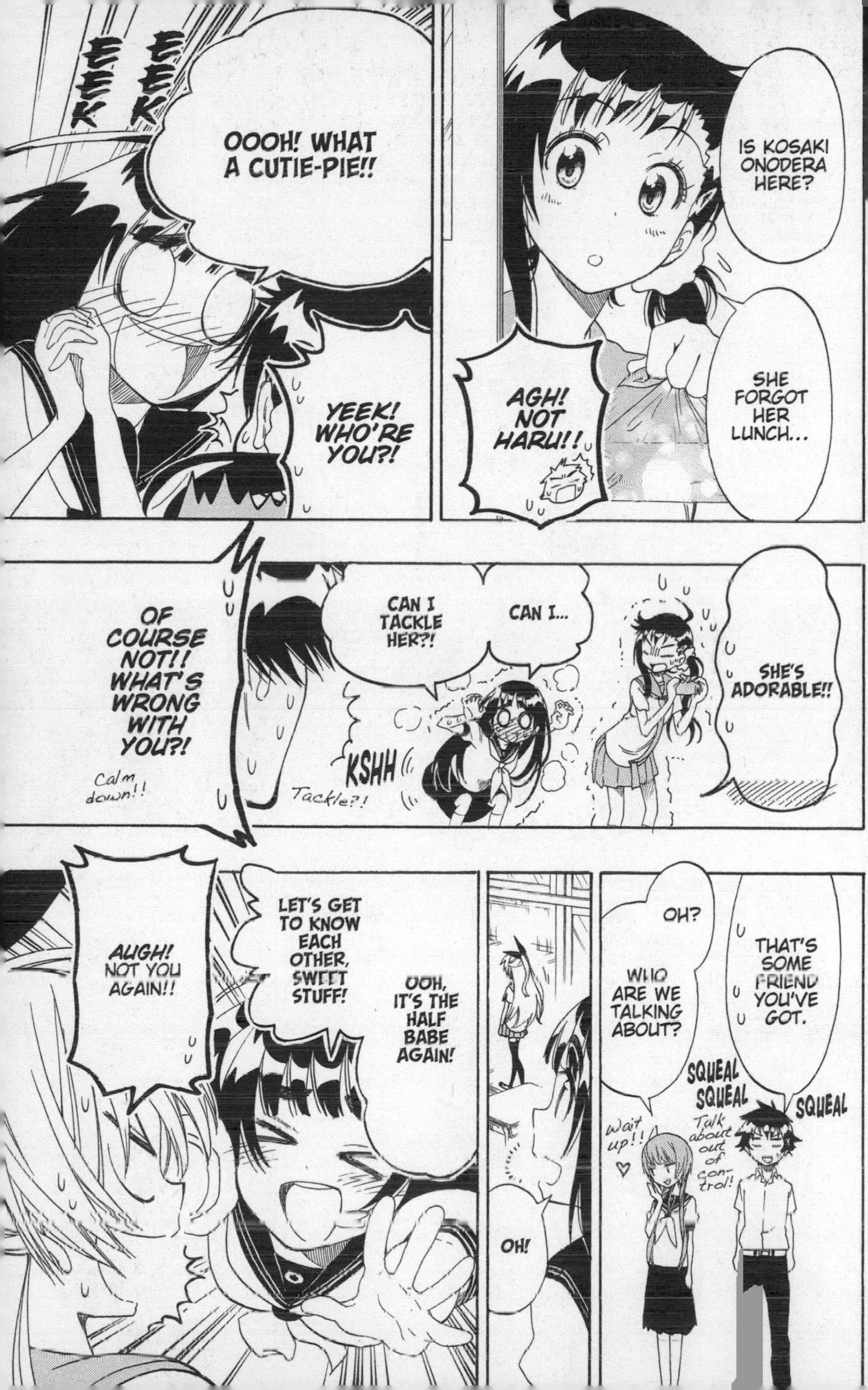
IS KOSAKI ONODERA HERE?
SHE FORGOT HER LUNCH...
AGH! NOT HARU!!
EEK EEK
OOOH! WHAT A CUTIE-PIE!!
YEEK! WHO'RE YOU?!
SHE'S ADORABLE!!
CAN I...
CAN I TACKLE HER?!
KSHH
Tackle?!
OF COURSE NOT!! WHAT'S WRONG WITH YOU?!
Calm down!!
THAT'S SOME FRIEND YOU'VE GOT.
OH?
WHO ARE WE TALKING ABOUT?
SQUEAL
SQUEAL SQUEAL
Talk about out of con-trol!
Wait up!!
OH!
OOH, IT'S THE HALF BABE AGAIN!
LET'S GET TO KNOW EACH OTHER, SWEET STUFF!
AUGH! NOT YOU AGAIN!!

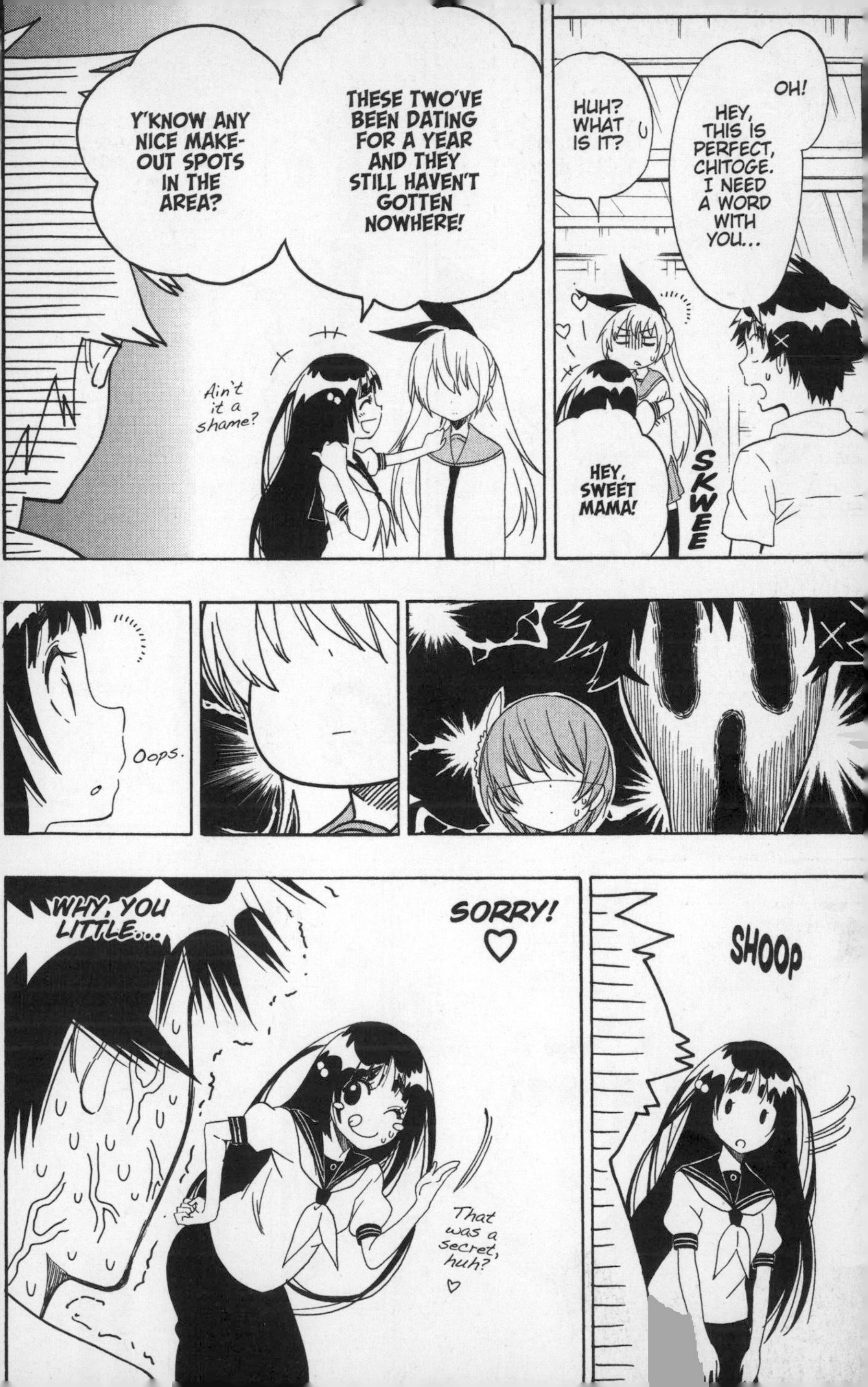
OH!
HEY, THIS IS PERFECT, CHITOGE. I NEED A WORD WITH YOU...
HUH? WHAT IS IT?
HEY, SWEET MAMA!
SKWEE
THESE TWO'VE BEEN DATING FOR A YEAR AND THEY STILL HAVEN'T GOTTEN NOWHERE!
Y'KNOW ANY NICE MAKE-OUT SPOTS IN THE AREA?
Ain't it a shame?
Oops.
SHOOP
SORRY! ♡
That was a secret, huh? ♡
WHY, YOU LITTLE...

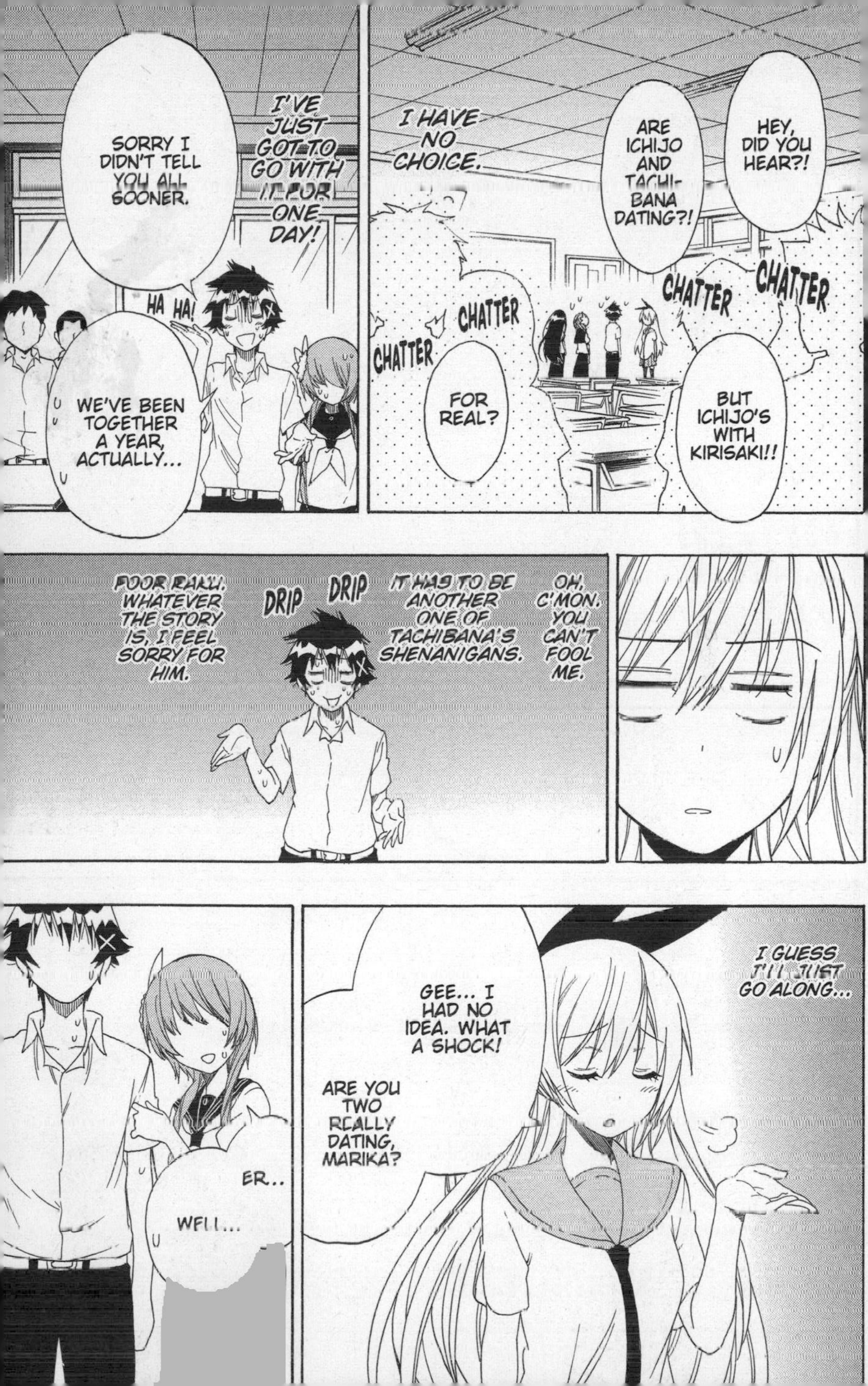
HEY, DID YOU HEAR?!
ARE ICHIJO AND TACHIBANA DATING?!
CHATTER
CHATTER
I HAVE NO CHOICE.
BUT ICHIJO'S WITH KIRISAKI!!
CHATTER
FOR REAL?
CHATTER
I'VE JUST GOT TO GO WITH IT FOR ONE DAY!
SORRY I DIDN'T TELL YOU ALL SOONER.
HA HA!
WE'VE BEEN TOGETHER A YEAR, ACTUALLY...
OH, C'MON. YOU CAN'T FOOL ME.
IT HAS TO BE ANOTHER ONE OF TACHIBANA'S SHENANIGANS.
DRIP
DRIP
POOR RAKU. WHATEVER THE STORY IS, I FEEL SORRY FOR HIM.
I GUESS I'LL JUST GO ALONG...
GEE... I HAD NO IDEA. WHAT A SHOCK!
ARE YOU TWO REALLY DATING, MARIKA?
ER...
WELL...

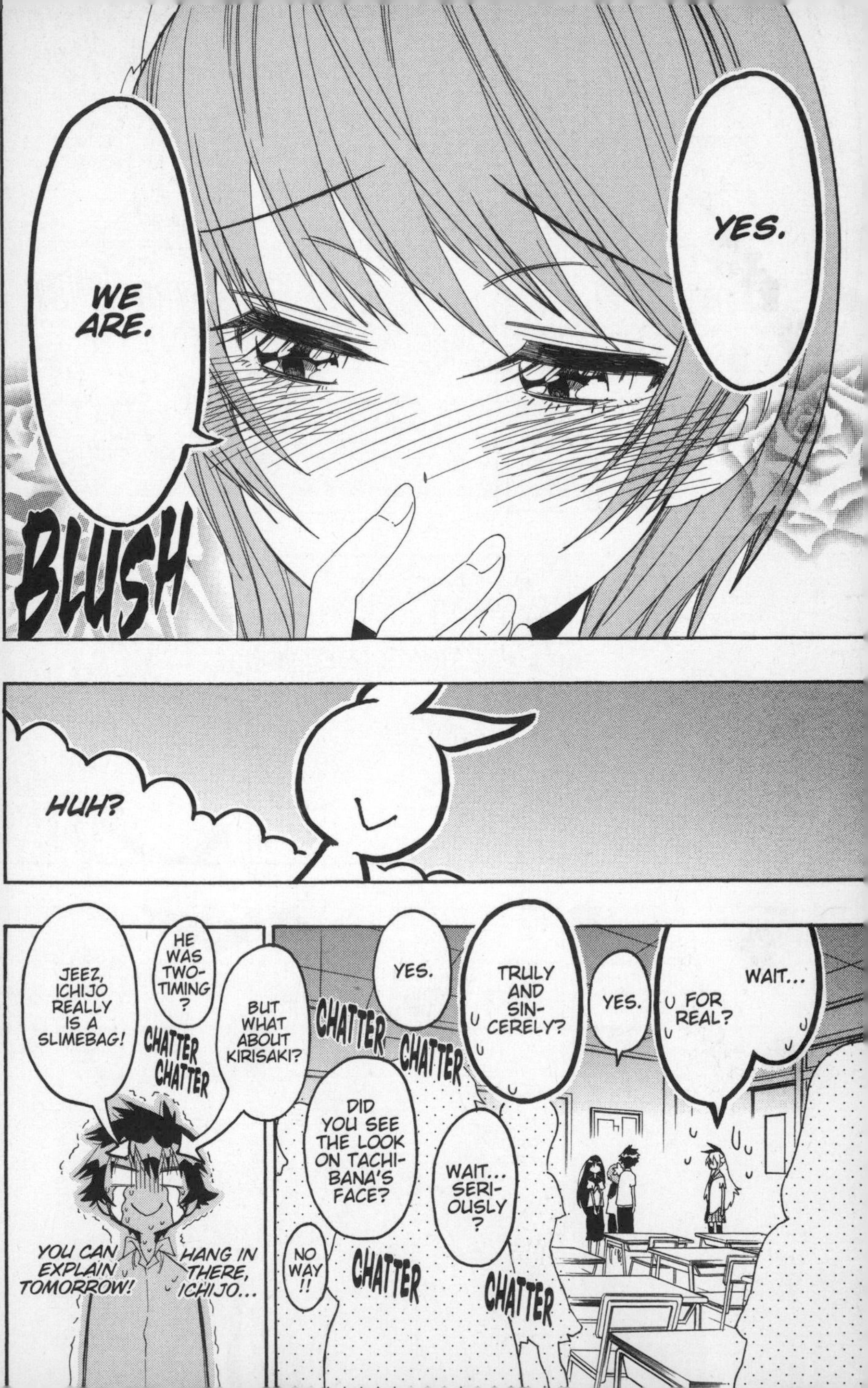
YES.
WE ARE.
BLUSH
HUH?
WAIT... FOR REAL?
YES.
TRULY AND SINCERELY?
YES.
CHATTER
CHATTER
DID YOU SEE THE LOOK ON TACHIBANA'S FACE?
WAIT... SERIOUSLY?
NO WAY!!
CHATTER
CHATTER
BUT WHAT ABOUT KIRISAKI?
HE WAS TWO-TIMING?
JEEZ, ICHIJO REALLY IS A SLIMEBAG!
CHATTER CHATTER
HANG IN THERE, ICHIJO...
YOU CAN EXPLAIN TOMORROW!

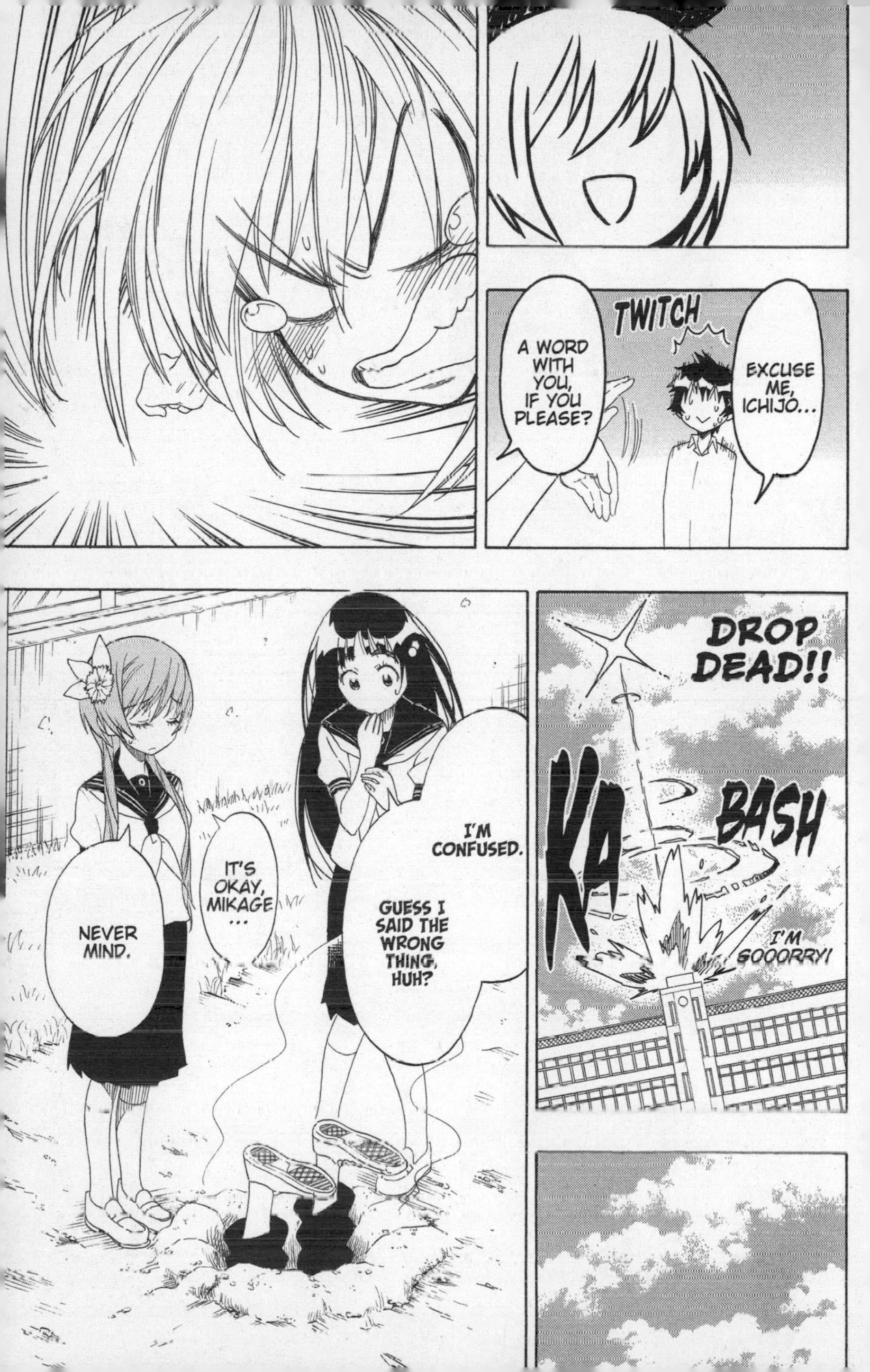
EXCUSE ME, ICHIJO...
TWITCH
A WORD WITH YOU, IF YOU PLEASE?
DROP DEAD!!
KA
BASH
I'M SOOORRY!
I'M CONFUSED.
GUESS I SAID THE WRONG THING, HUH?
IT'S OKAY, MIKAGE...
NEVER MIND.

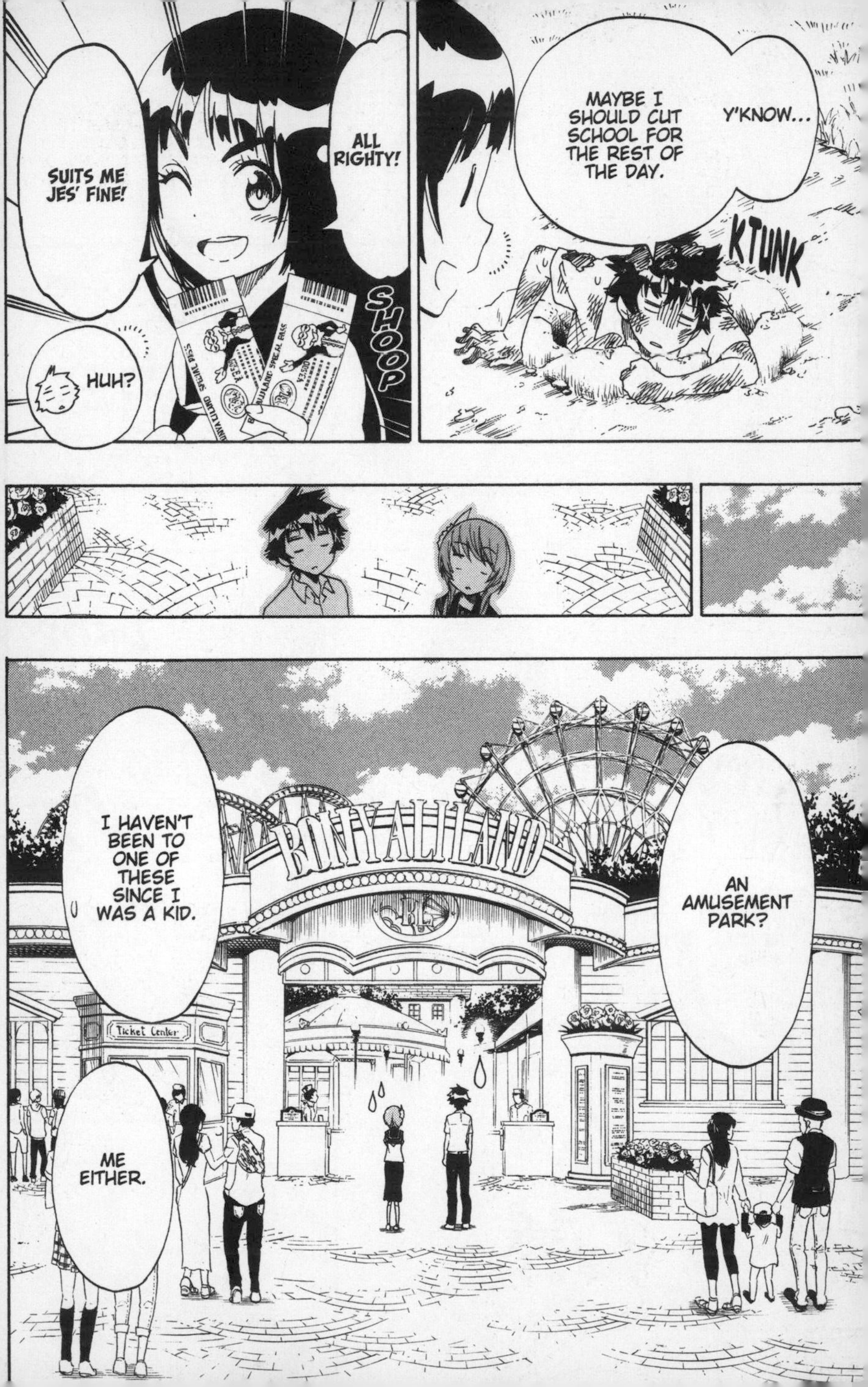
Y'KNOW...
MAYBE I SHOULD CUT SCHOOL FOR THE REST OF THE DAY.
KTUNK
ALL RIGHTY!
SHOOP
SUITS ME JES' FINE!
HUH?
AN AMUSEMENT PARK?
BONYALILAND
Ticket Center
I HAVEN'T BEEN TO ONE OF THESE SINCE I WAS A KID.
ME EITHER.

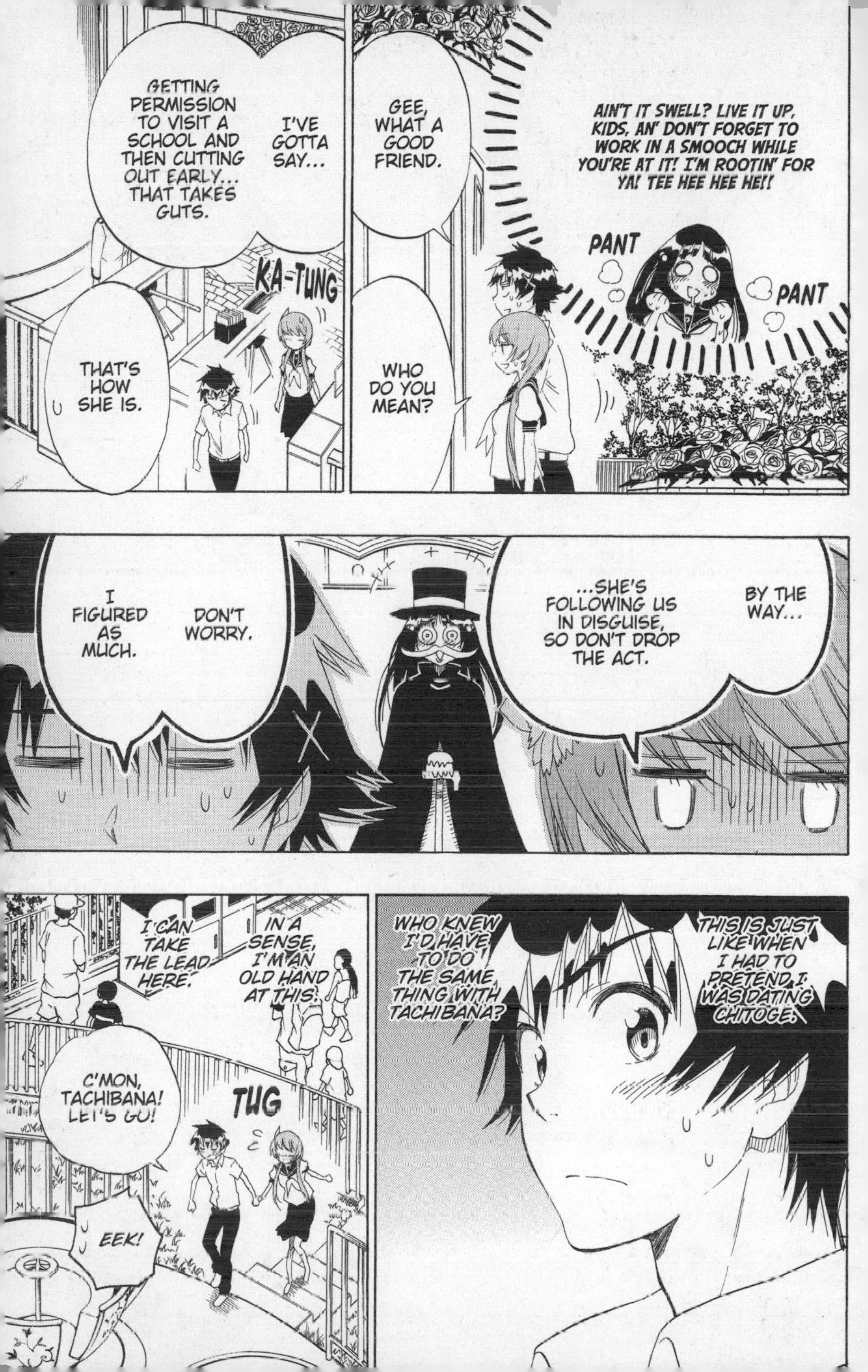

AIN'T IT SWELL? LIVE IT UP, KIDS, AN' DON'T FORGET TO WORK IN A SMOOCH WHILE YOU'RE AT IT! I'M ROOTIN' FOR YA! TEE HEE HEE HE!!
PANT
PANT
GEE, WHAT A GOOD FRIEND.
WHO DO YOU MEAN?
I'VE GOTTA SAY...
GETTING PERMISSION TO VISIT A SCHOOL AND THEN CUTTING OUT EARLY... THAT TAKES GUTS.
KA-TUNG
THAT'S HOW SHE IS.
BY THE WAY...
...SHE'S FOLLOWING US IN DISGUISE, SO DON'T DROP THE ACT.
DON'T WORRY.
I FIGURED AS MUCH.
THIS IS JUST LIKE WHEN I HAD TO PRETEND I WAS DATING CHITOGE.
WHO KNEW I'D HAVE TO DO THE SAME THING WITH TACHIBANA?
IN A SENSE, I'M AN OLD HAND AT THIS.
I CAN TAKE THE LEAD HERE.
TUG
C'MON, TACHIBANA! LET'S GO!
EEK!

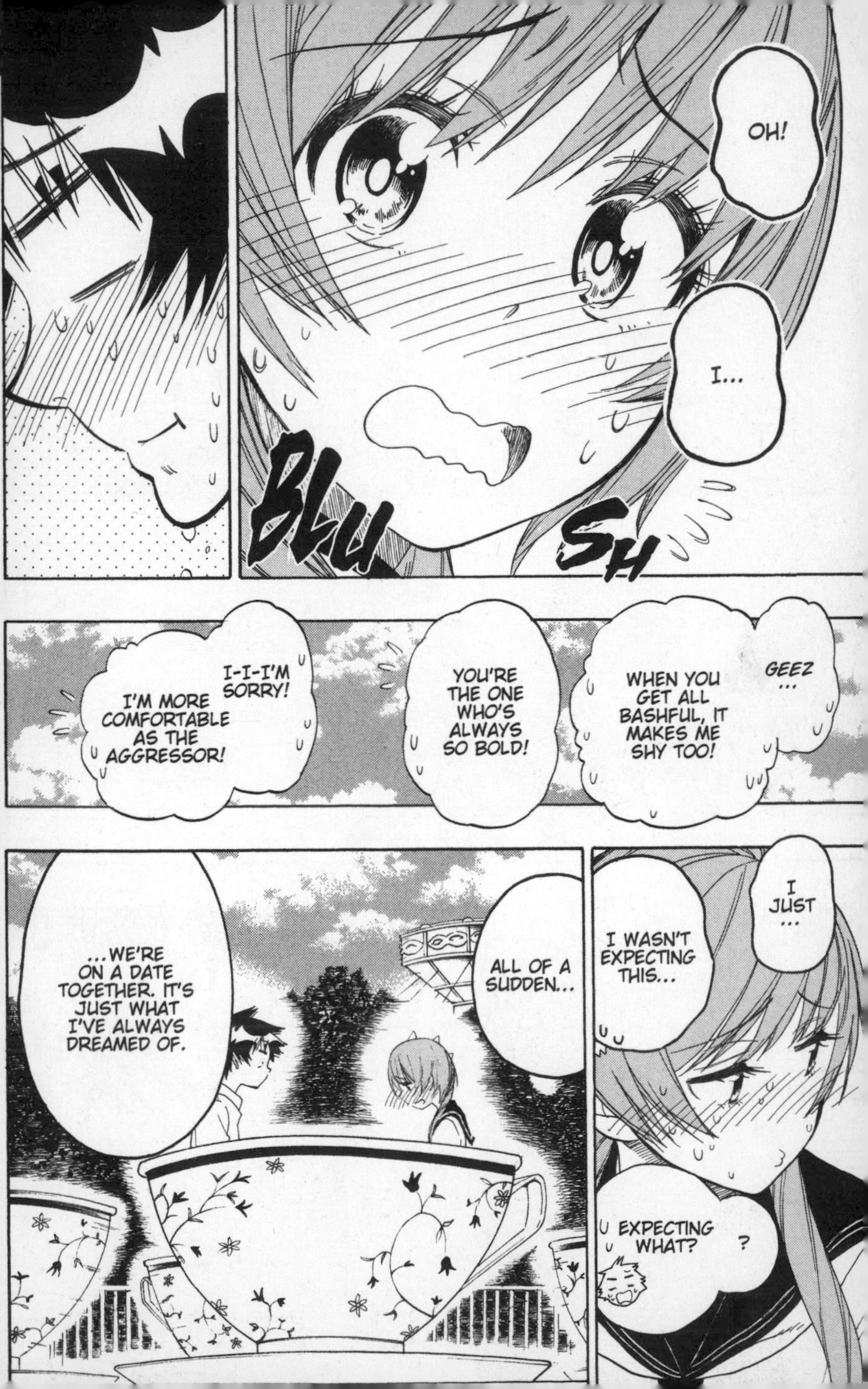
OH!
I...
BLUSH
GEEZ...
WHEN YOU GET ALL BASHFUL, IT MAKES ME SHY TOO!
YOU'RE THE ONE WHO'S ALWAYS SO BOLD!
I-I-I'M SORRY!
I'M MORE COMFORTABLE AS THE AGGRESSOR!
I JUST...
I WASN'T EXPECTING THIS...
EXPECTING WHAT?
?
ALL OF A SUDDEN...
...WE'RE ON A DATE TOGETHER. IT'S JUST WHAT I'VE ALWAYS DREAMED OF.

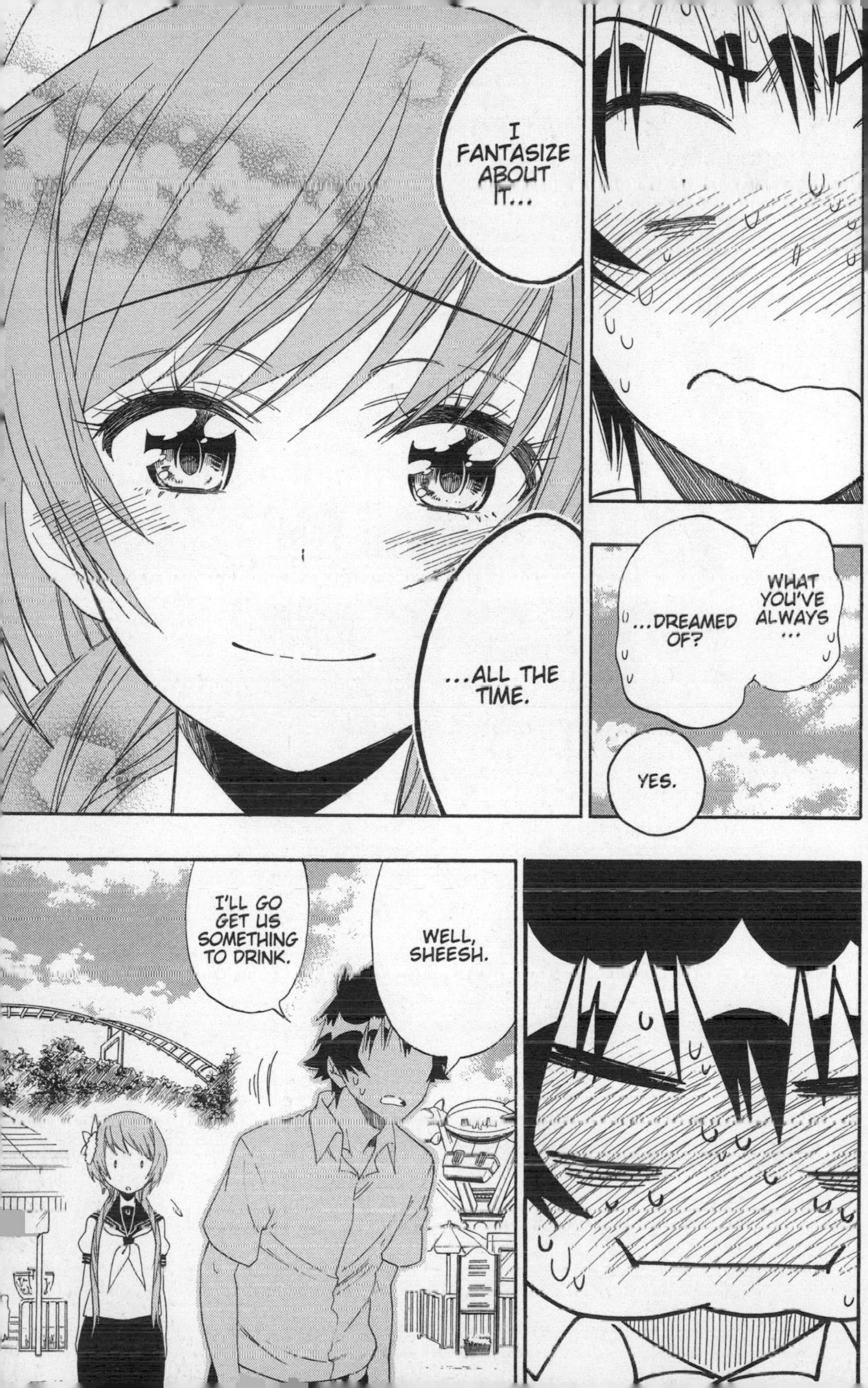
WHAT YOU'VE ALWAYS...
...DREAMED OF?
YES.
I FANTASIZE ABOUT IT...
...ALL THE TIME.
WELL, SHEESH.
I'LL GO GET US SOMETHING TO DRINK.

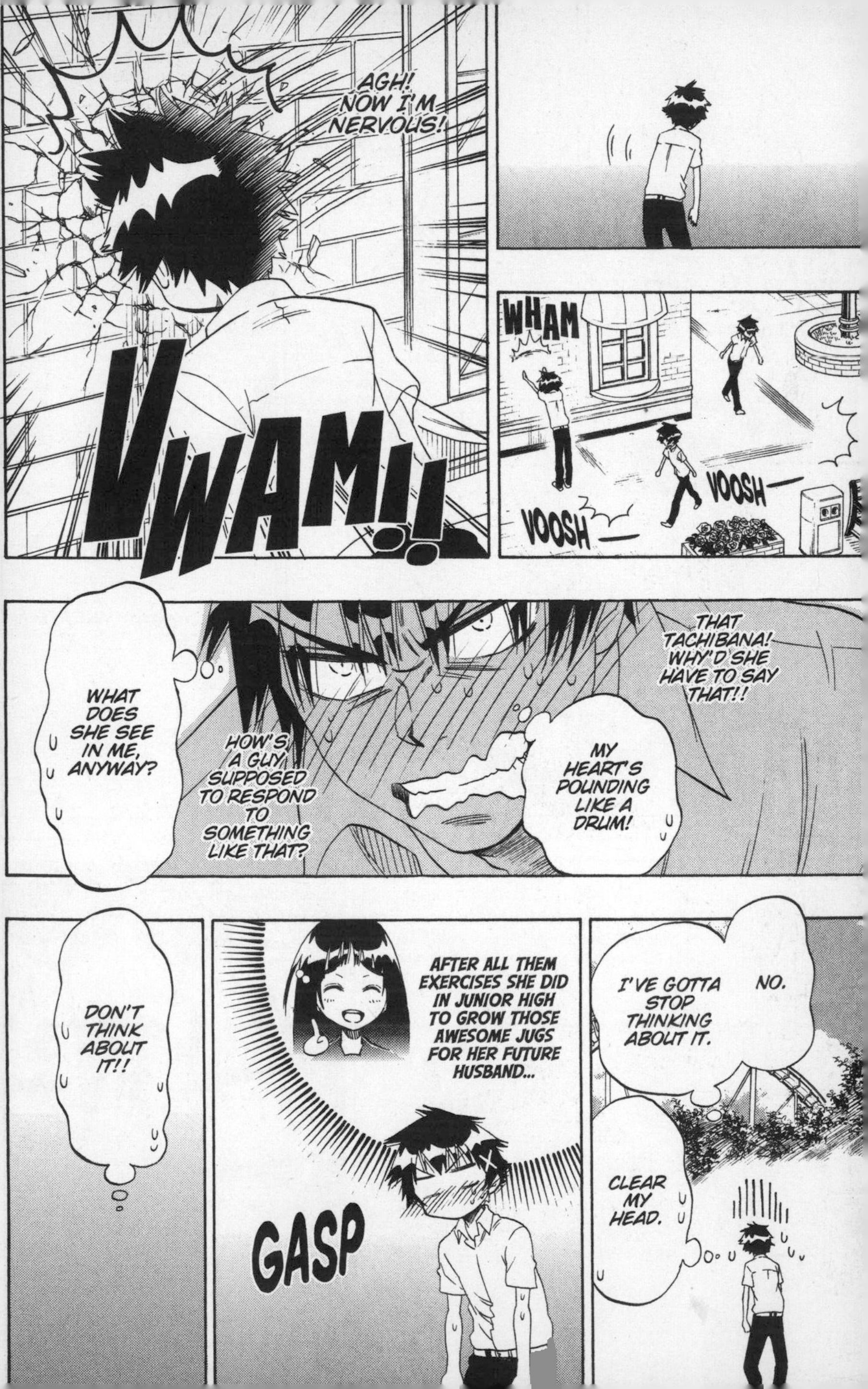
WHAM
VOOSH
VOOSH
AGH! NOW I'M NERVOUS!
VWAM!!
THAT TACHIBANA! WHY'D SHE HAVE TO SAY THAT!!
MY HEART'S POUNDING LIKE A DRUM!
HOW'S A GUY SUPPOSED TO RESPOND TO SOMETHING LIKE THAT?
WHAT DOES SHE SEE IN ME, ANYWAY?
NO.
I'VE GOTTA STOP THINKING ABOUT IT.
CLEAR MY HEAD.
AFTER ALL THEM EXERCISES SHE DID IN JUNIOR HIGH TO GROW THOSE AWESOME JUGS FOR HER FUTURE HUSBAND...
GASP
DON'T THINK ABOUT IT!!

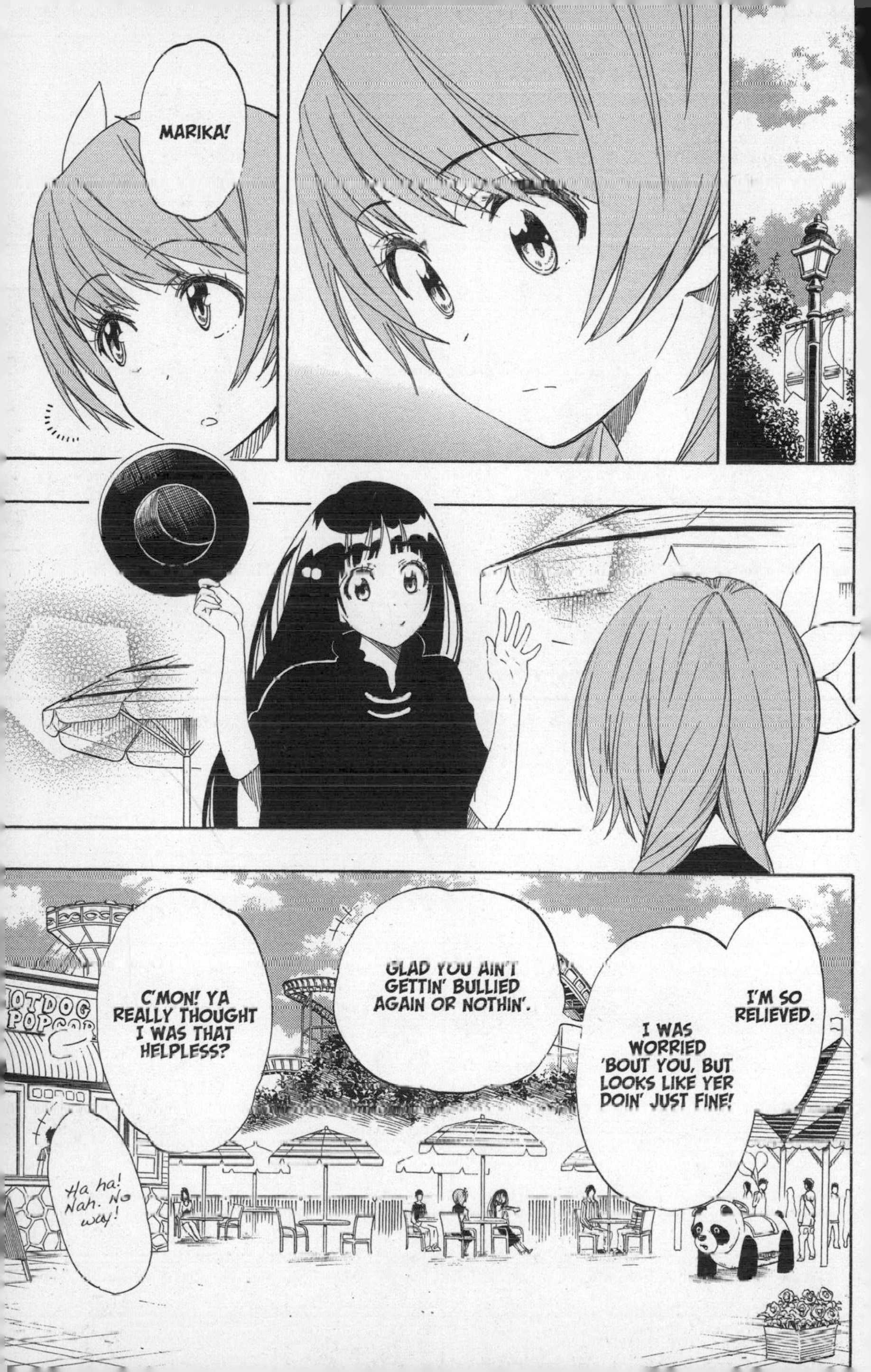
MARIKA!
I'M SO RELIEVED.
I WAS WORRIED 'BOUT YOU, BUT LOOKS LIKE YER DOIN' JUST FINE!
GLAD YOU AIN'T GETTIN' BULLIED AGAIN OR NOTHIN'.
C'MON! YA REALLY THOUGHT I WAS THAT HELPLESS?
Ha ha! Nah. No way!

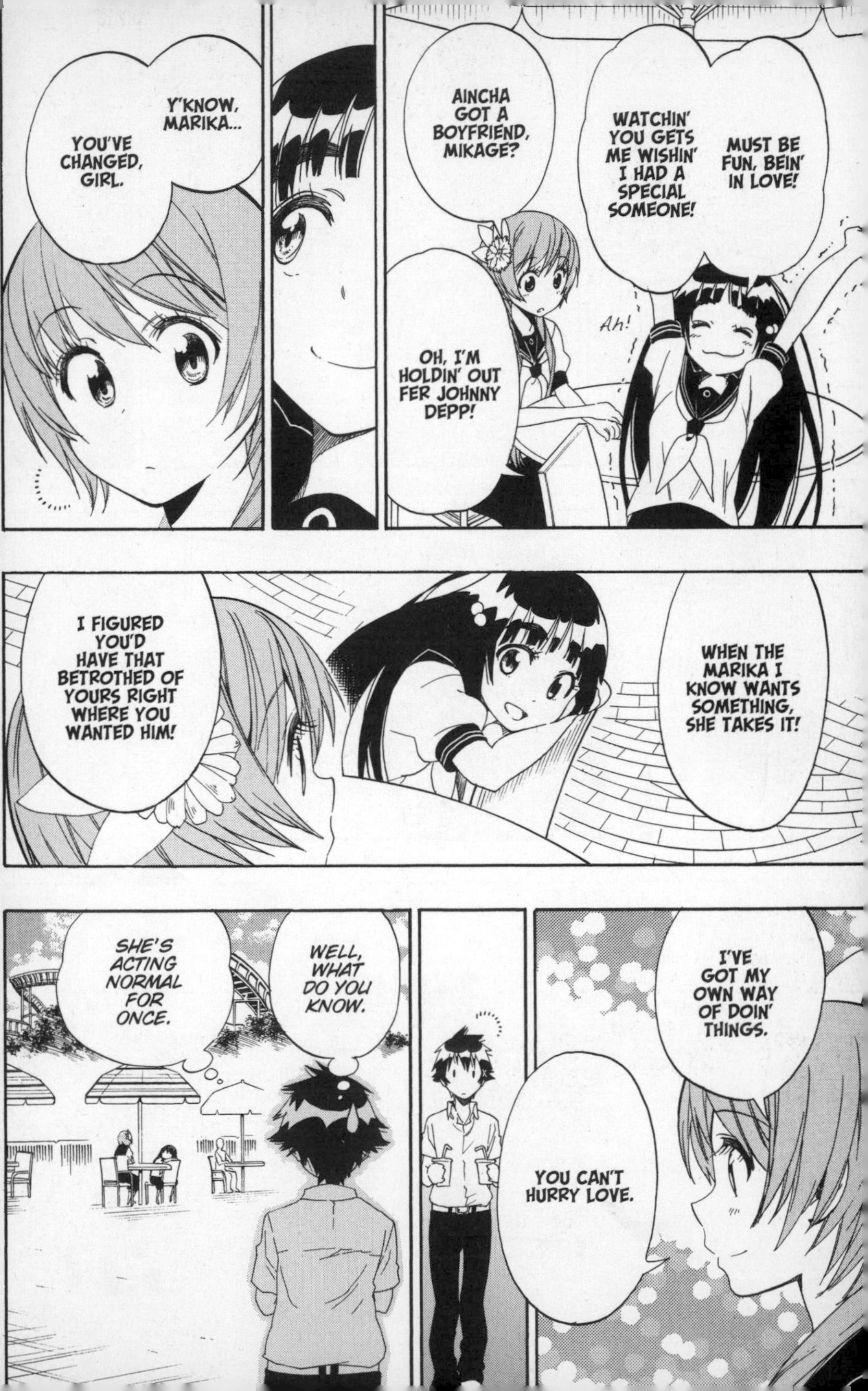
MUST BE FUN, BEIN' IN LOVE!
WATCHIN' YOU GETS ME WISHIN' I HAD A SPECIAL SOMEONE!
Ah!
AINCHA GOT A BOYFRIEND, MIKAGE?
OH, I'M HOLDIN' OUT FER JOHNNY DEPP!
Y'KNOW, MARIKA...
YOU'VE CHANGED, GIRL.
WHEN THE MARIKA I KNOW WANTS SOMETHING, SHE TAKES IT!
I FIGURED YOU'D HAVE THAT BETROTHED OF YOURS RIGHT WHERE YOU WANTED HIM!
I'VE GOT MY OWN WAY OF DOIN' THINGS.
YOU CAN'T HURRY LOVE.
WELL, WHAT DO YOU KNOW.
SHE'S ACTING NORMAL FOR ONCE.

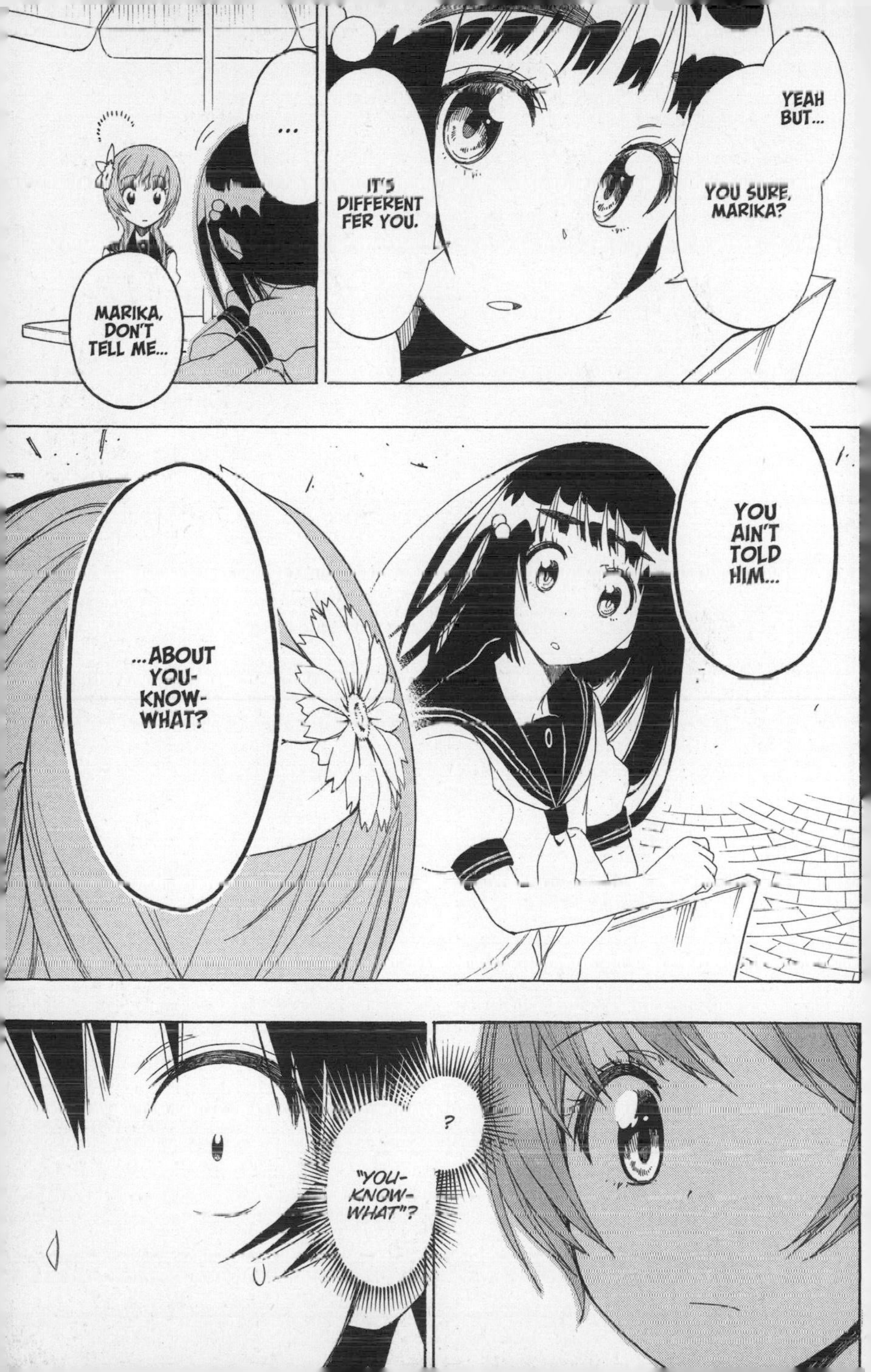
YEAH BUT...
YOU SURE, MARIKA?
IT'S DIFFERENT FER YOU.
...
MARIKA, DON'T TELL ME...
YOU AIN'T TOLD HIM...
...ABOUT YOU-KNOW-WHAT?
?
"YOU-KNOW-WHAT"?

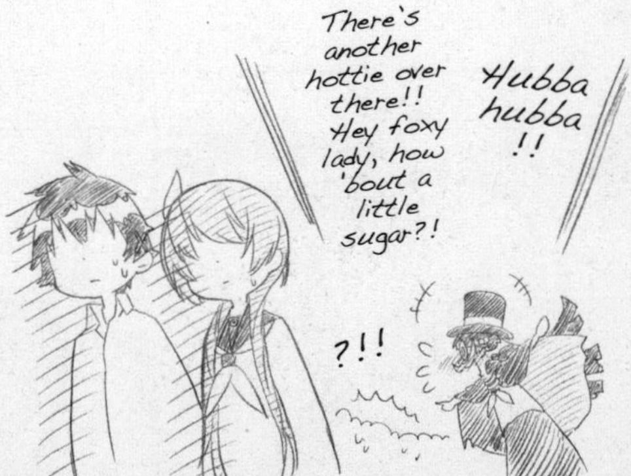
Hubba hubba!!
There's another hottie over there!! Hey foxy lady, how 'bout a little sugar?!
?!!

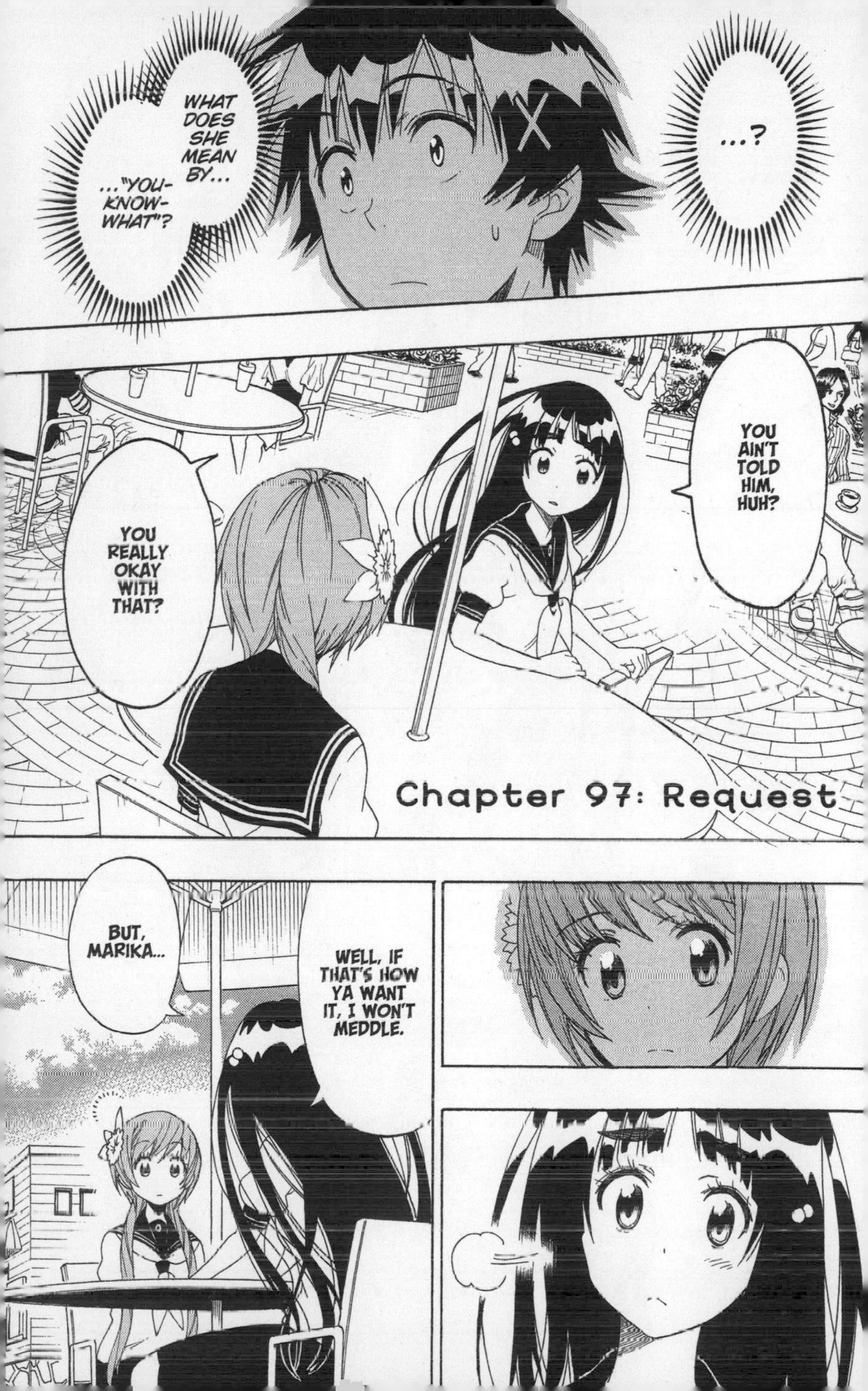
...?
WHAT DOES SHE MEAN BY... ..."YOU-KNOW-WHAT"?
YOU AIN'T TOLD HIM, HUH?
YOU REALLY OKAY WITH THAT?
Chapter 97: Request
WELL, IF THAT'S HOW YA WANT IT, I WON'T MEDDLE.
BUT, MARIKA...

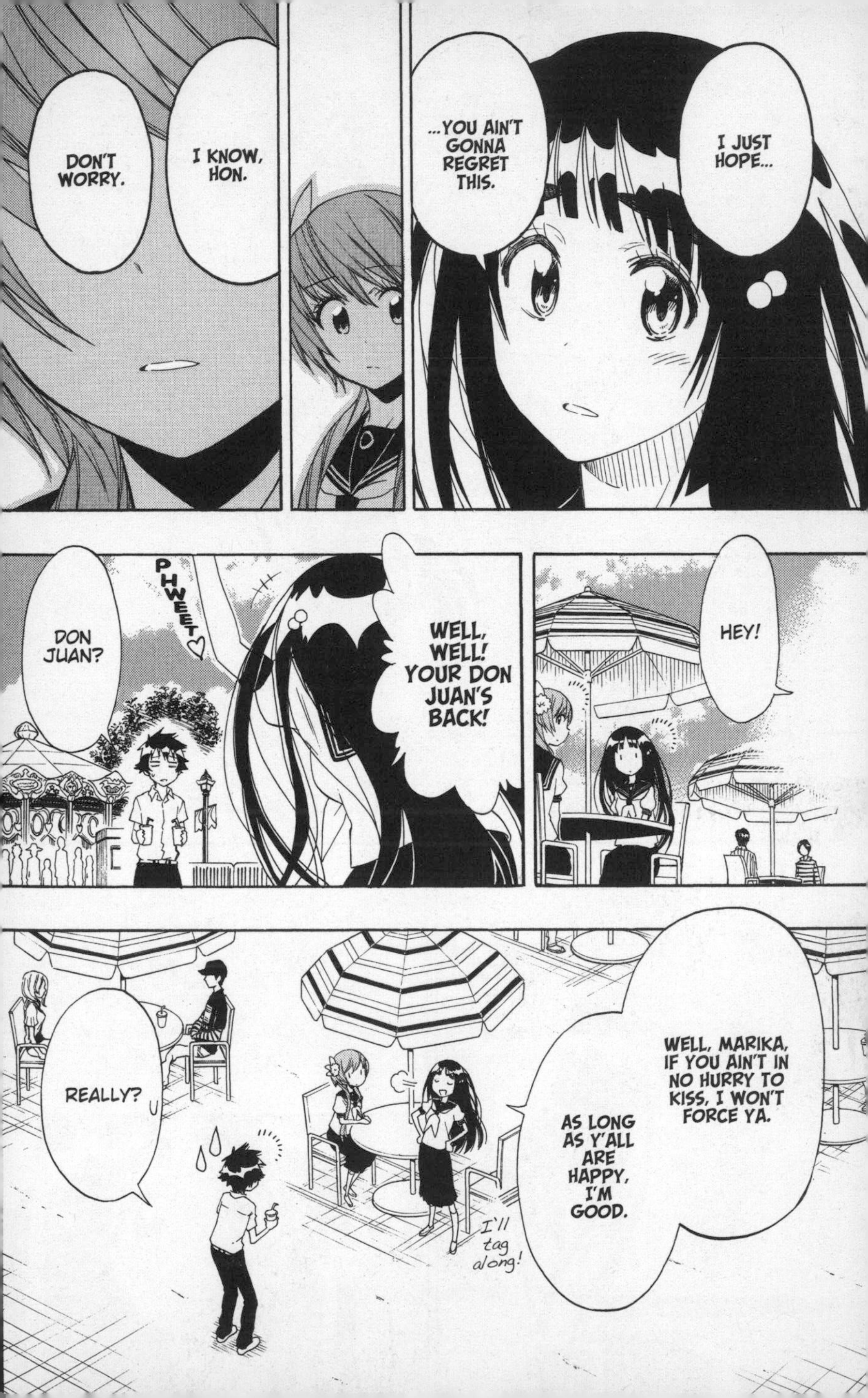
I JUST HOPE...
...YOU AIN'T GONNA REGRET THIS.
I KNOW, HON.
DON'T WORRY.
HEY!
WELL, WELL! YOUR DON JUAN'S BACK!
PHWEET♡
DON JUAN?
WELL, MARIKA, IF YOU AIN'T IN NO HURRY TO KISS, I WON'T FORCE YA.
AS LONG AS Y'ALL ARE HAPPY, I'M GOOD.
I'll tag along!
REALLY?

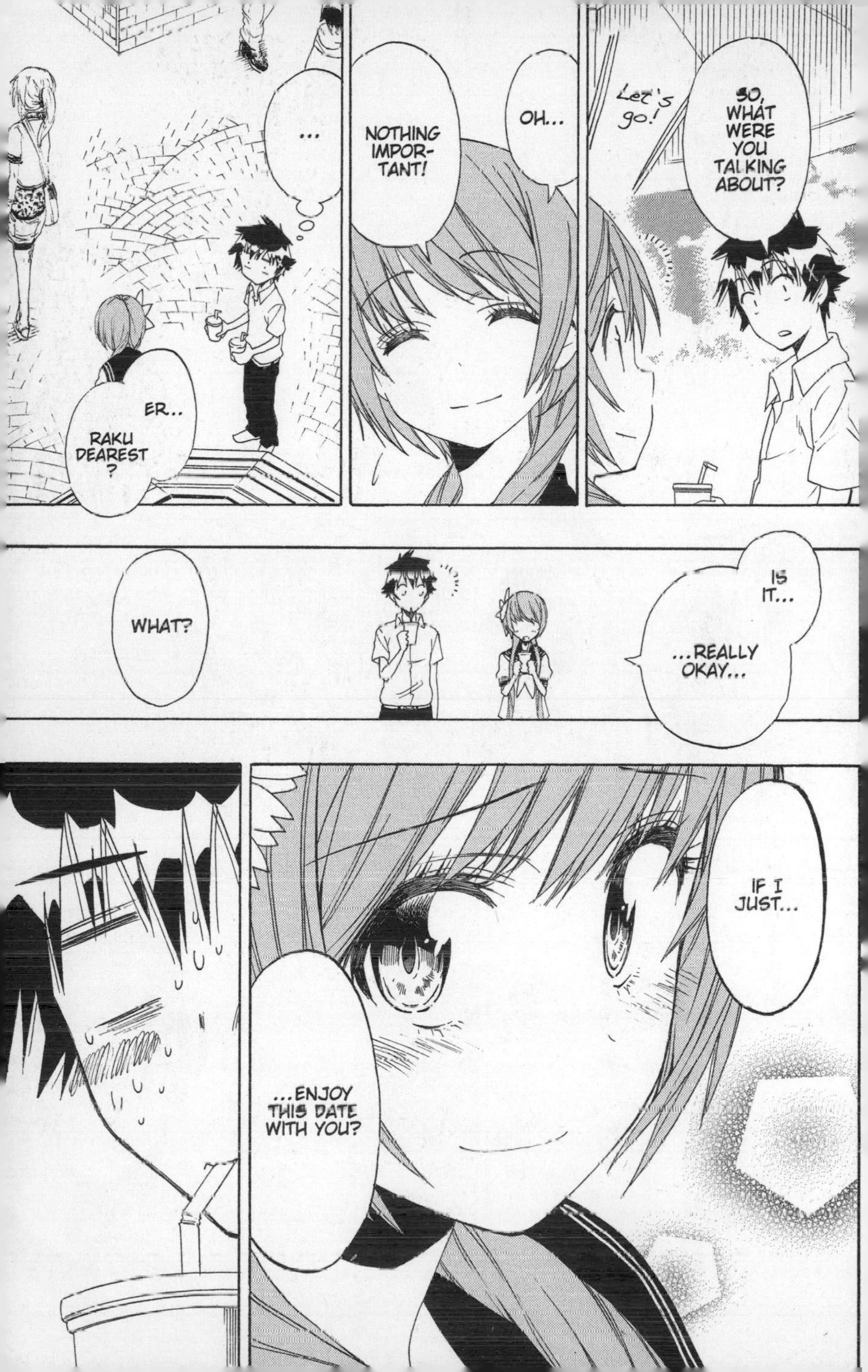
SO, WHAT WERE YOU TALKING ABOUT?
Let's go!
OH...
NOTHING IMPOR-TANT!
...
ER...
RAKU DEAREST?
IS IT...
...REALLY OKAY...
WHAT?
IF I JUST...
...ENJOY THIS DATE WITH YOU?

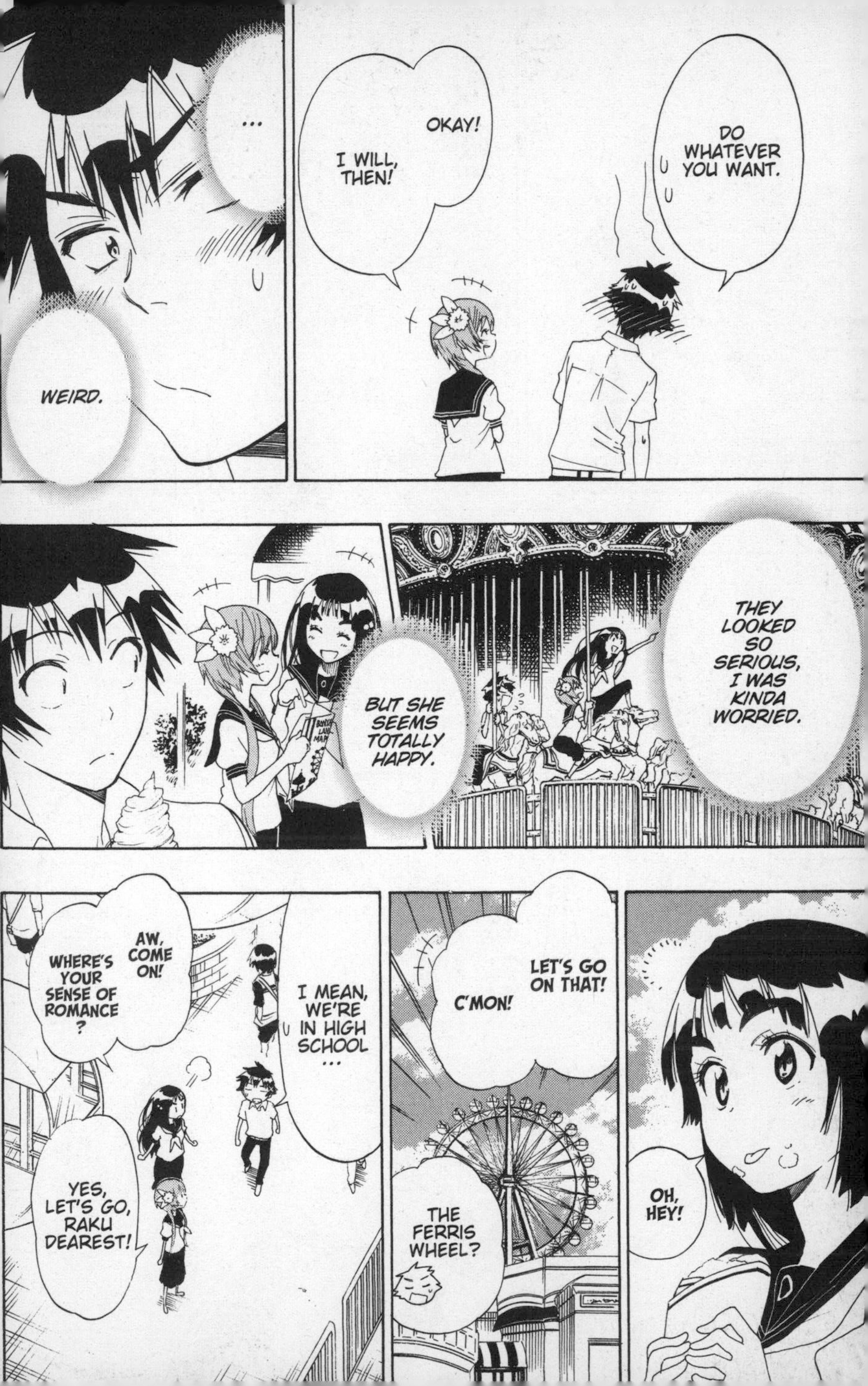
DO WHATEVER YOU WANT.
OKAY!
I WILL, THEN!
...
WEIRD.
THEY LOOKED SO SERIOUS, I WAS KINDA WORRIED.
BUT SHE SEEMS TOTALLY HAPPY.
OH, HEY!
LET'S GO ON THAT!
C'MON!
THE FERRIS WHEEL?
I MEAN, WE'RE IN HIGH SCHOOL...
AW, COME ON!
WHERE'S YOUR SENSE OF ROMANCE?
YES, LET'S GO, RAKU DEAREST!

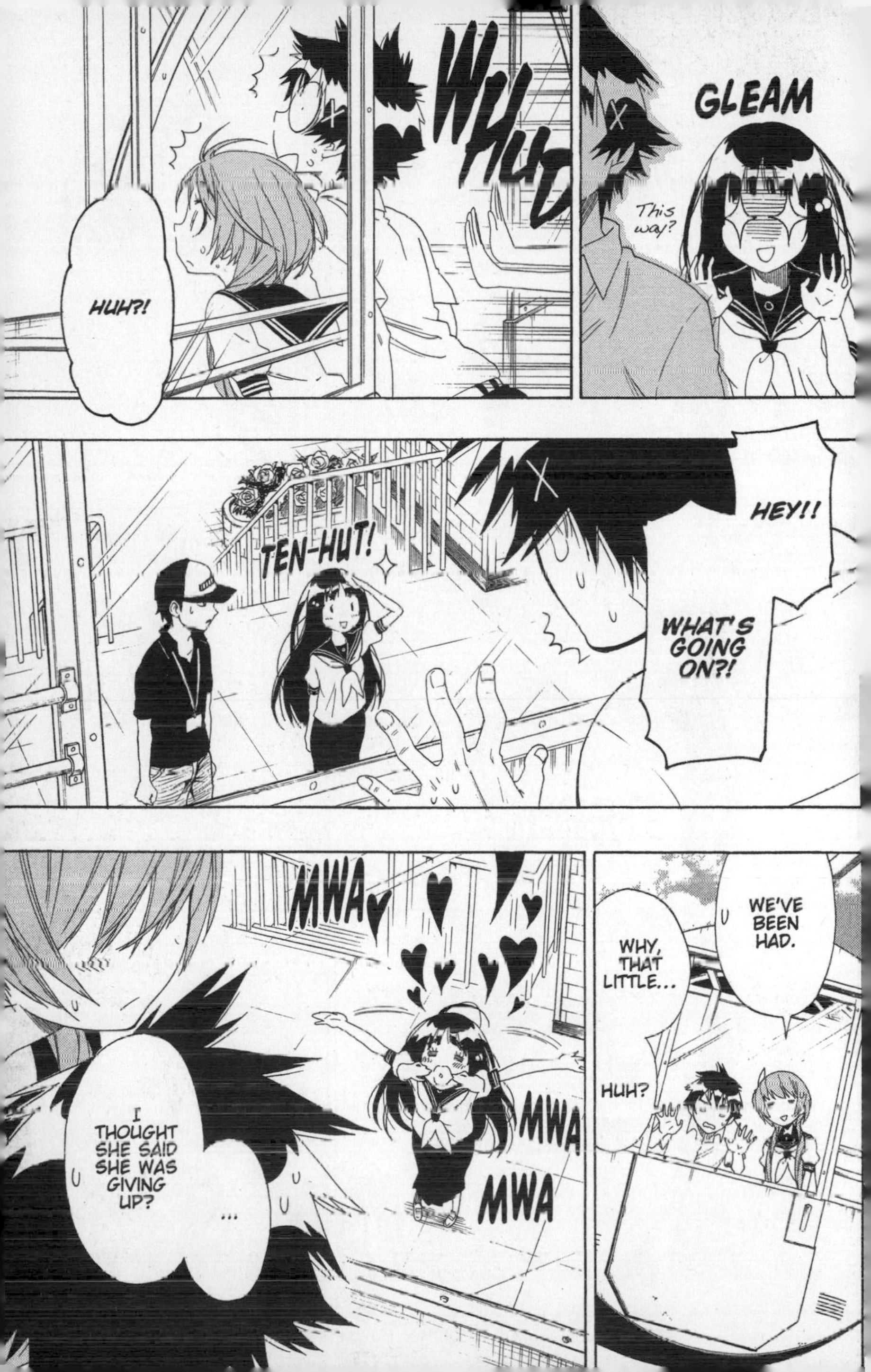
GLEAM
This way?
WHUT
HUH?!
HEY!!
WHAT'S GOING ON?!
TEN-HUT!
WE'VE BEEN HAD.
WHY, THAT LITTLE...
HUH?
MWA
MWA
MWA
I THOUGHT SHE SAID SHE WAS GIVING UP?
...

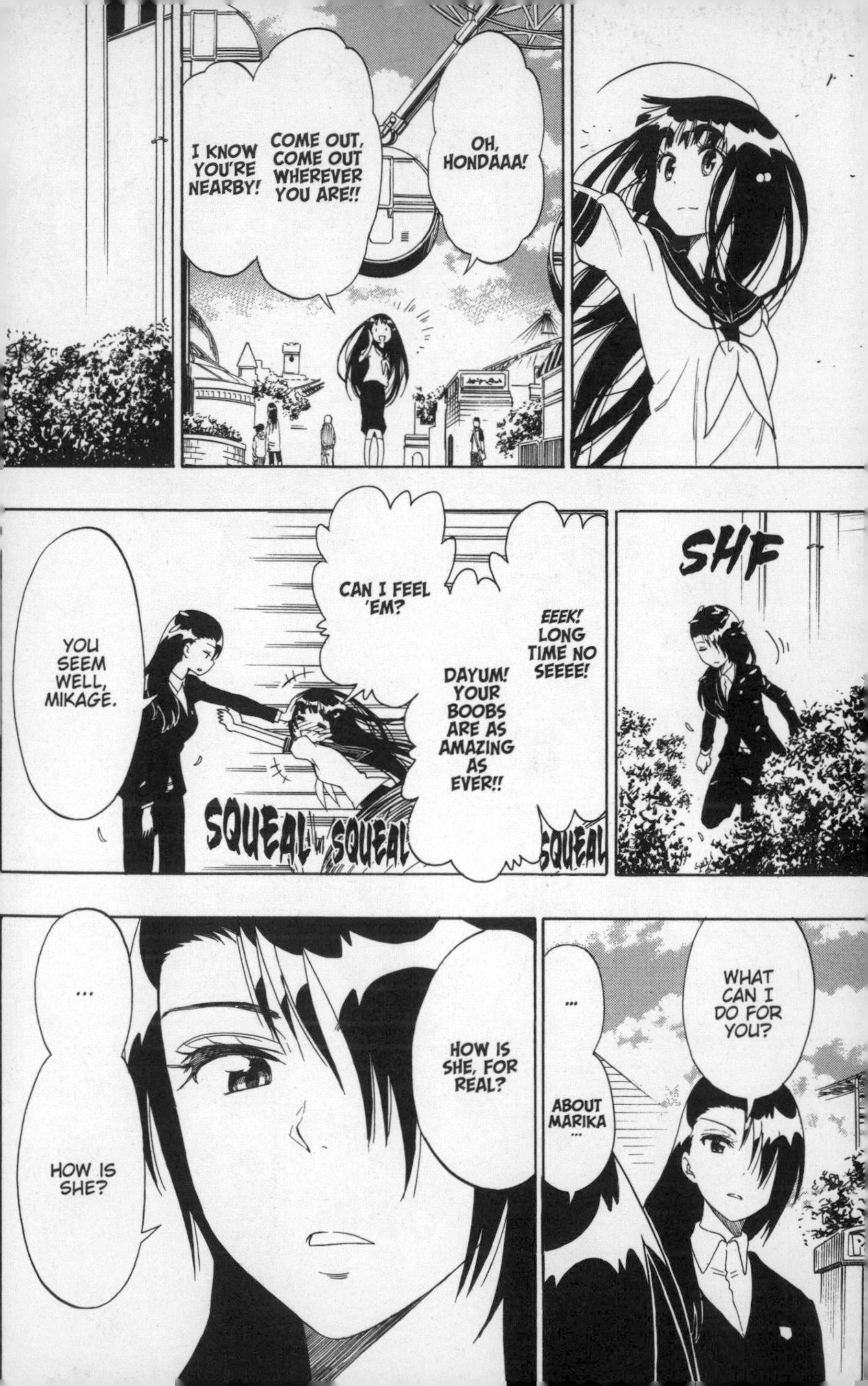
OH, HONDAAA!
COME OUT, COME OUT WHEREVER YOU ARE!!
I KNOW YOU'RE NEARBY!
SHF
EEEK! LONG TIME NO SEEEE!
DAYUM! YOUR BOOBS ARE AS AMAZING AS EVER!!
CAN I FEEL 'EM?
SQUEAL
SQUEAL SQUEAL
YOU SEEM WELL, MIKAGE.
WHAT CAN I DO FOR YOU?
...
ABOUT MARIKA ...
HOW IS SHE, FOR REAL?
...
HOW IS SHE?

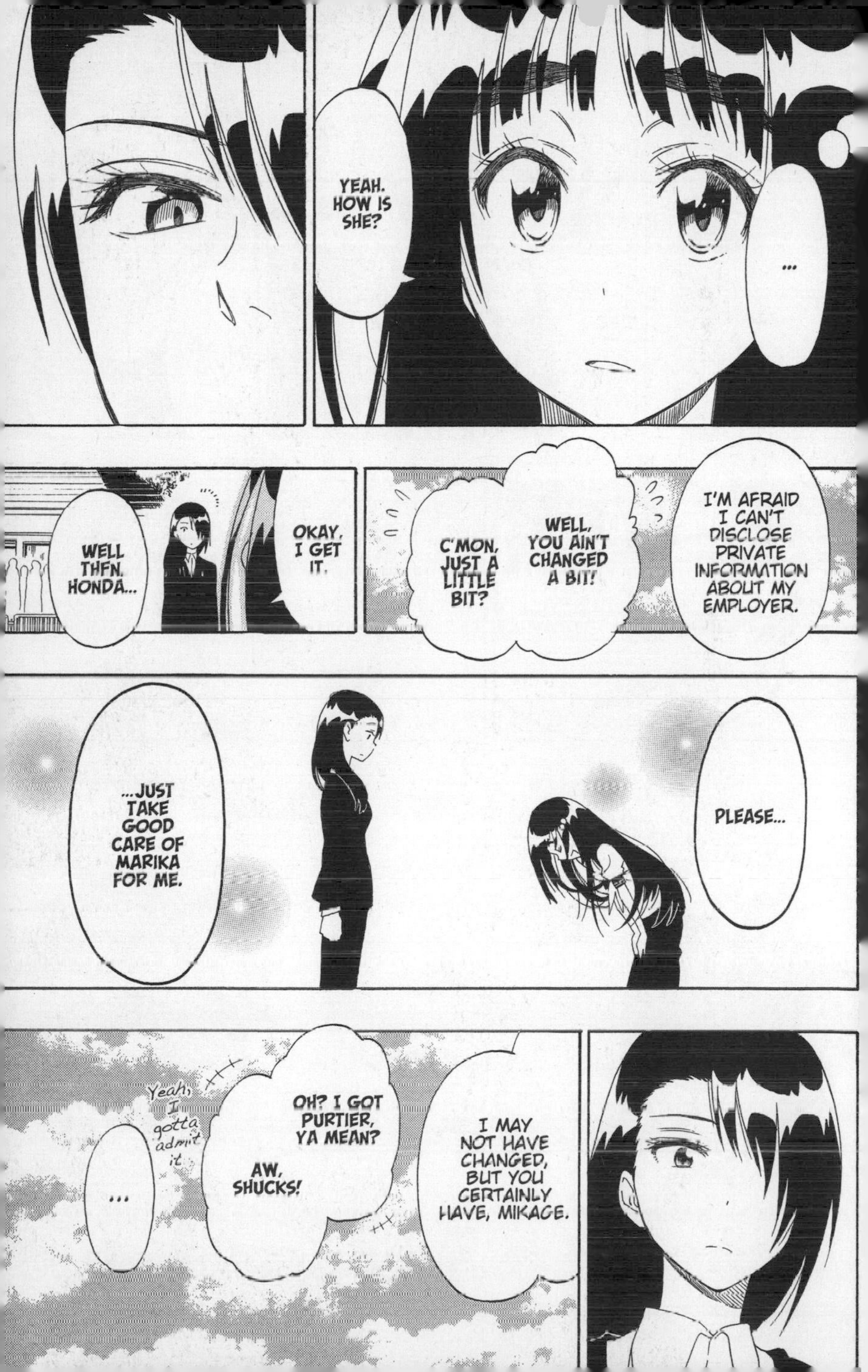
...
YEAH. HOW IS SHE?
I'M AFRAID I CAN'T DISCLOSE PRIVATE INFORMATION ABOUT MY EMPLOYER.
WELL, YOU AIN'T CHANGED A BIT!
C'MON, JUST A LITTLE BIT?
OKAY, I GET IT.
WELL THEN, HONDA...
PLEASE...
...JUST TAKE GOOD CARE OF MARIKA FOR ME.
I MAY NOT HAVE CHANGED, BUT YOU CERTAINLY HAVE, MIKAGE.
OH? I GOT PURTIER, YA MEAN?
AW, SHUCKS!
Yeah, I gotta admit it
...

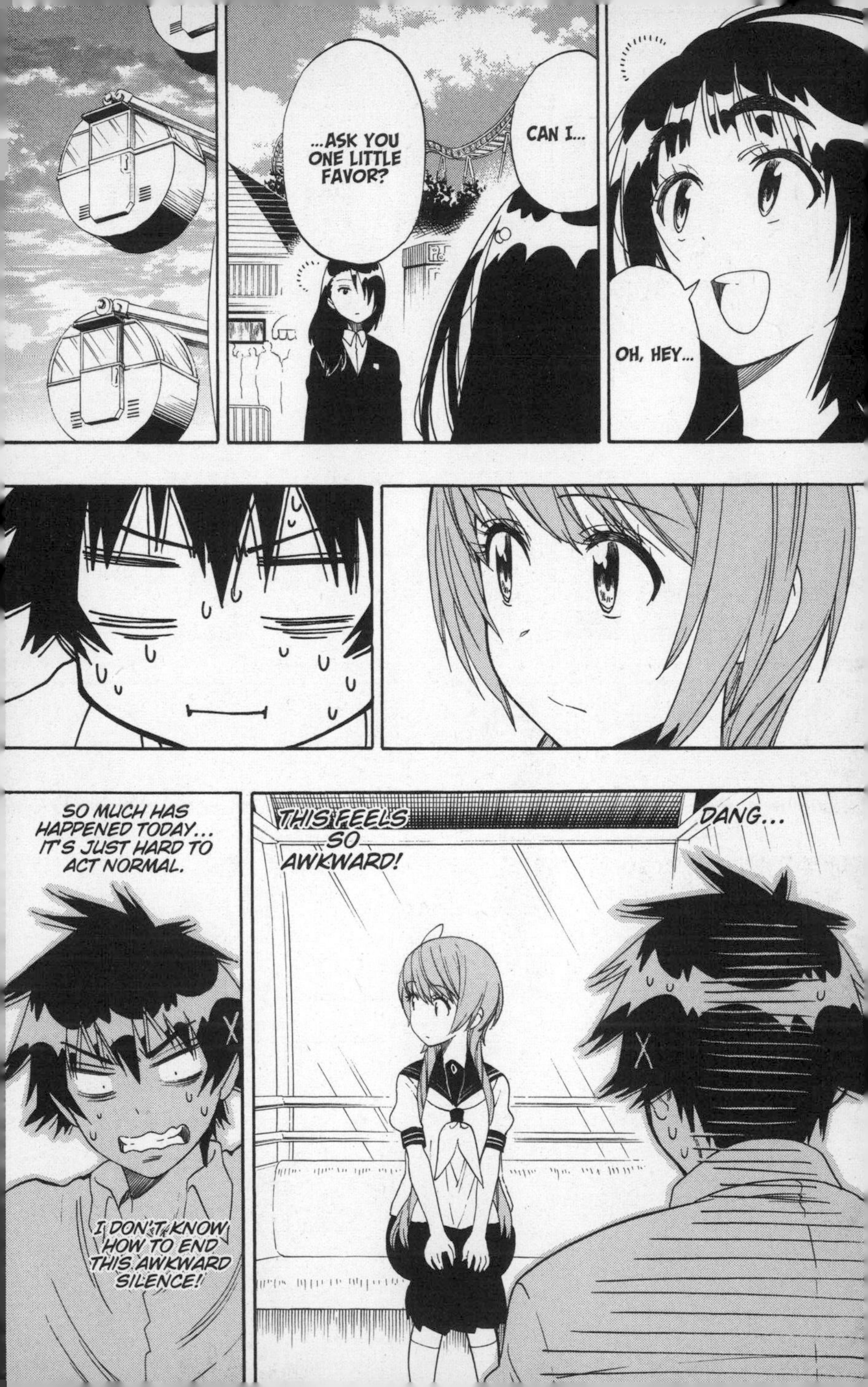
OH, HEY...
CAN I...
...ASK YOU ONE LITTLE FAVOR?
DANG...
THIS FEELS SO AWKWARD!
SO MUCH HAS HAPPENED TODAY... IT'S JUST HARD TO ACT NORMAL.
I DON'T KNOW HOW TO END THIS AWKWARD SILENCE!

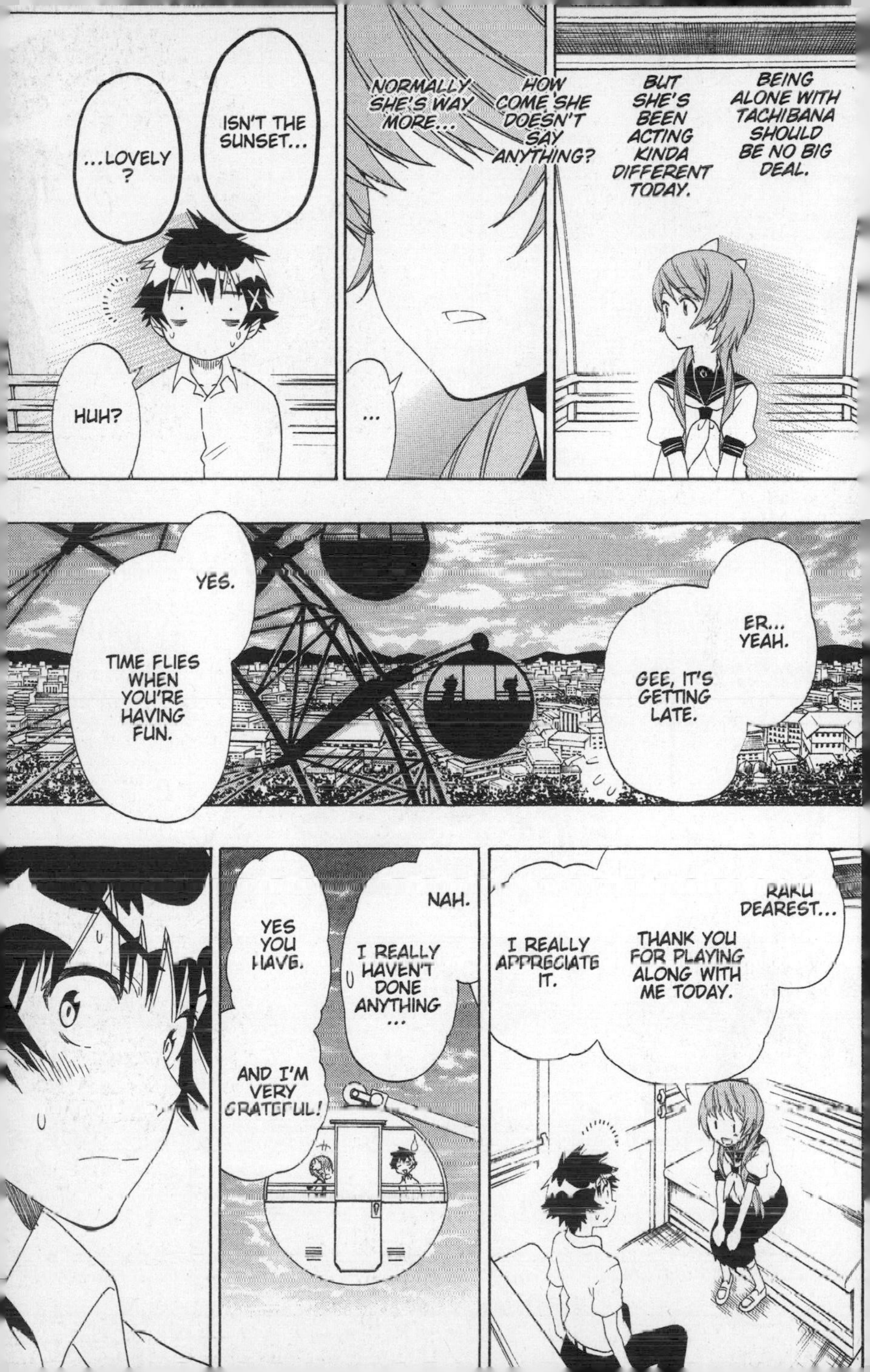
BEING ALONE WITH TACHIBANA SHOULD BE NO BIG DEAL.
BUT SHE'S BEEN ACTING KINDA DIFFERENT TODAY.
HOW COME SHE DOESN'T SAY ANYTHING?
NORMALLY SHE'S WAY MORE...
...
ISN'T THE SUNSET...
...LOVELY?
HUH?
ER... YEAH.
GEE, IT'S GETTING LATE.
YES.
TIME FLIES WHEN YOU'RE HAVING FUN.
RAKU DEAREST...
THANK YOU FOR PLAYING ALONG WITH ME TODAY.
I REALLY APPRECIATE IT.
NAH.
I REALLY HAVEN'T DONE ANYTHING...
YES YOU HAVE.
AND I'M VERY GRATEFUL!

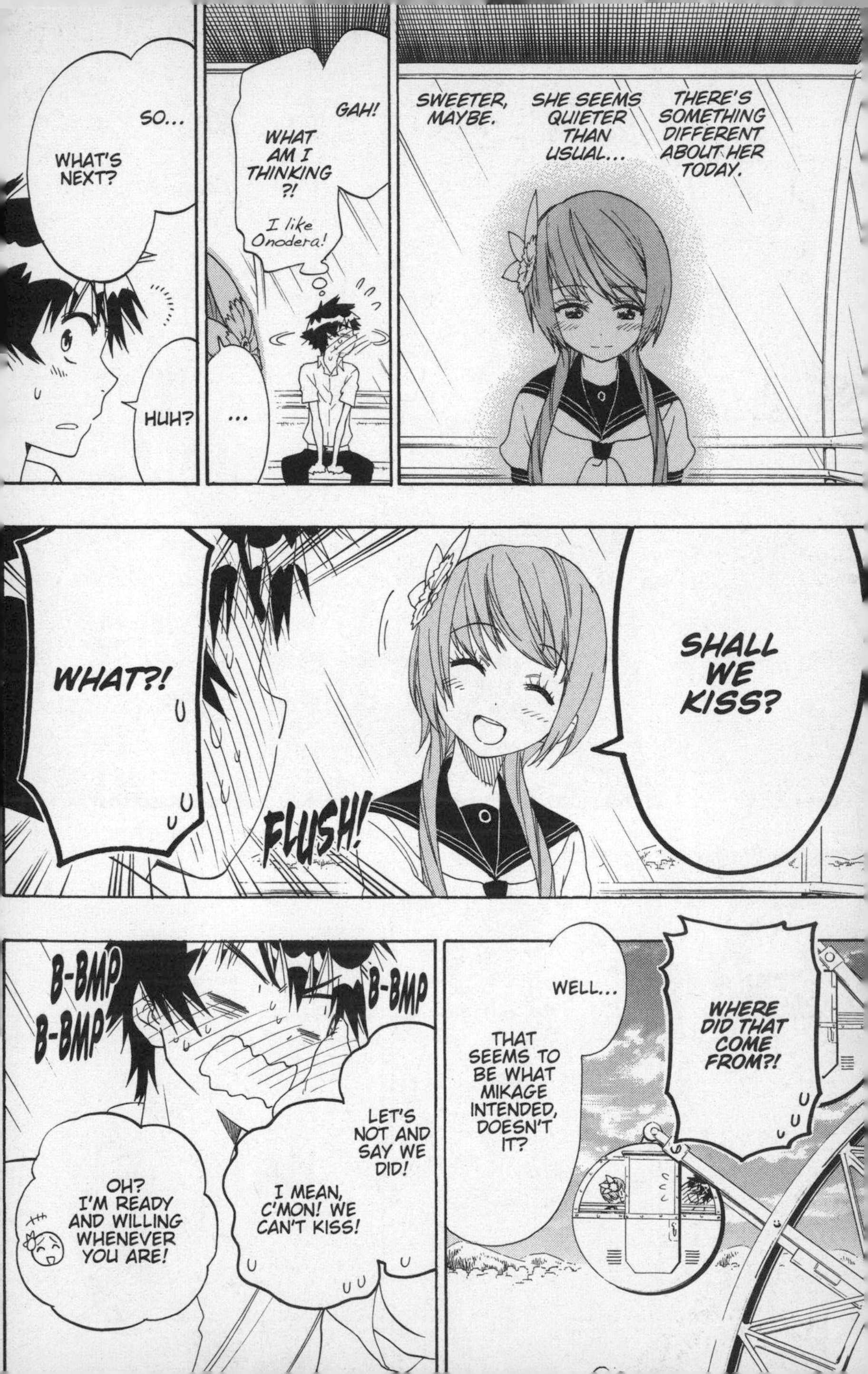
THERE'S SOMETHING DIFFERENT ABOUT HER TODAY.
SHE SEEMS QUIETER THAN USUAL...
SWEETER, MAYBE.
GAH!
WHAT AM I THINKING?!
I like Onodera!
...
SO...
WHAT'S NEXT?
HUH?
SHALL WE KISS?
FLUSH!
WHAT?!
WHERE DID THAT COME FROM?!
WELL...
THAT SEEMS TO BE WHAT MIKAGE INTENDED, DOESN'T IT?
B-BMP
B-BMP
B-BMP
LET'S NOT AND SAY WE DID!
I MEAN, C'MON! WE CAN'T KISS!
OH? I'M READY AND WILLING WHENEVER YOU ARE!

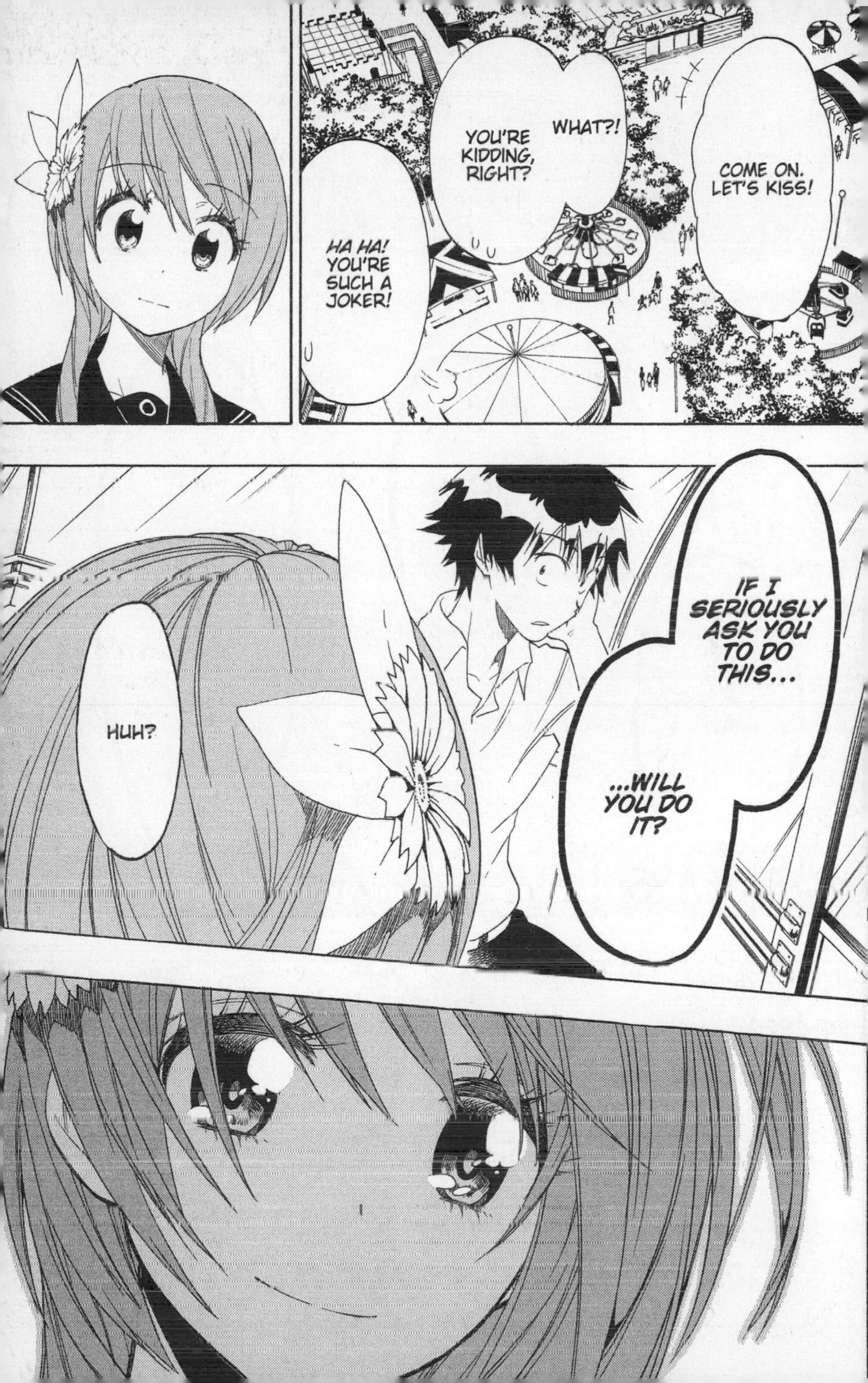
COME ON. LET'S KISS!
WHAT?!
YOU'RE KIDDING, RIGHT?
HA HA! YOU'RE SUCH A JOKER!
IF I SERIOUSLY ASK YOU TO DO THIS...
...WILL YOU DO IT?
HUH?

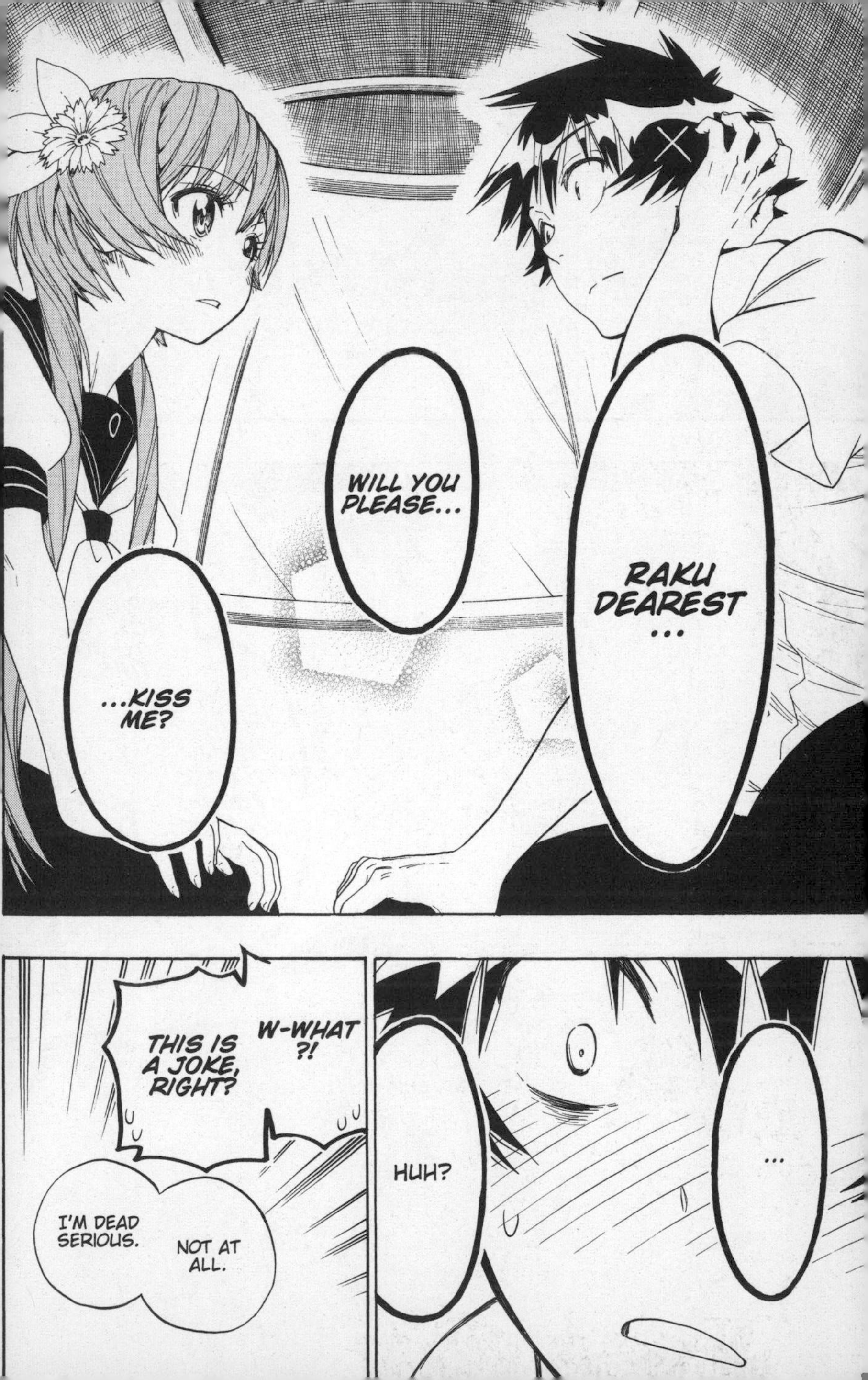
RAKU DEAREST ...
WILL YOU PLEASE...
...KISS ME?
...
HUH?
W-WHAT ?!
THIS IS A JOKE, RIGHT?
NOT AT ALL.
I'M DEAD SERIOUS.

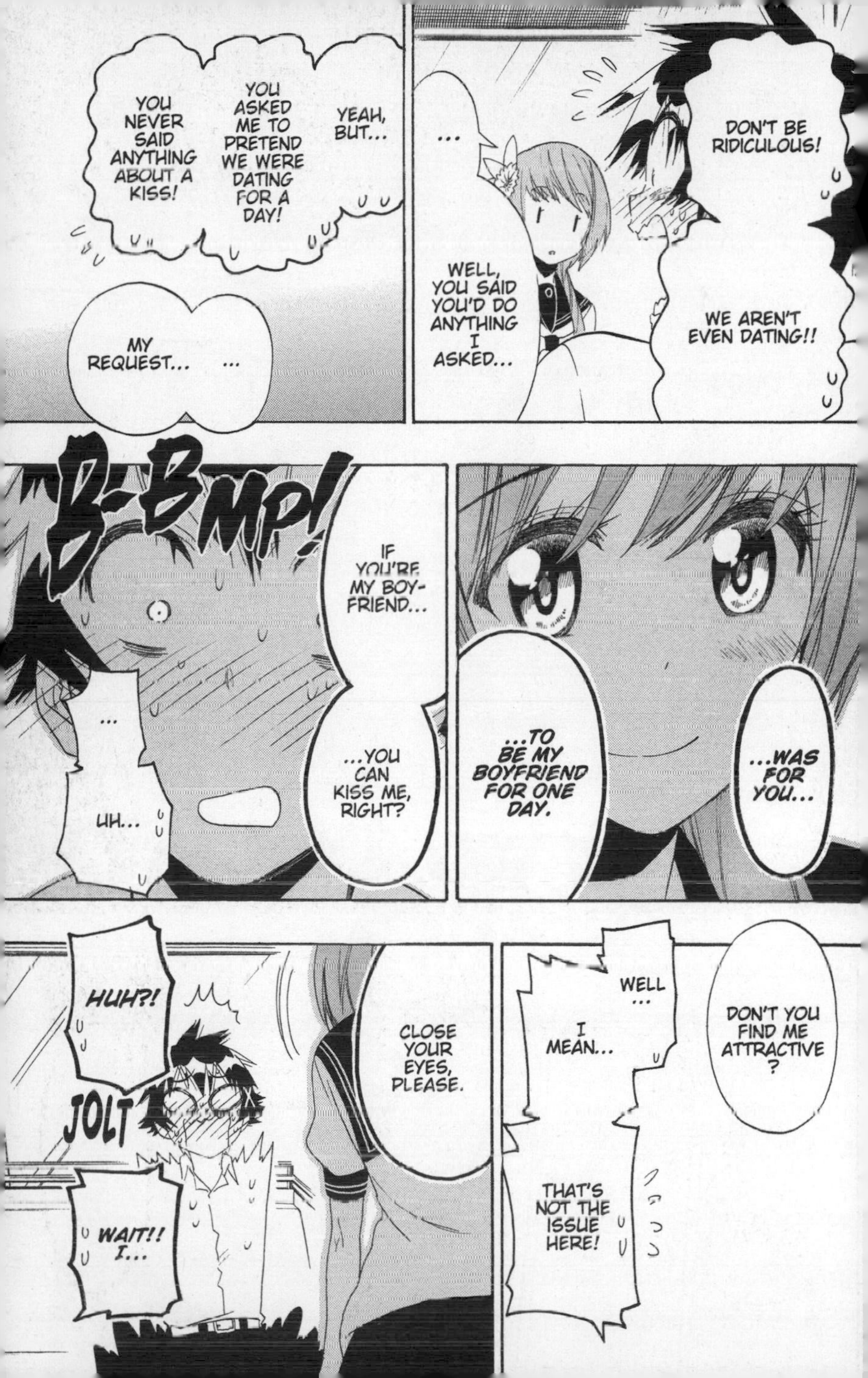
DON'T BE RIDICULOUS!
WE AREN'T EVEN DATING!!
...
WELL, YOU SAID YOU'D DO ANYTHING I ASKED...
YEAH, BUT...
YOU ASKED ME TO PRETEND WE WERE DATING FOR A DAY!
YOU NEVER SAID ANYTHING ABOUT A KISS!
MY REQUEST... ...
...WAS FOR YOU...
...TO BE MY BOYFRIEND FOR ONE DAY.
B-BMP!
IF YOU'RE MY BOY-FRIEND...
...YOU CAN KISS ME, RIGHT?
...
UH...
DON'T YOU FIND ME ATTRACTIVE?
WELL...
I MEAN...
THAT'S NOT THE ISSUE HERE!
CLOSE YOUR EYES, PLEASE.
HUH?!
JOLT
WAIT!! I...

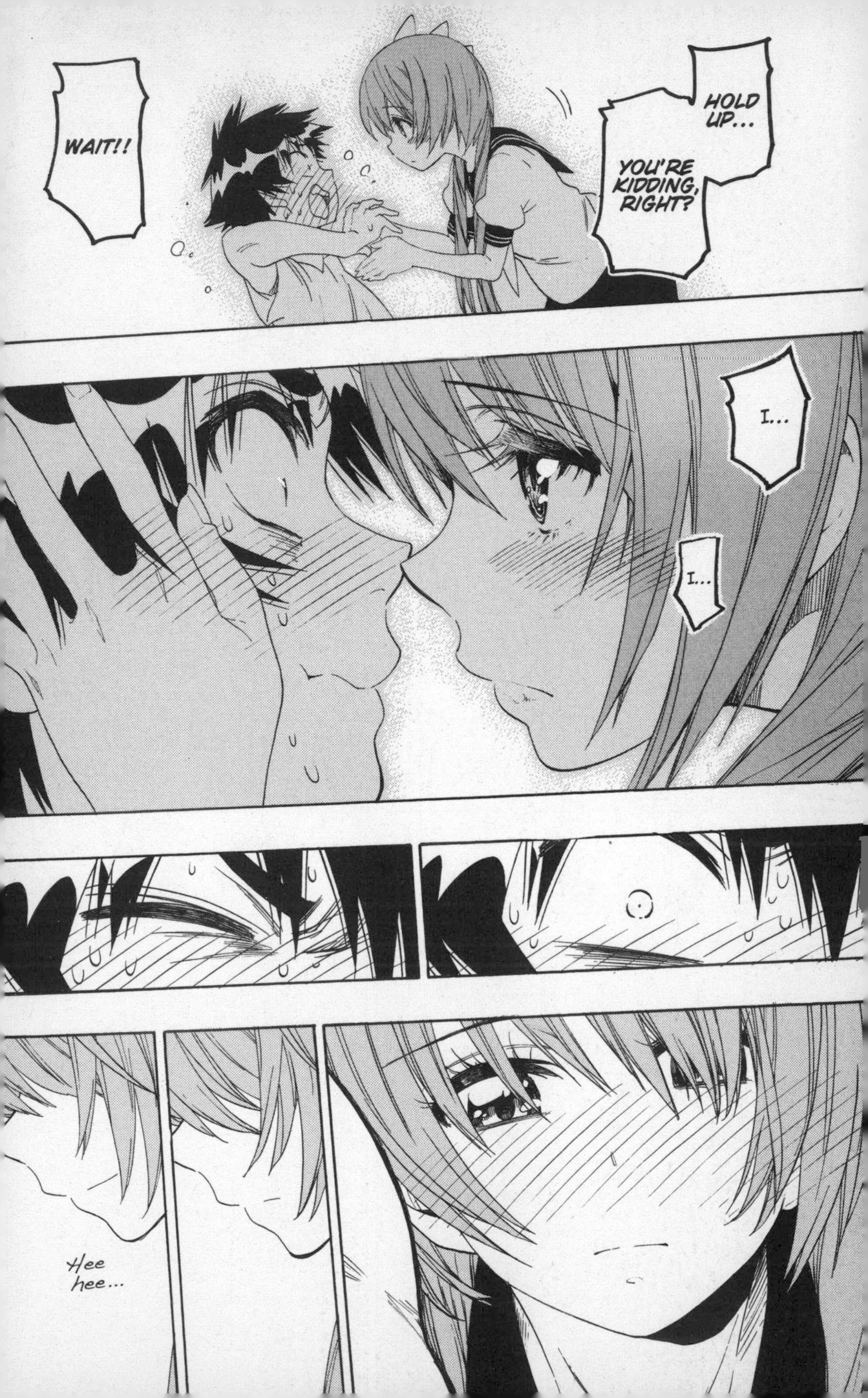
HOLD UP...
YOU'RE KIDDING, RIGHT?
WAIT!!
I...
I...
Hee hee...

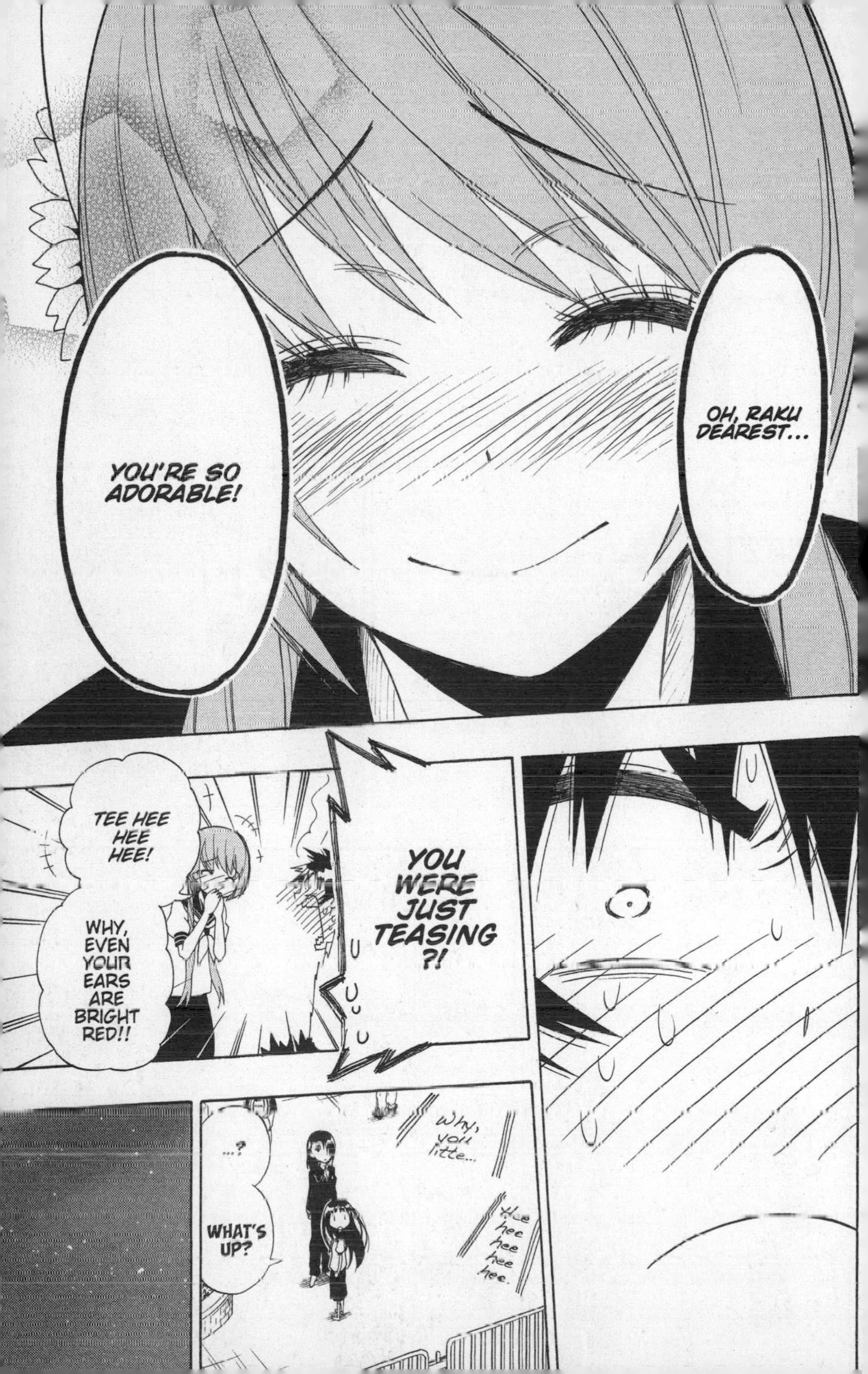
OH, RAKU DEAREST...
YOU'RE SO ADORABLE!
YOU WERE JUST TEASING?!
TEE HEE HEE HEE!
WHY, EVEN YOUR EARS ARE BRIGHT RED!!
Why, you litte...
Hee hee hee hee hee.
...?
WHAT'S UP?

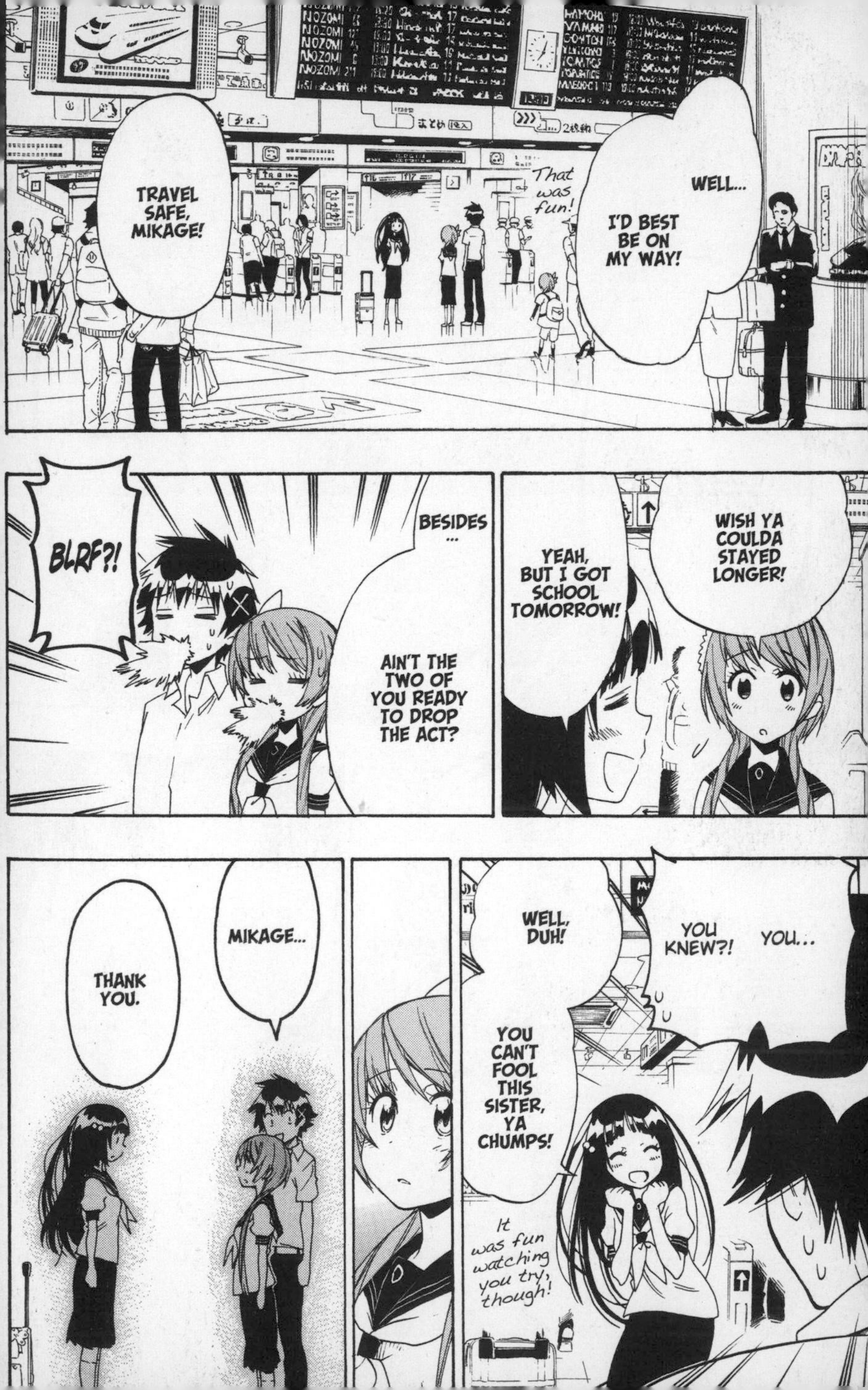
WELL...
I'D BEST BE ON MY WAY!
That was fun!
TRAVEL SAFE, MIKAGE!
WISH YA COULDA STAYED LONGER!
YEAH, BUT I GOT SCHOOL TOMORROW!
BESIDES ...
AIN'T THE TWO OF YOU READY TO DROP THE ACT?
BLRF?!
YOU...
YOU KNEW?!
WELL, DUH!
YOU CAN'T FOOL THIS SISTER, YA CHUMPS!
It was fun watching you try, though!
MIKAGE...
THANK YOU.

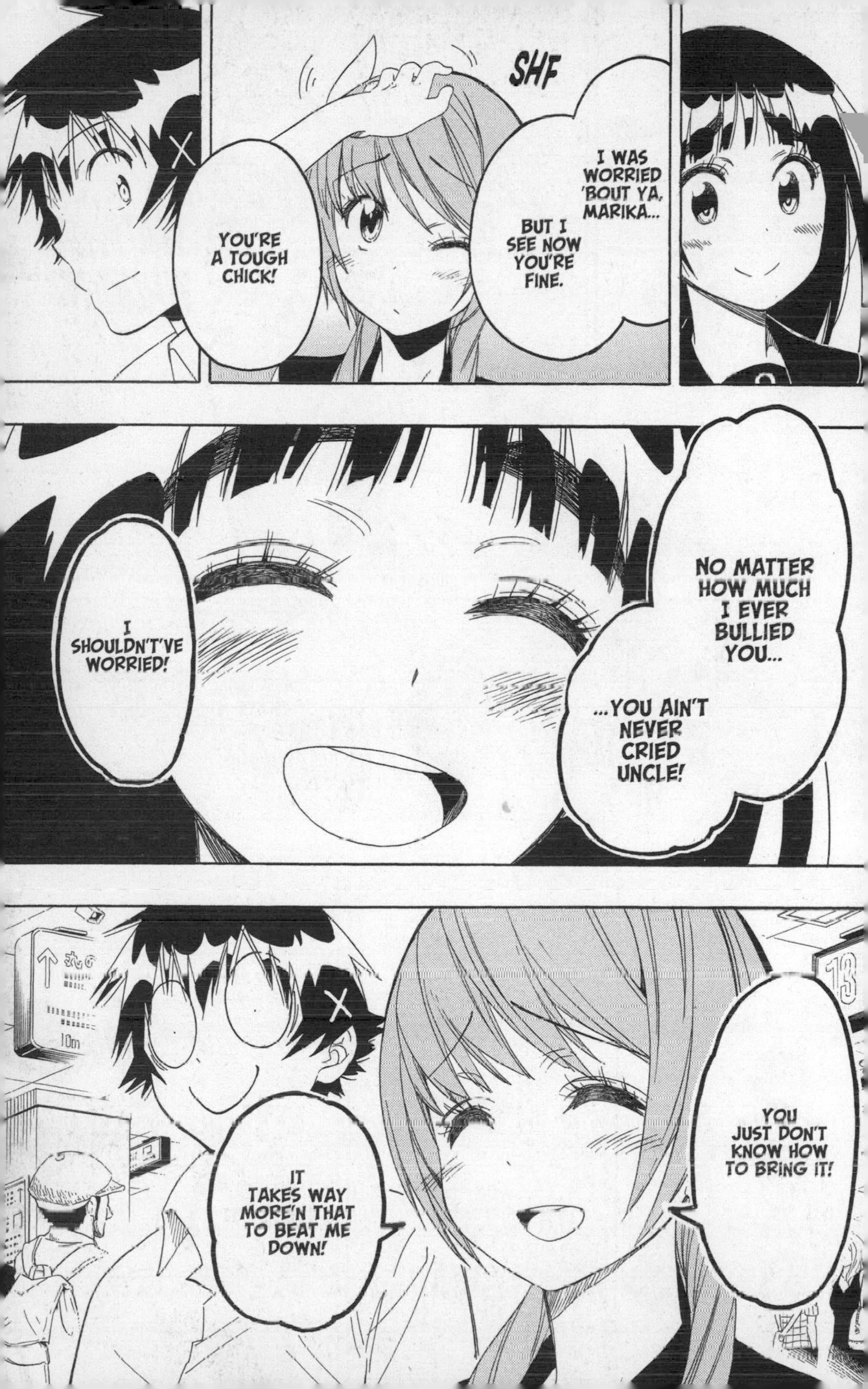
SHF
I WAS WORRIED 'BOUT YA, MARIKA...
BUT I SEE NOW YOU'RE FINE.
YOU'RE A TOUGH CHICK!
NO MATTER HOW MUCH I EVER BULLIED YOU...
...YOU AIN'T NEVER CRIED UNCLE!
I SHOULDN'T'VE WORRIED!
13
10m
YOU JUST DON'T KNOW HOW TO BRING IT!
IT TAKES WAY MORE'N THAT TO BEAT ME DOWN!

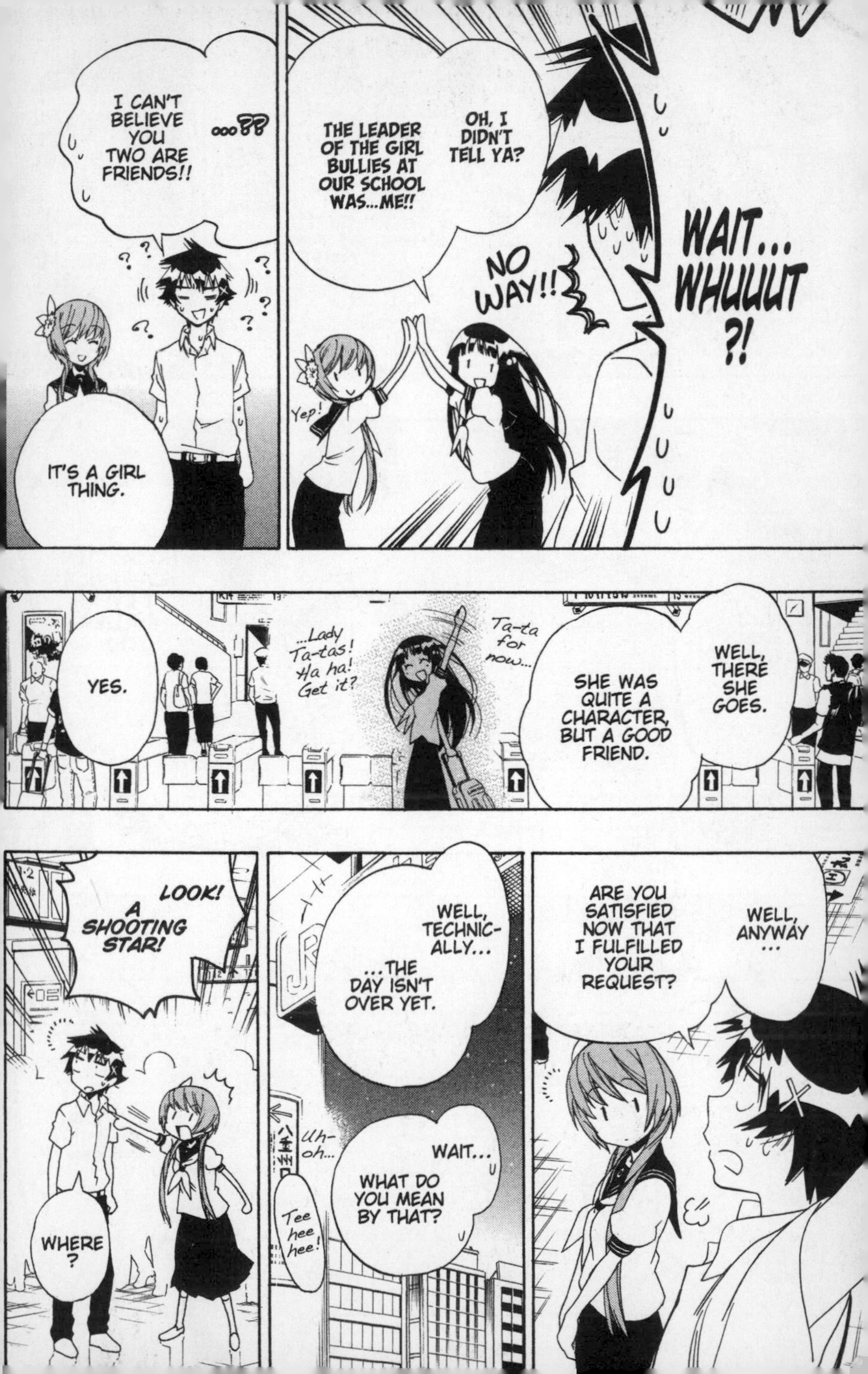
WAIT... WHUUUT ?!
NO WAY!!
OH, I DIDN'T TELL YA?
THE LEADER OF THE GIRL BULLIES AT OUR SCHOOL WAS...ME!!
Yep!
...??
I CAN'T BELIEVE YOU TWO ARE FRIENDS!!
IT'S A GIRL THING.
WELL, THERE SHE GOES.
SHE WAS QUITE A CHARACTER, BUT A GOOD FRIEND.
Ta-ta for now...
...Lady Ta-tas! Ha ha! Get it?
YES.
WELL, ANYWAY...
ARE YOU SATISFIED NOW THAT I FULFILLED YOUR REQUEST?
WELL, TECHNIC-ALLY...
...THE DAY ISN'T OVER YET.
WAIT...
WHAT DO YOU MEAN BY THAT?
Uh-oh...
Tee hee hee!
LOOK! A SHOOTING STAR!
WHERE?

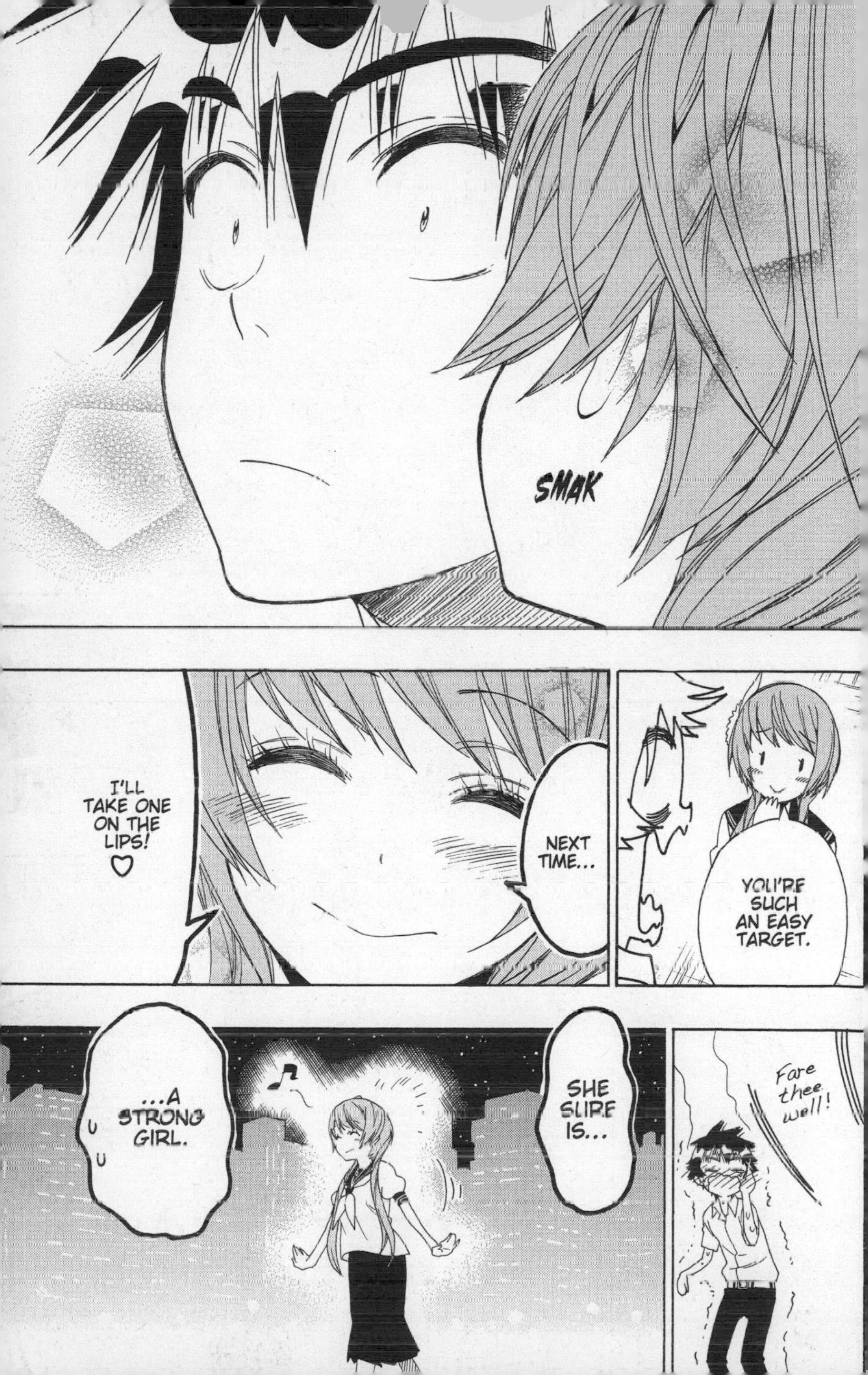
SMAK
YOU'RE SUCH AN EASY TARGET.
NEXT TIME...
I'LL TAKE ONE ON THE LIPS! ♡
Fare thee well!
SHE SURE IS...
...A STRONG GIRL.

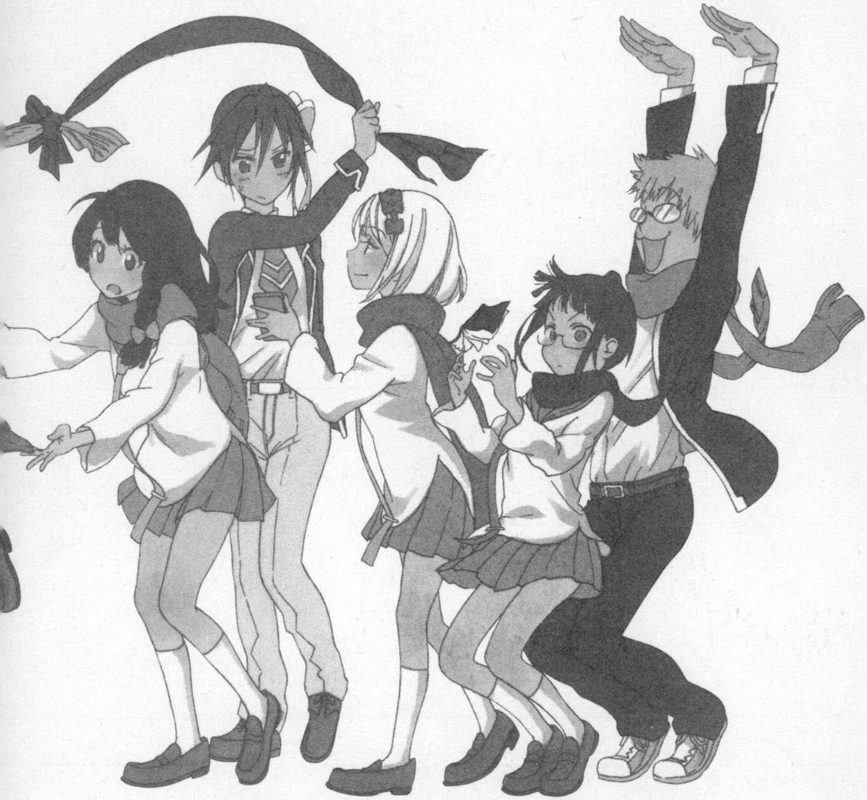

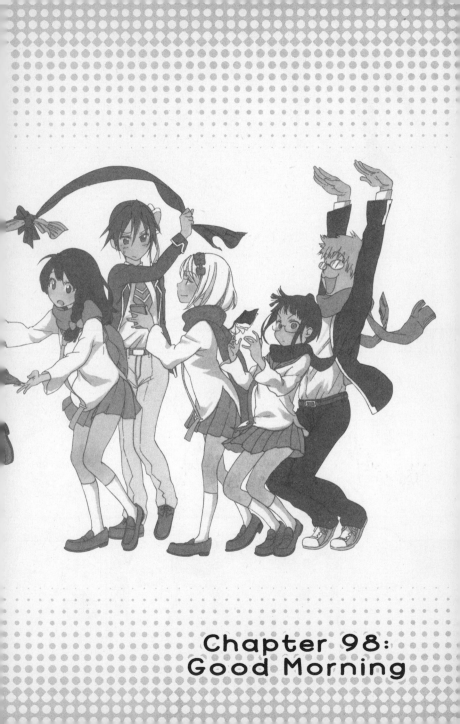

Chapter 98: Good Morning

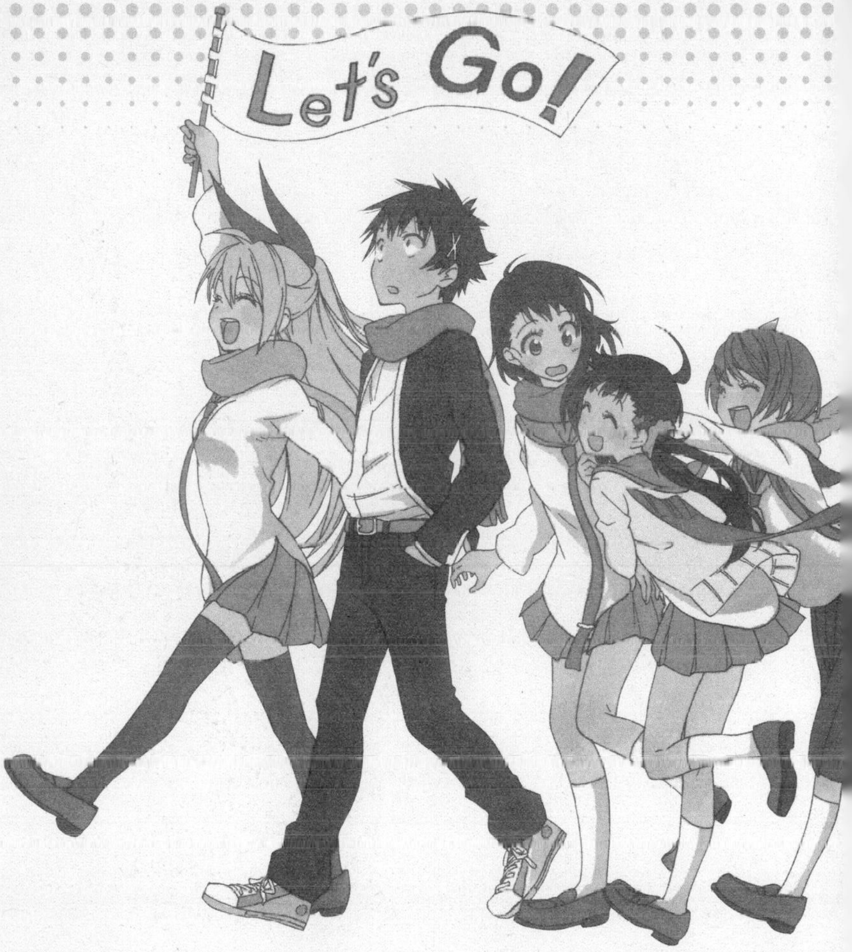
Let's Go!

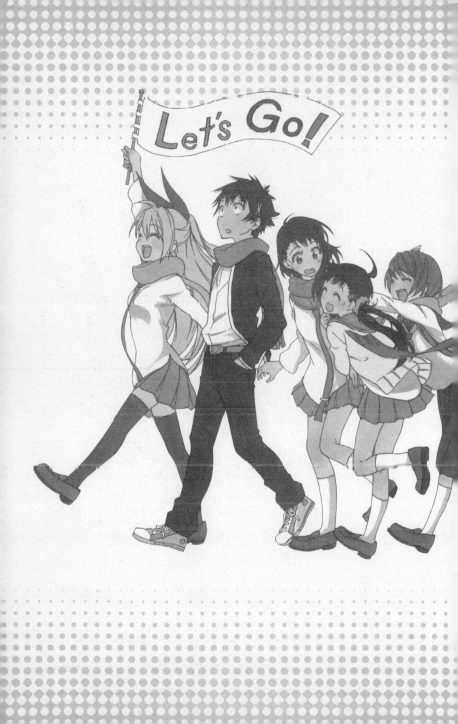

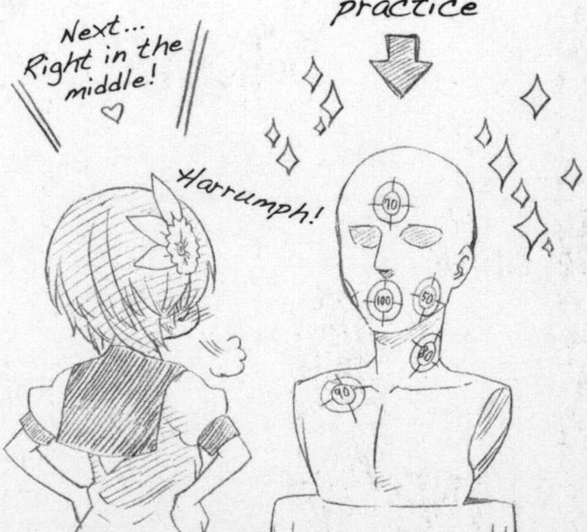
Kissing practice
Next... Right in the middle! ♡
Harrumph!
70
100
50
80
90

From Chapter 97: Request

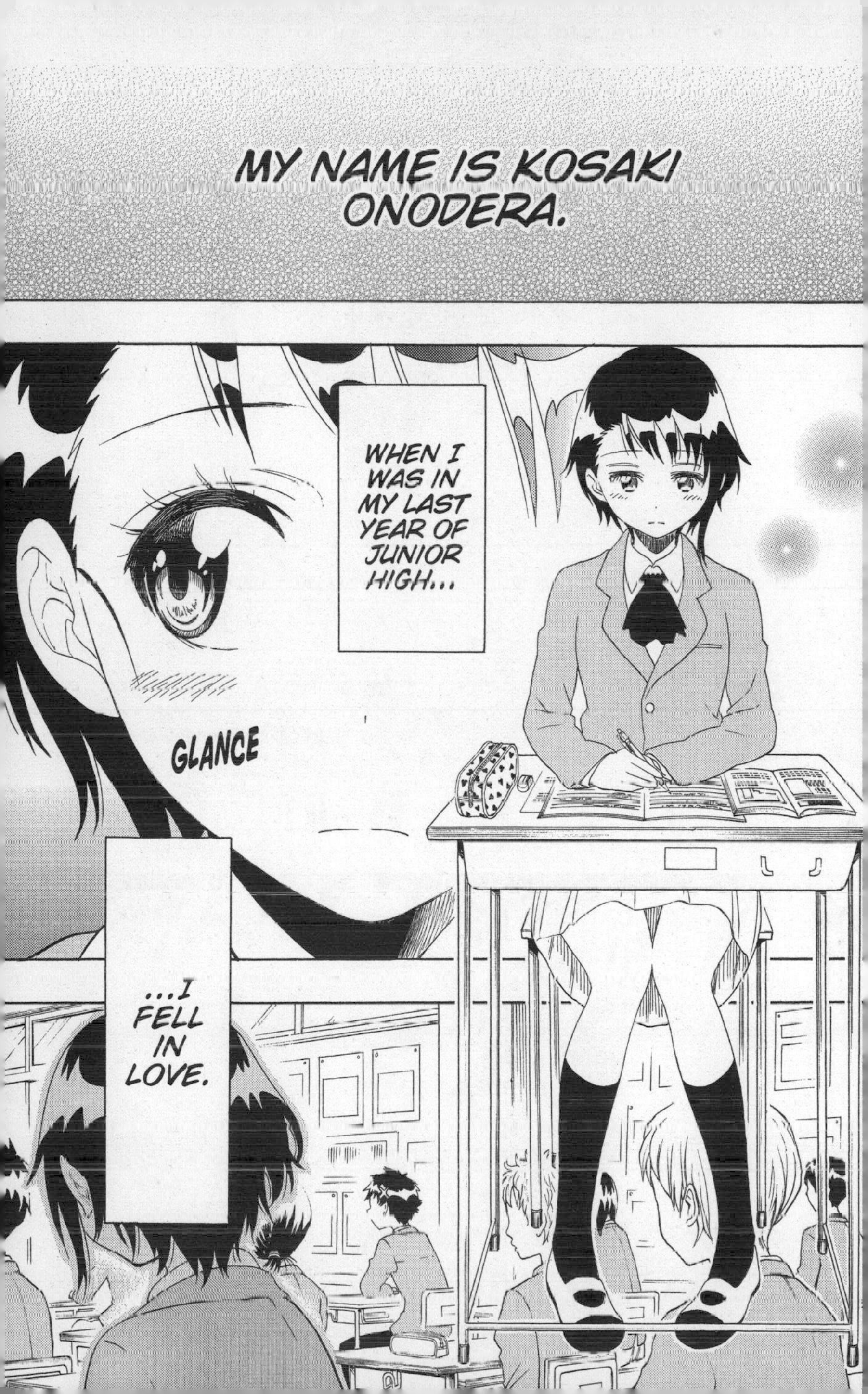
MY NAME IS KOSAKI ONODERA.
WHEN I WAS IN MY LAST YEAR OF JUNIOR HIGH...
GLANCE
...I FELL IN LOVE.

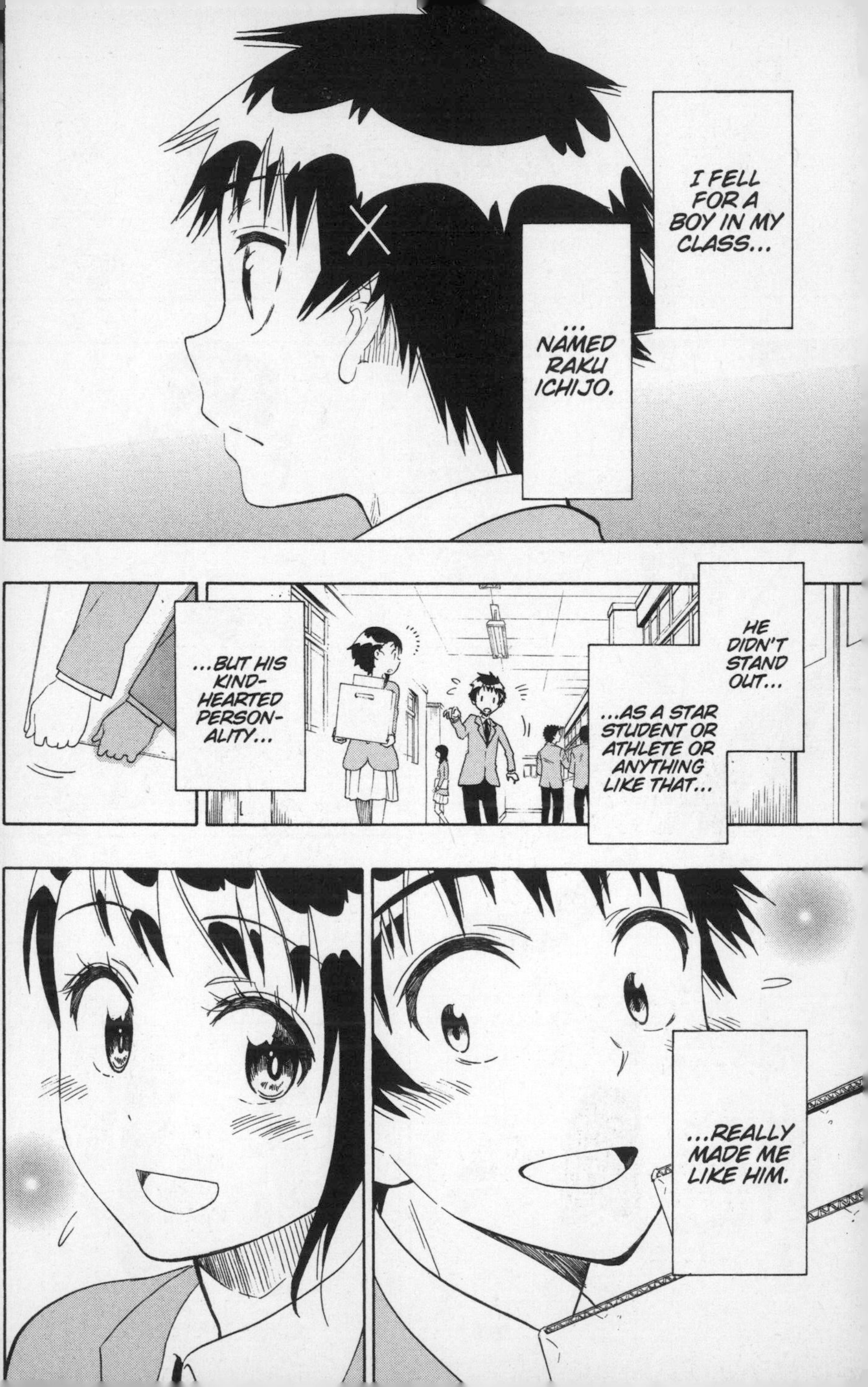
I FELL FOR A BOY IN MY CLASS...
...NAMED RAKU ICHIJO.
HE DIDN'T STAND OUT...
...AS A STAR STUDENT OR ATHLETE OR ANYTHING LIKE THAT...
...BUT HIS KIND-HEARTED PERSONALITY...
...REALLY MADE ME LIKE HIM.

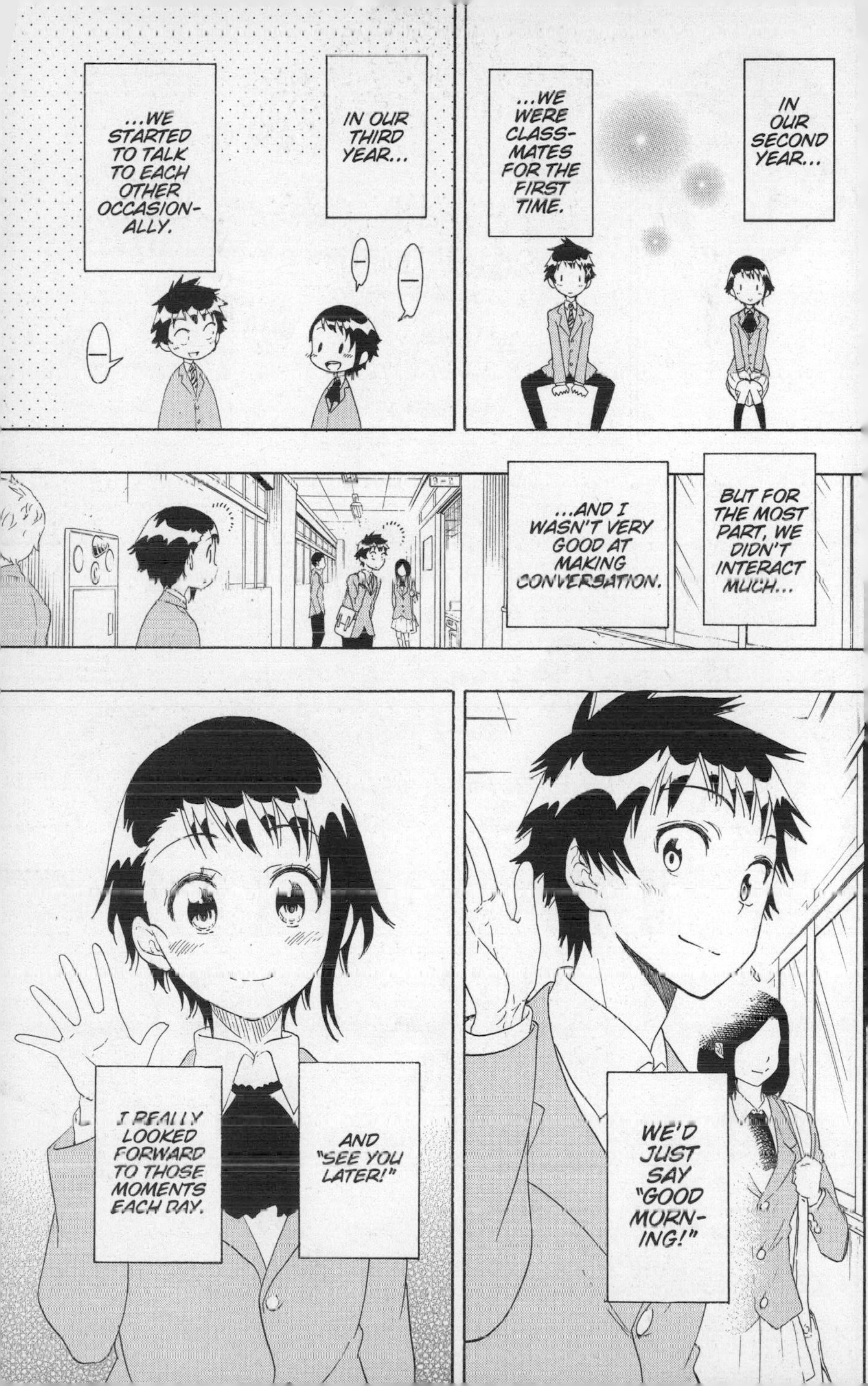
IN OUR SECOND YEAR...
...WE WERE CLASSMATES FOR THE FIRST TIME.
IN OUR THIRD YEAR...
...WE STARTED TO TALK TO EACH OTHER OCCASIONALLY.
BUT FOR THE MOST PART, WE DIDN'T INTERACT MUCH...
...AND I WASN'T VERY GOOD AT MAKING CONVERSATION.
WE'D JUST SAY "GOOD MORNING!"
AND "SEE YOU LATER!"
I REALLY LOOKED FORWARD TO THOSE MOMENTS EACH DAY.

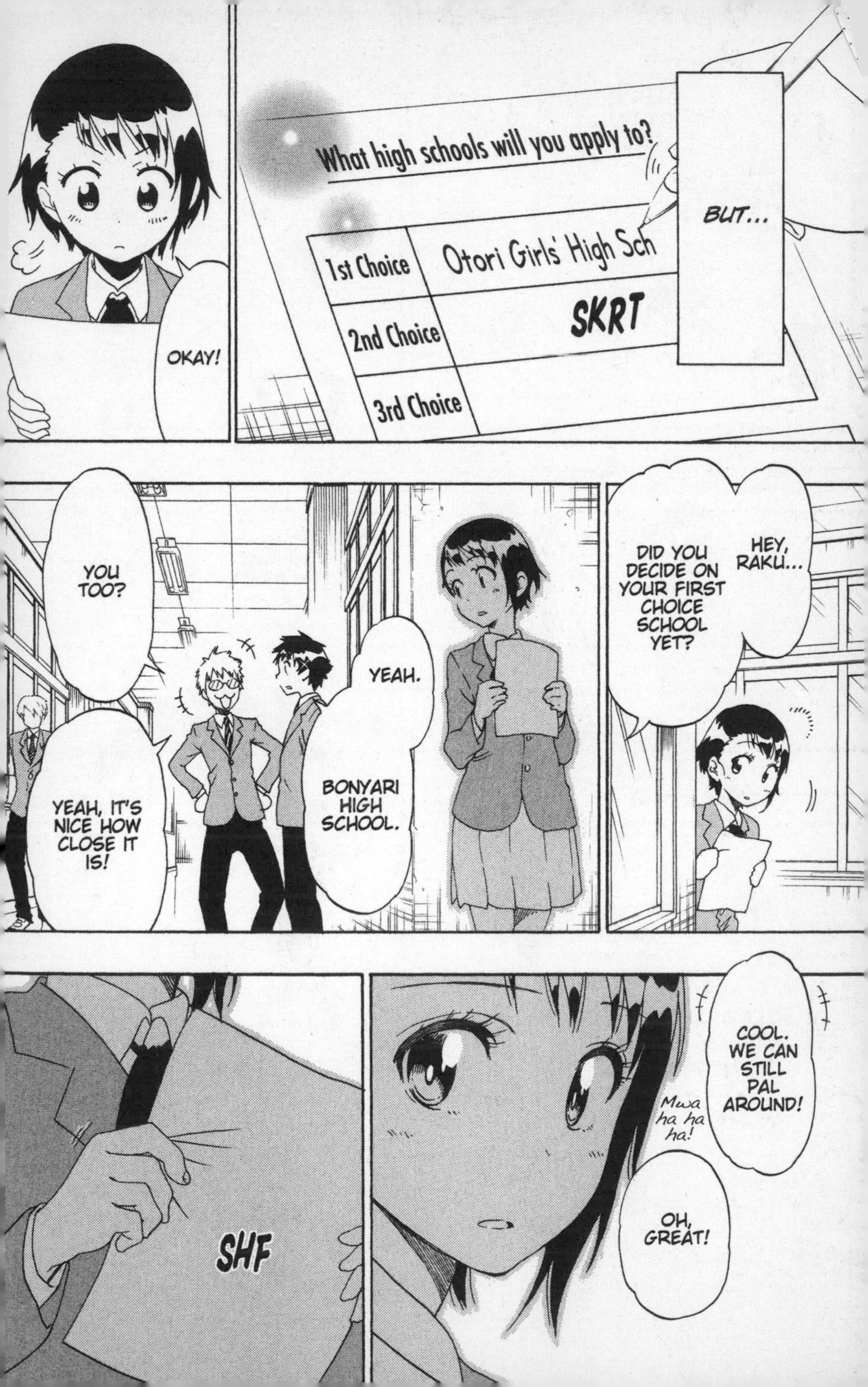
What high schools will you apply to?
1st Choice
Otori Girls' High Sch
2nd Choice
SKRT
3rd Choice
BUT...
OKAY!
HEY, RAKU...
DID YOU DECIDE ON YOUR FIRST CHOICE SCHOOL YET?
YEAH.
BONYARI HIGH SCHOOL.
YOU TOO?
YEAH, IT'S NICE HOW CLOSE IT IS!
COOL. WE CAN STILL PAL AROUND!
Mwa ha ha ha!
OH, GREAT!
SHF

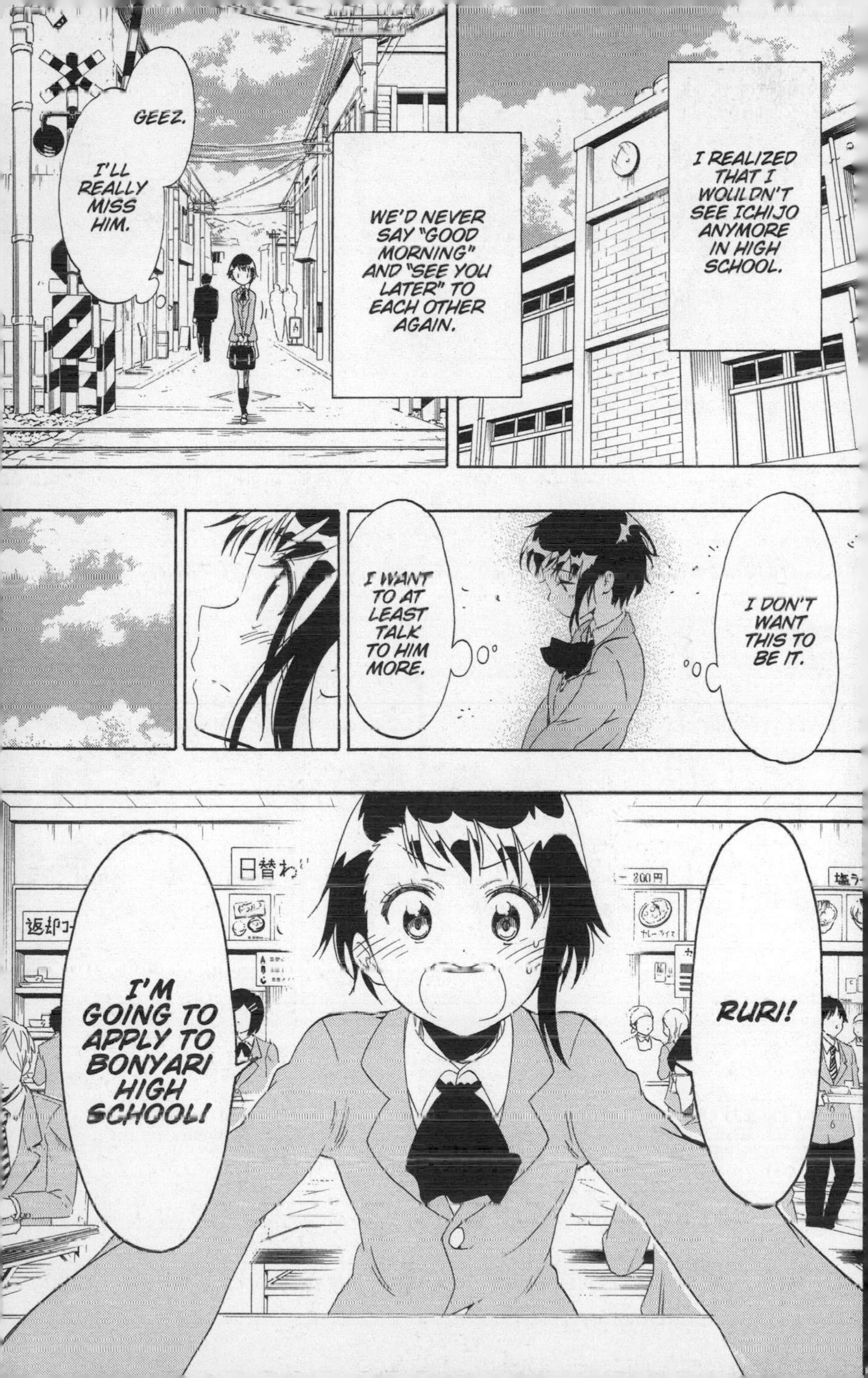
I REALIZED THAT I WOULDN'T SEE ICHIJO ANYMORE IN HIGH SCHOOL.
WE'D NEVER SAY "GOOD MORNING" AND "SEE YOU LATER" TO EACH OTHER AGAIN.
GEEZ.
I'LL REALLY MISS HIM.
I DON'T WANT THIS TO BE IT.
I WANT TO AT LEAST TALK TO HIM MORE.
RURI!
I'M GOING TO APPLY TO BONYARI HIGH SCHOOL!

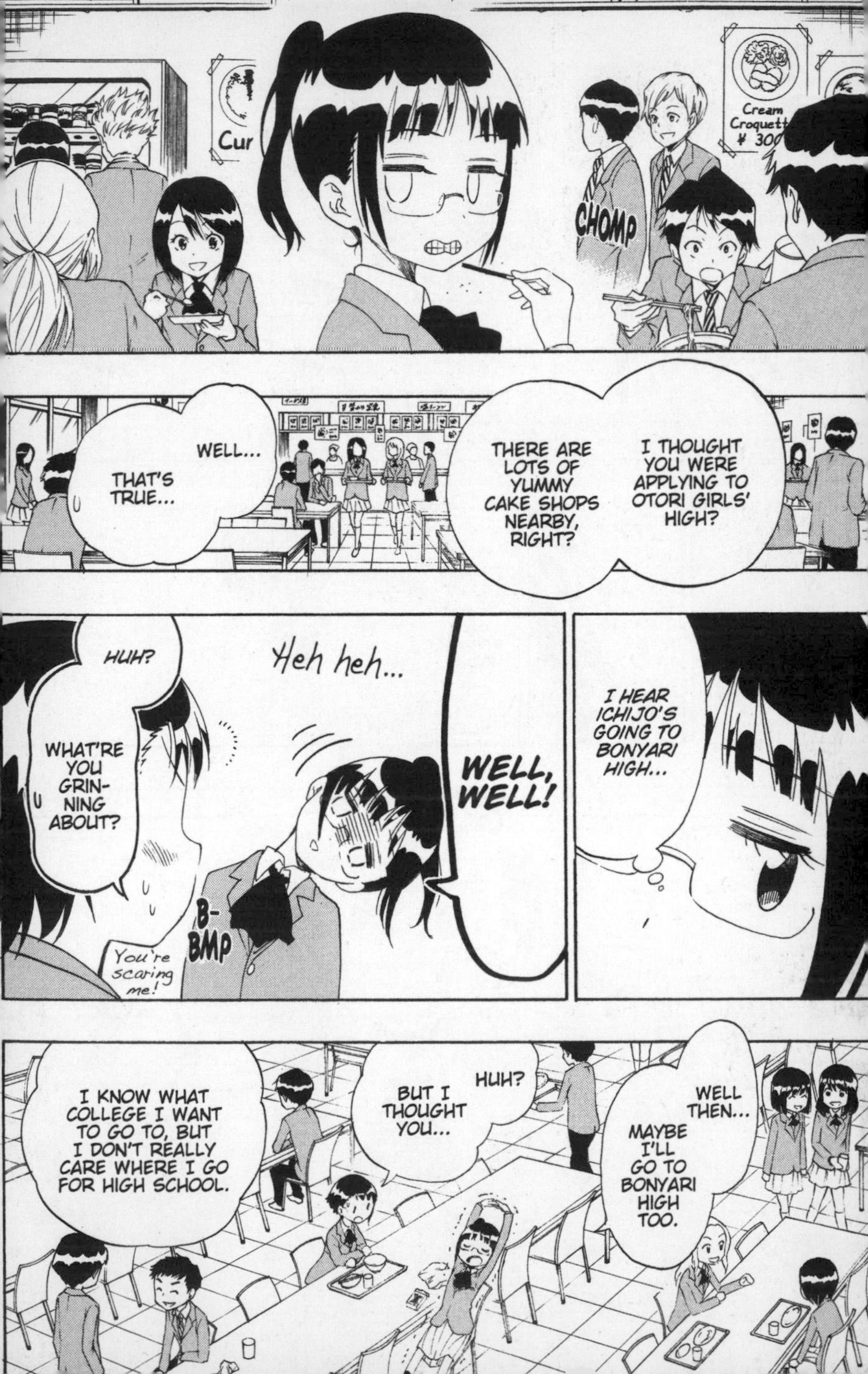
Cream Croquett
¥ 300
CHOMP
Cur
I THOUGHT YOU WERE APPLYING TO OTORI GIRLS' HIGH?
THERE ARE LOTS OF YUMMY CAKE SHOPS NEARBY, RIGHT?
WELL...
THAT'S TRUE...
I HEAR ICHIJO'S GOING TO BONYARI HIGH...
WELL, WELL!
Heh heh...
HUH?
WHAT'RE YOU GRIN-NING ABOUT?
B-BMP
You're scaring me!
WELL THEN...
MAYBE I'LL GO TO BONYARI HIGH TOO.
HUH?
BUT I THOUGHT YOU...
I KNOW WHAT COLLEGE I WANT TO GO TO, BUT I DON'T REALLY CARE WHERE I GO FOR HIGH SCHOOL.

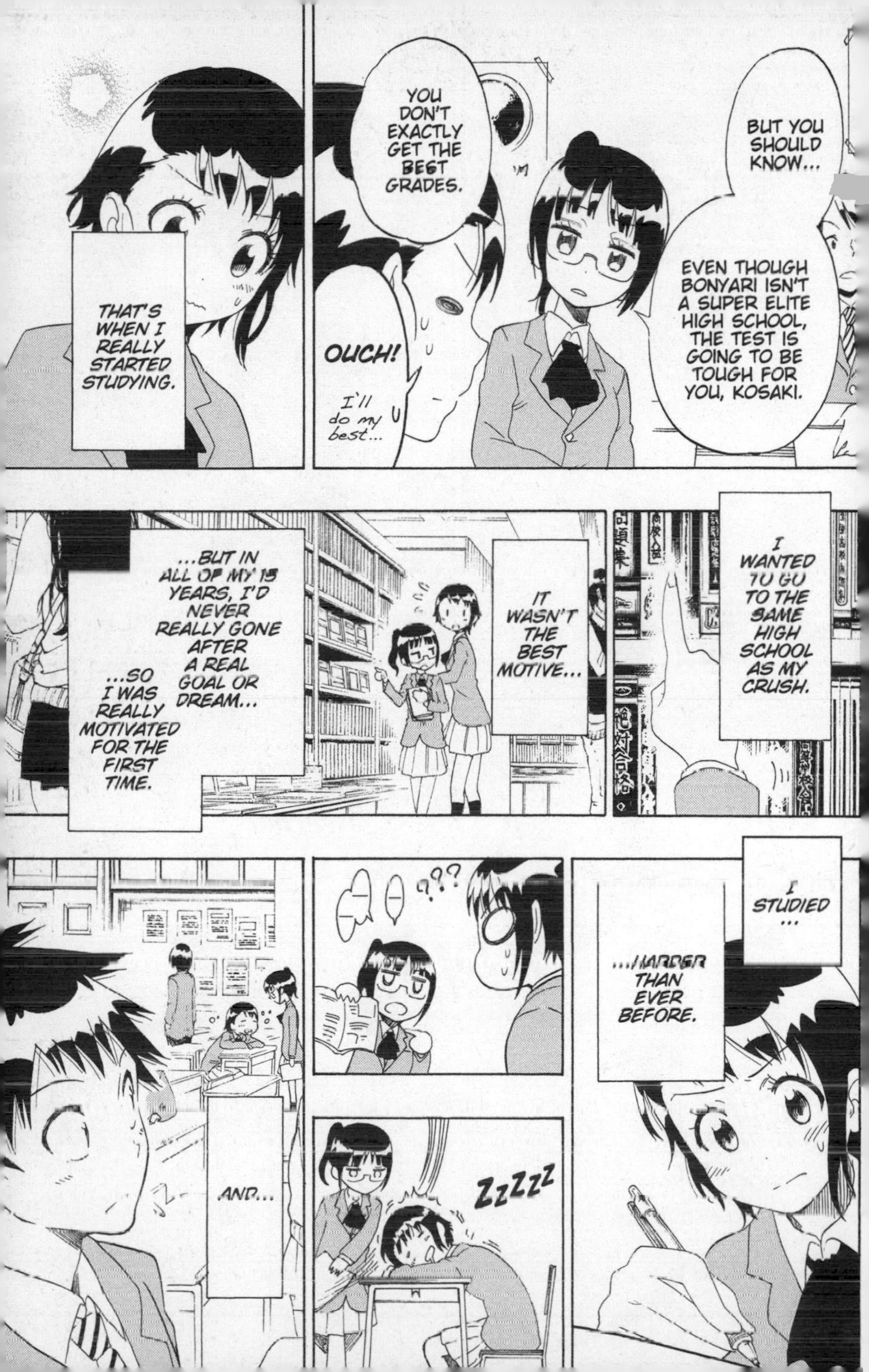
BUT YOU SHOULD KNOW...
EVEN THOUGH BONYARI ISN'T A SUPER ELITE HIGH SCHOOL, THE TEST IS GOING TO BE TOUGH FOR YOU, KOSAKI.
YOU DON'T EXACTLY GET THE BEST GRADES.
OUCH!
I'll do my best...
THAT'S WHEN I REALLY STARTED STUDYING.
I WANTED TO GO TO THE SAME HIGH SCHOOL AS MY CRUSH.
IT WASN'T THE BEST MOTIVE...
...BUT IN ALL OF MY 15 YEARS, I'D NEVER REALLY GONE AFTER A REAL GOAL OR DREAM...
...SO I WAS REALLY MOTIVATED FOR THE FIRST TIME.
I STUDIED...
...HARDER THAN EVER BEFORE.
???
ZZZZZ
AND...

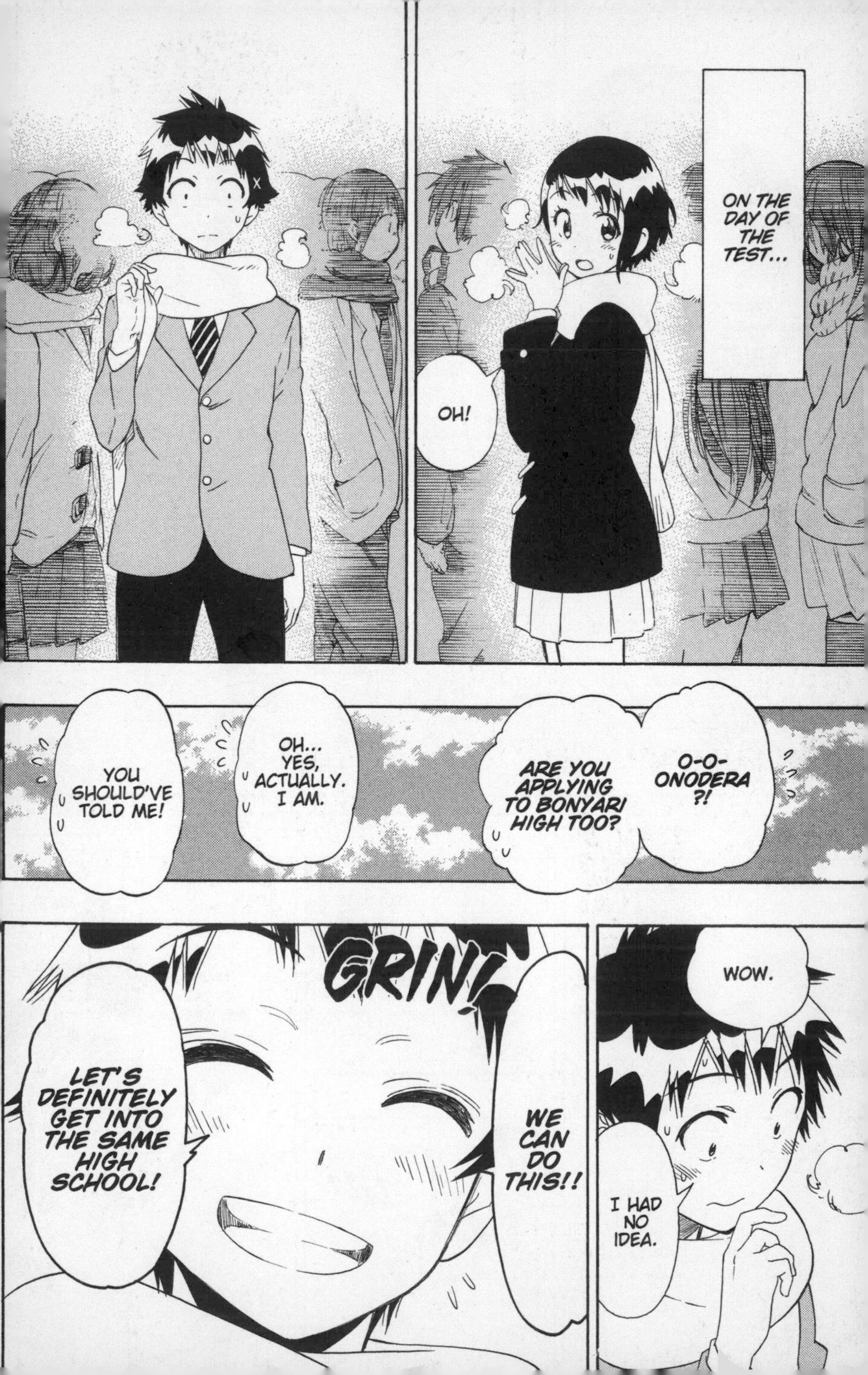
ON THE DAY OF THE TEST...
OH!
O-O-ONODERA?!
ARE YOU APPLYING TO BONYARI HIGH TOO?
OH... YES, ACTUALLY. I AM.
YOU SHOULD'VE TOLD ME!
WOW.
I HAD NO IDEA.
GRIN!
WE CAN DO THIS!!
LET'S DEFINITELY GET INTO THE SAME HIGH SCHOOL!

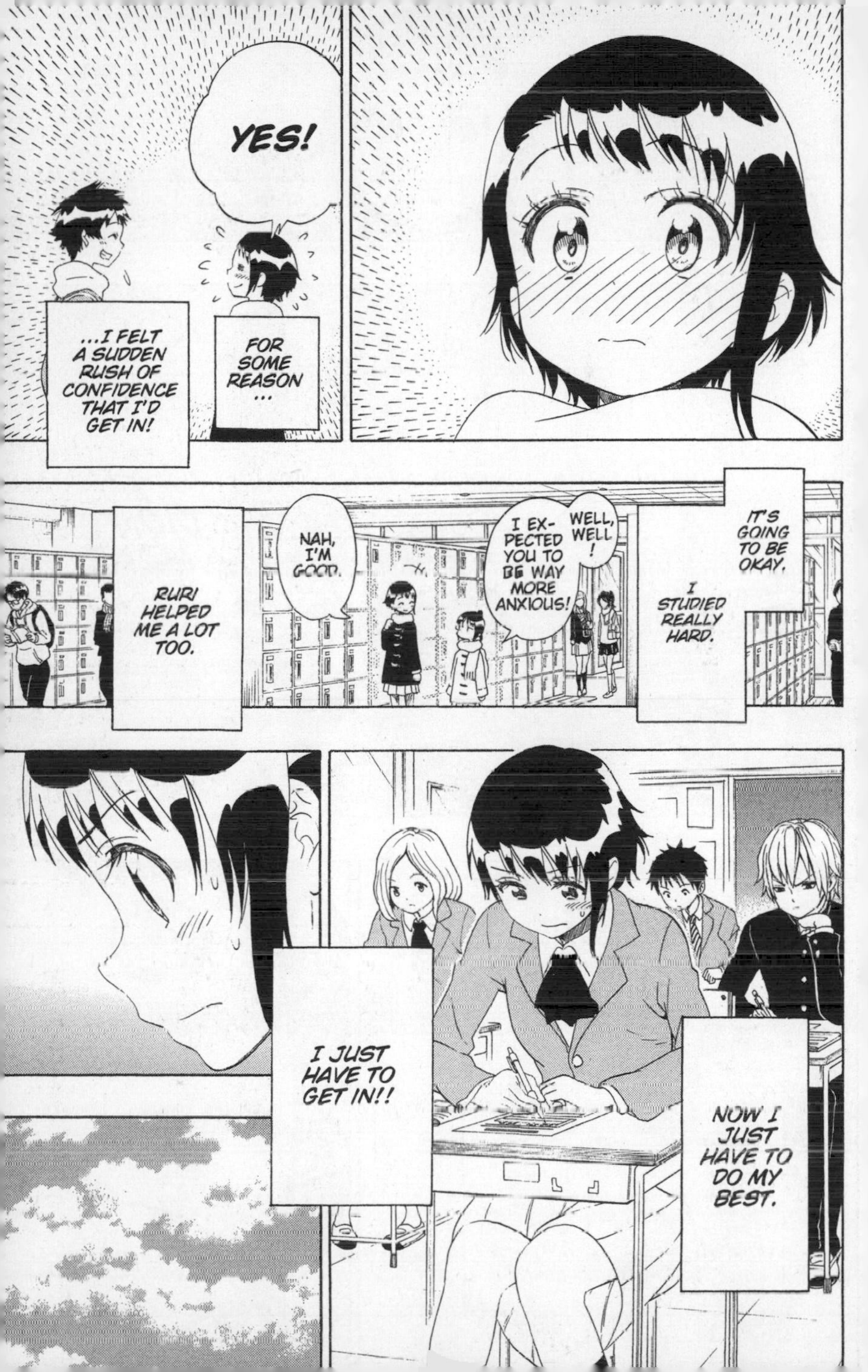
YES!
FOR SOME REASON ...
...I FELT A SUDDEN RUSH OF CONFIDENCE THAT I'D GET IN!
IT'S GOING TO BE OKAY.
I STUDIED REALLY HARD.
WELL, WELL!
I EX-PECTED YOU TO BE WAY MORE ANXIOUS!
NAH, I'M GOOD.
RURI HELPED ME A LOT TOO.
NOW I JUST HAVE TO DO MY BEST.
I JUST HAVE TO GET IN!!

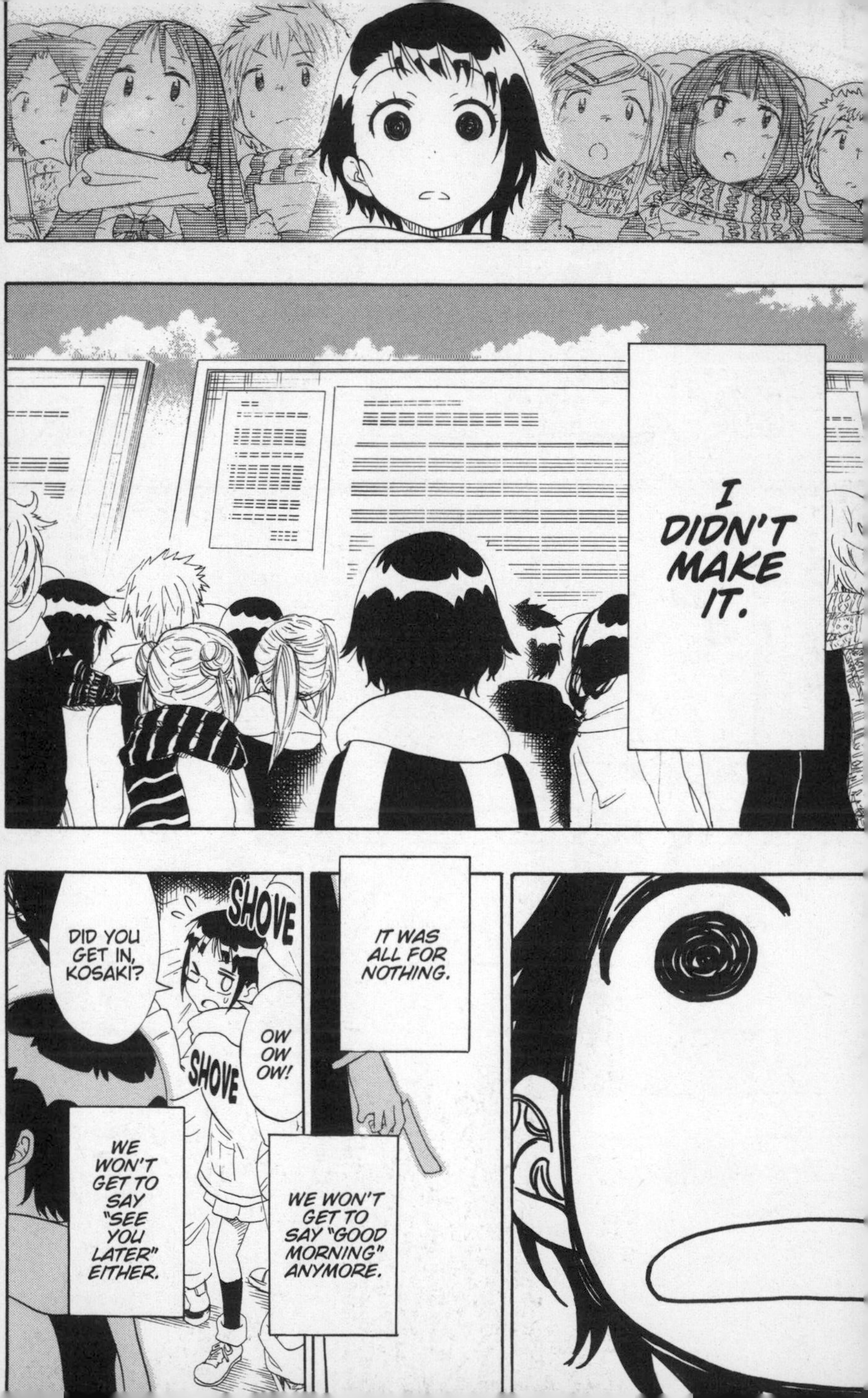
I DIDN'T MAKE IT.
IT WAS ALL FOR NOTHING.
WE WON'T GET TO SAY "GOOD MORNING" ANYMORE.
SHOVE
DID YOU GET IN, KOSAKI?
OW OW OW!
SHOVE
WE WON'T GET TO SAY "SEE YOU LATER" EITHER.

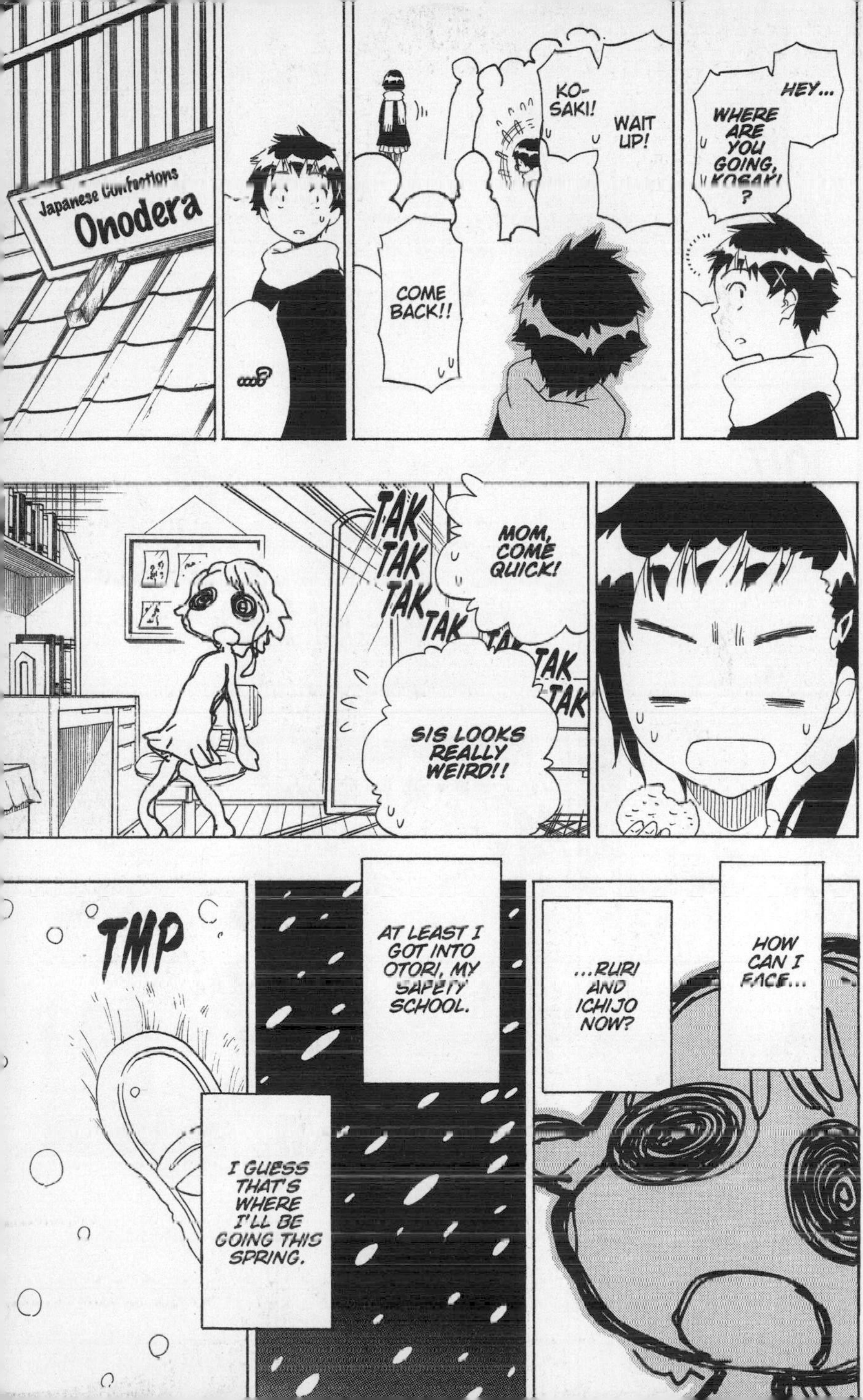
HEY... WHERE ARE YOU GOING, KOSAKI?
KO-SAKI!
WAIT UP!
COME BACK!!
Japanese Confections
Onodera
MOM, COME QUICK!
SIS LOOKS REALLY WEIRD!!
TAK TAK TAK TAK TAK TAK TAK
HOW CAN I FACE...
...RURI AND ICHIJO NOW?
AT LEAST I GOT INTO OTORI, MY SAFETY SCHOOL.
I GUESS THAT'S WHERE I'LL BE GOING THIS SPRING.
TMP

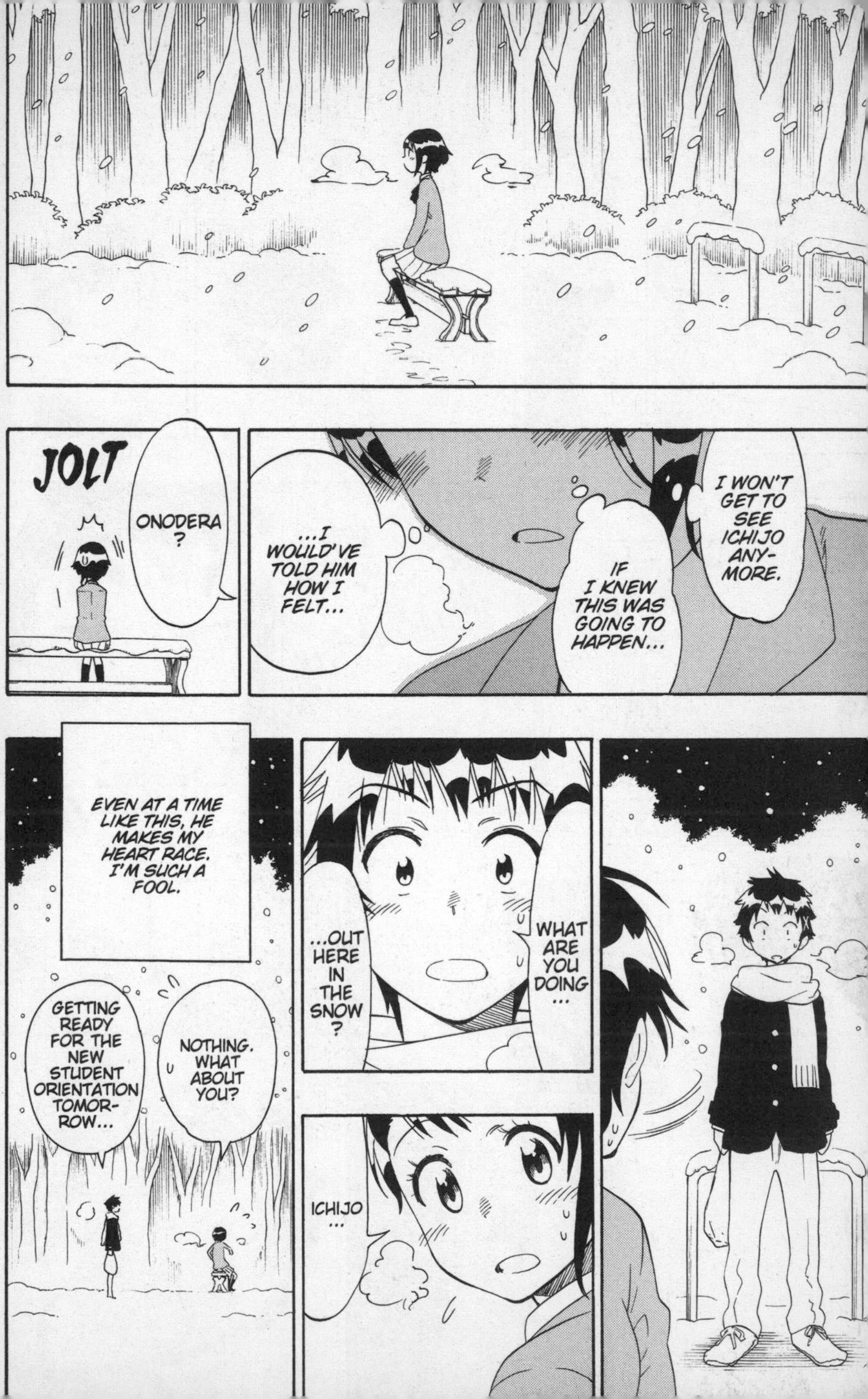
I WON'T GET TO SEE ICHIJO ANYMORE.
IF I KNEW THIS WAS GOING TO HAPPEN...
...I WOULD'VE TOLD HIM HOW I FELT...
JOLT
ONODERA?
WHAT ARE YOU DOING...
...OUT HERE IN THE SNOW?
ICHIJO...
EVEN AT A TIME LIKE THIS, HE MAKES MY HEART RACE. I'M SUCH A FOOL.
NOTHING. WHAT ABOUT YOU?
GETTING READY FOR THE NEW STUDENT ORIENTATION TOMORROW...

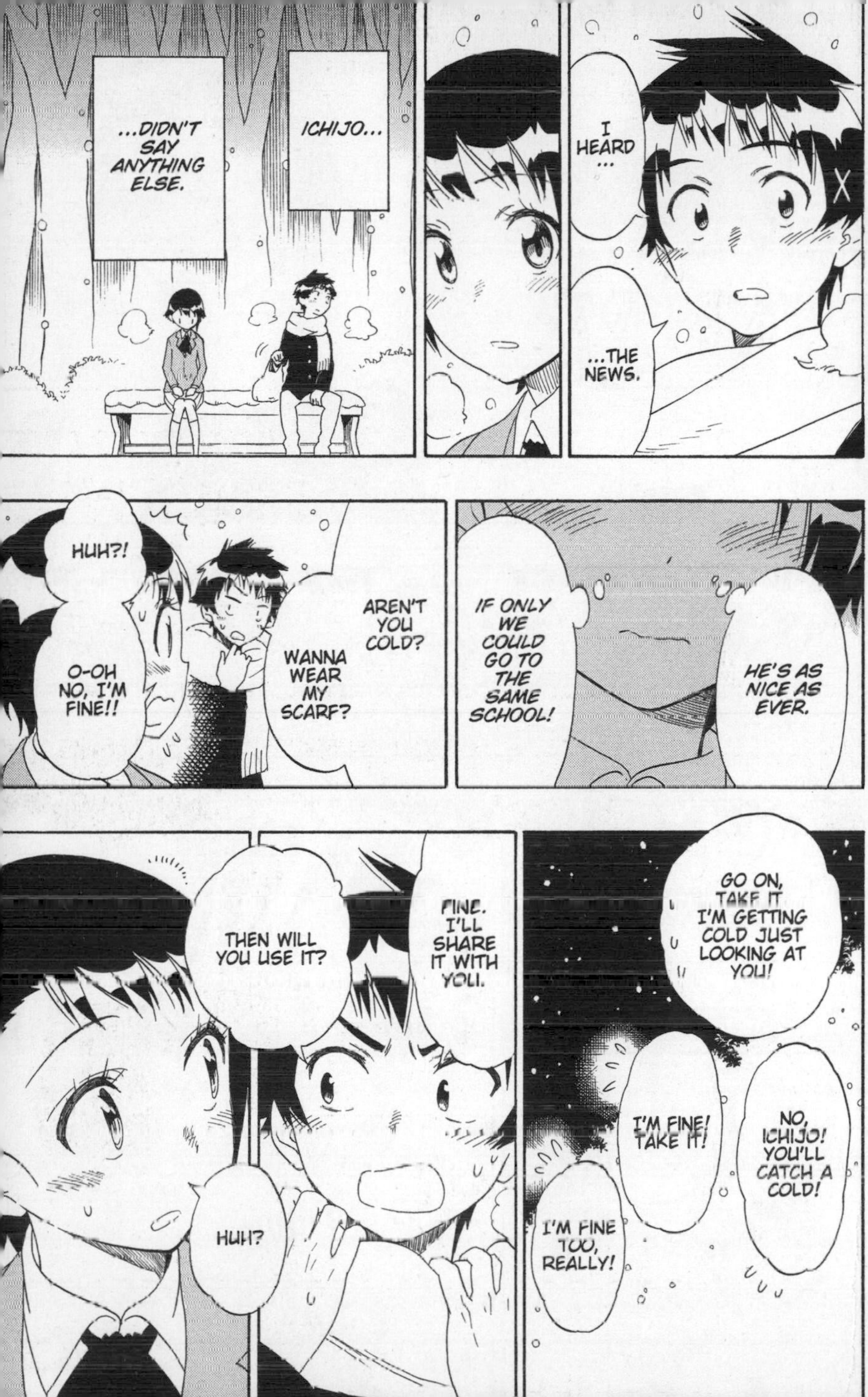
I HEARD...
...THE NEWS.
ICHIJO...
...DIDN'T SAY ANYTHING ELSE.
HE'S AS NICE AS EVER.
IF ONLY WE COULD GO TO THE SAME SCHOOL!
AREN'T YOU COLD?
WANNA WEAR MY SCARF?
HUH?!
O-OH NO, I'M FINE!!
GO ON, TAKE IT I'M GETTING COLD JUST LOOKING AT YOU!
NO, ICHIJO! YOU'LL CATCH A COLD!
I'M FINE! TAKE IT!
I'M FINE TOO, REALLY!
FINE. I'LL SHARE IT WITH YOU.
THEN WILL YOU USE IT?
HUH?

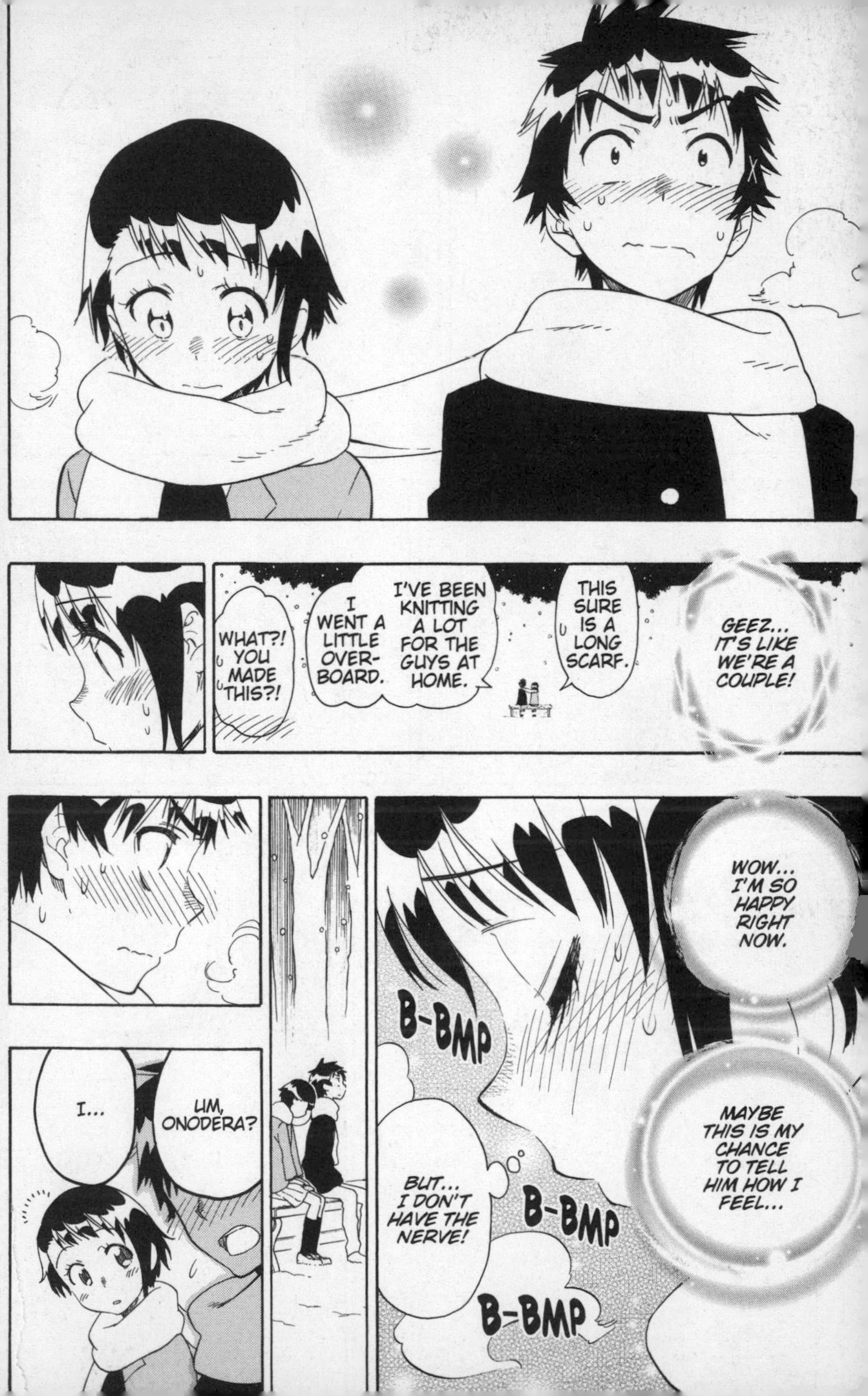
GEEZ... IT'S LIKE WE'RE A COUPLE!
THIS SURE IS A LONG SCARF.
I'VE BEEN KNITTING A LOT FOR THE GUYS AT HOME.
I WENT A LITTLE OVER-BOARD.
WHAT?! YOU MADE THIS?!
WOW... I'M SO HAPPY RIGHT NOW.
B-BMP
MAYBE THIS IS MY CHANCE TO TELL HIM HOW I FEEL...
BUT... I DON'T HAVE THE NERVE!
B-BMP
B-BMP
UM, ONODERA?
I...

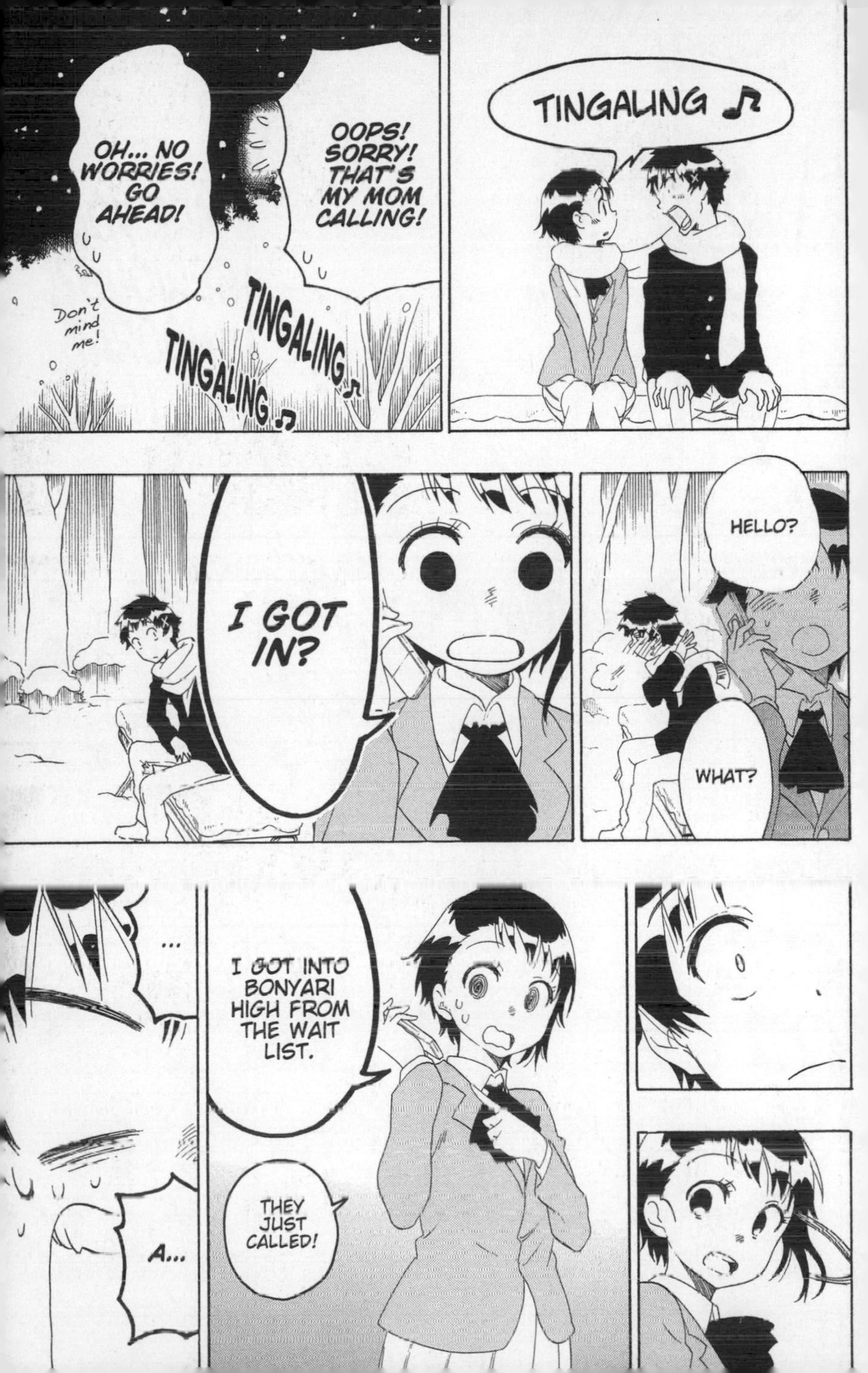
TINGALING ♪
OOPS! SORRY! THAT'S MY MOM CALLING!
OH... NO WORRIES! GO AHEAD!
Don't mind me!
TINGALING ♪
TINGALING ♪
HELLO?
WHAT?
I GOT IN?
I GOT INTO BONYARI HIGH FROM THE WAIT LIST.
THEY JUST CALLED!
...
A...

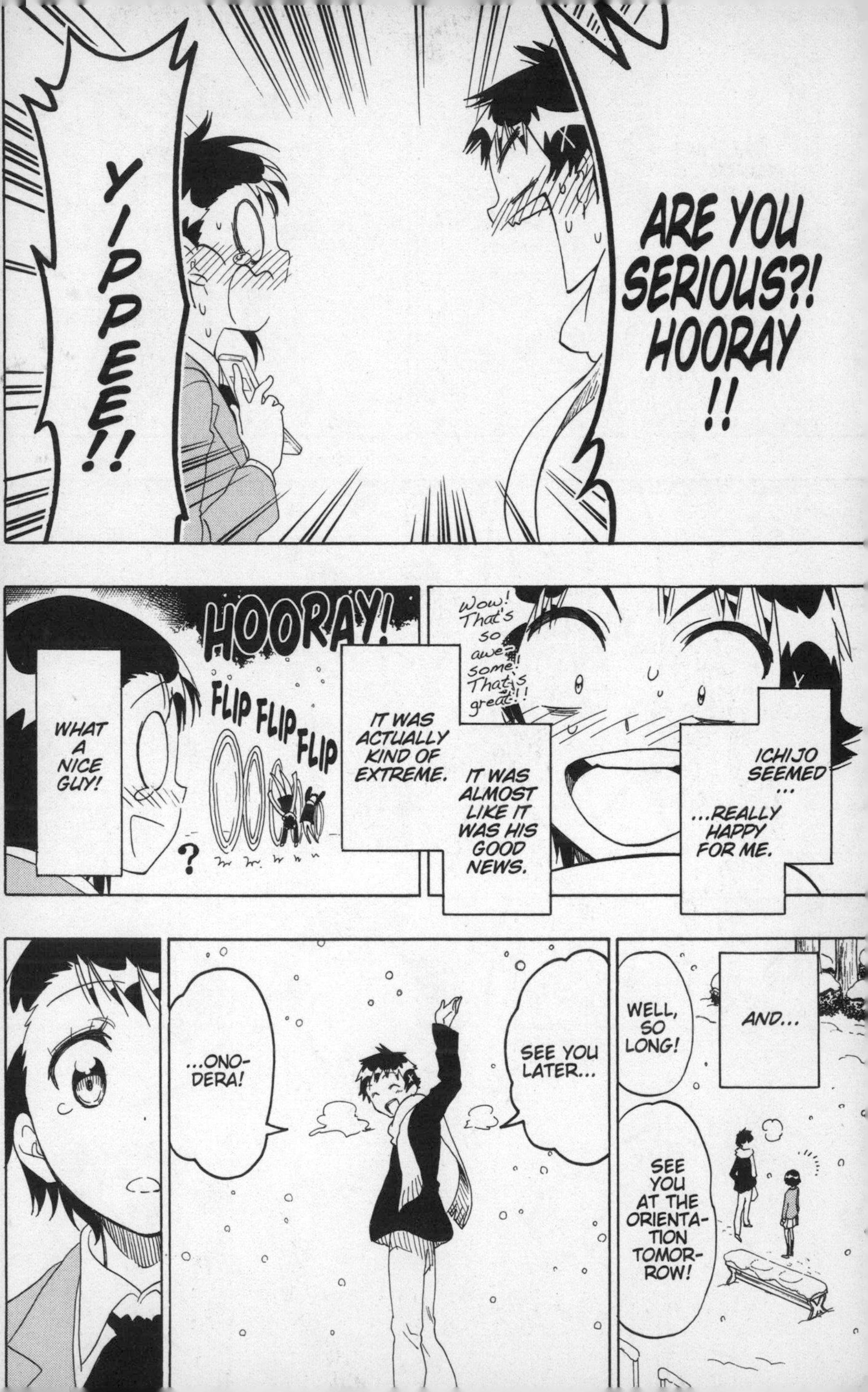
ARE YOU SERIOUS?! HOORAY !!
YIPPEEE!!
ICHIJO SEEMED...
...REALLY HAPPY FOR ME.
Wow! That's so awesome! That's great!!
IT WAS ALMOST LIKE IT WAS HIS GOOD NEWS.
IT WAS ACTUALLY KIND OF EXTREME.
HOORAY!
FLIP FLIP FLIP
WHAT A NICE GUY!
?
AND...
WELL, SO LONG!
SEE YOU AT THE ORIENTATION TOMORROW!
SEE YOU LATER...
...ONODERA!

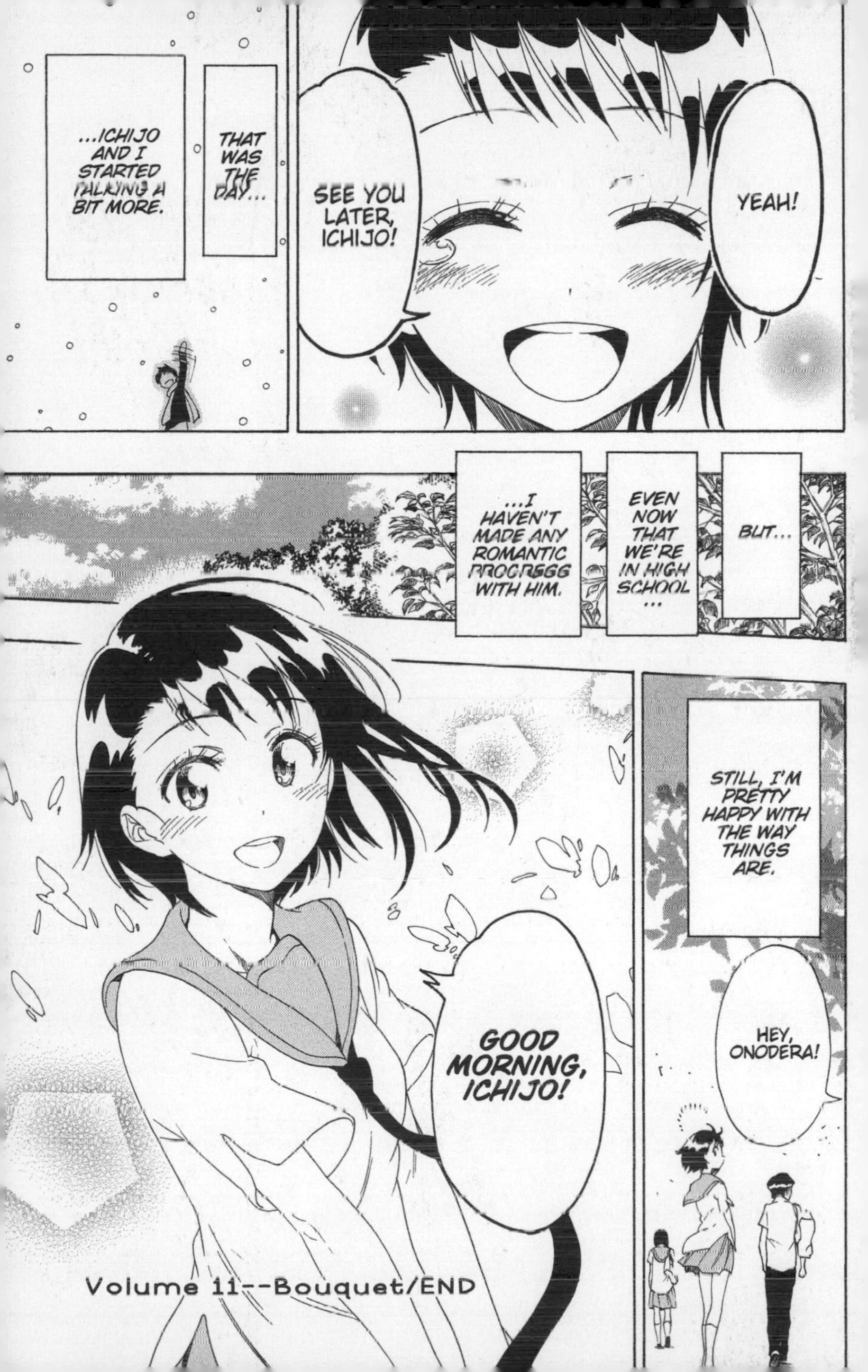
YEAH!
SEE YOU LATER, ICHIJO!
THAT WAS THE DAY...
...ICHIJO AND I STARTED TALKING A BIT MORE.
BUT...
EVEN NOW THAT WE'RE IN HIGH SCHOOL...
...I HAVEN'T MADE ANY ROMANTIC PROGRESS WITH HIM.
STILL, I'M PRETTY HAPPY WITH THE WAY THINGS ARE.
HEY, ONODERA!
GOOD MORNING, ICHIJO!

Volume 11--Bouquet/END

Bonus Comic!!

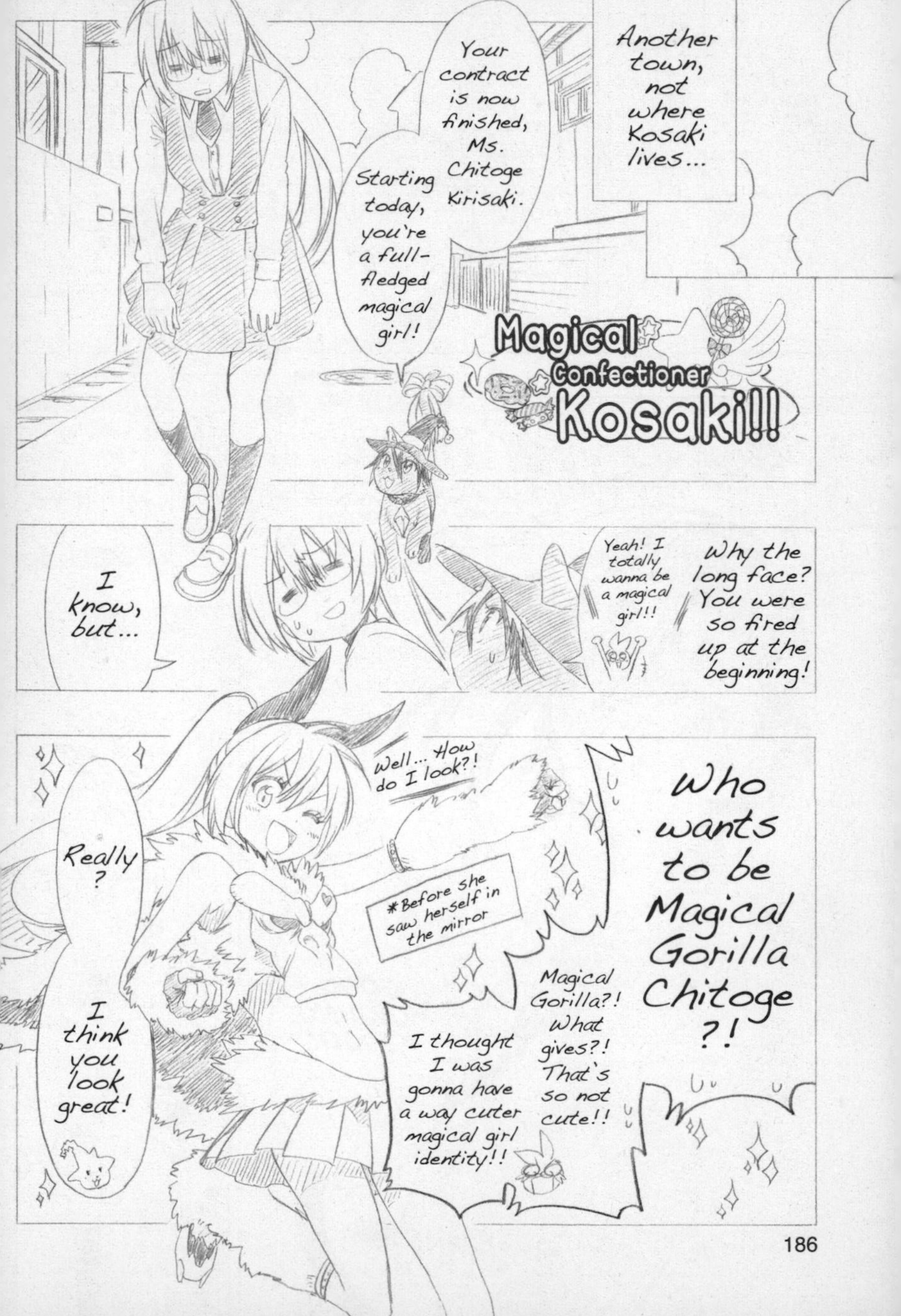

Another town, not where Kosaki lives...
Your contract is now finished, Ms. Chitoge Kirisaki.
Starting today, you're a full-fledged magical girl!
Magical Confectioner Kosaki!!
Why the long face? You were so fired up at the beginning!
Yeah! I totally wanna be a magical girl!!
I know, but...
Who wants to be Magical Gorilla Chitoge?!
Magical Gorilla?! What gives?! That's so not cute!!
I thought I was gonna have a way cuter magical girl identity!!
Well... How do I look?!
*Before she saw herself in the mirror
Really?
I think you look great!

Your Magical Gorilla form is highly adept at close combat!
There's nothing I can do... Your costume is based on your own hidden potential!!
Well...
I was surprised when I was able to shatter concrete slabs with the flick of a finger...
Uh-oh!
We're not allowed to have animals in the apartment.
What will I tell my mom?
Should I transform into human form then?
You can do that?
Sure. Sometimes I need to blend in with the human world...
Trans-form!
FWOO
FWASH!
KASHW
VOOSH
KA VWISH
FWASH
Whoa!
OOO

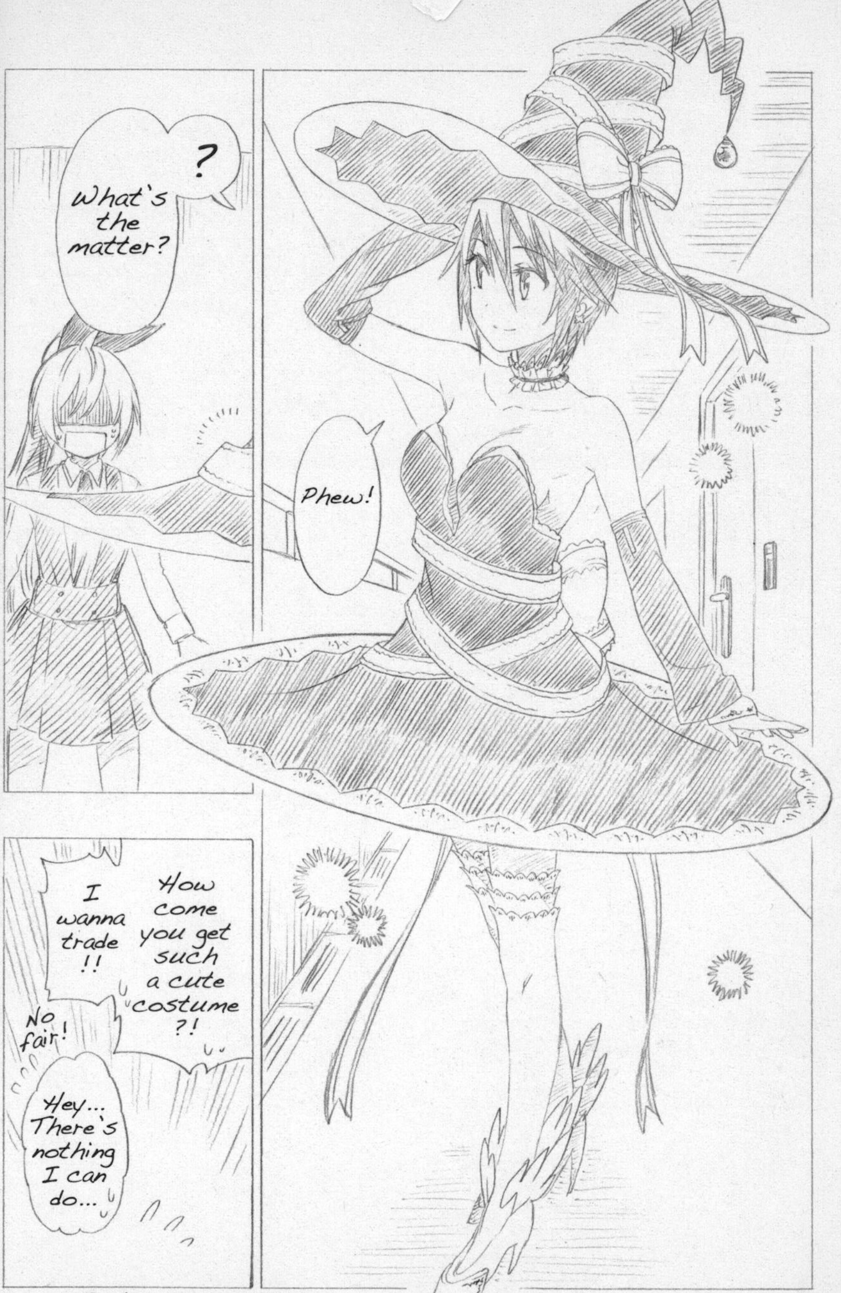

To be continued!!
(Or not to be continued...)

Hi! I'm Tsugumeow, the Magical Cat!
I love sun-bathing!
I hate fighting and mean mice who pick on me!
I'm looking forward to experiencing the human world—I've always wanted to!
Pleased to meet you!!

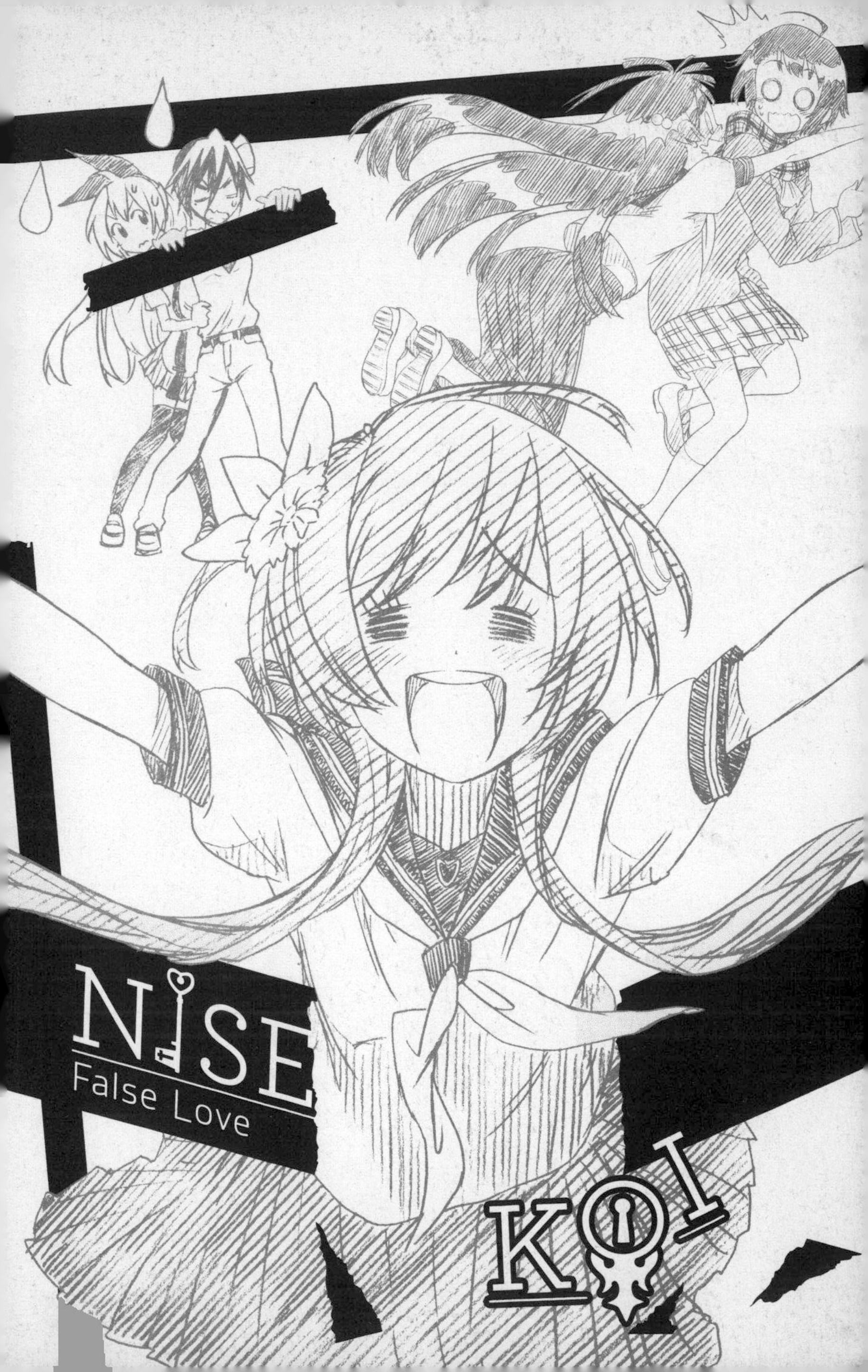
NISE
False Love
KOI

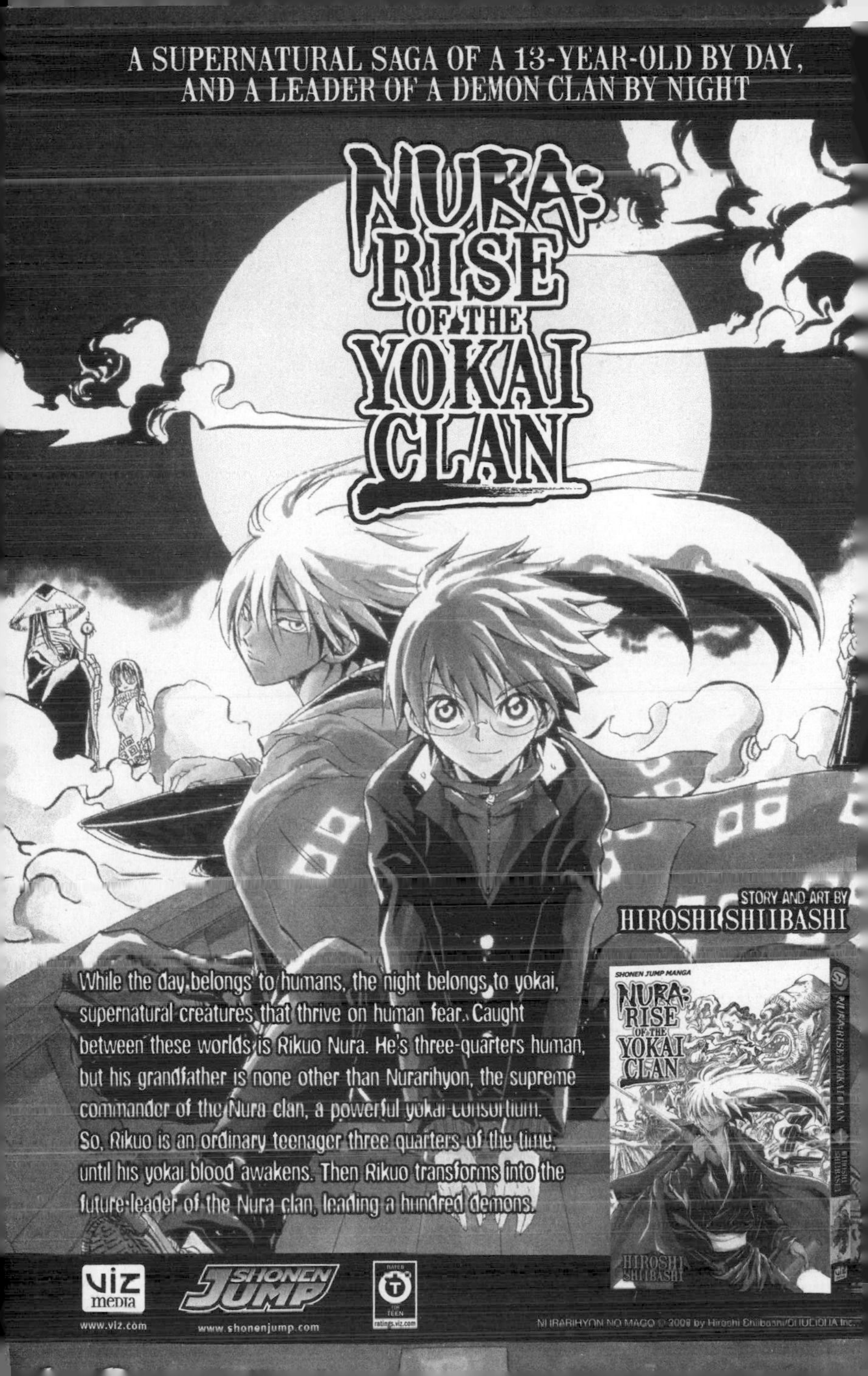

A SUPERNATURAL SAGA OF A 13-YEAR-OLD BY DAY,
AND A LEADER OF A DEMON CLAN BY NIGHT
NURA: RISE OF THE YOKAI CLAN
STORY AND ART BY
HIROSHI SHIIBASHI
While the day belongs to humans, the night belongs to yokai, supernatural creatures that thrive on human fear. Caught between these worlds is Rikuo Nura. He's three-quarters human, but his grandfather is none other than Nurarihyon, the supreme commander of the Nura clan, a powerful yokai consortium. So, Rikuo is an ordinary teenager three quarters of the time, until his yokai blood awakens. Then Rikuo transforms into the future leader of the Nura clan, leading a hundred demons.
SHONEN JUMP MANGA
NURA: RISE OF THE YOKAI CLAN
HIROSHI SHIIBASHI
viz media
www.viz.com
SHONEN JUMP
www.shonenjump.com
RATED T FOR TEEN
ratings.viz.com
NURARIHYON NO MAGO © 2009 by Hiroshi Shiibashi/SHUEISHA Inc.

You're Reading the
WRONG WAY!

SEP   2015

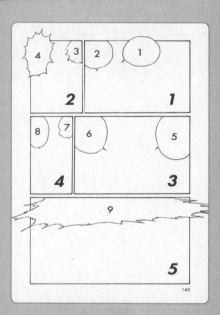

NISEKOI reads from right to left, starting in the upper-right corner. Japanese is read from right to left, meaning that action, sound effects, and word-balloon order are completely reversed from English order.